D0998448

CHURCH COURTS AND THE PEOPLE DURING THE ENGLISH REFORMATION
1520-1570

by
RALPH HOULBROOKE

OXFORD UNIVERSITY PRESS
1979

Oxford University Press, Walton Street, Oxford OX2 6DP

OXFORD LONDON GLASGOW
NEW YORK TORONTO MELBOURNE WELLINGTON
KUALA LUMPUR SINGAPORE JAKARTA HONG KONG TOKYO
DELHI BOMBAY CALCUTTA MADRAS KARACHI
NAIROBI DAR ES SALAAM CAPE TOWN

British Library Cataloguing in Publication Data
Houlbrooke, Ralph Anthony
Church courts and the people during the English
Reformation, 1520–1570. – (Oxford historical
monographs).
1. Ecclesiastical courts – England – History –
16th century
I. Title   II. Series
262.9   KD8680   78-41126

ISBN 0-19-821876-1

*set by Hope Services, Wantage
and Printed in Great Britain by
Billing & Son Ltd., Guildford & Worcester*

To my
Parents

PREFACE

My first thanks are due to Mr. Keith Thomas for his patient, watchful and stimulating supervision of my work upon the doctoral thesis out of which this book has grown. To my examiners, Professor Christopher Hill and Mrs. Dorothy Owen, I owe much valuable advice and the suggestion that I undertake further work on diocesan records which might be used as the basis of a broader study. In the preparation of subsequent drafts I relied heavily upon Mrs. Owen's unfailing encouragement and advice. Ultimately I was guided by her suggestions in making necessary reductions in length, chiefly by means of drastic compression of the portion dealing with the organisation and personnel of the courts. During the final stages of preparation Miss Barbara Harvey gave me much profitable counsel. I have been helped by the comments of a number of other people who have been kind enough to read thesis or book in whole or in part, especially Dr. Anne Whiteman, Dr. R. A. Marchant, Dr. Penry Williams, Professor Donald Logan, Professor Richard Helmholz, Dr. Steven Lander and Dr. Christopher Haigh. I have not followed the advice given me in all respects, and the responsibility for remaining errors and shortcomings is my own.

My research has been greatly assisted by the ready and friendly co-operation of the staffs of a number of libraries and archives, amongst them the Bodleian Library, the Reading University Library, the British Library, the Greater London Record Office and the Department of Palaeography and Diplomatic of Durham University. But my most heartfelt thanks are due to those who made so happy my long periods of work in the Hampshire and Norfolk and Norwich Record Offices.

The completion of the research upon which this book is based was made possible by my election to a Stone-Platt Studentship at New College, Oxford and a Research Fellowship at the University of Reading. The Research Board of the University of Reading has responded generously to my further requests for financial assistance.

Miss N. Merrifield typed both my thesis and the final draft of this book with calm cheerfulness and outstanding efficiency.

This preface must end with grateful mention of my wife, without whose support and encouragement this book could never have been completed. Had I named all those friends who, over the years, have helped me directly or indirectly, it would have been twice as long as it is.

Reading,
March 1979.

CONTENTS

ABBREVIATIONS

BIHR	*Bulletin of the Institute of Historical Research*
BL	British Library (under London in Bibliography)
CHJ	*Cambridge Historical Journal*
DNB	*Dictionary of National Biography*
EcHR	*Economic History Review*
EHR	*English Historical Review*
GLRO	Greater London Record Office (under London in Bibliography)
HJ	*Historical Journal*
HRO	Hampshire Record Office (under Winchester in Bibliography)
JEH	*Journal of Ecclesiastical History*
LP	*Letters and Papers, Foreign and Domestic, of the Reign of Henry VIII*
NCC	Norwich Consistory Court
NNRO	Norfolk and Norwich Record Office (under Norwich in Bibliography)
PRO	Public Record Office (under London in Bibliography)
SCH	*Studies in Church History*
TRHS	*Transactions of the Royal Historical Society*
VCH	*Victoria County History*

NOTES

All books cited in footnotes were published in London unless otherwise stated.

Dates are given in the old style except that the year has been taken to begin on January 1.

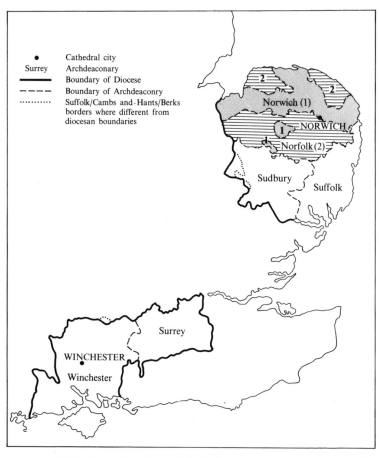

Based on *Tabula Generalis* in *Valor Ecclesiasticus*, vi, facing p. 1. The boundaries of the archdeaconries in Norwich diocese have been sketched in from the map at the end of volume iii. The deaneries shown are assigned to archdeaconries on pp. 281–498 of the same volume.

INTRODUCTION

Opinion has long been divided over the effects of the Reformation on the ecclesiastical courts. There can be little doubt that in the long run it weakened them. Religious uniformity, which they helped to maintain, and to which they owed much of their authority, was undermined and finally destroyed by the Reformation and the changes which flowed from it. The church courts relied heavily upon spiritual sanctions which lost much of their effect when a sizeable proportion of the population became indifferent or hostile towards the established church. It can nevertheless be argued that the royal supremacy gave the courts a new authority in the short term. They became more closely identified with the crown, more closely integrated into the administrative structure of the Tudor state.[1] Along with other courts, they enjoyed a great increase in business during the second half of the sixteenth century. A reliable assessment of the changing role of the courts during this momentous period must rest upon a careful examination of each aspect of their work.

Until recently the church courts received comparatively little attention from historians in their own right. Modern study of the ecclesiastical law in England may still be said to date from the closing decades of the nineteenth century, and in particular from the famous controversy between W. Stubbs and F. W. Maitland over the position of Roman canon law in

---

[1] For speculation and general views on the importance of the church courts in sixteenth-century England, see G. R. Elton, *The Tudor Constitution* (Cambridge, 1960), pp. 214-16; J. E. C. Hill, *Society and Puritanism in Pre-Revolutionary England* (1964), pp. 299-307; A. G. Dickens, *The English Reformation* (1964), p. 250; P. Collinson, *The Elizabethan Puritan Movement* (1967), pp. 38-41.

the medieval English church.[2] A new epoch in the study of the history of ecclesiastical administration was marked by Professor A. Hamilton Thompson's Ford lectures of 1933 and the appearance in the same year of I. J. Churchill's *Canterbury Administration*.[3] But not until 1952 did a study devoted specifically to ecclesiastical courts appear, that of B. L. Woodcock on the Canterbury diocesan courts.[4] Before this, to be sure, many editions of ecclesiastical records and collections of extracts from them had been published. In this field, the collections of W. H. Hale and J. Raine from the records of the dioceses of London and Durham, both published in the 1840s, were major landmarks.[5] The fifty years before the completion of Woodcock's work had seen the publication of a number of editions of court act books, and the continuation of the Hale tradition by such devoted local historians as F. S. Hockaday.[6] During the previous decade, F. D. Price had begun to publish a most important series of articles on the consistory court of Gloucester in the second half of the sixteenth century, which throw much light on such matters as the use of excommunication and the careers of the personnel

[2] Parliamentary Papers 1883 (c. 3760), xxiv, *Report of the Commissioners appointed to inquire into the Constitution and Working of the Ecclesiastical Courts*, pp. 21–51; W. Stubbs, *Seventeen Lectures on the Study of Medieval and Modern History* (Oxford, 1887), pp. 335–64; F. W. Maitland, *Roman Canon Law in the Church of England* (1898).

[3] A. Hamilton Thompson, *The English Clergy and their Organisation in the Later Middle Ages* (Oxford, 1947); I. J. Churchill, *Canterbury Administration*, 2 vols. (1933).

[4] B. L. Woodcock, *Medieval Ecclesiastical Courts in the Diocese of Canterbury* (1952).

[5] W. H. Hale, *Precedents in Causes of Office against Churchwardens and others* (1841); *A Series of Precedents and Proceedings in Criminal Causes, 1475–1640* (1847); *Depositions and other Ecclesiastical Proceedings from the Courts of Durham, extending from 1311 to the Reign of Elizabeth*, ed. J. Raine (Surtees Soc. xxi, 1845).

[6] Amongst the most important editions were *Act Book of the Ecclesiastical Court of Whalley, 1510–1538*, ed. A. M. Cooke (Chetham Soc. n. s. xliv, 1901); *Act Book of the Archdeacon of Taunton*, ed. C. Jenkins (Somerset Record Society, xliii, 1928) and *The Archdeacon's Court Liber Actorum, 1584*, ed. E. R. C. Brinkworth (Oxfordshire Record Soc. xxiii–iv, 1942–6). See also F. S. Hockaday, 'The Consistory Court of the Diocese of Gloucester', *Transactions of the Bristol and Gloucs. Arch. Soc.* xlvi (1924). E. R. C. Brinkworth compiled a very full and useful survey of work done in his 'The Study and Use of Archdeacons' Court Records, illustrated from the Oxford Records (1566–1759)', *TRHS* 4th ser.xxv (1943).

of the courts.[7] But Woodcock was the first to describe in some detail how the late medieval church courts were staffed and run, and to estimate the volume and types of business dealt with at different times. The years since Brian Woodcock's early death have seen a steady trickle of publications concerned with the church courts, the most important of which is Dr. Ronald Marchant's analysis of the work of the courts of York in the century after the Reformation.[8] The present study, therefore, joins a lengthening series of works on the church courts. But it also aims to do something not previously attempted, that is to trace in some detail the development of certain courts through the period of the Reformation.

Most historians of the ecclesiastical courts have, for good reasons, based their work on diocesan archives. Above the diocesan level there were two sets of provincial courts, and after the Reformation cases from all over England were heard in London by the judges delegate and the royal ecclesiastical commissioners. The sixteenth-century records of the province of York have survived in some quantity, and have been used to good effect by Dr. Marchant and others, but most of those

[7] 'Gloucester Diocese under Bishop Hooper', *Transactions of the Bristol and Gloucs. Arch. Soc.* lx (1939); 'The Abuses of Excommunication and the Decline of Ecclesiastical Discipline under Queen Elizabeth', *EHR* lvii (1942); 'An Elizabethan Church Official — Thomas Powell, Chancellor of Gloucester diocese', *Church Quarterly Review*, cxxviii (1939); 'Elizabethan Apparitors in the Diocese of Gloucester', ibid. cxxxiv (1942); 'Biship Bullingham and Chancellor Blackleech: a Diocese divided', *Trans. Bristol and Gloucs. Arch. Soc.* xci (1972).

[8] R. A. Marchant, *The Church under the Law: Justice, Administration and Discipline in the Diocese of York, 1560–1640* (Cambridge, 1969). See also the numerous works of Canon J. S. Purvis, esp. his *Select Sixteenth Century Causes in Tithe from the York Diocesan Registry* (Yorkshire Arch. Soc. Record Ser. cxiv, 1949); *An Introduction to Ecclesiastical Records* (1953); C.I.A. Ritchie, *The Ecclesiastical Courts of York* (Arbroath, 1956); R. W. Dunning, 'The Wells Consistory Court in the Fifteenth Century', *Proc. Somerset Arch. and Nat. Hist. Soc.* cvi (1962); R. Peters, *Oculus Episcopi: Administration in the Archdeaconry of St. Albans, 1580–1625* (Manchester, 1963); S. Lander, 'Church Courts and the Reformation in the Diocese of Chichester, 1500–58', in *Continuity and Change: Personnel and Administration of the Church in England, 1500–1642*, ed. R. O'Day and F. Heal (Leicester, 1976). Amongst recent editions of court records, see particularly *An Episcopal Court Book for the Diocese of Lincoln*, ed. M. Bowker (Lincoln Rec. Soc. lxi, 1967); *The Commission for Ecclesiastical Causes within the Dioceses of Bristol and Gloucester, 1574*, ed. F. D. Price (Publications of the Bristol and Gloucs. Arch. Soc. Records Section, x, 1972); *The Courts of the Archdeaconry of Buckingham*, 1483-1523, ed. E. M. Elvey (Bucks. Rec. Soc. xix, 1975).

kept by the London courts perished long ago. On the basis of what survives, together with such material as commissions of appointment, contemporary descriptions of procedure, correspondence, and references in the records of other institutions, the broad outline of the development of the superior southern courts in the sixteenth century can be traced, and the judges delegate, the ecclesiastical commissioners, and the prerogative court of Canterbury, have all been studied.[9] But a full analysis of the proceedings of the most important ecclesiastical courts in the period of the Reformation will never be possible. Those who wish to study the everyday work of the courts at this critical time and to examine in the most intimate detail their contacts with the people they served, must turn to the diocesan archives. What follows is an analysis of the activities of the church courts in two dioceses during the period of the Reformation.

The choice of the dioceses of Norwich and Winchester as the bases for the present study was determined primarily by the need for a body of material covering the period fairly fully and the desire to explore virgin territory. The former ruled out those dioceses whose records do not go back beyond the Reformation, the latter those whose records have already received attention from historians of the ecclesiastical courts. Good sets of comparatively little-known sixteenth-century court records survive at both Norwich and Winchester; in each case, excellent series of consistory court act and deposition books form the core of the material. The Norwich body of records is however much the larger of the two, both because it is the more complete, and because Norwich was by far the bigger diocese. For these reasons, the diocese of Norwich looms rather larger in this study than does that of Winchester.

In order to be able to distinguish the more important developments of the period from those of merely local significance, it was desirable to choose for study two dioceses of different character. There were clear social and economic

[9] G. I. O. Duncan, *The High Court of Delegates* (Cambridge, 1971); R. G. Usher, *The Rise and Fall of the High Commission* (Oxford, 1913); C. Kitching, 'The Prerogative Court of Canterbury from Warham to Whitgift', in *Continuity and Change*, ed. O'Day and Heal.

contrasts between the areas covered by the two dioceses. At
first sight, the differences within each may seem more important than those which distinguished one from the other. Each,
for instance, embraced farming areas of widely different
types, such as sheep-corn and wood-pasture.[10] In each there
were poor, sparsely populated areas as well as major urban
settlements. Nevertheless, the region covered by the diocese
of Norwich (Norfolk, Suffolk, and part of Cambridgeshire)
was on the whole richer and more densely populated than
that of the diocese of Winchester (Hampshire and Surrey).[11]
The former contained the second city of the kingdom and a
number of important cloth-making towns; its long coastline
was studded with ports, three of which (Lynn, Yarmouth, and
Ipswich) were of outstanding importance. The latter's major
urban centres (outside the London suburb of Southwark,
which lay on its northern periphery) were comparatively
small, and the two biggest, Winchester and Southampton, were
in economic decline.[12]

The early vigour of Protestantism in East Anglia owed much
to the strength of the region's industrial and commercial links
with London and the continent. Much of the diocese of
Winchester, on the other hand, lay in an area relatively thinly
populated and remote from major lines of communication,
where Catholic recusancy was later to be strong.[13]

The diocese of Norwich was much bigger than that of
Winchester, and in 1535 was reckoned to contain more than
three times as many parishes. Nevertheless, the see of Winchester, the wealthiest in England, was more than twice as
well endowed as that of Norwich, and remained by far the

[10] *The Agrarian History of England and Wales*, iv, ed. J. Thirsk (Cambridge,
1967), pp. 49-9, 64-6, 69-70.
[11] See map facing p. .
[12] R. S. Schofield, 'The Geographical Distribution of Wealth in England,
1334-1649', *EcHR* 2nd ser. xviii (1965), esp. 502-6. The over-all level of wealth
in Surrey was probably affected by the fact that Southwark lay within its borders.
See also W. G. Hoskins, *Local History in England* (1959), pp. 176-7; T. Atkinson,
Elizabethan Winchester (1963), pp. 29-33, 199, 248-51; A. Ruddock, 'London
Capitalists and the Decline of Southampton in the Early Tudor Period' *EcHR* 2nd
ser. ii (1949-50).
[13] J. Bossy, *The English Catholic Community, 1570-1850* (1976), pp. 100,
102-3.

richer of the two after the Reformation.[14] Wealth did much
to enhance episcopal authority, especially when, as was the
case with the bishops of Winchester, much of it was derived
from estates within the diocesan boundaries. Of the two
dioceses, that of Winchester was much the easier to supervise,
not only because it was the smaller, but also because the
bishops were permitted much more frequent visitations than
were their Norwich colleagues. Differences of this kind contributed to the contrast noted nearly seventy years ago by
W. H. Frere between the 'willing diocese of Winchester and
the ever recalcitrant diocese of Norwich'.[15]

[14] P. Hughes, *The Reformation in England* (5th edn. 1963), i. 31-6; *Registra
Stephani Gardiner et Johannis Poynet*, ed. H. Chitty and H. E. Malden (Canterbury
and York Soc. xxxvii, 1930), xix-xx; *Valor Ecclesiasticus temp. Henrici VIII
Auctoritate Regia institutus*, ed. J. Caley, J. Hunter (Record Commission,
1810-34), ii. 2; iii. 282; J. Strype, *Annals of the Reformation and Establishment
of Religion.. during Queen Elizabeth's Happy Reign* (Oxford, 1824), i, pt. 1, 227.
[15] *Visitation Articles and Injunctions of the Period of the Reformation* ed.
W. H. Frere and W. M. Kennedy (Alcuin Club Publications, xiv-xvi, 1910), i. 169.

1

ECCLESIASTICAL JURISDICTION AND THE REFORMATION

Today it is unlikely that more than a tiny minority of the English people is aware of the continued existence of ecclesiastical courts. Few could describe their work. To the bulk of the sixteenth-century population, however, the officers of the church courts were amongst the most familiar representatives of authority external to their own communities. The train of the archdeacon's official could be seen travelling remote lanes in all weathers, penetrating the countryside more deeply, traversing it more frequently, than did the representatives of any other comparable court. Ecclesiastical jurisdiction is now no more than the palest shadow of what it once was. Four centuries ago, some of the most intimate aspects of everyday life were subject to the scrutiny of church courts. Ecclesiastical judges dealt with matrimonial problems and punished those who entered into irregular sexual relationships. They settled disputes arising out of wills and prosecuted those who meddled with dead men's goods without authority. They helped to maintain harmony in the community by proceeding against those who reviled their neighbours. In the sixteenth century everybody was bound to accept the church's teachings, to participate in its rites, and to help to meet its expenses. The church courts punished those who denied orthodox doctrines. They enforced the observance of the Sabbath and of saints' days, attendance at church and decorous behaviour while there. They exacted when necessary the payment of tithes and offerings to the clergy, of various rates levied to maintain church fabrics and

furnishings, and of sundry dues received by bishops and archdeacons.

This study will concentrate upon litigation and correction
in the church courts, but it must not be forgotten that a large
part of the work of ecclesiastical judges consisted of acts of
validation, admission, and authorization. They approved wills,
admitted clergymen to benefices, and issued a wide range of
licences and dispensations. The scribes of the courts probably
spent as much of their time on such non-contentious acts as
they did upon work connected with litigation and correction,
and earned much more from them.[1]

The law of the church courts was the common law of
Christendom, much of it supplemented by local custom or reinforced by local legislation. The operation of this
law in England had been modified in important ways by
decisions of the royal courts and by acts of parliament during
the course of the later middle ages. Writs of prohibition had
been developed as a means of removing from the church
courts cases over which the king's courts claimed jurisdiction,
in particular those concerned with real property, rights of
presentation to churches, and debts and chattels not connected with marriages or testaments. Acts of parliament had
dealt with matters as diverse as papal provision to English
benefices, the tithability of wood, and benefit of clergy. But
perhaps the most important were the statutes of *Praemunire*,
passed in the fourteenth century in order to prevent suits
which should have been determined in the king's courts from
being drawn out of England. The third of them (1393) was
later to be turned against the church courts in England.[2] Despite *Praemunire*, however, the pope remained the ultimate
judge in matters which were agreed to be of ecclesiastical cognizance, and this fact was underlined by the events leading up
to Henry VIII's divorce from Catherine of Aragon.

The fifty years which preceded Henry's attack on the
church were eventful ones for the ecclesiastical courts.
Under Edward IV, they apparently enjoyed a brief spell of

[1] Marchant, *Church under the Law*, p. 15.
[2] R. L. Storey, *Diocesan Administration in Fifteenth-Century England* (St.
Anthony's Hall Pubn. xvi, 2nd edn. York, 1972), p. 27.

exceptional prosperity. Suffered to entertain suits against men who broke faith by failing to pay debts or fulfil contracts (matters long regarded as temporal by the royal judges), the consistory court at Canterbury increased its business enormously. Other courts probably did so too. But not long after Henry VII's accession there took place a notable revival of *Praemunire* as a weapon against the ecclesiastical courts, in which the attorney-general, Sir James Hobart, played a leading part. As a result of the officially inspired attacks upon them, the church courts lost much of the lucrative business they had enjoyed under Edward IV. The number of cases of breach of faith entertained by the Canterbury consistory court fell sharply after 1492, and the writ was used to halt certain suits of other types too.[3]

The ecclesiastical lawyers may have taken steps to meet this challenge, but if so they were on the whole unsuccessful. The foundation, apparently in the early 1490s,[4] of the association which was later to develop into Doctors' Commons, was perhaps inspired in part by the threat to their professional interests. A bill 'for the liberties of the English church', probably designed amongst other things to safeguard ecclesiastical jurisdiction, was introduced in Henry VIII's first parliament, but it proved abortive.[5] Bishop Nykke of Norwich was so deeply angered by certain *Praemunire* prosecutions that he expressed to Archbishop Warham, some time between 1504 and 1507, his desire to excommunicate as heretics those responsible.[6] Direct action of this sort would almost certainly have been counter-productive. Behind the notorious heresy proceedings of 1514 against Richard Hunne, merchant of London, there may have lain a determination to protect ecclesiastical jurisdiction, for the charges against him were believed to have resulted from his commencing a *Praemunire* action. If this was indeed so, the authorities in

---

[3] Woodcock, *Medieval Ecclesiastical Courts*, pp. 84, 89-92; Storey, *Diocesan Administration*, pp. 29-32; W. Rastell, *A Collection of Entrees, of Declarations, Barres, Replications* (1596 edn.), fo. 468.

[4] G. D. Squibb, *Doctors' Commons. A History of the College of Advocates and Doctors of Law* (Oxford, 1977), pp. 5-7.

[5] Storey, op. cit., p. 32.

[6] PRO SC 1/44/83.

the diocese of London were acting in this case in the spirit of Nykke's earlier letter to Warham. Proceedings against the chancellor of the diocese for Hunne's murder raised the vexed question of benefit of clergy, pruned by statutes of 1489 and (temporarily) 1512, and it was by citing Henry Standish before it to answer questions concerning, amongst other things, the immunity of clergy from secular prosecution, that convocation laid itself open to the penalties of *Praemunire* in the view of the chief common law judges.[7]

Thomas Wolsey's period of supremacy has often been seen as a time when the English church's last opportunity for reforming itself before the impending crisis was tragically wasted. Wolsey used his legatine powers to carry out visitations, diverted cases from episcopal courts to his own legatine court, and forced bishops to share with him the profits of their jurisdictions. The main aim of these activities is usually seen as self-aggrandizement; they have not yet been studied fully enough for us to be sure what good, if any, came of them. But it is becoming increasingly clear that Wolsey's interference was neither as damaging to episcopal morale nor as prejudicial to administrative efficiency as was once thought. The period of his supremacy was one in which a number of outstanding bishops (some of whom had retired from central government on his accession to power) took a keen interest in the efficient running of their dioceses. The improvement in the quality of administration which took place in some areas at this time had been most convincingly illustrated by a careful study of the diocese of Chichester. Here Bishop Robert Sherburne built up a particularly capable executive team and brought the courts under closer personal control. More cases were heard than in the years before Sherburne's arrival, and suits were more swiftly despatched than hitherto. Standards of discipline were improved. Less is known about other dioceses, but the bishops of Lincoln, Ely, Norwich, and Winchester certainly took a close interest in diocesan administration at this period. To some extent,

---

[7] J. A. F. Thomson *The Later Lollards, 1414-1520* (Oxford, 1965), pp. 238, 162-71; A. F. Pollard, *Wolsey* (1929), pp. 26-58; S. F. C. Milsom, 'Richard Hunne's "Praemunire"', *EHR* lxxvi (1961), 80-2.

therefore, the years of Wolsey's supremacy can be viewed as a period of recovery and reconstruction after the damaging attacks and consequent demoralization which had marked the later years of Henry VII.[8]

There is however nothing to show that during these years ordinaries tried to appease the passions aroused by the events of 1509-15. These smouldered on, to burst forth with renewed virulence when the Reformation parliament met in 1529. However attractive they may have been to humble litigants, the ecclesiastical courts had influential enemies. The families of wealthy men in the towns, whose estates consisted for the most part of moveable goods, resented probate fees. The common lawyers, whose business had been dwindling,[9] viewed rival jurisdictions with jealousy. The belief that ordinaries were ready to use heresy charges to bring to heel those who threatened ecclesiastical jurisdiction, given plausibility by Hunne's case, aroused a new fear of the ecclesiastical courts amongst comparatively substantial men who may not have had much sympathy with the humble people who made up the bulk of 'Lollard' suspects.[10] Amongst the earliest statutes passed by the Reformation parliament were acts dealing with probate fees and mortuaries, which had figured prominently in the suits and controversies of the first fifteen years of the century.[11]

Whereas Henry VIII had in his early years affected the role of impartial arbiter, he now encouraged the attack upon the church. Late in 1530, not long before the opening of the second session of the Reformation parliament, *Praemunire* proceedings undertaken against certain churchmen including

---

[8] Pollard, op. cit., pp. 165-216; S. Lander, 'Church Courts and the Reformation in the Diocese of Chichester, 1500-58', in *Continuity and Change*, ed. O'Day and Heal, esp. pp. 217-28; M. Bowker, *The Secular Clergy in the Diocese of Lincoln, 1495-1520* (Cambridge, 1968), pp. 17-23; F. M. Heal 'The Bishops of Ely and their Diocese, 1515- c. 1600' (Cambridge Ph.D. thesis, 1972), pp. 47-67.

[9] E. W. Ives, 'The Common Lawyers in Pre-Reformation England', *TRHS* 5th ser. xviii (1968), 165-70.

[10] M. Bowker, 'The Commons' Supplication against the Ordinaries in the light of some Archidiaconal *Acta*', *TRHS* 5th ser. xxi (1971), 75-6.

[11] On Londoners' earlier discontent with church courts' exercise of their testamentary jurisdiction, see H. Miller, 'London and Parliament in the Reign of Henry VIII', *BIHR* xxxv (1962), 134.

a number of Queen Catherine's sympathizers, broadened into an attack on the whole body of the clergy. The two convocations were forced early next year to pay substantially for their pardon, whose statutory confirmation alleged that they had incurred the penalties of *Praemunire* by exercising ecclesiastical jurisdiction. The two convocations had also to accept Henry as supreme head of the church 'as far as the law of Christ allows'.[12]

A much more important development in the attack on the church was to take place the following year. In March 1532 the *Commons' Supplication against the Ordinaries*, which included grievances first aired three years earlier, was presented to the king. A number of the complaints which it contained were concerned with the exercise of ecclesiastical jurisdiction. But the first article, pointing out that many of the ordinances of the church were repugnant to the laws of the realm, was the crucial one from Henry's point of view. In subsequent weeks he used the *Supplication* to bully a rump convocation into the so-called 'Submission of the Clergy', by which it agreed to enact no ecclesiastical laws without the king's permission and accepted the royal demand that the existing spiritual laws be examined by a commission appointed by Henry in order to discover which of them were compatible with the laws of the realm. In 1534 the Submission was incorporated in a statute. This provided that the existing ecclesiastical laws might still be executed, in so far as they were compatible with the king's prerogative and the laws and customs of the realm. In fact, the laws of the church had as we have seen long been subject in practice in a number of major respects to limitation by the laws of the realm. The Submission made this position much more explicit, and it seemed that the development of the English ecclesiastical laws would henceforth be subject to much closer royal control.[13]

A satisfactory solution of Henry's matrimonial problems in accordance with what he held to be the correct interpretation

---

[12] J. J. Scarisbrick, 'The Pardon of the Clergy, 1531', *CHJ* xii (1956); S. E. Lehmberg, *The Reformation Parliament, 1529–1536* (Cambridge, 1970), pp. 107–8, 118–19, 126–8.

[13] M. J. Kelly, 'The Submission of the Clergy', *TRHS* 5th ser. xv (1965); 25 Henry VIII, c. 19.

of God's law had still to be achieved. It became increasingly apparent that only an English tribunal could provide such a solution. The act in restraint of appeals, which received the royal assent in April 1533, left the final determination of most appeals in the hands of the archbishops; in matters touching the king, the party grieved might make further appeal to the upper house of convocation. Next year, the act for the submission of the clergy provided for the final determination of appeals by judges delegate commissioned under the great seal. Another statute passed in this session transferred the authority to grant dispensations and licences from Rome to Canterbury.[14]

The break with Rome was completed in the same year. Archbishop Cranmer undertook a metropolitical visitation one of whose main aims was to exact from many of the more important clergy a specific renunciation of papal authority. At the end of the year the act of royal supremacy was passed, which acknowledged that the king was supreme head of the church of England, and declared his power to redress and reform all errors, heresies and abuses in it. Early in 1535 Henry appointed Thomas Cromwell his vicegerent in spirituals, in order, so it has been argued, to resolve doubts about the source of jurisdictional authority in the church which the metropolitical visitation of 1534 brought to light.[15] Between February and June 1535, most of the bishops surrendered their bulls of appointment and received commissions which empowered them to exercise jurisdiction during the royal pleasure. In September, in order to underline the practical implications of these grants, the bishops were forbidden to proceed with their visitations pending a general royal visitation and were suspended from the exercise of their spiritual jurisdiction, which was gradually restored to them in a series of subsequent grants. Cromwell exercised his authority through a vicegerential court which, amongst other things, issued the licences to the bishops to exercise jurisdiction and

[14] 24 Henry VIII, c. 12; 25 Henry VIII, cc. 19, 21. The act in restraint of appeals made no specific mention of certain types of cause, for example defamation.
[15] M. Bowker, 'The Supremacy and the Episcopate: The Struggle for Control, 1534-1540', *HJ* xviii (1975), esp. 228; 26 Henry VIII, c. 1.

approved wills disposing of certain categories of more substantial estate. This court lapsed on Cromwell's fall in 1540.[16]

The church courts could not but be seriously affected by
this series of dramatic changes. They had been subjected with
official encouragement to repeated parliamentary criticism,
and new areas of their jurisdiction had been regulated by
statute. Their activities had been formally suspended. Leading
ordinaries, amongst them that Richard Nykke who had,
thirty years before, favoured the excommunication as heretics
of those who impugned the liberties of the church, had been
bullied and humiliated.[17] The whole fabric of ecclesiastical
jurisdiction had been shaken.

In 1534-5 the future shape of the church courts must have
appeared highly uncertain. A number of schemes were put
forward which involved the transfer of a large part of their
work to the temporal courts. Dr. William Petre, for instance,
Cromwell's commissary, in charge of the vicegerential court,
was in favour of leaving the church courts with only the
settlement of matrimonial and divorce cases and the probate
of small testaments. In the event, however, the courts were
allowed to retain most of their jurisdiction. The break with
Rome had clearly brought them more directly under royal
control than the temporal courts, and Henry had no desire
to see the diminution of his new powers.[18] The courts survived in their old shape. The governments of both Edward
and Elizabeth temporarily suspended episcopal jurisdiction
and carried out royal visitations on the model of the one
begun in 1535, but the vicegerential court was not revived,
and Elizabeth dropped the practice of issuing commissions to
the bishops which had, between 1535 and 1553, underlined
their jurisdictional dependence on the crown.[19] Mary I,
indeed, by the act of December 1554 repealing anti-papal

---

[16] Hughes, *The Reformation in England*, i. 272-3, 391-2; S. E. Lehmberg,
'Supremacy and Vicegerency: A Re-examination', *EHR* lxxxi (1966); C. J.
Kitching, 'The Probate Jurisdiction of Thomas Cromwell as Vicegerent', *BIHR*
xlvi (1973); G. R. Elton, *Policy and Police* (Cambridge, 1972), pp. 247-8.

[17] J. J. Scarisbrick, *Henry VIII* (1968), pp. 329-31.

[18] G. R. Elton, *Reform and Renewal: Thomas Cromwell and the Common
Weal* (Cambridge, 1973), pp. 133-5.

[19] R. B. Manning, 'The Crisis of Episcopal Authorty during the Reign of
Elizabeth I', *Journal of British Studies*, xi (1971), 3.

legislation, discarded the royal supremacy and in form restored
the relationship between the pope and the church courts to
what it had been before the legislation of the Reformation
parliament. But this restoration was not to have any lasting
significance in the history of the courts.

The development of the Reformation from 1536 onwards
brought the courts new tasks. The burden of enforcing religious changes fell largely upon them. It was under their
pressure, to a great extent, that churches were re-equipped
for Protestant worship. Until well after Elizabeth's accession
it was the church courts, too, that played the main part in
such attempts as were made to enforce attendance at church
services, a task which became increasingly onerous as conservative resistance to the Protestant settlement hardened.
The important part the church courts were called upon to
play in the enforcement of the Reformation made it desirable,
to say the least, that they should command respect. Yet very
little was done directly to strengthen them. Henry VIII's
government realized very swiftly how far the authority of the
ordinaries had been undermined. As early as 1536, a statute
passed by the Reformation parliament in its last session deplored what it described as unprecedented contempt of the
courts in tithe cases, and gave ordinaries the right to ask justices of the peace to attach contumacious defendants.[20] But
this expedient was not developed. In the long run, the crown,
while recognizing the importance of lay co-operation with
the ordinaries, especially in the crucial field of religious uniformity, preferred to promote it by making ordinaries members of special commissions rather than by assisting the church
courts directly. In 1539 the act of six articles gave such appointments statutory authority. The governments of Edward
VI and Mary I relied on the crown's spiritual prerogatives in
issuing similar commissions. The type was developed to its
fullest extent under Elizabeth I. The central commissions
which she established on a statutory as well as prerogative
basis from 1559 onwards became known as the 'high commission'. Similar commissions were also established for the
northern province and, by the middle of the reign, in most

---

[20] 27 Henry VIII, c. 20.

dioceses. The commissioners' power to fine and imprison made them more effective than the normal ecclesiastical courts, which had to rely upon spiritual sanctions. Designed in the first place to uphold religious uniformity, the commissions attracted in the course of time an increasing amount of instance business.[21] The ecclesiastical courts proper continued to deal with most cases of spiritual cognizance; the special powers of the commissioners were not, of course, available to them, but the latter probably helped to strengthen the confidence of a number of ecclesiastical judges who knew that, in the last resort, the most obstinate offenders might be referred to the commissioners. An attempt was made to strengthen the sanctions at their own disposal when in 1563 a statute was passed which was intended to improve the procedure for the arrest of the persistently contumacious.[22]

After an initial period of uncertainty, then, the church courts found an assured place in the post-Reformation judicial and administrative structure. The enforcement of the Reformation changes greatly increased their disciplinary work. A rapidly growing number of litigants brought cases before the courts, so that by the 1560s they were handling more cases between parties than at any time since the beginning of the century.

*   *   *   *   *

After the Reformation the common law of the medieval western church and the provincial statutes and constitutions remained the core of the substantive law enforced by the English ecclesiastical courts. Thus, despite the fact that Thomas Cromwell as vicegerent forbade the study of canon law *as hitherto organized*,[23] the judges and better-qualified lawyers in the post-Reformation ecclesiastical courts were

---

[21] R. G. Usher, *The Rise and Fall of the High Commission*, introd. P. Tyler (Oxford, 1968), pp. xi–xxxi, 21–31.

[22] 5 Elizabeth I, c. 23.

[23] W. Stubbs, *Seventeen Lectures on the Study of Medieval and Modern History* (Oxford, 1887), p. 366.

well acquainted with both civil and ecclesiastical law.[24] In 1551 Thomas Pelles, a former ecclesiastical judge of Norwich diocese, expressed in his will the hope that a young protégé of his would learn to write 'all manner of Instrumentes concerning Ecclesiasticall lawes' by working for a year or two as a proctor's clerk in the court of Arches before proceeding to one of the universities to study the civil law.[25]

It was at first intended that the reformed *Ecclesia Anglicana* should be provided with a revised code of ecclesiastical law. When the rump convocation submitted to the king in 1532, it agreed to the royal demand that the laws be scrutinized by a commission of thirty-two men, and this provision was incorporated in the statute of 1534. The king's powers to appoint commissioners were renewed by statute in 1536 and 1544; in the last act a collection of new laws was for the first time envisaged.[26] By then, however, a body of canons had already been prepared in draft, probably before October 1535.[27] It is likely that Cranmer was referring to this collection when, writing to the king in January 1546, he mentioned a book of ecclesiastical laws which had been completed. No further steps were taken to give these canons effect. When, in Edward's reign, a statute of 1550 renewing the crown's powers was at last followed by the nomination of commissioners in October 1551, an entirely new code was drawn up.[28] This code was printed with slight changes in 1571 as the *Reformatio Legum Ecclesiasticarum*, the title by which it has been known ever since. The code was designed to improve the efficiency of the ecclesiastical courts and to tighten up the discipline which they administered. It included, too, provisions designed to strengthen the church against lay encroachments. Tithe payments, for instance, were to be more rigorously enforced than was possible under the existing

---

[24] B. P. Levack, *The Civil Lawyers in England 1603-1641* (Oxford, 1973), pp. 16-21; J. D. M. Derrett, *Henry Swinburne (?1551-1624) Civil Lawyer of York* (Borthwick Paper, xliv, York, 1973).

[25] NNRO NCC will register Corant, fos. 163ᵛ-6.

[26] By 27 Henry VIII, c. 15 and 35 Henry VIII, c. 16.

[27] F. D. Logan, 'The Henrician Canons', *BIHR* xlvii (1974), esp. 103.

[28] J. Ridley, *Thomas Cranmer* (Oxford, 1962), pp. 331-2; Hughes, *Reformation in England*, ii. 128-34; *The Reformation of the Ecclesiastical Laws*, ed. E. Cardwell (Oxford, 1850), pp. iii-xvi.

law.[29] Under the circumstances, it would hardly be surprising if indeed the duke of Northumberland did tell Cranmer that the project should come to nothing when he presented it in parliament in 1553.[30] Never again were hopes for the comprehensive reform of the ecclesiastical laws to come so close to fruition. A bill for the renewal of the commission introduced in 1559 failed to become law, and an attempt to obtain statutory sanction for the *Reformatio* in 1571 met with no success.[31]

No thorough revision of the ecclesiastical laws inherited from the middle ages was achieved during the Reformation, but they were modified and added to by means of a number of new measures. Royal injunctions were issued in 1536, 1538, 1554, and 1559. Proclamations and royal or conciliar letters dealing with matters ecclesiastical were published in large numbers, especially during periods of rapid religious change, such as Edward VI's reign. Articles and orders were also issued by the archbishops, often with episcopal concurrence. Royal and episcopal orders and injunctions were concerned in particular with liturgical practice, the duties of the clergy and the maintenance and equipment of churches. It was largely through them that England's church was given the outward face of Protestantism. Later on a series of convocations, culminating in that of 1604, were to approve important canons and articles. But from 1529 onwards parliamentary legislation was the most important source of change in the ecclesiastical law, and the changes made were much more extensive than those achieved before that date. Statutes altered the laws enforced by the church courts, gave secular courts concurrent jurisdiction in some cases and removed others from ecclesiastical cognizance. Use of the new liturgy of the Protestant church of England was from the start enforced by acts of parliament. The course of appeals, the qualifications and status of judges, the regulation of marriage, the correction of sexual misbehaviour, procedure in the probate of testaments, the levying of tithes and mortuaries, the

---

[29] Ibid., pp. 130–1.
[30] *Calendar of State Papers Spanish*, xi, ed. R. Tyler (1916), 33.
[31] J. E. Neale, *Elizabeth I and her Parliaments, 1559–1581* (1953), pp. 194–7.

control of clerical pluralism and non-residence, the punishment of religious nonconformists, usurers, witches, and criminous clerks — all of these and other important matters were affected by statutes passed within the first half-century after the opening of the Reformation parliament.

During our period no English civilian or canonist of the first rank attempted to describe and analyse the bewildering changes which were taking place or to comment in detail upon their implications for the practice of ecclesiastical lawyers. The legislation of the medieval church, though modified in a number of important respects by the changes of the Reformation, remained the core of the ecclesiastical laws till the end of our period. Of the late-medieval English canonists the foremost were John Ayton (d. 1349) and William Lyndwood (1375?-1446) who completed his commentary upon the constitutions of the province of Canterbury in 1430.[32] Lyndwood's work remained the leading authority on the English ecclesiastical law right through the period of the Reformation, the legal textbook which was probably most often consulted by the middle and lower ranks of the ecclesiastical legal profession. Not until the 1590s was the first serious post-Reformation attempt made to expound the ecclesiastical laws for the benefit of English readers by a group of men familiar with the work of the ecclesiastical courts. The most outstanding of these was Henry Swinburne, advocate of York (?1551-1624), whose great *Treatise of Testaments and Last Wills* was published in 1590-1. He also wrote a *Treatise of Spousals* which was to remain unpublished till 1686. These works are particularly useful to the historian of the courts, since they deal with aspects of the law on which Lyndwood had had little to say. At last Swinburne has received his due.[33] Dr. Derrett has shown him to be 'a true follower of Bartolus and Baldus, and a genuine colleague of the celebrated jurists of the European continent, a *rara avis*

---

[32] *Provinciale (seu Constitutiones Angliae) ... cum Summariis atque Eruditis Annotationibis ... Auctore Gulielmo Lyndwood ... Cui adjiciuntur Constitutiones Legatinae D. Othonis et D. Othoboni ... cum Profundissimis Annotationibus Johannis de Athona ...* (Oxford, 1679).

[33] In Derrett, *Henry Swinburne*. For passages cited here, see pp. 2, 13, 17-19, 27.

indeed.' Swinburne brought to bear in his work an immense knowledge of the studies of previous canonists and civilians. He summed up the existing state of opinion on difficult questions concisely and judiciously, and was not afraid to add his own view, one which gains added weight from his long practical experience. He wrote beautifully, at times with a sharp sense of humour, while at the same time 'making no improper concession to the lay mind'. Swinburne had no rivals amongst his English contemporaries, but a number of other important works were produced at this time. Richard Cosin's *Apologie* (1591) was a detailed defence of ecclesiastical court proceedings against the attacks of puritans and common lawyers. An anonymous civilian, in a work heavily indebted to Lyndwood, set out the law of tithes in concise form.[34] Francis Clarke completed in 1596 the most detailed post-Reformation treatise on the practice of an English ecclesiastical court, based on the procedure of the court of Arches.[35] His work, though not published for seventy years, circulated widely in manuscript form within a few years of its completion, and enjoyed a high esteem. Clarke's work was rearranged and translated by Henry Conset, who incorporated very little of his own in *The Practice of the Spiritual or Ecclesiastical Courts* (1685) which is thus, despite its date of publication, one of the most accessible guides to the procedure of the courts shortly after the end of our period.[36] The authors of the 1590s provide the historian with his most useful introduction to the practice of the ecclesiastical courts and the law they administered in the years following the Reformation, though their works have of course to be used with care, since the law never stood still.

---

[34] R. Cosin, *An Apologie: of, and for Sundrie Proceedings by Jurisdiction Ecclesiasticall* (1591); *Tithes and Oblations according to the Lawes established in the Church of England* (1595). The latter was compiled by W. C., bachelor of the civil law, who had already, in 1591, published a *Decimarum tabula*.

[35] F. Clarke, *Praxis in Curiis Ecclesiasticis* (Dublin, 1666).

[36] Because Conset's *Practice* is easier to consult, I have generally referred to it rather than to Clarke's *Praxis* in the course of this study, though occasionally I have drawn upon the latter in order to clear up doubtful points. The second edition of the *Practice* (1700) has been used.

2

THE COURTS AND THEIR PROCEDURE

ORGANIZATION AND PERSONNEL

(i) *The bishops and their courts*

The efficiency of diocesan administration varied greatly from time to time and from one diocese to another. It was determined not only by inherited custom and organization, but also by the character of the men who ruled each diocese. Of the two here studied, the diocese of Winchester was the easier to run, above all because of its smaller size and because of the exceptionally frequent visitations which the bishop and his chief judge were allowed to make by long-established custom. But the differences between the experiences of the two dioceses during the period of the Reformation were accentuated by the fact that it was Norwich's misfortune to suffer under the rule of two particularly ineffective bishops.

In the years before the break with Rome, both dioceses were governed by experienced and well-qualified men. Richard Fox of Winchester (1501-28) and Richard Nykke of Norwich (1501-35) were both civilians who after their years of close involvement in public affairs devoted much of their old age to the oversight of their dioceses. Both men took part in visitations and heard some cases in person during at least part of their episcopates.[1] They belonged to a generation of distinguished

---

[1] *DNB*; A. B. Emden, *A Biographical Register of the University of Oxford to A.D. 1500* (Oxford, 1957-9), ii. 715-19, 1381-2; BL Add. MS. 48022, fo. 88; *Letters of Richard Fox, 1486-1527*, ed. P. S. and H. M. Allen (Oxford, 1929), pp. 82-4, 86-8, 95, 115, 150-1; *Visitations of the Diocese of Norwich*, ed. A. Jessopp (Camden Soc. n. s. xliii, 1888); NNRO ACT 4B; GLRO microfilm X 11, fos. 1, 4, 6, 7^V-8, 11, 14^V-15, 21^V, 56, 96^V, 152.

episcopal administrators which included West at Ely, Sherburne at Chichester, and Atwater at Lincoln.

The fortunes of the two dioceses during the early years of the Reformation were however very different. Though Stephen Gardiner of Winchester (1531-51, 1553-5) was active in royal service for most of his episcopate and gave little of it to the care of his diocese, the task of supervision seems on the whole to have been effectively discharged by his appointees. At Norwich the ineffectual William Rugge, promoted on account of his support for the royal divorce, succeeded Nykke in 1536. His incompetence led to his enforced resignation just under fourteen years later, but his extravagance inaugurated a much longer period of financial difficulty for the bishops of Norwich. His embarrassment was not entirely his own fault, for an exchànge of lands with the crown had sharply reduced the income of the see. But the bishops of Winchester adapted far better to reduced circumstances than did their Norwich colleagues despite a drastic diminution in the value of their bishopric during the Reformation.[2]

None of the bishops who ruled the two dioceses in the 1550s retained his position very long. Neither John Ponet (1551-3) nor John White (1556-9) left much trace of his involvement in the administration of the diocese of Winchester.[3] Thomas Thirlby, an important servant of the crown, visited Norwich seldom and briefly during his episcopate (1550-4). Of these bishops, only John Hopton of Norwich (1554-8), who was closely interested in the suppression of heresy, left the stamp of his personality upon his diocese.[4]

The first Elizabethan bishops of Winchester and Norwich, Robert Horne (1561-79) and John Parkhurst (1560-75) were

---

[2] J. A. Muller, *Stephen Gardiner and the Tudor Reaction* (1926); F. Blomefield and C. Parkin, *An Essay towards a Topographical History of the County of Norfolk* (2nd edn. 1805-10), iii. 547-9; *Reg. Gardiner et Poynet*, xix. Wolsey held Winchester *in commendam*, 1529-30.

[3] W. S. Hudson *John Ponet (1516?-1556), Advocate of Limited Monarchy* (Chicago, 1942), esp. pp. 48-60; *DNB*; A. B. Emden, *A Biographical Register of the University of Oxford, A.D. 1501 to 1540* (Oxford, 1974), pp. 621-2; *Registrum Johannis Whyte, Episcopi Wintoniensis*, ed. W. H. Frere (Canterbury and York Soc. xvi, 1914).

[4] T. F. Shirley, *Thomas Thirlby, Tudor Bishop* (1964); NNRO ACT 7A, fos. 77-8; ACT 7B, fos. 127-34; *DNB*; Emden, *Oxford, 1501-40*, p. 298.

both wholehearted supporters of godly reformation. But there the resemblance between them ended. Horne was a tough, pugnacious but realistic ecclesiastical politician and administrator, whose hostility towards remnants of popery was coupled with a healthy respect for superior powers. He belonged, together with Jewel, Cox, and Grindal to a group of early Elizabethan bishops whose energy and zeal enabled them to exploit with some success the machinery of diocesan government inherited from the pre-Reformation church. John Parkhurst, on the other hand, was a poor administrator and judge of men, over-dependent on officials who exploited his lenity and naivety, whose incompetence earned him stinging rebukes.[5]

Bishops often took a personal interest in the work of conciliation and correction for whose success they were ultimately responsible. A number of the bishops of Winchester and Norwich sometimes presided over consistory courts during our period.[6] Some bishops also heard cases elsewhere, and courts of audience existed in both dioceses.[7] It seems probable, however, that the Winchester and Norwich courts of audience were never as important as their counterpart at Lincoln, a vital instrument in the government of a huge diocese, where bishops and chancellors regularly undertook important cases *ex officio* and heard appeals from inferior courts in the archdeaconries.[8] There is indeed no evidence that such a court functioned in the diocese of Winchester between 1528 and 1580 or in that of Norwich between 1550 and 1575, though later bishops of Norwich certainly attempted to revive their court. In each diocese the lapse of the audience

[5] *DNB*; J. Le Neve, *Fasti Ecclesiae Anglicanae 1541–1857*, iii, comp. J. Horn (1974), 80; Emden, *Oxford, 1501–40*, pp. 433–4; *The Letter Book of John Parkhurst, Bishop of Norwich*, ed. R. A. Houlbrooke (Norfolk Record Soc. xliii, 1974-5), 17-57.

[6] HRO CB 5, fo. 49; CB 17, p. 101; CB 29, fos. 7^v, 25, 62^v, 86^v, 111; CB 31, fos. 1, 56^v, 67^v, 91^v, 98^v, 137; CB 35, *passim*; NNRO ACT 7A, fos. 77-8; ACT 7B, fos. 127, 129-30, 132^v-3, 134; ACT 8, fos. 263, 267; ACT 9 (unfoliated) Michaelmas term of 1561.

[7] HRO CB 3, fos. 68^v, 72^v; CB 5, fo. 87; NNRO ACT 3A, fo. 110; ACT 4A, fos. 19^v, 87^v, 94, 116, 117^v, 238; ACT 4B fos. 16^v, 139; ACT 5, fos. 14, 21^v, 39^v, 54, 77^v, 134^v, 170^v, 214^v; ACT 6, fos. 78^v, 85^v, 89; institution book xiv, fos. 60a-p; NCC will register Thyrkyll.

[8] *Lincoln Episcopal Court Book*; Bowker, *Secular Clergy*, p. 19.

court seems to have occurred during the episcopate of an absentee bishop.

The bulk of the bishop's judicial responsibilities were discharged by his official principal. In both dioceses, throughout our period, this office was held with that of vicar general by one man, usually a beneficed clergyman, who was described as the chancellor. His most important functions were the hearing of cases of every sort, inquiry into and punishment of every type of offence, institution of clergymen to benefices and (if necessary) their deprivation of them, the probate of testaments and concession of letters of administration. He was empowered to name his own deputy and to make certain other appointments.[9] These weighty responsibilities demanded high qualifications, and most of the chancellors of our period were doctors of law at the time of their appointment or received doctorates during their terms of office.

In both dioceses it was the rule for chancellors to be granted revocable commissions, and most incoming bishops made their own appointments. Few parted with their appointees during their episcopates, but chancellors occasionally got into trouble or failed to measure up to their jobs, and some of them resigned or were dismissed. The first Elizabethan bishops, who seem to have been exceptionally unfortunate in this respect, parted with five chancellors. The resignations or dismissals of at least four of them were caused by personal disagreements, incompetence or misbehaviour.[10] Clearly these appointments increased the already formidable administrative difficulties of Horne and Parkhurst.

None of the men who held office as chancellors in the two dioceses during our period is known to have been a vigorous supporter of the Reformation. The two who remained longest in office, Edmund Stuarde (Winchester, 1531-51, 1553?-7) and Miles Spencer (Norwich, 1531-70) were both conservatives

[9] NNRO institution book xviii, fos. 1-2, 84ᵛ-5; institution book xix, fos. 4, 120ᵛ, 278ᵛ-9, 283ᵛ-4; HRO Reg. Fox, v. fo. 21; *Registrum Thome Wolsey*, ed. H. Chitty (Canterbury and York Soc. xxxii, 1926), 8-12; *Reg. Gardiner et Poynet*, 9-16, 49-52, 80-1; *Reg. Whyte*, 9-17.

[10] BL Lansdowne MS. 18, fo. 20; *Letter Book of Parkhurst*, 116; Cambridge, Corpus Christi College MS. 114, pp. 951, 955; PRO E 135/25/31, fos. 5-8; HRO, CB 28, 19 Jan. 1569; CB 30, 28 Sept. 1569; CB 32, 19 June 1570; below, p. 53.

who differed only in the extent to which they were prepared to bend before the wind. Shortly before Gardiner's trial, in November 1550, Stuarde was committed to the Marshalsea for failing to make adequate acknowledgement of certain offences against the royal proceedings. Spenser was retained as sole chancellor by Bishop Rugge, and as joint chancellor by Rugge's successors; he continued to hold office with perhaps one short break until his death in 1570. Either Spenser's experience made him appear indispensable or he had been granted some sort of life tenure exceptional at that time by his beloved master Richard Nykke. His will reveals that leading church papists and future recusants were amongst his closest associates. Spenser was while chancellor archdeacon of Sudbury for over thirty years.[11] Both he and Stuarde no doubt did much to stamp with their own conservatism the courts over which they presided.

The principal registrar was the chancellor's most important partner in the work of running the diocese. It was his responsibility to write out, or see written out, acts of court, testaments, and all the instruments employed in diocesan administrative and judicial processes. He was necessarily a public notary, whose testimony was equal to that of two ordinary witnesses and sufficient guarantee of the validity of acts of court for whose entry he was responsible. It has been well said that in so far as the efficiency of a church court depended on any one man, that was the registrar. His control over the process of citation, to take but one example, enabled him to discourage trivial or ill-considered litigation.[12] The work of the office was far too great to be done by one man, and registrars entrusted much of it to their deputies. All the registrars appointed during our period were laymen who received episcopal patents for life; Norwich registrars secured

[11] NNRO NCC will register Alpe, fo. 127; institution book xviii, fos. 1-2, 84ᵛ-5; institution book xix, fos. 4, 120ᵛ, 278ᵛ-9; *Reg Gardiner et Poynet*, xvii-xviii, 9-16, 49-52, 80-1; *Reg. Whyte*, 9-14; *Acts of the Privy Council of England*, iii. ed. J. R. Dasent (1891), 138, 163, 226; PRO PROB 11/52, fos. 49-50; J. Le Neve, *Fasti Ecclesiae Anglicanae 1300-1541*, iv, comp. B. Jones (1963), 32.

[12] Woodcock, *Medieval Ecclesiastical Courts*, pp. 38-40; *Letter Book of Parkhurst*, p. 263; below, pp. 40, 53.

the inclusion of sons or servants in their patents.[13] Such patents naturally conferred upon those who received them greater independence than did revocable commissions, and relations between bishops and registrars were often unhappy. John Parkhurst had cause to be dissatisfied with the service given him by two registrars, William Mingay and his son John. At Winchester John Cooke, principal registrar from 1524 until at least 1564, caused trouble for most of the bishops under whom he served, notably Gardiner, Ponet and Horne. Abhorring the 'pure religion' set forth by Horne, he tried to discredit the bishop by spreading a rumour that he had been seen in adultery.[14]

These were not the only dioceses in which officials remained in their posts through successive changes in religious policy. Continuity was maintained by long-serving chancellors at York, Chester, Chichester, and Gloucester.[15] Registrars, shielded by their patents, were of course harder to remove than chancellors. Bishop Tunstall's registrar at Durham survived all the vicissitudes of the Reformation to serve two Elizabethan bishops. It is not surprising that Bishop Scambler of Peterborough should have suggested in 1564 that bishops should be authorized to remove registrars who 'for the most parte haue there office by patent, being corrupt in religion', doing 'more hurt knowing the state of the diocesse and being in greate estimacion with the aduersaries of good religion than the prechers are able to do good otherwayes ...'[16] It was hardly to be expected that men like these would execute

[13] NNRO dean and chapter patent book 1, fos. 95-6; *The Registrum Vagum of Anthony Harison*, ed. T. F. Barton (Norfolk Record Soc. xxxii-xxxiii, 1963-4), i. 88-90.

[14] NNRO institution book xix, fo. 120; *Letter Book of Parkhurst*, 172; HRO Reg. Fox, v, fo. 84; BL Lansdowne MS. 7, fo. 139; *Reg. Gardiner et Poynet*, xxiii-iv; *Narratives of the Days of the Reformation*, ed. J. G. Nichols (Camden Soc. o. s. lxxvii, 1859), 49-51.

[15] Marchant, *Church under the Law*, pp. 41-2; C. Haigh, *Reformation and Resistance in Tudor Lancashire* (Cambridge, 1975), pp. 12-13, 196; Lander, 'Church Courts and the Reformation', p. 233; Price, 'Gloucester Diocese under Bishop Hooper', 68-9.

[16] *The Registers of Cuthbert Tunstall, Bishop of Durham, 1530-59, and James Pilkington, Bishop of Durham, 1561-76*, ed. G. Hinde (Surtees Soc. clxi, 1946), xiv-xv; *A Collection of Original Letters from the Bishops to the Privy Council, 1564*, ed. M. Bateson (Camden Soc. n. s. liii, 1895), 34.

with equal vigour and relish the different policies which followed each other with such baffling rapidity in the middle years of the sixteenth century.

The most important court in both dioceses was the consistory court. In settling disputes, the Norwich court was by far the busier of the two, because it dealt with causes originating in all parts of the great eastern diocese, while its counterpart at Winchester heard very few cases from outside Winchester archdeaconry. On the other hand, much more correctional work was done at Winchester, because here many of the offenders presented in visitations (which were far more frequent than they were in Norwich diocese) were dealt with in the consistory court. In a number of other large dioceses, including London, Lincoln, and York, the consistory courts left most of the work of correction to the courts in the archdeaconries, while in certain relatively small dioceses, such as Canterbury, Chichester, and Ely, the principal court dealt, as at Winchester, with both types of business.[17]

In both dioceses the consistory court usually sat in the cathedral, but sometimes elsewhere, in an episcopal residence, the chancellor's house, or another church in the cathedral city. In the diocese of Winchester post-visitation sessions were held in a number of local centres, while in that of Norwich they sometimes took place at Ipswich in synod time. During our period the regular pattern of term-time sessions was only rarely interrupted: by royal and metropolitical visitations, by Kett's rebels, who in 1549 pressed the Norwich diocesan registrar into their service, and by the troubles of Bishop Gardiner and Chancellor Stuarde of Winchester in 1550-1.[18]

[17] Woodcock, *Medieval Ecclesiastical Courts*, pp. 31-4; Lander, 'Church Courts and the Reformation', pp. 216, 223; M. E. Aston, *Thomas Arundel* (Oxford, 1967), pp. 41, 53-68; J. P. Anglin, 'The Court of the Archdeacon of Essex, 1571-1609; An Institutional and Social Study' (Univ. of California Ph. D. thesis, 1965), chs. 2, 3; C. Morris, 'A Consistory Court in the Middle Ages', *JEH* xiv (1963), 155, 157-8; Marchant, *Church under the Law*, p. 62. The Winchester consistory court nevertheless dealt with relatively few *ex officio* cases from Surrey save during the 1560s.

[18] NNRO ACT 6, fos. 271-2; PRO Star Chamber 3/1/74; *Reg. Gardiner et Poynet*, vii; HRO CB 9 (unfoliated) entries for 8 Nov. 1550, 10 Oct. 1551. On synods, see below p. 30; on troubles of Stuarde, above, p. 25.

The number of lawyers (proctors) regularly employed in the conduct of cases rose with the expansion of business from about three at the beginning of the period in both consistory courts to four or five at Winchester and about six at Norwich by 1570. Other men practised intermittently. The majority of proctors gained degrees or admission to practice as notaries public in the course of their careers; some both. Of the men with degrees, a number went on to become judges, mostly in archdeaconry courts. Those notaries who did not hold degrees usually spent longer as proctors. Some of them became registrars or deputy registrars in various courts. A number of proctors held other posts in the course of their careers, such as schoolmaster or town clerk.[19] Long service as a proctor could be quite lucrative in periods when business was expanding rapidly; some men built up for themselves considerable positions in local society.

In all dioceses there were officers known as apparitors, mandataries, or summoners whose job it was to serve the mandates of the courts. The bishops of Winchester and Norwich appointed the most important apparitors within their jurisdictions, but the deanery apparitors appointed in both dioceses by the archdeacons or their officials did much of the work for both consistory and archdeaconry courts. The numbers of apparitors may have increased in our period; the volume of complaint about their activities certainly did. A Norwich memorandum, probably drawn up not long after 1600, was to complain that a number of 'extraordinary' apparitors had 'crept' into the diocese in recent years by virtue of commissions issued by the chancellor. The author complained that these men found time to 'range about the countrie for gayne', troubling people for trivial offences.[20]

---

[19] The proctors practising at Norwich in this period are listed in R. A. Houlbrooke, 'Church Courts and People in the Diocese of Norwich, 1519-1570' (Oxford Univ. D. Phil. thesis, 1970), pp. 394-7. One man who practised at Winchester, Robert Knaplocke, had previously been master of Southampton Grammar School. He later became town clerk and mayor, 1575-6; see HRO CB 14, *passim*.; C. F. Russell, *History of King Edward VI School Southampton* (Cambridge, 1940), pp. 24-5.

[20] NNRO HAR 3, p. 311; Winchester Cathedral dean and chapter ledger book 2, fos. 82^v, 94^v, 113; ledger book 4, fos. 92^v-3, 101^v; HRO Reg. Edington, i, fos. 12-13; Reg. Fox, ii, 149; v, 66^v-7; *Registrum Vagum*, i. 46-8.

Zealous apparitors could provide the central administration with useful antennae, and additional appointments, whatever their unfortunate consequences, were no doubt due in large part to a determination to improve the supervision of the diocese.[21] But their inquiries were no substitute for that measure of personal acquaintance with what was going on in outlying areas which visitations alone could provide.

Visitations were supposed to be triennial. In the diocese of Norwich, however, they were sexennial before the Reformation and later septennial. The long gaps between visitations made supervision of its vast area difficult even for diligent and able bishops. In the diocese of Winchester, however, they took place every year.[22] The essential features of a visitation as described in a Norwich paper of about 1604 were as follows. During the visitation sessions, held in a few important churches in each archdeaconry, the bishop or his deputies charged those responsible to make true presentments in answer to articles of inquiry. The registrar or his deputy then called forward the clergy, schoolmasters, physicians, and others, who handed in for examination their letters of orders, licences, dispensations, and other relevant documents. Next the churchwardens and other lay representatives of each parish were called forward and sworn; before they left they went in turn to make their returns to the articles of inquiry.[33] The records of both dioceses suggest that a visitation routine resembling this in the most important respects was in operation before the break with Rome. Cases between parties were also heard during Norwich visitations. Most of the correctional business arising out of visitations of the archdeaconry of Winchester seems to have been dealt with in later sessions of the consistory court. In 1532 Bishop Nykke and his chancellor dealt with some weighty cases during the visitation, but

---

[21] For additional appointments made before the Reformation in the diocese of Canterbury, see Woodcock, *Medieval Ecclesiastical Courts*, p. 48.

[22] *Visitations of the Diocese of Norwich; Letter Book of Parkhurst*, 116; R. M. Haines, 'Adam Orleton and the Diocese of Winchester', *JEH* xxiii (1972), 21-2; *Hampshire Churchwardens' Accounts*, ed. J. F. Williams (1913), pp. xli-xliii. In the 1520s Bishop Fox seems to have left most of the work involved in visiting the archdeaconry of Winchester to his chancellor, who was assisted by the commissary in the archdeaconry; see HRO VB 2, 3.

[23] NNRO HAR 3, pp. 384-5.

appear to have left much of the correctional work to local commissaries. Nykke, like some other bishops, seems to have reserved his closest personal attention for the religious houses.[24] The upheavals of the Reformation brought some temporary dislocation of routine and consequent deterioration in efficiency, while inflation and the loss of some of their manors helped make the bishops' visitational task financially more onerous. In the long run, however, visitations became more thorough and systematic in a number of dioceses.[25]

In the diocese of Norwich, the synod of the clergy, which met twice a year at both Norwich and Ipswich, went some way towards compensating for the infrequency of episcopal visitations. Unfortunately it is not clear how many of the clergy attended the synods in person rather than by proxy.[26] But it seems clear that the synods were not as vigorous or important as they were in the neighbouring diocese of Ely, whose small compass allowed synods to be real meetings of the clergy for consultations, reception of injunctions, nomination of rural deans, and the festivities of the synodal dinner.[27] In Winchester diocese the name synod was given to a quarterly meeting of the clergy of each deanery, whose most important function at the end of the period was to enable the archdeacon, who convened it, to examine the clergy's progress in scriptural study.[28]

(ii) Archdeaconries and rural deaneries

The archdeaconries (four in the diocese of Norwich, two in that of Winchester) were the units of the second layer of

[24] NNRO ACT 4B fos. 14^V, 53^V, 55^V, 131, 135; *Visitations of the Diocese of Norwich; Bishop Geoffrey Blythe's Visitations, c. 1515-1525* (Collections for a History of Staffordshire, 4th ser. vii, 1973), xiii and *passim*.

[25] Marchant, *Church under the Law*, pp. 116-17; H. G. Owen, 'The Episcopal Visitation: Its Limits and Limitations in Elizabethan London', *JEH* xi (1960); Woodcock, *Medieval Ecclesiastical Courts*, p. 69.

[26] NNRO ACT 4A, fo. 226; ACT 4B, fo. 134^V; ACT 5, fos. 15, 36, 57, 72, 80^V, 105; ACT 6, fo. 116^V; ACT 7A, fo. 41; ACT 8, fo. 167^V; *Registrum Vagum*, i. 123.

[27] D. M. Owen, 'Synods in the Diocese of Ely in the latter Middle Ages and the Sixteenth Century', *SCH* iii (1966).

[28] *Articles to be ministred by the right Reuerend ... Robert ... Bishop of Winchester ... in his Visitation, to be kept and holden ... Anno 1570* (1570), sig. A iv^V; *Visitation Articles and Injunctions*, iii. 13-4.

diocesan administration. The apportionment of jurisdiction between bishop and archdeacon varied from one diocese to another, and often from one archdeaconry to another within the same diocese. In both the dioceses under consideration the archdeacons and their officials were debarred from the probate of certain wills and the hearing of certain types of weighty case. Other sources of profit, too, were reserved to the bishops.[29] A crucial difference between the dioceses was that in that of Winchester archidiaconal jurisdiction was inhibited during the annual visitations for several weeks, a fact which gave the bishops a means of exercising closer and more effective supervision than was possible in the diocese of Norwich. In 1508-10 Richard Fox enjoined both his archdeacons to carry out their visitations in person, told the archdeacon of Winchester to call certain incumbents into residence, and warned his colleague of Surrey to see to it that incumbents repaired their churches. Both archdeacons were later summoned to answer for their neglect of episcopal orders, and the archdeacon of Winchester was eventually brought to resign.[30]

Disputed boundaries between episcopal and archidiaconal jurisdiction had often given rise to prolonged and acrimonious conflict in the middle ages. Such disputes sometimes burst into new life after the Reformation, as they did in the diocese of Lincoln and York.[31] In Bishop Ponet's time Archdeacon Philpot of Winchester was charged with contempt of episcopal jurisdiction. It was allegedly Registrar Cooke[32] who set the two reformers by the ears by drawing to Ponet's attention the fact that Philpot had failed to pay him a pension due to him out of the profits of the archdeaconry. Testamentary jurisdiction may have been another bone of contention between the two, and in April 1564 Bishop Horne's chancellor

[29] HRO Reg. Edington, i, 12-13; Reg. Fox, v, fox. 16ᵛ; *Valor Ecclesiasticus*, ii. 3; NNRO institution book xviii, fo. 4; HAR 3, pp. 311-12.
[30] HRO Reg. Fox, ii, fos. 97ᵛ-9, 145-6; iii, fo. 3; GLRO microfilm X 11, fos. 17, 131.
[31] Marchant, *Church under the Law*, pp. 152-7; J. Strype, *The Life and Acts of John Aylmer* (Oxford, 1821), pp. 15-16; *The Life and Acts of Matthew Parker* (Oxford, 1821), iii. 189-93.
[32] Above, p. 26.

strictly inhibited Archdeacon Cheston from granting administrations of intestates' estates or approving clergymen's wills.[33]

One of the chief means which later medieval bishops used
to safeguard their jurisdictional rights within archdeaconries
was the appointment of episcopal sequestrators or commissaries. In the diocese of Norwich it was during our period
common for the same man to be both episcopal commissary
and archdeacon's official. In 1572 the archdeacon of Norfolk
claimed that the custom in his time had been for the bishop
to accept the archdeacon's appointee as his commissary, and
this probably happened in other archdeaconries too.[34] The
prime loyalty of such official-commissaries was probably
given to the archdeacon who had first placed them; this must
in turn have reduced their effectiveness as episcopal watch-
dogs in the archdeaconries, a particularly serious development in a diocese such as Norwich which was so large and
difficult to supervise.

Loss of most of the records of the archdeaconries within
the diocese of Winchester makes it impossible to list all the
episcopal commissaries of our period. Between 1524 and
about 1552 the archdeaconry of Winchester was, like those
in the diocese of Norwich, under the supervision of episcopal
commissaries who were also archdeacons' officials. At least
one episcopal sequestrator in the archdeaconry of Surrey was
also the archdeacon's official. Between 1511 and 1514 an
episcopal court sat in Southwark under the presidency of
episcopal commissaries, the chancellor of the diocese and,
occasionally, Bishop Fox himself. But no records of such a
court survive from the years between 1520 and 1570.[35]

Some archdeacons took a personal share in the running of
their archdeaconries. But many of them had other responsibilities in church or state which kept them away most of the

[33] J. Strype, *Ecclesiastical Memorials relating chiefly to Religion, and the
Reformation of it ... under King Henry VIII, King Edward VI and Queen Mary*
(Oxford, 1822), iii, pt. 1, 439; HRO CB 9, 14, 20, 27 Jan. 1553, and on verso of
penultimate folio; CB 13, p. 77; CB 17, pp. 87, 123–6.

[34] C. Morris, 'The Commissary of the Bishop in the Diocese of Lincoln',*JEH*
x (1959); Blomefield, *Norfolk*, iii. 655–61; PRO E 135/25/31, fo. 16.

[35] HRO Reg. Fox, v, fos. 6, 66ᵛ; Winchester archdeaconry will registers D,
fo. 11; G, fos. 2, 9, 199, 245, 330, 332; J, fo. 113; GLRO DW/PA/7/2, fos. 174,
175ᵛ, 179ᵛ, 185ᵛ, 190ᵛ, 193; microfilm X 11. For some post-visitation correctional
sessions held at Southwark in the later 1560s, see HRO CB 11.

time. We have already seen that Bishop Fox of Winchester was dissatisfied with two of his archdeacons. In 1573 Bishop Horne complained that he had hitherto had little help from his archdeacon of Surrey. Alluding to the old metaphorical description of the archdeacon as *oculus episcopi*, he pointed out that if he had to do without one of his eyes, he 'must continue half blinde, or at the least more then poore blinde.'[36] Many archdeacons left the discharge of their administrative and judicial duties to their officials. The type of man chosen varied slightly from time to time and from one jurisdiction to another, but most of them were beneficed ecclesiastical lawyers with degrees. Each archdeaconry also had a registrar appointed by the archdeacon, usually by life patent confirmed by bishop and chapter.[37]

In each diocese regular visitations were supposed to be carried out by the archdeacons or their officials. In Norwich diocese the archdeaconry courts were the main correctional instruments. The archdeacons' officials probably held two general inquisitions each year and travelled on circuit to deal with outstanding business during most of the rest of the year as well.[38] In the diocese of Winchester, where the work of correction was shared with the chancellor, the archdeacons or their officials were supposed to conduct annual visitations.[39] In each diocese the most serious offences were probably referred to higher courts.

Certain archdeacons had lost the right to hear cases between

[36] Above, p. 31; BL Lansdowne MS. 17/49.

[37] *Registrum Vagum*, i. 84-9; Winchester Cathedral dean and chapter ledger book 2, fo. 136; 4, fos. 39ᵛ-40.

[38] Two 'generals' and a visitation to inquire about fabrics, ornaments, and books were held each year in Sudbury archdeaconry early in the seventeenth century. In the archdeaconry of Norwich in our period inquiries concerning fabrics and ornaments seem to have been made in the course of the general inquisitions. In a number of years two of these certainly took place, but it is impossible to say whether this was always the case. There is no evidence that 'quarter courts' were held in this archdeaconry as they later were in that of Suffolk. Each archdeaconry court was held in more than one centre, but the court in the archdeaconry of Norwich may have been more mobile than its counterparts in the Suffolk and Sudbury archdeaconries. (See NNRO AI 1532; 1551, deaneries of Blofield and Flegg; *Registrum Vagum*, pp. 27-8, 48, 75; Houlbrooke, 'Church Courts and People', pp. 386-8; Marchant, *Church under the Law*, p. 30).

[39] *Articles to be ministred by Robert Bishop of Winchester*, sig. A iv.

parties.[40] It seems probable that most if not all such causes
originating in the archdeaconry of Winchester came before
the consistory court, which was fairly accessible from all
parts of the archdeaconry. The courts in all the other archdeaconries, however, certainly settled causes between parties.
By far the busiest was the Surrey court, which seems to have
dealt with nearly all such causes originating in the archdeaconry of that name; by 1585 they numbered about 150 a
year.[41]

The rural deans formed the third and lowest tier of diocesan
administration above the parochial level. Their importance
was greatest in the northern province, for there, in large,
thinly populated archdeaconries it was convenient to entrust
them with many tasks normally discharged by archidiaconal
courts, including probate and correction. Evidence that deans
were still being appointed on the eve of the Reformation,
that they still executed citations, forwarded mandates and
carried out inquiries, has survived from a large number of
southern dioceses, including both Norwich and Winchester.
In the latter diocese they also acted in a number of matters
which involved the taking of oaths.[42] Just before the Reformation, the Norwich deans (few of them holding benefices
with cure of souls, some not priests at all) were collated to
their benefices by the bishop. Most Winchester chancellors of
our period were empowered by their commissions to appoint
deans; yet in this diocese the clergy of some deaneries were in
1572 electing their deans from amongst themselves.[43]

In each diocese there were certain parishes or larger areas

[40] Marchant, op. cit., pp. 14, 122; Lander, 'Church Courts and the Reformation', pp. 216–17, 221.

[41] GLRO DW/PA/2/1.

[42] R. W. Dunning, 'Rural Deans in England in the Fifteenth Century', BIHR xl
(1967); Haigh, Reformation and Resistance, pp. 13–14; Marchant, Church under
the Law, pp. 88–90, 120–1, 127–8; Foxe, Acts and Monuments, vi. 218; Articles
to be ministred by Robert Bishop of Winchester, sig. Bi; NNRO DEP 12, fo. 114;
HRO CB 2, fos. 64ᵛ, 66, 114, 115; CB 3, fo. 156ᵛ; CB 4, fo. 132ᵛ; CB 8, 6 June
1545; CB 16, 5 Feb. 1563, Netby c. Cooper.

[43] NNRO institution book xiv, fos. 200, 209ᵛ, 221ᵛ, and fo. 6 of new series at
end; A. H. Thompson, 'Diocesan Organisation in the Middle Ages; Archdeacons
and Rural Deans', Proceedings of the British Academy, xxix (1943), 189–91;
Reg. Gardiner et Poynet, 9–16; Reg. Wolsey, 8–12; Reg. Whyte, 15–7; HRO VB
11.

exempt from control through the normal machinery of diocesan government. It is now difficult to ascertain the exact status of some of these. For the sake of convenience one may establish two main categories: those which were free from episcopal supervision, and those which, though subject to episcopal visitation, were free of archidiaconal supervision. The number of parishes in these dioceses which fell into the former category was small, though before the Reformation it also included some monastic houses. In the latter category there were in the diocese of Winchester over forty parishes, in that of Norwich about twenty and (before the Reformation) certain deaneries. Loss of records precludes confident judgement of the question, but on the whole it seems likely that exempt jurisdictions were not a major obstacle to good government in either diocese during our period, and that episcopal judges maintained adequate control over most of them.[44]

(iii) *The dioceses and superior authorities*

From time to time dioceses came under the temporary supervision of judges appointed by archiepiscopal or royal authority. The archbishop appointed in each vacant diocese keepers of the spiritualities to whom he delegated most of the powers normally entrusted by a bishop to his chancellor. He could also order a metropolitical visitation. Vacancies seldom disturbed the even tenor of diocesan administration; indeed local men were often appointed keepers. In 1550, however, Thomas Cranmer committed his powers to visit the diocese of Norwich after Rugge's resignation to two men from outside the diocesan administration (including the prominent reformer Rowland Taylor), probably because he knew all too well the state to which the rule of the incompetent bishop had reduced the diocese. But during the long vacancies at the beginning of Elizabeth's reign religious neuters were appointed keepers, men who were disposed to

---

[44] Parliamentary Papers 1845 (249), xxxvi, 44-7, 56-9; *Reg. Gardiner et Poynet*, 66-7, 154; *Valor Ecclesiasticus*, ii, 507; BL Lansdowne MS. 6/60; *Registrum Vagum*, i. 77-81; V. B. Redstone, 'South Elmham Deanery', *Proc. Suffolk Institute of Archaeology and Natural History*, xiv (1912), 326-31; NNRO institution book xix, fo. 271[v]; HAR 3, p. 419; ACT 5, fo. 170; ACT 8, fo. 177[v].

do little more than keep diocesan administration ticking over at a time when enormous problems were waiting to be tackled.[45] Metropolitical visitations have left relatively few traces in the records. If an archbishop had complete confidence in his suffragan he might abstain from using this opportunity to intervene in the affairs of his diocese; thus in 1556 Bishop Hopton visited his own diocese of Norwich as Reginald Pole's deputy. On the other hand Thomas Cranmer's visitation led to a suspension of the correctional sessions of the Winchester consistory court between May and September 1535, while in 1567 Parker's Norwich visitation opened the archbishop's eyes to the parlous state of the diocese under John Parkhurst, and led to the attempted deprivation of many absentee clergy.[46]

The supremacy of the crown in matters spiritual was asserted by means of three royal visitations, undertaken in 1535, 1547, and 1559. These visitations were probably to those who witnessed them impressive evidence of the power of the crown over the church. After the first royal inhibition of September 1535, the full restoration of episcopal jurisdiction was only gradually accomplished.[47] But the visitors passed quickly through the dioceses, and though there was certainly something of a break in normal routine at Winchester in the Michaelmas terms of 1535 and 1547, as the consistory court records show,[48] the Norwich 'old hands' ran the consistory court of that diocese without any considerable interruption through the periods of the Henrician and Edwardian visitations. After the visitors had gone on their way, the further enforcement of new policies, on whose vigour the

[45] Churchill, *Canterbury Administration*, i. 163-4, 196-9, 590-1; BL Add. MS. 48022, fo. 88; Lambeth Palace Library Reg. Cranmer, fos. 107ᵛ-15; Reg. Pole, fos. 38ᵛ-39ᵛ; *Registrum Matthei Parker*, ed. W. H. Frere (Canterbury and York Soc. xxxv-vi, xxxix, 1928-33), i. 181-4, 202.

[46] NNRO ORR/1(b), fos. 1-27; HRO CB 7; *Reg. Parker*, ii. 720-67; *Correspondence of Matthew Parker*, ed. J. Bruce and T. T. Perowne (Parker Soc. xlii, 1853), 478; below, pp. 190-1, 199, 255.

[47] Lehmberg, 'Supremacy and Vicegerency', 227-9; Bowker, 'Supremacy and the Episcopate', 234-8; *Visitation Articles and Injunctions*, i. 121-6; Foxe, *Acts and Monuments*, vi. 212, 216, 218, 219-20, 248-52; C. G. Bayne, 'The Visitation of the Province of Canterbury, 1559', *EHR* xxviii (1913), esp. 646-9, 652; *LP* xii. pt. 1, 80; NNRO ACT 5, fo. 171.

[48] HRO CB 7 and CB 8.

success of the Reformation so largely depended, was left to men who were at best lukewarm towards the government's aims.

(iv) *Conclusions*

A comparison of these two dioceses brings out one of the most serious weaknesses in the structure of the sixteenth-century English church: the great variety in the size of its administrative units. The smaller and medium-sized dioceses were inevitably the easiest to run efficiently. Some of the bigger ones, such as Norwich, Lichfield, York, and Lincoln, were too large for effective personal supervision save by the most energetic bishops. The bishops of Norwich laboured under an additional handicap in being limited by custom to sexennial visitations. Diocesan organization was not completely stereotyped in our period, and it was possible to make certain improvements. There were a number of organizational experiments and changes, ranging from an important new composition between bishop and archdeacons in the diocese of Chichester to the establishment of a mobile post-visitation correction court in the diocese of York.[49] But the Reformation made harder the task of the men entrusted with the greater dioceses by reducing their estates and making difficult if not impossible the sort of peripatetic government characteristic of efficient later medieval bishops. The benefits of Henry VIII's partial reorganization were meagre by comparison.

The Reformation also damaged the efficiency of diocesan administration by demoralizing those responsible for it. The atmosphere of uncertainty created by the series of bewildering changes begun in 1529 helped to reduce the business of the church courts in the mid-1530s. Everywhere their records tell the same story: at Canterbury, Chichester, and Durham, as at Winchester and Norwich, the flow of cases was drastically reduced.[50] The courts were retained, and business began to

---

[49] Lander, 'Church Courts and the Reformation', pp. 216–17, 221; Marchant, *Church under the Law*, pp. 116–17.

[50] Woodcock, *Medieval Ecclesiastical Courts*, p. 84; Lander, op cit., p. 231; Durham University Department of Palaeography and Diplomatic DR III/1, fos. 13ᵛ–39, 68–82, which show that nearly 200 instance causes entered the Durham consistory court in 1532, 87 in 1535.

revive, but lasting damage had been done. From 1536 onwards, and particularly after 1547, diocesan officials were called upon to implement a series of reforms which many of them did not support. In most sees conservative Henrician bishops survived well into Edward's reign. In few dioceses were chancellors of reforming sympathies appointed before Elizabeth's accession. Some court registrars, holding office for life, remained formidable obstacles in the path of reforming bishops much longer than this.[51] An instinct for self-preservation, rather than the keenness for improvement often seen in the 1520s, was what now actuated most of those who staffed the administrative machinery of the English dioceses. Only in those dioceses such as London and Ely, which contained major centres of English Protestantism, were early-Elizabethan bishops able to build up teams of administrators in sympathy with their aims. Most of their colleagues, who had to run their dioceses with the help of men largely indifferent to their aims, found it hard to enforce reforming measures. Under these circumstances it was hardly surprising that the puritans should demand more or less radical remodelling of the organisation inherited from the pre-Reformation church.[52]

PROCEDURE

Judges in the ecclesiastical courts proceeded against offenders *ex officio* and settled disputes *ad instantiam partium*. In office cases the judges acted either *ex officio mero* or *ex officio promoto*, in which case the individual who promoted the judge's action was supposed to bear the costs if the charge proved unfounded.[53] Many of the matters within the cognizance of the church courts could be dealt with by means of either instance or office procedure. The course chosen in a particular case was determined to a great extent by the custom of the court in question, the volume of business, the standing of the parties and the way in which the matter had come to the judge's notice.

[51] Above, pp. 25-6.
[52] P. Collinson, 'Episcopacy and Reform in England in the later Sixteenth Century', *SCH* iii (1966), 103-11; *The Elizabethan Puritan Movement* (1967), pp. 300-1.
[53] Conset, *Practice*, pp. 388-9, 395.

Matrimonial, testamentary, tithe, and defamation cases accounted between them for over nine-tenths of the identifiable instance business of the courts in these two dioceses during our period. In both there was during the Reformation a striking increase in the volume of tithe and testamentary litigation. By the beginning of our period judges in these dioceses had almost ceased to entertain certain types of suit which had brought much business to fifteenth-century church courts, notably those concerned with breach of faith. Such suits were being heard elsewhere, at Canterbury and at Durham (where they made up the great majority of cases dealt with by the consistory court as late as the 1530s) but their numbers dwindled rapidly during our period.[54] The defamation cases heard by these courts were no longer concerned, as many had been in the previous century, with accusations of such secular crimes as theft and murder. Imputations of sexual misconduct lay behind the great majority of cases, though a few plaintiffs had been accused of other offences of ecclesiastical cognizance, such as embezzlement of church property, scolding, or witchcraft. The evident reluctance of ecclesiastical judges to touch certain causes with which their fifteenth-century predecessors had dealt was no doubt due in the main to pressure from the royal courts.[55]

Amongst the large number of offences dealt with *ex officio*, some were particularly numerous. One historian of the courts speaks for all when he refers to 'the great weight of cases of immorality which burdened the courts from year to year'.[56] These, together with quarrelling and malicious gossip, neglect of the fabric and furnishings of the parish church, and unauthorized meddling with the goods of the dead dominate the records of pre-Reformation *ex officio* proceedings. The Reformation laid heavy new burdens on the courts: the

[54] Woodcock, *Medieval Ecclesiastical Courts*, p. 84; Durham University Department of Palaeography and Diplomatic, DR III/1, 2.

[55] Storey, *Diocesan Administration*, pp. 29–32; R. H. Helmholz, 'Canonical Defamation in Medieval England', *American Journal of Legal History*, xv (1971), 260. The Durham consistory court still heard cases relating to defamation of secular crimes in our period; see Durham University Department of Palaeography and Diplomatic, DR III/1, fos. 14, 32, 61, 64, 73ᵛ, 77. On pressure from royal courts, see also above, p. 9.

[56] Woodcock, *Medieval Ecclesiastical Courts*, p. 82.

neglect of new duties imposed upon the clergy, failure to purchase new equipment for churches and a growing problem of absence from services had to be tackled and now took up a large amount of judges' time. Many other delicts, including usury, sacrilege, and witchcraft, were dealt with only comparatively rarely. At no time was it possible for the courts to exact equally scrupulous observance of all ecclesiastical regulations. As Hamilton Thompson pointed out, visitation returns 'reflect the topics which for the time being were uppermost in the mind of the visitor', and the same is true of all correctional records. 'Drives' against one particular type of offender played an important part in judges' correctional strategies.[57]

In an instance cause the plaintiff initiated proceedings by asking that the defendant be cited to appear. Service of the citation was very often enough to bring about a settlement, and in many years a third or more of the suits introduced went no further. When service of the citation was certified (if no settlement was yet in sight) the plaintiff's proctor exhibited his proxy and asked to be assigned a day on which to offer a libel setting out his case. That done, the defendant's proctor contested the suit, usually negatively. The judge admitted the libel and repeated it 'in full force of positions and articles'. The positions and articles administered to the defendent and witnesses respectively were statements of the elements of the plaintiff's case which had to be answered on oath.[58]

Only a minority of cases were settled as a result of the answers given by defendants. Having come this far, plaintiffs usually attempted to produce further proof. A plaintiff's proctor had up to three terms probatory in which to produce witnesses or documents in support of his case. The term probatory varied in length from court to court and could be extended for reasons such as difficulty in securing the attendance of witnesses. The concurrent testimony of two witnesses was sufficient in theory to settle most types of cause in the

[57] *Visitations in the Diocese of Lincoln, 1517-31*, ed. A. H. Thompson (Lincoln Record Soc. xxxiii, xxxv, xxxvii, 1940-7), i. xxiv; Woodcock, op. cit., pp. 80-1.
[58] See the excellent discussion in R. H. Helmholz, *Marriage Litigation in Medieval England* (Cambridge, 1974), pp. 13-18.

ecclesiastical courts. In practice it was usually necessary to produce more than two witnesses, save in the simplest types of suit, either because two could not testify on the whole range of matters covered by the libel, or because their testimony was challenged. Certain types of document, too, might in theory be sufficient to establish a case, but in practice witnesses were nearly always needed to supplement or elucidate written evidence.[59] After testifying, witnesses were usually examined upon interrogatories submitted by the adverse party's proctor which were designed to reveal discrepancies between and within their depositions, and to show that they were not disinterested. Two other weapons were available to the defendant (and later, in his turn, to the plaintiff). These were the allegation or *materia* drawing attention to some relevant fact not mentioned in the libel. The plaintiff and his witnesses could be produced to answer positions and articles based upon it.[60] Even more commonly used were exceptions (which could be supported by testimony) against the characters or depositions of witnesses.

After the evidence of both sides had been produced and published, the formal pleadings in court came to a close with the assignation of terms to 'propound all acts' and to 'conclude'. The judge then assigned a term to hear sentence which was often delayed by a series of postponements.[61] In many cases these were probably due to the prolongation of the unrecorded discussions in which the proctors thrashed out before the judge the legal points at issue.

It was open to the judge to decree the use of 'summary' procedure, which was distinguished from the 'plenary' procedure so far described by the omission of certain of the major stages.[62] But one should not make too much of the distinction, which was not always rigorously observed in the diocesan courts. Judges were highly flexible in their handling

[59] For a fuller description of the grading of proofs in ecclesiastical law see Conset, *Practice*, pp. 107-9.
[60] NNRO DEP 5B, 192-3; DEP 6A, fo. 109^V; DEP 11B, fo. 38.
[61] In e.g. *Appleyarde c. Petham*, NNRO ACT 7B, fos. 8^V, 29^V, 56^V, 80^V, 93, 109.
[62] Conset, *Practice*, pp. 22-3, 177-8.

of cases. Formalities were often compressed without an order for the use of summary procedure. Judges shortened and lengthened terms as the circumstances of cases required; examiners departed from set articles in interrogating witnesses, if this seemed convenient.[63] On the other hand, uncooperative parties and their proctors could slow down the hearing of causes even when summary proceedings had been ordered. Much depended upon the firmness and dexterity of judges. A judge could do much to prevent delays and abuses of procedure by ordering a party to pay expenses so far incurred by the other side, or by tendering to a proctor an oath that he would not deny anything he believed to be true, or request a delay fraudulently or in a malicious spirit.[64]

Of the causes pursued as far as sentence, most were finished within a year from the day on which the libel was given, many in a few months. The speeds maintained in the dispatch of causes by the courts in the diocese of York in the eighty years before the civil war appear to have been broadly similar.[65] Efficiency in dealing with cases naturally varied somewhat from court to court and from one decade to the next. Much depended upon the volume of cases currently being handled, the skill of individual chancellors and the attitudes of litigants. The Winchester consistory court, which had a smaller load of instance cases than its Norwich counterpart and met more frequently, tended to settle suits somewhat more expeditiously. At Norwich, Bishop Thirlby's efficient chancellor John Fuller managed in the 1550s to speed up the dispatch of cases despite a great increase in the volume of litigation, while there are some signs of deliberate prolongation

---

[63] Woodcock, *Medieval Ecclesiastical Courts*, pp. 53-4; Helmholz, *Marriage Litigation*, pp. 16-18, 112-13, 119-23; for good examples of flexibility and high speed in going through the formal stages of a case, see HRO CB 5, fo. 32^v; CB 8, 5 Dec. 1545, *Foster c. Northe*; NNRO ACT 6, fo. 201^v.

[64] NNRO ACT 6, fos. 141, 199; Conset, *Practice*, pp. 90-2; HRO CB 8, 18 Nov. 1542, *Fynne c. Wilmot, Leeghe c. Drewet*; 17 Jan. 1545, *Haycrofte c. Hodson*.

[65] Ritchie, *Ecclesiastical Courts of York*, pp. 183-5; Marchant, *Church under the Law*, p. 65.

of causes under the weak rule of Bishop Parkhurst.[66] When Archbishop Grindal consulted his leading lawyers about abuses in his own courts shortly after Parkhurst's death, he was told that there was 'more griping of gains than ever before; handling of causes is made an art of gain, and prolonging of suits a point of cunning; styles and customs formed for commodity, observed as laws ...'[67] The malaise which had begun to afflict the Norwich consistory court under Parkhurst could not have been better described. Every system of judicial procedure is open to abuse. Much depends upon the calibre of those who operate it and the spirit in which they approach their work. The procedure of the ecclesiastical courts yielded very good results when under the firm yet flexible control of experienced and scrupulous judges. The decline in efficiency which took place at Norwich during the later years of our period was due above all to a loosening of judicial control over inferior scribes and lawyers and waning respect among litigants.

The judge might terminate proceedings either with the reading of a formal sentence proffered by the victorious party[68] or, if the case was a simple and straightforward one, with a less formal order or decree in favour of one of the parties. Winchester judges very often gave orders of this sort. It is usually possible to tell which party won a case which came this far. But the records say nothing directly of the grounds upon which the sentence or decree was given. These can often be inferred from depositions, but such inferences must very often be tentative. Appeals from sentences were fairly common, but in many cases it is impossible to say whether or not they were prosecuted.

It was the duty of the ecclesiastical judge to encourage the peaceful settlement of most types of dispute by compromise or arbitration. In the consistory courts of both dioceses far

<hr />

[66] PRO E 135/25/31, fo. 7. For some cases in which delaying tactics seem to have been used, see NNRO ACT 11, *Fosdick c. Fosdick*, 16 Nov., 7, 8, Dec. 1568, 11 Feb. 1569; *Carne c. Jaye*, 12 July 1569; *Wentworth c. Tylnye and Aylmer*, 21 June, 5 Oct. 1569; *Manne c. Manne*, 12 May, 12 July 1569; DEP 11B, *Farmer of Stonham Aspall c. Blomefield*, 18 Jan. 1570; *Sawer c. Wade*, 14 Feb. 1570.
[67] J. Strype, *The Life and Acts of Edmund Grindal* (Oxford, 1821), p. 308.
[68] Clarke, *Praxis*, pp. 305-6; Conset, *Practice*, p. 166.

fewer cases were pushed as far as the expensive formality of final sentence than were settled by peaceful agreement. As the leading authority on the late medieval English ecclesiastical courts has recently pointed out, medieval litigants went to law more quickly than their modern counterparts. 'But they were no less ready to compromise in the end. Agreement of the parties was the most satisfactory way of ending a dispute.'[69]

The great majority of correctional proceedings in both the dioceses here studied probably originated in presentments made in visitations by the lay representatives of the parishes, the churchwardens and the 'questmen', 'sworn men' or 'enquirers', whose particular responsibility it was to report prosecutable offences. The latter were probably chosen in most parishes by parishioners and incumbent. Their numbers depended upon the size of the parish concerned; their standard term of office (not always strictly observed) was a year.[70] The size of most jurisdictions and the number of offences to be dealt with prevented the authorities from carrying out a thorough investigation of presentments, and in the majority of cases it was difficult to check their veracity. Failure to make adequate returns might be due to a conspiracy of silence on the part of a united community or to the sworn men's fear of reprisals by fellow parishioners, who sometimes made life difficult for their representatives by threatening or abusing them.[71] Nevertheless, the records are studded with notes that questmen and sworn men had concealed offences or had failed to make accurate presentments, and it is clear that judges received information from other sources, such as the clergy or apparitors, who were presented with good opportunities for making inquiries in the parishes they visited in the course of executing court mandates.[72] Their importance

[69] Lyndwood, *Provinciale*, pp. 72-4, canon *Caeterum districtius*; Helmholz, *Marriage Litigation*, p. 137; below, pp. 112, 138-9, appendix 2.

[70] HRO Reg. Fox, ii, fo. 149v; *Registrum Vagum*, i. 48.

[71] NNRO AI (1548), Harpley; NAGB 2A (1563), Gt. Snoring, Mileham, Yarmouth.

[72] HRO CB 2, fo. 73v; CB 3, fos. 45, 63v-4; CB 17, p. 42; NNRO AI (1550), original letter surviving amongst Walsingham deanery *acta*; NAGB 2A (1563), Thursford, Bastwick; (1564), Snoring.

may have grown in our period because the enforcement of sometimes unpopular official demands (for alterations in the furniture and equipment of churches, for example) entailed closer supervision by the courts. Apparitors, though insufficient in number for the detailed surveillance of the lives of parishioners, could fairly easily view the fabric and contents of churches. But the official view of the Elizabethan church remained that visitation presentments, not apparitors' reports, should be judges' chief sources of information.[73]

Some faults could be dealt with by means of warnings to set them right by a certain date, given immediately after the presentments had been received.[74] Defects in the structure or contents of churches were often tackled in this way, because the churchwardens responsible would be present in court. But the majority of those concerned would not have appeared, and would have to be cited. In a typical court book of this period there is no record of appearance before the court on the part of a large minority of those whose names had been entered in it.[75] In many cases it is impossible to tell what action, if any, was taken against those concerned.

A person who appeared was charged upon oath to make a true answer concerning his supposed offence, unless indeed he admitted it without further ado. If he denied the charge he was ordered to 'purge' himself by means of his own oath and those of a given number of compurgators who would swear that they believed him. Suspects were usually ordered to produce between three and six compurgators, though as many as ten were occasionally required in the case of grave offences.[76] The results of something like two-thirds of the purgation orders issued were recorded. Between two-thirds and three-quarters of those known to have attempted purgation succeeded in clearing their names. When men failed in

---

[73] Marchant, *Church under the Law*, p. 180; *Registrum Vagum*, i. 31, 43, 46-8; Ritchie, *Ecclesiastical Courts of York*, pp. 172-3.

[74] Below, pp. 159-60.

[75] In the Norwich archdeaconry court books the proportion ranges between *c.* 15 per cent and *c.* 40 per cent. Careless record keeping is largely responsible for these figures; they are not reliable indicators of contumacy levels.

[76] Lyndwood, *Provinciale*, pp. 313-14, canon *Item licet*, esp. n. g; NNRO VIS 1 (1569), fo. 62^{v}.

purgation they usually did so because they were unable to produce a sufficient number of compurgators, or because those they did bring refused to take the oath, not because of objections by interested parties, which were rare. Purgation was a primitive and unreliable means of discovering the truth,[77] but a useful means of avoiding conflict and maintaining social harmony. It allowed the putative offender to produce those of his neighbours who were willing to speak in his favour under an external supervision which gave the proceedings solemnity and reduced the likelihood that gross fraud or injustice would be perpetrated.

The individual who failed in purgation was usually ordered to perform penance, barefoot and dressed in a sheet. He often had to declare why he was doing penance or carry an explanatory placard or symbol. The typical pre-Reformation penitent preceded the cross borne in procession round the church, carrying a candle which he subsequently placed before the principal image or took to the high altar at the time of the offertory. Winchester penances frequently included a beating administered by the penitent's parish priest or rural dean. But in some other dioceses, including that of Norwich, this type of punishment had practically gone out of use by the early sixteenth century.[78] The Protestant church re-emphasized the ceremony's didactic purpose; penitents were often ordered to make very full declarations or to stand in an appropriate place while a homily was read.[79] The degree of publicity in penance generally depended upon the seriousness of the offence. Penance might have to be performed twice or even three times, in other churches besides the penitent's own parish church, and perhaps in the local market place as well. In performing penance, those whose conduct had offended the local community gave it satisfaction. The ritual served to resolve tensions and perhaps to save individuals from the consequences of a more informal popular judgement.

[77] Cf. the remarks in F. G. Emmison, *Elizabethan Life: Morals and the Church Courts* (Chelmsford, 1973), pp. 291-9.

[78] HRO CB 2, fos. 14^v, 16^v, 17^v, 70^v, 126^v-7; Woodcock, *Medieval Ecclesiastical Courts*, p. 98, Bowker, *Secular Clergy*, pp. 21-2.

[79] Cf. Price, 'Gloucester Diocese under Bishop Hooper', 87-94.

Penance was a humiliating experience, especially for anyone of standing. Judges were sometimes prepared to commute it into a money payment, and in this way quite substantial sums were raised for pious uses such as the relief of the poor and prisoners, the support of scholars at the universities, and the equipment of parish churches.[80] Before the Reformation private penances were also given, especially to clergy, whose authority judges were unwilling to impair. The standard elements of such penances were fasting, regular recitation of prayers or psalms, and pilgrimage to a local shrine. It was also open to judges to exercise their discretion and treat some offenders with leniency. Those who showed obvious contrition were sometimes dismissed with a warning. Others escaped penance through the intercession of friends or relatives, local incumbents, deans or gentlemen.[81]

The church courts could hardly have performed their correctional work without the co-operation of the representatives of the local communities, who in their presentments had to take their neighbours' opinions into account. The effectiveness of steps taken against those presented was determined by popular views as much as by the official scale of priorities. In so far as it is possible to make the distinction, 'social' offences were more severely punished than 'church' offences in the archdeaconry courts.[82] Failure to receive the communion (in Elizabeth's reign) or to observe the Sabbath, defilement of the churchyard, and disturbances in church, were comparatively lightly punished. But somebody who was alleged to have defamed her neighbours or sown discord amongst them was an unpopular figure whose prosecution was readily supported by fellow parishioners, and was amongst those offenders more likely to be forced to clear their names or to do penance. Sexual delicts were the most thoroughly investigated and most vigorously punished of all.

[80] HRO CB 7, 9 Dec. 1534, *L. Barwike*; CB 9, 7 Dec. 1551, *A. Bensted*; CB 16, 19 Mar. 1563, *G. Warner*; VB 10, fo. 28; NNRO ACT 7B, fos. 17, 142; VIS 1 (1569), fos. 26ᵛ, 57, 77ᵛ, 87ᵛ. Cf. Marchant, *Church under the Law*, p. 176.

[81] NNRO AI (1538), Binham/*T. Loode, M. Wilkyns*; (1548), Beetley/*K. Heringe*, Terrington/*J. Parkyn*, Erpingham/*R. Smith*; (1549) Hoo/*E. Pedder*, Marsham/*E. Wake*, Yarmouth/*W. Glewe*; (1550), Lynn/*J. Makenter*, West Walton/ *M. Tate*.

[82] Below, pp. 86-7 and appendix 3.

The church courts used two sanctions to enforce obedience to their orders: suspension and excommunication. The suspended man was forbidden to enter a church; the excommunicate was in addition barred from the company of all Christians. Somebody who failed to appear in court or to comply with a decree or monition was declared contumacious and ordered to be either suspended or excommunicated. Sometimes the penalty was held over till another day; very often the sentence was read at the end of the day, so as to give the party plenty of chance to appear. In order to give the sentence full publicity a mandate was sent to the offender's priest, ordering him to declare it in his church.[83] Continued contumacy or outstanding insolence might compel the judge to employ more solemn and public excommunication. The insolence of one man who failed to appear despite excommunication and said 'we lif like dogges and it is better not to come to church' warranted daily publication of his excommunication in all the churches of the deanery.[84] But absolution was nearly always readily granted to those who appeared in court to submit and to pay the requisite fees.

Suspension was normally the first censure employed against the recalcitrant before the Reformation. Excommunication was however decreed when serious acts of contempt had been committed. It was also the automatic canonical penalty for many offences, including perjury, defamation, violence to clergy, simony, sacrilege, heresy, impeding the execution of wills, and withholding tithe. Four times a year parish clergy had to read a 'general sentence' of excommunication covering these offences, though in practice an excommunication *lata a canone* did not become effective until a judge declared that an individual had incurred it.[85]

---

[83] Lyndwood, *Provinciale*, pp. 78, n. b, 264, n. r, 266, 329-30, 349, esp. n. c, 350, esp. n. z, 352, n. k; E. Gibson, *Codex Juris Ecclesiastici Anglicani* (Oxford, 1761), ii. 1046-51; Conset, *Practice*, pp. 36-7, 47-8; Woodcock, *Medieval Ecclesiastical Courts*, pp. 93-5; Ritchie, *Ecclesiastical Courts of York*, pp. 98-102; NNRO ACT 3A, fos. 117ᵛ, 118, 121, 124ᵛ; ACT 3B, fo. 107; ACT 4B, fo. 43; ACT 7A, fos. 91, 105ᵛ; ACT 7B, fos. 162, 178, 187ᵛ.

[84] NNRO AI (1550), Wighton/*S. Feeke.*

[85] Lyndwood, *Provinciale*, pp. 353-4, canon *Cum malum*; supplement, pp. 73-4. For absolution from such a sentence, see HRO CB 2, fo. 123; CB 3, fo. 86ᵛ.

The effectiveness of spiritual censures had been waning for a long time before the Reformation, but during the upheavals which followed the break with Rome open contempt became much commoner. In 1541 a certain Robert Sparkes protested in the Winchester consistory court 'that noman hath powre to acursse', while in 1548 a man of Ormesby St. Michael (Norfolk) told his judge 'your assoylinge can do me no good.' In 1563 a man of Empshott (Hants) confessed that he did not know what excommunication and absolution were. The successful attack on the church, the break with the pope, to whom the ultimate power to bind and loose had previously belonged, and the increasing popular ignorance about excommunication (the reading of the general sentence was discontinued in 1534) all helped to weaken popular respect for spiritual censures.[86] In a number of dioceses judges responded by making excommunication instead of suspension their first weapon against contumacy. The process began in the diocese of Chichester in the 1530s; in the diocese of Norwich the middle years of Edward's reign were the crucial phase. In the short run this measure had some effect, but it was not long before excommunication too began to lose its edge.[87] Some stalwart judges continued to use suspension long after our period, but everywhere the Reformation gravely weakened the power of spiritual censures. In the diocese of Gloucester more than two-thirds of those cited to appear before the consistory court in the middle of Elizabeth's reign failed to appear on a first summons; for a time the situation in Norwich diocese under Bishop Rugge was almost as bad.[88]

[86] R. Hill, 'The Theory and Practice of Excommunication in Medieval England', *History*, xlii (1957); NNRO AI (1548), Ormesby St. Michael/*John Fowlser*; HRO CB 8, 18 June 1541, *North c. Sparkes*; CB 17, p. 51; *Miscellaneous Writings and Letters of Thomas Cranmer*, ed. J. E. Cox (Parker Soc. xvi, 1846), 281-2, 461.

[87] Lander, 'Church Courts and the Reformation', p. 232; NNRO ACT 6, ACT 7A. In the archdeaconry of Norwich the percentages of offenders failing to appear in court even when suspended or excommunicated were as follows: 1532-3, 5 per cent; 1549-50, 8 per cent; 1551-2, 4 per cent; 1569, 13 per cent. (These figures are based on the same samples as appendix 3.)

[88] Heal, 'Bishops of Ely', p. 145n; Marchant, *Church under the Law*, p. 124; Price, 'The Abuses of Excommunication', 107, 109-11. Suspension was still occasionally used in these dioceses; see e.g. HRO CB 47, fo. 35.

If an individual remained excommunicated for over forty days, the bishop and those judges to whom he delegated the requisite authority could apply by means of a letter of signification for a royal writ *de excommunicato capiendo* which ordered the sheriff to imprison him. The judge would request his release after arrangements had been made for the payment of contumacy expenses. Neither the Chancery files of letters of signification nor the diocesan records appear to give a complete picture of the use of the procedure. But the two classes of record taken together give the impression that during the middle years of our period significations were very rarely dispatched. Later on, there was an increase in their use, in the 1550s in the case of Norwich, the 1560s in that of Winchester.[89] But greater use of the signification procedure and an attempt made by means of a statute of 1563 to improve the machinery for the arrest of excommunicates failed to revive respect for the major spiritual censure. Indeed, Archbishop Whitgift was later to write that the procedure was 'so chargeable, and so slenderly performed, throughe the corruption of inferior officers and ministres, that men are discouraged to pursue it.' The proportion of excommunicates signified remained small in these and other dioceses.[90]

The work of the church courts was financed by the fees levied from those who appeared before them. Not much information on this subject can now be found in the archives of either diocese, and most of what does survive dates from Elizabeth's reign.[91] It is clear however that sentences were relatively expensive, and this fact helps to explain why so few cases were pushed that far. It did not cost much to engage a proctor and his fee for one appearance in court was small, but the number of such appearances which bore small fruit could mount rapidly if one's opponent proved unco-operative. The costs of the plaintiff's proctor's appearances and of sen-

[89] The totals of surviving significations of 1520-70 in the files (PRO C 85/140-2, 157-8) are as follows: Norwich 55 (120 individuals, 113 reported after 1552); Winchester 23 (28 individuals, 14 reported after 1561).
[90] 5 Eliz. I, c. 23; J. Strype, *The Life and Acts of John Whitgift* (Oxford, 1822), iii. 129; Ritchie, *Ecclesiastical Courts of York*, pp. 189-92, 234.
[91] *Registrum Vagum*, i. 69-73; HRO CB 12, 8 June 1560, loose slip; CB 18, list at end of book; CB 23, 16 Nov. 1566, expenses in *Wakelinge c. Osborne*.

tence are the two largest items on a Norwich bill of expenses of 1545-6; next come the personal expenses claimed by witnesses who had to travel a long way to the consistory court.[92] The initiation of litigation was inexpensive; given a disposition to settle on both sides it need not cost much to finish. But the burden grew rapidly in the later stages of a hard fought suit, especially one which went as far as sentence.

Parties could be admitted *in forma pauperis* and pay nothing for the services of the courts. The litigant who wished to claim admission had to swear that he was worth only 40s. (at Norwich) or £5 (at Winchester). The privilege was claimed comparatively rarely in either court, though naturally enough by a higher proportion of Winchester than of Norwich litigants. The majority of claimants were defendants.[93]

Both judges and registrars, though dependent upon the courts for their living to a far greater extent than the bishops or archdeacons who appointed them, gained much more from their non-contentious work (institutions and the grant of probates, dispensations, and licences) than from litigation or correction.[94] Of all the personnel of the courts the proctors were the most dependent upon lawsuits for their living, and the largest share of fees paid in most cases probably went to them. But at Norwich the increases in proctors' fees in the second half of this inflationary period may have lagged behind those which the registrar managed to secure for himself and his deputies. The fee they received for one appearance in a case remained the same, while the scribes gained a new fee of 2d. for the drawing up of each act of court, agreed upon in 1562.[95]

Most scribes and proctors did better out of litigation than they did out of correctional proceedings.[96] Instance causes were usually more prolonged and involved the drafting of a

[92] NNRO DEP 4A, fo. 225.
[93] NNRO ACT 3A, fo. 119ᵛ; ACT 4A, fos. 38ᵛ, 65ᵛ, 79, 239; ACT 7A, fo. 39; HRO CB 5, fos. 136ᵛ, 151, 172ᵛ. Woodcock, too, found that requests were rare; see *Medieval Ecclesiastical Courts*, p. 62.
[94] Ibid., pp. 75-8; Marchant, *Church under the Law*, pp. 15, 29, 246; *Registrum Vagum*, i. 69-73.
[95] Ibid., loc. cit.; *Letter Book of Parkhurst*, 263-4; NNRO DEP 4A, fo. 225; ACT 9, 22 Apr. 1562.
[96] Cf. Woodcock, *Medieval Ecclesiastical Courts*, p. 79.

much greater number of legal instruments; many more fees were levied. The chances of securing payment of sums due were far better, since plaintiffs came freely to the courts and could be asked to pay promptly or even in advance, while presented offenders came unwillingly, and their attendance, let alone the payment of their dues, might be difficult to enforce. Scribes and proctors thus had an interest in encouraging parties to resort to litigation rather than to seek redress through the questmen in cases where they had some choice. Only the deanery apparitors stood to gain much by stimulating correctional business.

Of all court personnel the apparitors were the most open to temptation and the most difficult to supervise. Some evidence of their misbehaviour, in the shape of allegations of bribery and suspensions from duty, can be found in the records of the courts themselves. In 1578 the chancellor of Norwich diocese referred to wholesale corruption on the part of apparitors as a notorious fact.[97] But during our period it was only under the weak rule of Bishop Parkhurst that other Norwich personnel were accused of malpractice on a large scale. Parkhurst's third chancellor, Stephen Nevinson, in a letter written to the bishop shortly after his resignation in 1569, referred to 'bribrie and extortion in all your courtes, falsifiynge and corruptynge of your recordes' and more specifically to the prolongation of causes by proctors and the practice of giving them tips when cases had been brought to a successful conclusion. He seems to have believed the 'whelpes' of registrars responsible for the worst malpractices which plagued the courts. One of the registrars allegedly caused a false entry to be made in the episcopal register. A memorandum drawn up by the bishop himself described further misdeeds. The most serious of these were premature grants of probate and administration which facilitated embezzlement and stimulated litigation. The scribes were also responsible for granting citations without due investigation of

[97] HRO CB 19, p. 14; NNRO DEP 5B, fo. 218ᵛ; NCC will register Thyrkyll, 5 and 27 Oct. 1543; Strype, *Annals*, ii, pt. 2, 699.

the circumstances of causes.[98] Adequate judicial supervision was lacking for most of Parkhurst's episcopate. His first chancellor was unequal to his job, his second he dismissed, his third, who wrote so angrily about registrars, was himself accused of gross irregularities.[99] Things had clearly gone badly wrong at Norwich. The almost certainly exceptional state of affairs in this diocese was due in large part to the fact that it had been ruled by weak and ineffectual bishops for much of the time since 1535. There is no comparable evidence of deterioration in the running of the Winchester courts. The experience of Norwich was not, however, unique. At Gloucester, too, a pervasive rot set in under the weak Bishop Cheyney and the corrupt chancellor Powell.[100]

The instance procedure of the ecclesiastical courts was a flexible instrument which when well used facilitated the swiftest dispatch of cases compatible with the full examination of relevant evidence and gave every opportunity for their peaceful settlement. The correctional work of the courts was dependent upon popular co-operation: the types of case dealt with and the outcomes of proceedings reflected not only the demands of the authorities but also the concerns and prejudices of the people. The changes of the mid-sixteenth century had three major adverse effects upon the courts. First, they seriously weakened respect for the spiritual censures upon which the courts relied in the main to secure compliance with their orders. Secondly, they sapped the morale of the men who ran the courts and undermined the efficiency of administration in some dioceses. Proctors, scribes, and apparitors, less well supervised than hitherto, sought to make more business for themselves, and some of them engaged in damaging malpractices. Lastly, the spate of new demands which followed the Reformation placed new correctional and supervisory

[98] PRO E 135/25/31, fos. 6-8; NNRO institution book xix, fo. 120; *Letter Book of Parkhurst*, pp. 261-3; below, p. 109.
[99] Cambridge, Corpus Christi College MS. 114, pp. 951, 955; PRO E 135/25/35; *Letter Book of Parkhurst*, 116, 257-60. The men referred to were Thomas Brooke, Edward Gascoigne, and Stephen Nevinson.
[100] Price, 'An Elizabethan Church Official'.

burdens on the courts which in turn necessitated more interference in the parishes:[101] interference which threatened the delicate balance between official and popular demands.

[101] Below, esp. pp. 163–72.

3

MATRIMONIAL CAUSES AND THE PUNISHMENT
OF INCONTINENCE

No part of the work of the church courts affected so intimately
the lives of ordinary people as did their regulation of relations
between the sexes. The courts' activity in this sphere bulked
indeed so large in the popular imagination that it made them
known as the 'bawdy courts'. The satirists of the courts con-
jured up a picture of prying prurient summoners, scribes and
commissaries battening on the sins of the people, and indeed
the acts and depositions entered in cases of divorce and correction are a rich mine for the connoisseur of coarse stories.
But there was in the testimony heard by the courts ample
material for poignant tragedy as well as low farce. In nearly
every session the chancellor would hear the anguished plea of
a jilted suitor clutching at the fading mirage of marital happi-
ness, at each stopping-place on his circuit the commissary
would be confronted with the spectacle of the unmarried
mother-to-be, abandoned by a casual lover and cold-shouldered
by an unfriendly community. Their all too familiar situations are recorded in laconic court-book entries which the
process of statistical analysis reduces to mere figures. Yet
behind each line lies the sharp reality of individual misery,
which the judge might aggravate by automatic adherence to
chill routine or alleviate with a friendly mien and a kindly
word.

Most of the matrimonial causes dealt with by the church
courts were concerned with the validity of marriages. The
commonest type of suit was brought by a party to a matrimonial contract (an exchange of words making a couple man

and wife or binding them to marry) seeking its enforcement.[1] Far rarer were suits in which individuals sought to escape their marriage partners, seeking sentences of annulment. A marriage could only be annulled if technically flawed from the beginning. The church courts of the sixteenth century could grant no divorce (in the modern sense of the word) on account of its breakdown; in this situation a decree of separation was the most that could be hoped for.[2] Matrimonial questions were commonly brought to the notice of consistory court judges by plaintiffs in instance suits, but they could also be dealt with upon presentment. Thus we find individuals prosecuted for failing to have matrimonial contracts solemnized, for contracting invalid marriages, and for abandoning or maltreating their marriage partners. In addition fornication and adultery were nearly always dealt with by means of prosecution after presentment.[3] It was partly in order to clear their names, and thereby avoid prosecution, that people initiated suits against those who had defamed them of sexual immorality.[4]

BREACH OF CONTRACT

(i) *Types of contract and types of suit*

The explicit mutual consent of the partners had come to be considered an essential element of a marriage long before the sixteenth century. This consent was (and still is) expressed in a contract recited at the beginning of the service of solemnization, but in our period partners very often entered into a binding contract before this. The medieval church had had to face the fact that marriages often took place without priestly participation. But by punishing those who consorted together without having their marriages solemnized it had tried to change popular custom. It is likely that the vast majority of matrimonial contracts concluded in the early sixteenth century were viewed by one or both of the parties as merely

---

[1] Below, pp. 56–67, 83–5.
[2] Below, pp. 67–75, 84–6.
[3] Below, pp. 75–9, 86–7.
[4] Below, pp. 79–83, 87–8.

the first step towards solemnization in church.[5] The Council of Trent at last declared that no marriage not solemnized by a priest henceforth be considered valid, but not until 1753 did the British parliament follow suit.

There were two main types of matrimonial contract. The *de praesenti* contract, a good example of which is preserved in the present marriage service of the church of England, became immediately binding upon the contracting parties, who thereby joined themselves in marriage. The *de futuro* contract, on the other hand, was a promise of future performance, similar in intention to the modern engagement. It could be dissolved by mutual consent of the parties or a later *de praesenti* contract. But Henry Swinburne, who wrote the fullest English account of the forms of contract, had to admit that it was often extremely difficult in practice to make the theoretically crucial distinction between *de praesenti* and *de futuro*. Depositions of witnesses in matrimonial causes often suggest that parties were not fully aware of the difference between the two types of contract. By choosing the wrong form of words people committed themselves to marriage prematurely, or alternatively failed to secure the marriage they had hoped for.[6]

Matrimonial contracts of both sorts could have conditions attached to them, and suits over conditional contracts were very common. Pending the fulfilment of the condition, either party might withdraw consent, and the contract could be superseded by a later unconditional one. But once the condition had been fulfilled, the contract became binding.[7] The commonest condition was the party's ability to secure the goodwill of parents and friends.[8] Many contracts were made conditional upon the provision of house, lands, money, a suitable guarantee of eventual inheritance, or proof that a suitor's wealth was really what he claimed.[9] The conditional

[5] Helmholz, *Marriage Litigation*, pp. 26-31, 72-3, 167.
[6] Swinburne, *Spousals*, pp. 12-13, 67. 70-1, 75-6, 82, 88-9, 236-7, 239.
[7] Ibid., pp. 114, 122-3, 129-32.
[8] NNRO DEP 3, fo. 47; DEP 5A, fo. 282^v; DEP 5B, fo. 102^v; DEP 6A, fos. 86, 247; HRO CB 5, fos. 66^v-7; CB 6, p. 339; CB 24, fos. 46-7.
[9] NNRO DEP 3, fo. 381; DEP 7C, fo. 22; DEP 12, fo. 119; HRO CB 6, pp. 93, 134-5, 249.

form was particularly attractive to widows who had acquired the experience necessary to conduct for themselves negotiations more likely to be undertaken for a young girl by family or friends. They might use it, for instance, to guarantee the discharge of obligations inherited from previous marriages.[10]

Parties often wished to postpone marriage till the end of a period of service, or entry into a copyhold. In such cases the contract could be made conditional upon the other partner's waiting for the event in question, or, more simply, it could be 'referred to a day', so that it only took effect at a specified future date.[11]

In case of dispute, the ecclesiastical judge had to decide whether a contract was binding or not. If he found that it was, he gave an adjudicatory sentence declaring the defendant to be the plaintiff's spouse. If not, he gave an absolutory sentence dismissing the defendant from suit.

In order to be upheld in court, disputed contracts had to be witnessed by two people. A contract witnessed would usually be upheld against an earlier contract attested by only one witness and a common fame.[12] Depositions show that contracts often took place in the presence of the parents and friends of the parties, perhaps at a meal given to provide a suitable opportunity. Even when things had not been so well arranged, true well-wishers of the couple would impress upon them the seriousness of the step they were taking, attempt to dissuade them from acting hastily, and try to ensure that the time and place of the contract were fitting.[13] But all too frequently informal or inadequately witnessed contracts took place in shops, fairs, backyards and the fields, and these formed a large proportion of the ones that were disputed in the courts.[14] People sometimes went to court even though they were unable to produce witnesses. After hearing what a plaintiff without witnesses had to say, the judge could only

[10] NNRO DEP 6A, fos. 17^v-18, 106^v, 272-3; DEP 7C, fo. 2; DEP 7D, fo. 6.
[11] NNRO DEP 3, fo. 269; HRO CB 22, 1 Feb. 1566, *Aslatt c. Ede*; Swinburne, *Spousals*, p. 110.
[12] Ibid., pp. 198-201.
[13] NNRO DEP 4A, fos. 35-6, 92^v-3, 120, 358, 471^v-2; HRO CB 6, p. 197.
[14] NNRO ACT 4B, fo. 42; DEP 4A, fos. 110, 164^v, 373, 397.

put the defendant on oath. In such circumstances confessions were extremely rare.[15]

If the judge feared that the defendant might attempt during the course of suit to marry some person other than the plaintiff, he gave a solemn monition against contract or solemnization before sentence. In order to prevent a clandestine marriage he could order sequestration of the defendant in the house of some indifferent person, and if one may judge by the paucity of suits for breach of sequestration, the system worked fairly well.[16]

The commonest type of contract suit involved two people only. But three people often took part. Plaintiffs frequently initiated suit in order to challenge a contract between the defendant and a third party or to prevent solemnization of marriage between them. If the plaintiff's case proved a strong one, the suitor favoured by the defendant might well be forced to intervene in order to protect his interests and to produce witnesses. Suits involving three people sometimes began after the banns of marriage had been challenged, though the courts looked with some suspicion upon those who acted so late in the day, and the impugning of banns became much less common during our period.[17]

Suits concerned with matrimonial contracts were not always brought by those who sought their enforcement. The initiative sometimes came from a party who wished to prove conclusively that he had entered no previous contract because he feared that boasts of the existence of such a contract (the 'jactitation' of the law) would spoil his chances of marriage with a third party. Such a suit was normally terminated by a decree condemning the boaster to 'perpetual silence'. It was however open to him to propound a justificatory allegation that the contract had really taken place, though no such

[15] HRO CB 8, 14 Nov. 1545, 13 Feb. 1546, *Palmer c. Yatman*; NNRO AI (1533), Dunham Magna/*Sare c. Tailor*.
[16] Conset, *Practice*, pp. 265-6; HRO CB 5, fo. 121; CB 18, 10 June 1564, *Rainoldes c. Cleverley*; 8 July 1564, *Woddes c. Agullye*; CB 20, 4 June 1565, *Webbe c. Deane*.
[17] HRO CB 3, fo. 44; CB 5, fo. 156^V; CB 22, 6 Apr. 1566, *Cleverley c. Barbor, Colbroke pro interesse*, NNRO ACT 3A, fos. 75, 102; ACT 4A, fos. 129, 136^V-7; ACT 9, 30 July, 1 Oct. 1561, *Parisshe c. Dearne*.

allegations proved successful in these two dioceses during our period.[18]

(ii) *Carnal knowledge, tokens, and circumstantial evidence*

Some matrimonial contracts did not take immediate effect. But the extent of a couple's commitment did not depend only on the form of words they had exchanged. Certain actions could in theory make a *de futuro* contract immediately binding. Of these, carnal knowledge (which could not by itself create marriage) was by far the most important. Yet in no case can proof of carnal knowledge be said confidently to have played a decisive part. It was often alleged, especially by women who were unable to produce the two witnesses necessary to prove a contract.[19] In this sort of case, if the man swore that he had not entered a contract, even his confession that he had known a woman and got her with child did not entitle the judge to order him to marry her. The most he could do was to let it be understood that the couple would by marrying escape public penance, the normal penalty for fornication.[20]

Swinburne mentioned that a *de futuro* formula might also be given *de praesenti* effect by the placing of a ring on the fourth finger, though he admitted that 'this Conclusion is not very sound', and I have found only one case in which the giving of a ring apparently played a key part.[21] The importance of the ring (and of other tokens, such as gloves, coins, and kerchiefs, which in popular estimation often partook of the special character enjoyed by the ring) seems to have been much greater in the eyes of the parties, and more particularly

[18] HRO CB 8, 29 July 1542, *Wigmore c. Harte*; 30 Jan. 1546, *Ringe c. Struder*; CB 11, 30 Apr., 7 May, 2 July 1558, *Glosse c. Sander*; *Fayercliff c. Steward* in NNRO DEP 8, fos. 120, 135ᵛ-7; ACT 10, 9 Dec. 1562. For one successful counter-allegation, see Durham University Department of Palaeography and Diplomatic DR/III/1, fos. 38ᵛ, 41, 50.

[19] NNRO ACT 4A, fo. 129; ACT 7A, fo. 68; ACT 7B, fo. 303; HRO CB 8, 9 June, 23 Nov. 1543, *Hickes c. Laynston*; *Elmes c. Baker*, CB 19, p. 386; CB 22, 9 Nov. 1566; *Helyar c. James*, CB 19, pp. 233, 254–5; CB 22, 27 Apr. 1566; *Warren c. Irishe*, CB 24, fo. 43; CB 22, 7 Dec. 1566.

[20] NNRO ACT 4A, fos. 164ᵛ, 210ᵛ; HRO CB 2, fos. 86, 126; *Depositions and other Proceedings from Durham*, 102.

[21] Swinburne, *Spousals*, p. 71; *Allen c. Howling*, NNRO DEP 8, fos. 158ᵛ, 162–4; ACT 10, 2 Mar. 1563.

in the eyes of male suitors, than it was in the view of the law.[22] Men and the witnesses they produced often did their best to blur still further what seems to have been the always hazy distinction between tokens of 'good will' and symbols of binding agreement. Some suitors seem to have believed that tokens planted on women against their will, or even without their knowledge, might establish a claim.[23] The law gave such suitors no encouragement. But it did allow that a confession on the woman's part that gifts had been received might prove 'just cause for litigation' entitling the plaintiff, even if he had failed to prove his main contention, to be dismissed without paying costs, and to have his gifts, or their money value, returned to him.[24] The most prudent course, therefore, though one perhaps only taken by a strong-minded minority of women, was to return immediately the gifts of unwelcome suitors.

In theory, if the words of the contract itself were ambiguous, a case might be resolved by circumstantial evidence as to the parties' intentions. It is impossible to demonstrate that this happened in practice; indeed one is left with a distinct impression that such evidence had little or no influence on judges' decisions. Yet examination of it tended to become ever more detailed as time went by, to the benefit of the court scribes and the modern student of matrimonial customs, and the detriment of the parties. This evidence ranged from the concrete and obviously significant to the vague and irrelevant, from words spoken by the parties to mere rumours of their intentions.

It was common to allege that the parties had recognized the contract after it had been made, and apparently customary for judges to count such acknowledgement, if proved, as good ground for litigation.[25] Solemnization was normally preceded by the triple declaration of banns, and knowledge of a couple's intention to marry did give a conscientious

---

[22] NNRO DEP 3, fo. 256ᵛ; DEP 5A, fos. 35ᵛ, 104ᵛ, 117ᵛ, 278; HRO CB 6, pp. 201–2, 230–1, 237, 281, 329.

[23] NNRO DEP 5A, fo. 104ᵛ; DEP 5B, fo. 212; HRO CB 6, p. 423.

[24] NNRO ACT 3B, fos. 179, 203; ACT 5, fo. 53; HRO CB 2, fo. 127; CB 8, 13 Nov. 1546, *Rokeley c. Draper*.

[25] Cf. Conset, *Practice*, p. 271.

clergyman the opportunity to question them, to recommend a binding contract formula, and to ensure that it was properly witnessed. Yet women sometimes claimed that banns had been published without their consent, or even without their knowledge, so that even an announcement which might have been expected to provide the clearest evidence of intention could prove quite useless in this respect.[26] Witnesses were also called upon in many cases to describe arrangements made for the wedding feast and for the accommodation of the parties at the beginning of their married life.[27] Much of the evidence given was even less to the point, consisting for instance of descriptions of visits paid by one party to the other, or of rumours of their intentions in the neighbourhood.

(iii) *Limitations on contractual freedom*

A contract freely entered into was valid in the eyes of the church whatever efforts were subsequently made to frustrate it, while one brought about by coercion was invalid. Judges had to resolve questions raised both by attempts to limit contractual freedom and by the exertion of undue pressure in order to induce people to enter marriage.

In sixteenth-century society, attainment of the canonical ages of consent of fourteen (for men) and twelve (for women) did not in practice give people freedom to marry whom they liked. Feudal wardship lasted till the age of twenty-one in the case of males, sixteen in that of females, and the ward's refusal of the marriage partner chosen by the guardian could prove extremely costly.[28] Ecclesiastical law did not recognize parents' right to determine their children's choice of spouses, though in the case of adolescents the right was upheld by custom, the material sanctions at parents' disposal, and the

[26] Lyndwood, *Provinciale*, p. 271; NNRO DEP 5A, fo. 33; DEP 5B, fos. 120, 217v-18, 281; DEP 6A, fo. 154; DEP 7C, fo. 13; HRO CB 6, pp. 327, 366; CB 19, p. 109. For some marriage licences issued in 1516-17 see NNRO SUN 1(c), fo. 18 (most of these permitted marriage with only one reading of banns).

[27] NNRO DEP 4A, fo. 46v; DEP 6A, fos. 142, 148v; DEP 8, fos. 178-80; HRO CB 6, p. 509; CB 14, 3 Nov. 1562, *Byrrell c. Wotton*.

[28] J. Hurstfield, *The Queen's Wards: Wardship and Marriage under Elizabeth I* (1958), pp. 96-102, 134-5, 137-8, 142-3. Girls who were already fourteen when their fathers died did not enter wardship.

very strongly expressed views of Protestant divines.[29] Parents'
opposition to what they felt to be unsuitable marriages probably lay behind much matrimonial litigation. Differences in
social status and wealth (the latter often revealed by difficulties encountered in raising the stipulated dowry) were probably
the most important grounds for parental opposition. Witnesses
were often asked about differences in wealth between the
parties in the hope that their answers might throw doubt on
plaintiffs' claims.[30]

Some young people were ready, at least initially, to resist
parental pressure.[31] The full significance of their resistance
cannot be evaluated without more precise indications of age
and social status than the court books themselves provide.
There is however some evidence that the courts tried to uphold their right to make their own choice. The sequestration
of parties (usually women) who were likely to be unduly influenced by parents or friends was an oft requested precaution.
Occasionally we read of official proceedings promoted against
parents who had hindered marriages; one father had gone to
the length of carrying his son off to a place unknown to the
girl who hoped to marry him.[32] Some adjudicatory sentences
were given despite apparent parental opposition to the
matches proposed.[33] Yet it is possible that in other cases informal pressure of which no evidence survives in the court
books was brought to bear on parties to conform with their
parents' wishes. An interesting and oft quoted description of
persuasion of this type is given in one of the fifteenth-century

[29] Cf. Helmholz, *Marriage Litigation*, pp. 91-3. For the views of Protestant
divines see the following works (all refs. to Parker Soc. edns.); T. Becon, *The Cat-
echism, with other pieces*, ed. J. Ayre (xi, 1844), 355, 358, 371, 372; E. Sandys,
Sermons, ed. J. Ayre (ii, 1842), 50, 281, 325, 326, 455; W. Tyndale, *Doctrinal
Treatises and Introductions to different portions of the Holy Scripture*, ed. H.
Walter (xxxii, 1848), 169, 170, 199.

[30] NNRO DEP 3, fos. 67-8, 397; DEP 4A, fos. 36, 165^V-6, DEP 5A, fo. 6.

[31] For a striking example of a disagreement between child and parents, see
NNRO DEP 3, fos. 16^V-17^V.

[32] HRO CB 5, fos. 63^V, 101^V, 106, 126, 153; CB 7, 21 Oct. 1540, proceedings
against *Osborn*; CB 17, 11 June 1563, against *Newman*.

[33] *Fade c. Shipdham*, NNRO DEP 5B, fos. 86, 89-90, 94^V-6, ACT 7B, fos. 50,
99; *Auncell c. Warner*, NNRO DEP 5B, fos. 186^V-7; ACT 7B, fos. 155^V, 183; *Coo
c. Bawle*, NNRO DEP 5B, fos. 3-5; ACT 7A, fos. 266, 292; HRO CB 5, fos. 148^V,
150; *Fiberd c. Wilmot*, HRO CB 6, pp. 438-41; CB 8, 13 June 1545.

Paston letters. The bishop put it to Margery Paston that she could expect no help from her friends and kindred if she did not follow their advice, and told her that he would not be too hasty in giving sentence since evidence might yet be found that 'mythe cause the lettyng' of the marriage, although he seems to have been unable to do so, and in the end it went ahead.[34]

Marriages were brought about, as well as hindered, by external pressures. The sort of pressure which made a contract invalid seems most frequently to have been applied by masters who discovered that their maidservants had been carnally known, and perhaps made pregnant. Their lovers could find themselves threatened with summary proceedings before the justices of the peace unless they got married. One such unfortunate, already under arrest, was mockingly told 'thow must take and marye her onely for love'. Later he gained another girl's consent, and sentence was given for the second, free contract.[35] This outcome was typical. Judges upheld no contracts clearly shown by the evidence to have been vitiated by coercion.

(iv) *Trends in contract litigation: the effectiveness of the courts*

In both consistory courts, contract suits made up in the 1560s a much smaller proportion of the business dealt with than they had done in the 1520s.[36] In both the increase in matrimonial litigation was dwarfed by the enormous growth in the number of tithe and testamentary disputes. The latter development was in large part due to causes (to be examined in due course) which did not affect matrimonial suits.[37] The divergent trends were also to some extent connected with the courts' own approach to their work, especially to the fact

[34] *The Paston Letters*, ed. J. Gairdner (Edinburgh, 1910), ii. 364–5.
[35] NNRO DEP 5B, fos. 299ᵛ, 301ᵛ-4, 306-7; ACT 7B, fos. 308ᵛ, 312ᵛ; HRO CB 6, pp. 16-17, 479; CB 8, 6 Feb. 1546, *Foster c. North*.
[36] See appendix 2. Of the causes of the four major types, matrimonial cases amounted at Winchester to 33·33 per cent in sample years of the 1520s, to only 11·8 per cent in the 1560s; at Norwich to 22·34 per cent in the 1520s, to only 9·75 per cent in the 1560s.
[37] Below, pp. 105-12, 146-8.

that matrimonial suits as a class were considerably less profitable to the men who ran them than were other types of cause. The contract suit, especially if insufficient witnesses were produced, was usually straightforward, could often be dispatched in a single session, and provided the consistory lawyers with some of their least lucrative work, so that as they became busier with protracted and profitable tithe and testamentary causes, they may have become more willing to deter plaintiffs with weak cases from embarking on matrimonial litigation. A large majority of sentences given in both consistory courts were absolutory. It seems clear that the main reason for plaintiffs' failure was their own determination to press poor or hopeless cases. Many of the contracts alleged were ill attested, and much of the evidence which witnesses had to offer was, as has been pointed out, interesting but not determinative.[38]

Proceedings relating to unfulfilled matrimonial contracts could be initiated *ex officio*; enforcement did not necessarily have to be sought in a case between parties, especially if the circumstances of the case were simple. Some people were presented for delaying solemnization after contracting and living suspiciously meanwhile. The judge would order the couple to proceed to solemnization without delay, unless there were some doubt about the validity of the contract, in which case they might renew it before the court. When people did sue for breach of contract in the archdeaconry court, they had often been prodded into doing so by previous disciplinary proceedings for incontinence.[39] Between the later sixteenth century and the Civil War the numbers of matrimonial causes entering the consistory courts of Norwich and York fell markedly. This decline has been attributed to the 'change in marriage customs, simpler rules, and stricter enforcement of them'.[40] Yet it was the often ill-attested *de praesenti* matrimonial contract that gave rise to most matrimonial litigation. It is true that an act of 1540 provided that from thenceforth

---

[38] Above, pp. 60-2.
[39] NNRO AI (1548), Terrington/*Grenewoode and Elgare*, Middleton/*R. Russell*, Sall/*R. Alyns*; (1550), Gressenhall/*J. Gryffith*, Binham/*T. Frende*.
[40] Marchant, *Church under the Law*, pp. 20, 61-2.

a solemnized and consummated marriage should supersede an unsolemnized and unconsummated pre-contract, but this, the only legislation of the Reformation period concerned with matrimonial contracts, was repealed in 1549.[41] Thus litigation could not have been directly affected by legislation, though of course it is possible that the act's refusal to treat an unconsummated contract as a marriage exercised an influence over people's attitudes which survived its repeal.

The attitudes of churchmen themselves probably played a large part in the decline of contract litigation. The number of cases dealt with by the courts had already fallen quite dramatically between the fourteenth and the early sixteenth centuries. Despite its reluctance to disown altogether the private *de praesenti* contract, the medieval church had doubtless done much to bring about this outcome through its unremitting efforts to discourage cohabitation before solemnization.[42] On the eve of the Reformation, Richard Whytforde, author of one of the best-known of early domestic conduct books, warned his readers that the devil 'doth deceyue many persones by the pretence and colour of matrimony, in pryuate and secrete contractes', all too easily repudiated, he pointed out, once lust was slaked.[43] The note of disapproval became harsher and more emphatic in the writings of his Protestant successors. It seems likely that as a result ill-attested contracts grew less common, and that contracts came to be regarded ever more clearly as preliminaries to solemnization. Readiness to enter a binding contract before the service may indeed have been on the wane, if the sentiment expressed by a man of Lincoln diocese in 1576 was at all widespread. He was heard to say 'that he cared for no assuringe until he came to be marryed'.[44]

The decline of the ecclesiastical suit to enforce the matrimonial contract was no doubt hastened by the development of alternative remedies in secular courts. Long before the sixteenth century, manorial courts had settled suits over

---

[41] 32 Henry VIII, c. 38; 2 & 3 Edward VI, c. 23.

[42] Helmholz, *Marriage Litigation*, p. 167.

[43] R. Whytforde, *A Werke for Housholders* (1530), sig. E iii.

[44] *Lincoln Episcopal Records, in the time of Thomas Cooper, 1571 to 1584* ed. C. W. Foster (Lincoln Record Soc. ii, 1912), 130.

breaches of covenants made in anticipation of marriage. The common-law action for breach of promise, which became familiar in the sixteenth century, brought the successful plaintiff compensation, not performance. A number of church-court depositions reveal the initial readiness of parties to agree upon financial compensation through unofficial arbitrators without resorting to the courts at all. Only the breakdown of the agreements in question brought them to the notice of the courts, but the unsuccessful arrangements were probably greatly outnumbered by the successful ones.[45]

Most of the sentences given in breach-of-contract cases in the two consistory courts seem to have been worthy of respect and to have received it. Some sentences are hard to understand in the light of the recorded evidence, but the overwhelming majority of decisions seem to have conformed with the requirements of the law. Without examining other types of record (which might not in any case yield a conclusive answer) one cannot say how many adjudicatory sentences were obeyed; but the paucity of subsequent proceedings against recalcitrant defendants suggests that plaintiffs were usually satisfied.[46]

SEPARATION AND ANNULMENT

In the sixteenth century a valid marriage could not be dissolved save by death. Only those marriages flawed from the beginning could be annulled. Partners whose unions 'broke down' because of cruelty or infidelity could only be granted a separation incompatible with the remarriage of either husband or wife, the so-called divorce *a mensa et thoro*, and it was hoped that reconciliation would follow. The line between

---

[45] G. C. Homans, *English Villagers of the Thirteenth Century* (New York, 1941), pp. 161-2; S. T. C. Milsom, *Historical Foundations of the Common Law* (1969), p. 289; *Depositions and other Proceedings from Durham*, 52, 86; NNRO ACT 4A, fo. 178ᵛ, DEP 4A, fo. 156; DEP 11A, 23 Apr. 1567. For a peaceful conclusion in a matrimonial cause see HRO CB 8, 6, 20 Oct. 1543, *Edwardes c. Vicary*. It is not always clear from the record of peaceful conclusions like this whether the parties agreed upon compensation, or whether one party had conceded the other's case, as in HRO CB 8, 3 Nov. 1543, *Cocker c. Warne*. Cf. Helmholz, *Marriage Litigation*, pp. 136-8.

[46] But see NNRO ACT 4A, fo. 214ᵛ; ACT 5, fo. 28ᵛ; HRO CB 5, fos. 46ᵛ, 112ᵛ, 115 for some exceptions.

separation and annulment was probably blurred in the popular mind. Both were means of breaking away from an unwanted spouse. In our period the ideas of continental reformers who had made cruelty and infidelity grounds for annulment may also have had quite a widespread unsettling effect, even though the English church never followed their example.

(i) *Separation, desertion, and bigamy*

Divorce from bed and board, with the hope of ultimate reconciliation was granted on account of infidelity, cruelty, and inability to live together because of continual quarrels.[47] References to about twenty decrees of separation, most of them given at Norwich, have been found amongst the records of the two dioceses. The grounds for many of them cannot now be ascertained; no one pretext for separation predominates amongst the surviving records of suits. The majority of successful petitioners were women. If the parties agreed to seek a separation on the ground of their inability to live together because of continual quarrels, it was incumbent upon the judge to guard against collusion by carrying out a proper investigation of the case. Separation cases sometimes ended peacefully, but there is no convincing evidence of vigorous efforts to reconcile estranged spouses.[48]

An order for payment of alimony during these separation suits was usually made when the parties first came into court. Its scale was determined by the husband's wealth and the weekly payments ordered ranged from 10s. (in the case of one knight's daughter) to 7d. A separate payment for clothes might also be ordered. Sometimes these alimony orders were met by protests, and one case was considerably prolonged by ensuing wrangles.[49] But longer-term arrangements for the

---

[47] Cf. Helmholz, *Marriage Litigation*, pp. 100-7.

[48] For examples of the major types of separation case, see HRO CB 2, fos. 56, 63; CB 13, p. 149; *Goodwyn c. Goodwyn*, NNRO DEP 4A, fos. 327-9; DEP 9, fos. 76-82, 87-9; ACT 10, 14 Aug. 1564; *Loryson c. Loryson*, NNRO ACT 7A, fos. 163, 224; DEP 5A, fos. 243-4. For a peaceful conclusion, see NNRO ACT 5, fos. 155ᵛ, 178.

[49] Conset, *Practice*, pp. 277-8; NNRO ACT 5, fo. 225ᵛ; DEP 4A, fo. 327; ACT 7B, fo. 27; ACT 10, 25 May, 8 June, 6 July, 26 Oct., 8 Dec. 1563, *Goodwyn c. Goodwyn*.

maintenance of the wife after separation are only rarely mentioned in the court records.[50]

Suits for formal separations *a mensa et thoro* were rare in these two dioceses. Many cases of maltreatment of wives came to judges' notice as a result of presentments made during visitations and inquisitions. Those who sought decrees of separation were no doubt greatly outnumbered by those who simply abandoned or expelled their spouses. Abandonment was probably commonest at the lowest social levels where the courts' control was weakest. Over 8½ per cent of the married women included in the survey of the poor drawn up by the city of Norwich in 1570 or 1571 had allegedly been deserted by their husbands.[51] Cases of abandonment or expulsion were often treated as matter for correction both in the Winchester consistory court and in the inferior courts of Norwich diocese. It was also open to an expelled or abandoned wife to sue or promote proceedings for the restitution of conjugal rights, though few did so.[52] Such cases usually ended with a monition to the husband to receive the wife or go back to her and to treat her with marital affection, or a decree of restitution. Occasionally the *de facto* separation was confirmed by a formal decree or absolutory sentence. Such was probably the outcome of a suit which a woman named Helen Grigges commenced against her husband in the Norwich consistory court in 1551. An exceptionally full set of personal answers throws a shaft of light upon the destitution into which she had fallen. Her last desperate attempt, on the threshold of old age, to reclaim the husband whom she had allegedly tried to murder over twenty years before, had been preceded by a series of casual liaisons, two spells in prison, domestic service, three years of sickness and beggary, and a period of spinning in a rented chamber.[53]

[50] HRO CB 2, fo. 56; CB 17, p. 73; CB 28, 4 Dec. 1568, *Spering c. Spering*; CB 35, fo. 52^V.

[51] *The Norwich Survey of the Poor*, ed. J. F. Pound (Norfolk Record Soc. xl, 1971), 95.

[52] HRO CB 11, 2, 9, July 1558, *Gibbes c. Gibbes*; CB 16, 16 Oct., 4 Dec. 1562, *OP c. Isarne*; CB 22, 8 Mar. 1567, *Newneham c. Newneham*; NNRO ACT 5, fos. 205^V, 250; ACT 7B, fo. 27.

[53] NNRO DEP 5A, fos. 132, 229^V-30, 273.

Judges occasionally proceeded against suspected bigamists, and in at least one case a party to a bigamous marriage herself instituted proceedings after discovering that her husband had previously been married to another woman.[54] Official proceedings were in a number of cases sparked off by the arrival of a stranger from another parish or even another diocese, dogged by a suspicion, perhaps fed by an incautious word let slip by himself, that he had another wife alive. Alternatively they might be brought about by the remarriage of a woman long abandoned by her husband, whom she conveniently assumed to be dead. The haze of rumour could sometimes be dispersed by ordering the recently arrived stranger to produce letters testimonial from municipal authorities or the bishop of his former diocese, or by tracing the originator of the story and ordering him to substantiate it. The Winchester judges seem to have been readier than their Norwich counterparts to undertake these investigations. Some of these cases petered out without any definite conclusion being reached.[55] But the offence, if proved, was one which the courts sometimes treated with great severity. A bigamist was the one Norwich offender of our period who may have received corporal punishment. In 1517 a man of Winchester diocese was ordered to do public penance on as many as nine separate feast days. These bigamists were warned to go back to their previous partners; their irregular unions were of course regarded as being utterly void.[56]

So far we have been dealing with bigamists who no doubt hoped that their action would pass unnoticed. Under the influence of new ideas, however, a few men openly repudiated their wives on account of their adultery and made second marriages which they were prepared to justify. The existing law of the church did not of course sanction such marriages. However, the draft ecclesiastical laws drawn up in the second half of Edward VI's reign provided for divorce in cases of

---

[54] NNRO ACT 10, 20 Jan. 1563, *Arundell c. Arundell*.

[55] NNRO AI (1550), Martham/*R. Johnson*, Caister St. Edmund/*T. Elston*, Yarmouth/*W. West*; ACT 4A, fos. 210ᵛ, 288; DEP 4A, fos. 344–5; ACT 7A, fo. 17; ACT 7B, fos. 77ᵛ, 90ᵛ; HRO CB 2, fos. 30ᵛ, 86ᵛ, 92, 112ᵛ; CB 3, fos. 12ᵛ, 149, 150, 150ᵛ, 181ᵛ; CB 4, fos. 10ᵛ, 194ᵛ; VB 3, p. 164.

[56] NNRO AI (1532), Edgefield; HRO VB 1, fo. 16ᵛ; cf. CB 2, fo. 72.

adultery, desertion and extreme ill treatment, and sanctioned the remarriage of the innocent party. In 1552 a special act of parliament was passed to confirm the second marriage of the marquis of Northampton after he had divorced his first wife for adultery.[57]

Thomas Thirlby was one of the two bishops who opposed Northampton's bill,[58] and when he and his chancellor John Fuller encountered the influence of the new ideas in Norwich diocese they resisted it vigorously. They dealt with at least three men, including an alderman of Norwich and a resident of nearby Sall, who had attempted to marry again after separation from their first wives. These were not cases of clandestine bigamy. Two of the men concerned, whose wives had committed adultery (the reason for the third separation was not stated), held that their wives' infidelity made their second marriages lawful. Two of the three cases were distinguished by the care taken to prevent the men concerned from living with their new 'wives' — first warned in December 1550, they were still being harried in Mary's reign.[59] Thirlby faced what he regarded as matrimonial indiscipline with a more forthright resistance than he ever dared offer to doctrinal novelties, and it was no coincidence that his two short spells as judge in his own consistory court should largely have been devoted to the hearing of matrimonial causes.

(ii) *Annulment*

All decrees of annulment known to have been given in the two dioceses were based on one of three grounds: a precontract entered into by one of the parties, coercion applied to one or both of them, or an impediment of affinity between them.

Strictly speaking, a valid matrimonial contract *de praesenti*

[57] R. Haw, *The State of Matrimony* (1952), pp. 74-89; L. Dibdin, C. E. H. Chadwyck Healey, *English Church Law and Divorce* (1912), pp. 23-30, 67-9; *Reformatio Legum*, pp. 50-5.

[58] G. Burnet, *History of the Reformation of the Church of England*, ed. N. Pocock (Oxford, 1865), ii. 325.

[59] NNRO ACT 6, fos. 142ᵛ, 152ᵛ, 156; ACT 7A, fos. 77-8, 206ᵛ, 224, 303ᵛ-4; ACT 7B, fos. 14, 133, 187; ACT 8, fos. 14ᵛ-5, 150ᵛ; DEP 5B, fos. 51ᵛ, 135ᵛ, 146, 147ᵛ-51, 153ᵛ-5, 157ᵛ-8; ORR 1(b), fo. 10.

made bigamous any marriage subsequently entered into by one of the partners with a third party during the lifetime of the other partner. But people who entered into such marriages despite pre-contracts were not treated in these two dioceses in our period with the severity often accorded to bigamists. Judges must have made the charitable assumption that defendants in such cases had acted in good faith, genuinely believing that they were free to marry.

Seven sentences of annulment because of pre-contracts are known to have been given in the two dioceses.[60] The paucity of decrees of annulment is fairly striking in view of criticisms levelled against the existing law in the preamble of an ostensibly reforming statute of 1540. This complained that allegations of unconsummated pre-contracts had often led to the dissolution of marriages solemnized in church and blessed with children. It went on to provide that solemnized and consummated marriages should in future supersede unconsummated pre-contracts. The real reason for these provisions was to safeguard Henry VIII's marriage with Catherine Howard against attempts to impugn it on the grounds of pre-contracts entered into by either party. The fact that only one annulment decree is known to have been pronounced in the two dioceses on the ground of pre-contract in the period between 1520 and 1540 casts some doubt on the justice of the preamble's complaints.[61]

In 1549 the provisions of the 1540 statute relating to pre-contracts were repealed on the ground that they had encouraged people to break contracts in order to satisfy bodily lusts. There is rather more evidence in favour of the complaints of the 1549 act than there is for the allegations made in the preamble to the previous act. A Winchester case of 1541 showed that a defendant could nullify a contract alleged by a plaintiff

[60] *Dalderbye c. Parker and Clerk*, NNRO DEP 7B, fos. 45, 65; ACT 9, fo. 3; *Baldwyn c. Baldwyn*, ACT 9, 5 Feb. 1561; *Babbye c. Kynderslye*, NNRO ACT 10, 6–8 May 1563; DEP 9, fos. 45–6; *Bale c. Thurstone*, DEP 11B, fos. 78ᵛ–80ᵛ; ACT 11, 13 May 1568; *Heydon c. Fenne*, ACT 7A, fos. 101–2; *Reg. Gardiner et Poynet*, 58–63; *Deane c. Goodwyn als. Lamdene & Lamdene*, HRO CB 13, pp. 23, 35–7, 71–3; CB 14, 31 Jan. 1562.

[61] 32 Henry VIII, c. 38; H. A. Kelly, *The Matrimonial Trials of Henry VIII* (Stanford, 1976), pp. 262–4, 273–5.

by solemnizing and consummating marriage even after the commencement of suit. It is hardly surprising to find that the numbers of suits for breach of contract declined swiftly during the forties at both Norwich and Winchester.[62]

Coercion and marriage before the age of consent were further grounds for annulment (often linked) which were involved in three Norwich cases. In one of the cases the parties were trying to escape a marriage arranged by their parents before they had reached the age of consent. The provisions of the ecclesiastical law relating to marriages of this sort were amongst its most complex and least satisfactory.[63] Somebody who wished to escape a marriage solemnized in his or her childhood was supposed to protest against it formally immediately after reaching the age of consent. After this (when most adolescents would still be very much under their parents' influence) living together, kissing, and other marks of intimacy were held to constitute signs of consent unless they could be shown to have been compelled. Consummation did not need to take place for some years; a man had to be at least eighteen before a judge could decide whether or not he was impotent. The law left much to the discretion of judges, but still made it extremely difficult to escape a marriage solemnized before the age of consent, and it is therefore hardly surprising that so few suits for annulment of such marriages came before the courts. One Norwich couple wedded some years before the age of consent achieved the dissolution of their marriage in 1552 only because an immediate, deep-rooted, and lasting mutual antipathy buoyed up their resolution to refuse signs of consent at any cost. Physically compelled by the girl's mother to go to bed together some years after the marriage, they would not consummate it.[64] A second marriage within age was dissolved in 1562 after evidence had been produced that the couple had never treated each other as man and wife.[65] The third case involving the issue of consent sprang from the abduction and

---

[62] 2 & 3 Edward VI, c. 23; HRO CB 8, 5 Mar. 1541, *Page c. Selwood.*

[63] Swinburne, *Spousals,* pp. 40-4, 49.

[64] *Homerston c. Crane,* NNRO DEP 5B, fos. 87v-8, 155v-6, 165-9, 183v-4; ACT 7B, fos. 42, 47v, 208v.

[65] *Flowerdewe c. Drurye,* NNRO DEP 8, fo. 90; ACT 9, 14, 16 July 1562.

forced marriage of a Norwich girl in 1548. When her abductor sought restitution of conjugal rights three years later an absolutory sentence was given for her which was tantamount to a declaration that the marriage was void.[66]

Contravention of the church's prohibited degrees was the fourth ground for recorded annulment decrees. On the eve of the Reformation, consanguinity or affinity created by marriage or fornication barred marriage as far as the fourth degree. Spiritual affinity, created by sponsorship at baptism or confirmation, prevented marriage with the person whom one sponsored or her parents and one's sponsor or her children. The church had added a large number of prohibited relationships to those specified by 'God's law' in Leviticus 18, which lay within the first and second degrees of consangunity and affinity. At first the break with Rome brought no change in the law save that dispensations to marry within the degrees specified in Leviticus 18 (as interpreted by Henry VIII and his advisers) were utterly prohibited in 1534 and 1536. Then, in 1540, it was laid down that *only* the prohibitions included in Leviticus 18 were to be observed in future; henceforth no dispensations would be necessary for marriages previously forbidden by ecclesiastical as opposed to divine law and spiritual impediments disappeared from English church law altogether.[67]

It has often been suggested that the medieval church's structure of prohibited degrees made it only too easy to find grounds for annulment when one of the partners wanted to escape from a marriage.[68] But the paucity of suits for the annulment of marriages contracted within the prohibited degrees recorded in the registers and court books of the two

---

[66] *Atkinson c. Atkinson als. Randoll*, NNRO DEP 5A, fos. 227-9, 230^v-6, 249-55, 262, 263^v-4; DEP 5B, fos. 34-6, 97^v-100, 103; ACT 7A, fo. 206; ACT 7B, fo. 159.

[67] Helmholz, *Marriage Litigation*, p. 78; *Faculty Office Registers, 1534–1549*, ed. D. S. Chambers (Oxford, 1966), xxxiii-xxxvi; 25 Henry VIII, c. 22; 28 Henry VIII, c. 7 (which made it clear that fornication and adultery, as well as marriage, created affinity); 32 Henry VIII, c. 38. The table of kindred and affinity published by Matthew Parker in 1563 follows Calvin's interpretation of Leviticus 18, i.e. that marriage is forbidden between any two persons related more closely than, or as closely as, any pair there mentioned, rather than the literal interpretation favoured by Henry VIII; *Oxford Dictionary of the Christian Church*, 2nd edn., ed. F, L. Cross and E. A Livingstone (Oxford, 1974), p. 781.

[68] Helmholz, op. cit., p. 75n.

dioceses casts some doubt on this suggestion so far as the diocesan courts are concerned.

No annulments on the ground of consanguinity have been discovered in Norwich or Winchester records. At Norwich four marriages were held void on the ground of an impediment of affinity.[69] The relationships had been created by godparenthood in two cases, fornication in one, and marriage in the last. In a fifth case Bishop Thirlby's role was limited to enforcing separation, for the marriage of Henry Reppes, a gentleman of Mendham (Suffolk), had already been judged invalid by Thomas Cranmer and his advisers. After seeking the opinions of John Hooper, Nicholas Ridley, and John à Lasco, Reppes had wedded his nephew's widow who claimed that she had not been carnally known by her first husband.[70] In this case too, therefore, we see Thirlby in conflict with new ideas. I have found no annulments of solemnized marriages at Winchester, though in a few cases people tried to escape contracts by claiming that impediments existed.[71]

Whatever may have been the case higher up the social scale, it seems clear that in these two dioceses at least the complexity of the late-medieval marriage law did not make annulments easily available for the strata of society up to the lesser gentry who were served normally by the local church courts. Comparatively few marriages were annulled, and the most important single ground was the existence of a pre-contract, not one of the impediments of consanguinity or affinity, the only part of the marriage law to be simplified at the Reformation.

SEXUAL INCONTINENCE

Correction of sexual lapses took up more of the time of the church courts in these dioceses in the period of the Reformation than any other branch of their *ex officio* activities.

---

[69] NNRO ACT 5, fos. 105ᵛ, 176ᵛ, 287ᵛ; DEP 4A, fo. 115; *Toll c. Jolly* and *Toll c. Toll*, NNRO DEP 4B, fos. 26-31; ACT 7A, fos. 17ᵛ, 21, 42-3; *Myles and Filby*, NNRO ACT 10, 27 Oct. 1563 (for another possibly similar case see Act 8, fo. 309ᵛ).

[70] NNRO DEP 5B, fos. 131-45; ACT 7B, fo. 210.

[71] HRO CB 2, fos. 64ᵛ-5; CB 4, fo. 171ᵛ; CB 5, fos. 7, 8, 10, 19, 20ᵛ; CB 7, 20 Feb. 1535, *Androw.*

Improper sexual relationships were, in the eyes of the ecclesiastical law, crimes to be formally punished. They brought
with them tensions, quarrels, and disrepute, but for those involved and their neighbours and kindred unwanted children
were potentially their most serious consequence. Pregnancies
always figured prominently among the presentments made.
The local community naturally had a strong interest in having
relationships likely to lead to this outcome reported to the
church courts, if only to have the responsibility for filling an
extra mouth placed firmly on the shoulders of those to
whom it belonged. If an association had not resulted in a
pregnancy or birth, the partners were usually described as
noted for 'incontinence' or 'suspicious life'. The court books
usually supply no details of the basis for presentments. Those
who made them had sometimes heard nothing more than an
unsubstantiated accusation or rumour. Only rarely are the
court-book entries sufficiently specific to make it clear that
the parties had been caught in the act. In a great many cases
it is unclear whether offences were fornication or adultery,
and the court books very often fail to tell us whether the
individuals concerned were single or married, though amongst
those whose status was described, the former greatly outnumbered the latter.

Rather more women than men were normally presented,
because a pregnant woman was bound to be more conspicuous
than her partner. In the archdeaconry of Norwich about one-
third of the sexual delicts recorded in the commissary's court
books during our period came to the knowledge of the court
because a woman had been made pregnant. The man might
be a priest or married householder who had made the little
help he offered (perhaps a payment to a poor man to induce
him to marry her, or provision for her bed and board during
pregnancy) conditional on her keeping his name secret.[72] The
records suggest that pregnant girls were often packed off to
underground 'maternity homes' whose disreputable proprietors were ready, for a consideration, to help women in
need and perhaps to take their children off their hands.
Women were sometimes presented simply because they had

[72] NNRO DEP 5A, fos. 80ᵛ-1; DEP 6A, fo. 64ᵛ.

just left, or just arrived in, the area of a court's jurisdiction by themselves.[73] The parish employed its own crude methods to ascertain the father's identity. The most effective of these was probably the midwives' inquisition at the bedside of the woman in labour, unacceptably brutal though it appears to modern eyes. Here is an example of a testimonial sent by the midwife and her assistants:

> To sertyfye yowre mastershyppe of the throwthe of the mater consernynge the confessyon of Crystyan Smythe beyng in labor of chylld examyned by me the mydwyffe and the wyffes that were at her labor to the number of xiii[th] honest wyfes and the mydwyfe and we examyned hyr yn moste labor and trauaylle who was the chylldes father and she sayd that no nother man was the father but Thomas Ryder and we they [sic] sayd that we wold leue hyr excepte she wold tell the trewthe when she was yn hyr most labor and she dyd say that and yf we dyd leue hyr she wold neuer put yt wrongefully apone no nother man but he was the very father of hyr chyld as owre lady schode helpe her yn hyr moste nede and we do suppose thomas ryder that he ys the very father....[74]

Once the father's identity was established, the judge could order him to meet the expenses of confinement and purification, to support the child, and to provide the woman with a dowry, though the arrangements made varied widely, and only rarely were all these elements combined in the same decree. Recorded dowries ranged from £2 to £13, the period during which weekly sums (6d. was the commonest) for the child's maintenance were to be paid from two years to the whole time till it could earn its own living. In nearly every case maintenance was recognised to be the man's responsibility. Only if he could not be found might the woman's family be ordered to shoulder the burden, and then only provisionally. The Norwich courts seem to have neglected to supervise the fulfilment of these duties; more evidence, in the

---

[73] NRO AI (1538), Cawston/M. Skynner, Heydon/K. Aleyn; (1548), Wulterton/Isabella, servant with Mr. More, Calthorpe/Dorothy, servant with Robert Levett, Harpley/I. Martin; (1549), Blickling/T. Wylkenson.
[74] HRO CB 7, letter pinned amongst acts of Dec. 1541; for facial similarities between children and putative fathers, see NNRO DEP 4B, fo. 30^V; DEP 5B, fo. 173^V.

shape of orders to certify performance and excommunications for failing to do so, is to be found in the Winchester records.[75]

There was always a danger that a pregnancy might be terminated prematurely, or that the ministrations of an unskilful midwife or deliberate neglect later on might lead to a child's death. The Norwich courts seem to have abandoned any attempt at supervision in this field by our period, though until the thirties at least a number of people were cited before the Winchester consistory court for having concealed abortions, killed newborn children, or for having brought about miscarriages by means of herbal potions.[76] No registers of midwives' licences covering our period survive in either of the two dioceses, and the few entries in the Winchester court books relating to midwives have to do with combating papistry and prostitution rather than ensuring infant survival.[77]

A number of offenders had already 'made themselves sure' to one another in an informal manner or were prepared to consider marriage. The courts treated their cases in different ways at different times. Early in the period people were frequently punished for ante-nuptial fornication at Winchester, while in the 1560s the commissary in Norwich archdeaconry often dismissed couples who got married.[78] One should probably look for an explanation to the attitudes of individual judges, and possibly the heaviness of a court's workload at a given time, rather than to any significant long term change in outlook.

The courts often punished accessories to fornication and adultery. The father, master, husband, or landlord was held responsible for what went on under his roof, and could be held to have 'maintained bawdry' if misbehaviour went unchecked or unreported. Men who harboured pregnant girls also ran the risk of being called upon to do penance, though

[75] HRO CB 2, fos. 76, 77ᵛ, 99, 116; CB 7 (all cases taken from 1541), 21 Jan. *Roges*; 4 Feb. *Trumpe*; 19 Mar. *Burd*, 2 Apr. *Bell*; 29 Apr. *Flowde*; 23 July *Bruer*; 5 Nov. *Aunsell*; CB 17, p. 24; NNRO ACT 6, fo. 100ᵛ; ACT 8, fos. 146, 160, 249.

[76] HRO CB 2, fo. 59ᵛ; CB 3, fos. 24, 110, 123, 172, 192ᵛ; CB 4, fos. 46ᵛ, 105, 117ᵛ; CB 7, 3 Dec. 1534, *J. Hackman and wife*.

[77] HRO CB 35, fos. 100, 212ᵛ, 240ᵛ.

[78] HRO CB 3, fos. 6ᵛ, 118, 145ᵛ; CB 4, fos. 48ᵛ, 59; NNRO NAAB 2 (1569), Cley/*Hardinge and Stewarde*; Wells/*Forward*; Beetley/*Barrett and Warner*.

the court books suggest that judges were concerned to suppress clandestine boarding houses for pregnant women rather than to punish those who assisted individuals 'out of charity'.[79]

The courts could not supervise equally closely all aspects of relations between the sexes. Contraventions of the prohibited degrees, for instance, seem to have been presented very rarely. Offenders of substantial wealth or gentle birth were seldom dealt with by the courts in these dioceses. Thomas Thirlby of Norwich seems to have been quite exceptional in his readiness to tackle even fairly well-connected sexual offenders. In August 1552 he personally exhorted the mistress of Sir Roger Woodhouse of Kimberley (Norfolk) to mend her ways, and his chancellor, John Fuller, punished an alderman of Norwich for his adultery with his servant. It was Fuller, too, who in August 1550 censured the conduct of the countess of Surrey, mother of the future duke of Norfolk, albeit indirectly, when he punished the clergy responsible for her clandestine second marriage.[80]

Even in this area of its work (the one in which it could probably count on the warmest popular support) over half the proceedings initiated by the court in the archdeaconry of Norwich had no recorded outcome. There are signs, too, that in the short run at least the upheavals of the time had deleterious effects on its correctional work. The disordered state of the records and possible loss of material make it unsafe to rely upon totals of delicts presented as measures of efficiency. But it is noticeable that whereas a third of those reported in sample deaneries in 1532-3 purged themselves or were ordered to do penance, the corresponding proportion in the restless year of 1549-50 was smaller than one-seventh. At the end of our period it stood at just under a quarter.[81]

DEFAMATION OF SEXUAL INCONTINENCE

During the period of the Reformation, the overwhelming majority of defamation suits before the church courts were

---

[79] NNRO AI (1550), Grimston/*J. White*; DEP 5B, fos. 221ᵛ-2; HRO CB 3, fos. 45, 47ᵛ, 118ᵛ; CB 17, pp. 36-8; above, p. 76.

[80] NNRO ACT 7A, fos. 22ᵛ, 23ᵛ; ACT 7B, fos. 17, 131, 142.

[81] Appendix 3.

concerned with imputations of sexual misbehaviour. By the beginning of our period, ecclesiastical judges in most dioceses no longer entertained defamation suits concerned with crimes (such as theft and murder) which they could not themselves punish. But talk about a person's immoral conduct with members of the opposite sex could still lead to his or her presentment in visitation or inquisition. Poor men were not of course always forced to undertake defamation suits in order to clear their reputations. Malicious gossips and quarrellers were themselves often punished as a result of presentments. Much depended on the attitudes of questmen and judges.

The defamatory statements recorded ranged from the light-hearted jest and the hasty and ill-considered insult to the deliberate accusation. Two of four men of Terrington (Norfolk) who in 1549 met in an inn at Lynn to make merry were sued two years later for their part in a conversation in the course of which it was rehearsed 'how many men in Terrington were cuckolds'.[82] Abusive exchanges often arose out of quarrels over such things as small items of disputed property or what was felt to be slighting behaviour. In the heat of his anger a man might call a woman 'whore', and then perhaps explain somewhat lamely later on that he had only meant that she was a 'whore of her tongue', not a 'whore of her body'.[83] More serious were the spreading of unpleasant rumours or the making of bitter accusations in which long-nursed grudges or jealousies sometimes found vent.[84] The most deliberate accusations of all were made by people who had complained of plaintiffs' behaviour to sworn men or others in authority with a view to getting it punished. By divulging their complaints to friends and neighbours, some of them made themselves liable to be sued.[85]

Married people, especially middle-aged women, seem to have been the commonest litigants, and adultery the offence

[82] NNRO DEP 5A, fos. 267ᵛ-270.
[83] NNRO DEP 4A, fo. 203; DEP 5B, fos. 16ᵛ-17; ACT 7B, fo. 203; DEP 8, fo. 137; DEP 9, fos. 18-9; HRO CB 6, pp. 445-52.
[84] NNRO DEP 4A, fo. 233; DEP 5A, fos. 260-1; DEP 7D, fos. 59, 61; DEP 12, fo. 116; HRO CB 13, pp. 115, 121.
[85] HRO CB 3, fos. 36ᵛ, 37ᵛ-8, 52; CB 6, pp. 517, 518-20; NNRO DEP 8, fos. 94-5; DEP 12, fos. 47, 117ᵛ; ACT 12, 19 Apr. 1570, *Blisbye c. Kinge*.

most often imputed. In the first half of the period, the most popular single term of abuse was 'priest's whore'. Fornication was seldom the subject of a defamatory statement. At Norwich women ceased to rival men in the number of suits started in the course of the period, and the proportion of male plaintiffs at Winchester grew. It is tempting to put this down to some change in attitude, to men's becoming relatively more sensitive to imputations of sexual misconduct. A more likely explanation of the Norwich figures at least is that women were more apt to embark on a simple suit, sparked off for instance by a vigorous slanging match with a neighbour, which raised no complex legal issues and could easily be settled, the type of suit, in fact, which proctors might tend to discourage when the pressure of more complex and lucrative business was heavy.

When they heard defamation suits, ecclesiastical judges were concerned with the state of mind which lay behind the defendant's words, and the health of his soul, as well as with the damage to the plaintiff's good fame. The constitution *Auctoritate Dei Patris omnipotentis* (1222) decreed excommunication for all who maliciously imputed a crime to any man, thereby causing him to be defamed among good and grave men, or put to this purgation.[86] According to Lyndwood's gloss, it was to be interpreted broadly. Even true words might be spoken with malice, and only a formal accusation, or a judicial exception, could excuse their utterance. Lyndwood noted with disapproval the common excuse that the party's fame was already damaged. Every separate utterance of defamatory words could further injure a man's fame. The speaker was to be punished even if they had borne no fruit. It was sufficient that they had come to the notice of 'good and grave men' whether they believed them or not. Nevertheless, the speaker's general disposition ought to be taken into account, and Lyndwood suggested that judges were wont to deal leniently with those who had spoken such words drunkenly, or in jest.

Witnesses were often asked whether the words spoken had

---

[86] Lyndwood, *Provinciale*, pp. 345-8, esp. 346-7; Helmholz, 'Canonical Defamation', 256-7, 262; NNRO ACT 4A, fos. 24, 39ᵛ-40, 41-2.

damaged the plaintiff's fame, and whether they had been spoken in malice.[87] Testimony on these points favourable to defendants may have helped to bring about some peaceful settlements, though in other cases sentences were given for plaintiffs despite such evidence. But the defendant's own confession that the words had been spoken in the heat of anger, and his expression of readiness to ask forgiveness of the offended party might spare him the expense of sentence, and even the need to seek pardon before more than a few neighbours.[88] Indeed, sentence may have been given for one defendant who had already, before the start of suit, offered to declare the matter before the chancellor and ask the plaintiff's forgiveness in court.[89]

Many defendants were described as saying that they could prove their assertions. Only once, however, did a Norwich judge defer the defendant's penance till the plaintiff had cleared himself of the crime imputed to him,[90] and it is clear that most of the few absolutory sentences given at Norwich are to be explained not by the judge's acceptance of the truth of the defendants' accusations, but by some ambiguity in the words spoken, or insufficient proof that they had been uttered.[91] But at Winchester those defamed undertook, or were assigned, to purge themselves more often, and it is also clear that two absolutory sentences were given because the judge felt that the accusations made were at least partly proven.[92] As we might expect from Lyndwood's gloss, the great majority of sentences given were condemnatory. The comparatively few fully recorded sentences declared the defendants excommunicated and ordered them to desist from

[87] NNRO DEP 3, fos. 4ᵛ, 59ᵛ-61, 76ᵛ-77ᵛ, 174ᵛ, 177, 251, 253, 265ᵛ; HRO CB 13, p. 69; Helmholz, op. cit. 263-4.
[88] NNRO ACT 5, fo. 278ᵛ; ACT 7A, fo. 79ᵛ; ACT 7B, fo. 278; ACT 8, fos. 319, 319ᵛ.
[89] *Hunt c. Monye*, NNRO DEP 5B, fos. 47-8; ACT 7B, fos. 40, 176ᵛ.
[90] NNRO ACT 10, 18 July 1564, *Brown c. Smyth*.
[91] See e.g. *Myles c. Meys*, NNRO DEP 3, fo. 116; ACT 3B, fos. 117ᵛ-18; *Gamon c. Galt*, NNRO DEP 5A, fo. 201; ACT 7A, fo. 292ᵛ; *Hoberd c. Baxter*, NNRO DEP 5B, fos. 265ᵛ-6; ACT 7B, fo. 303.
[92] HRO CB 2, fos. 4ᵛ, 5ᵛ, 12, 14; *Redford c. Rede*, HRO CB 11, 30 Apr. 1558; *Holte c. Irishe*, HRO CB 22, 15 Dec. 1565; CB 19, pp. 201-3; *Tawke c. More*, HRO CB 22, 6 July 1566, 15 Feb. 1567; CB 19, pp. 354-6. Cf. Helmholz, 'Canonical Defamation', 263.

the defamatory words they had uttered.[93] Defendants' subsequent absolution and reception of suitable penance were sometimes recorded in the act books. At Winchester judges seem to have preferred until at least the 1540s not to give formal sentences in defamation suits, but rather to order defendants to seek plaintiffs' pardon with varying degrees of penitential formality.[94] At Norwich (though not at Winchester) the average annual number of defamation cases was lower at the end of the period than it had been at the beginning.[95] It seems possible that Norwich proctors occupied with a rapidly increasing number of tithe and testamentary suits (more complex and more lucrative than defamation causes) discouraged those who intended to seek restitution of their good name in the consistory court. One cynical critic of the church courts, writing in 1535, described defamation suits as 'but brabling' and 'only stuff to get money for the advocates and proctors'.[96] Yet it would be wrong to suggest that proctors could regulate the flow of defamation litigation at will. If individuals' concern for their reputations was not satisfied in the consistory court they turned elsewhere: in 1567-8 the commissary in Norwich archdeaconry heard more defamation suits than cases of any other type, and in 1569-70 unprecedented numbers of quarrellers and common defamers of neighbours were presented in the same court.[97]

CONCLUSIONS AND COMPARISONS

In the field of matrimonial litigation, the church courts of the sixteenth century had a very different task from that which faces today's courts, for most of the plaintiffs before them sought not the annulment or dissolution but the validation and enforcement of marriages. The majority of sentences given in such causes were absolutory.[98] Judges seem to have interpreted the law scrupulously and fairly, and so far as one can tell their sentences were worthy of respect. Many

---

[93] NNRO ACT 4A, fos. 203v-4, 209, 211, 212.
[94] HRO CB 5, fos. 53v, 124, 129.
[95] Appendix 2.
[96] LP ix, 1071.
[97] See book of instance causes in NNRO NAAB 1; appendix 3.
[98] Above, p. 65.

absolutory sentences were due to the failure of plaintiffs to produce sufficient witnesses. Yet the law suffered from one major defect: the lack of clear cut and easily understandable distinctions between *de futuro* and *de praesenti* formulae. The inability to make the distinction ensnared a number of those who subsequently sought redress in the courts. Nevertheless, the church's steady pressure in favour of publicity and solemnization, maintained through the Reformation, helped to discourage unwitnessed contracts and thus tended to reduce the volume of matrimonial litigation.[99]

The judges of the two dioceses very rarely annulled marriages in the age of the Reformation. Very few marriages were held to be void because prohibited degrees had not been observed. The commonest reason was a pre-contract. Despite what is sometimes suggested, the complexity of the church's rules relating to marriage did not make escape from unloved spouses an every day occurrence on the eve of the Reformation. This is not to claim that the rules were everywhere carefully observed. But whether they were observed or not, men very rarely sought annulments, and a number of such suits were unsuccessful. Separation suits were rare. Though it is impossible to claim on the basis of available evidence that the courts offered effective 'marriage guidance' and reconciliation facilities, judges seldom granted decrees.[100]

These findings reinforce the conclusions of recent historians of later medieval matrimonial litigation. In the fourteenth and fifteenth centuries, too, suits to enforce contracts (nearly all of them believed to be *de praesenti*) had predominated over suits for annulment in a number of dioceses. In the consistory court of Ely, towards the end of the fourteenth century, absolutory sentences had been in the majority, though admittedly a majority slenderer than that revealed by the sixteenth-century Norwich and Winchester records. As at Norwich and Winchester in the sixteenth century, parties' inability to distinguish clearly between *de futuro* and *de praesenti* formulae, and the attachment of conditions, were

---

[99] Above. pp. 57–8, 64–6.   [100] Above, pp. 67–75.

amongst the most important reasons for litigation in the later medieval church courts.[101]

'The most striking fact about divorce litigation in medieval England', writes Professor Helmholz in his excellent recent survey of matrimonial lawsuits, 'is how little of it there was.' That there were so few suits for annulment on grounds of consanguinity and affinity, Professor Helmholz suggests, was due in part to the great difficulty of assembling adequate proof of the more distant relationships within which marriage was forbidden, in part to the fourth Lateran Council's recognition that all but the closest prohibited degrees were ordained by human, not divine laws, and its consequent concession that 'It is more tolerable to leave couples joined together against the statutes of man than to separate, against the statutes of the Lord, those who are legitimately joined.'[102] Professor Sheehan has shown that at Ely in the late fourteenth century, as at Norwich and Winchester in the sixteenth, precontracts were raised in objection to marriages far more frequently than were consanguinity or affinity, and he shows too that fewer than half the annulment suits brought to the Ely consistory court in his period were successful.[103] Nor did medieval ecclesiastical judges compensate for their unwillingness to grant annulments by being ready to decree divorces *a mensa et thoro*: such divorces seem to have been ordered as rarely by most fourteenth- and fifteenth-century judges as they were by the chancellors of Norwich and Winchester in the period of the Reformation.[104] On this aspect of the courts' work temporal differences may have exercised less influence than geographical and social, for it is clear that the London consistory court was confronted in the mid-sixteenth century with many more cases concerning unsuccessful marriages than were other diocesan courts either then or in earlier centuries. Some 13 per cent of the cases dealt with by the London court between 1553 and 1555 whose nature is broadly

[101] M. M. Sheehan, 'The Formation and Stability of Marriage in Fourteenth-Century England: Evidence of an Ely Register', *Medieval Studies*, xxxiii (1971), 244-7, 257-8, 262; Helmholz, *Marriage Litigation*, pp. 25-6, 36-57.

[102] Op. cit., pp. 74, 81-2.

[103] Sheehan, 'Formation and Stability of Marriage', 258-9, 262.

[104] Helmholz, *Marriage Litigation*, pp. 100-7.

identifiable were brought by husbands or wives seeking either separation or restitution of conjugal rights.[105] There were nearly as many suits caused by marital breakdown as there were over breaches of matrimonial contract. The exceptional pressures of the metropolitan environment probably did most to produce a situation so strikingly different from that revealed by the act books of courts sitting in provincial towns.

As in the dioceses of Norwich and Winchester, the punishment of sexual immorality was one of the most important facets of correctional activity before the Reformation in the diocese of Canterbury and after it in the dioceses of York, Chester and London; sexual offences normally headed the list of those which engaged judges' attention.[106] Other courts seem to have resembled those of our two dioceses in their approach to offenders. Sexual offences were generally the most vigorously pursued. Dr. R. A. Marchant has claimed that the courts met a greater degree of recalcitrance in attempting to correct sexual feelings than they did in other aspects of their work. The reason for this state of affairs is not far to seek. The courts encountered resistance on the part of sexual offenders because they demanded more of them than they did of other individuals who appeared before them. Offenders of this class were amongst those least likely to get away with a simple warning. The point is brought out by Marchant's analysis of eight selected sets of *acta* dating from 1590 to 1633, the same sets which he uses to demonstrate the recalcitrance of sexual offenders. His figures show that these made up well under a third of those presented, a much higher proportion of those who 'performed penance or obeyed other orders'. In the court of the archdeaconry of Norwich during the period of the Reformation the proportion of such proceedings ending satisfactorily, i.e. in dismissal, successful purgation, or certified penance, fluctuated markedly from one year to another between 25 per cent and 40 per cent. Marchant's figures exhibit even wider variations, but

---

[105] It is not always possible to distinguish the two types of case in the act books. The figure given here is based on GLRO DL/C/additional, 1553-5.

[106] Woodcock, *Medieval Ecclesiastical Courts*, pp. 79-82; Owen, 'Ecclesiastical Jurisdiction', 211n; Emmison, *Morals and the Church Courts*, pp. 1-2; Marchant, *Church under the Law*, p. 219.

taken together do not suggest that the level of efficiency of the church courts in this sphere changed significantly between the Reformation and the early seventeenth century. In one deanery, however, that of Frodsham in Cheshire, the results achieved both in 1590 and 1633 were better than any apparent from the surviving records of the Reformation period from the archdeaconry of Norwich.[107]

The community's concern with sexual discipline helps to explain parties' sensitivity to imputations of sexual misconduct and their readiness to go to law upon what at first appear trivial grounds. The courts gave the successful plaintiff in a defamation cause a remedy whose appropriateness Helmholz has recently underlined.[108] What the plaintiff wanted was a public vindication of his reputation, and this an order to the defendant to seek his pardon achieved more effectively than money damages. At Winchester, in the first half of our period, judges were ready to assign such penances without the plaintiff's having to pay for a costly formal sentence, and this was the practice of the judge of the consistory court at Durham in the early 1530s. In the London consistory court in the mid-1550s as many such orders were given as formal sentences.[109] It has been suggested here that the pressure of more lucrative business may have led proctors in the Norwich consistory court to discourage defamation suits towards the end of our period.[110] By the 1630s, however, writs of prohibition had deprived the church courts of much of this more lucrative business, and defamation suits were once more the commonest type of case heard in the Norwich consistory court. In other consistory courts, such as those of Chester and York, defamation suits steadily increased in number for

---

[107] Op. cit., pp. 214-15, 219. My Norwich archdeaconry percentages cited here are based on categories different from those employed in appendix 3.

[108] Helmholz, 'Canonical Defamation', 265-7.

[109] Durham University Department of Palaeography and Diplomatic, DR/III/ 1, fos. 15, 65ᵛ, 73, 75ᵛ; GLRO DL/C/additional, 1553-5, e.g. 26 Jan. 1555, *Conway c. Wylkokkes, Hill c. Athewe*; 2 Mar. 1555, *Goldsalve c. Philippe and Wyttam.*

[110] Above. p. 83.

most of Elizabeth's reign.[111] Whatever the reasons for local
and temporary fluctuations in litigation of this type, it remains clear that people greatly resented imputations of sexual
misconduct and continued throughout our period and beyond
to seek redress in the ecclesiastical courts.

[111] Marchant, *Church under the Law*, pp. 20, 62; Haigh, *Reformation and Resistance*, p. 227; 'Slander and the Church Courts in the Sixteenth Century', *Transactions of the Lancs. and Cheshire Antiquarian Society*, lxxviii (1975).

4

TESTAMENTARY ADMINISTRATION
AND LITIGATION

The church had first become involved in the disposal of the property of individuals after death because his soul's health had originally been the primary motive for bequests made by the dying man.[1] The subsequent growth of testamentary freedom had made this aspect of the church's work much more important. There were two main tasks: to ascertain the dead man's wishes and to enforce them. In order to make a dead man's testament legally effective an ecclesiastical judge had to approve it, and entrust its execution to the testator's nominees (the executors) who remained answerable to him until they had discharged their trust. If the validity of the testament were challenged, or the executors failed to carry out their responsibilities, the resultant dispute might well come before the ecclesiastical judge for settlement. There were limits to what he could do, however, for he was power-less to determine title to land, and by the beginning of our period he had practically lost the right to enforce payment of debts due to the dead man. If somebody died without making a will, the judge entrusted the disposal of his estate to ad-ministrators who remained answerable to him in the same way that executors did. When it operated efficiently, the system of registration and supervision enforced by the church courts offered the families, legatees, and executors of the deceased tangible advantages. But probate had to be paid for;

---

[1] On the early development of the church's testamentary jurisdiction, see M. M. Sheehan, *The Will in Medieval England* (Toronto, 1963), esp. pp. 16–18, 163–76; T. F. T. Plucknett, *A Concise History of the Common Law* (5th edn. 1956), pp. 725–46.

some thought it excessively expensive, and it is hardly surprising that many should have attempted to escape the jurisdictional net, especially when estates were small and those
close to the decreased were able to co-operate in mutual trust.
Attempts to tighten the net and enforce ecclesiastical jurisdiction, in which apparitors played a prominent part, were
amongst the most resented activities of court personnel. But
against the grief and anger which their insensitive zeal caused
those close to the deceased must be set the succour which
the courts alone might be able to give to widows and orphans,
to the victims of unscrupulous executors, or to those worsted
in internecine family feuds.

THE JURISDICTION OF THE COURTS

The church courts' jurisdiction only covered the goods and
chattels of the dead. Chattels fell into two categories, personal
and real. Within the former came household goods, money,
plate, cattle, crops, and cut wood, within the latter leases and
rents.[2] But ecclesiastical judges had no jurisdiction over land
and the statute of 1529 concerning probate specifically ex-
cluded the proceeds of land sold by virtue of a testament
from the goods and chattels of the deceased.[3] The statute of
wills of 1540 provided that wills of land should be in writing,
but gave the ecclesiastical court no power to compel probate
of such wills. (A Norwich defendant in a case of 1567–70
who refused to produce a will on the ground that it concerned
his lands and tenements managed to secure a writ of prohibition.)[4] Provisions for the disposal of land were usually included by landholders of sufficient substance in the document
registered in the ecclesiastical court (though often in a separate
section described as the 'last will' to distinguish it from the
'testament' disposing of goods and chattels) but this was a
matter of convenience alone.

Some lay courts could grant probate, but the great bulk
of the work was divided between the church courts. The

[2] R. Burn, *Ecclesiastical Law* (1763), ii. 645.
[3] 21 Henry VIII, c. 5.
[4] 32 Henry VIII, c. 1; *Annott c. Symkins and Depden*, NNRO ACT 11, 21
Jan. 1568, 5, 25 Oct., 1569; DEP 11B, 20 Apr. 1570.

prerogative court of the archbishop of Canterbury claimed the probate of wills of those who died leaving goods worth £5 or more in more than one diocese except in those cases where a higher limit had been established by agreement. The disposal of certain more valuable estates was reserved to Wolsey as legate between 1522 and 1529 and to Cromwell between 1536 and 1540.[5] Below the limits set for provincial, legatine and vicegerential jurisdiction, the arrangements for the division of probate work between the courts of archdeacon, commissary, and bishop varied very much from one diocese to another. Within each diocese were a number of exempt jurisdictions to whose courts the probate of the wills of their inhabitants belonged. Relations between the various courts within the dioceses of Norwich and Winchester usually seem to have been amicable enough so far as probate was concerned. Jurisdictional boundaries may not have been observed with the utmost strictness, but only very rarely does one read of the quashing of a probate granted in error by an inferior court. The only major clashes took place as we have seen between the archdeacons and bishops of Winchester in the second half of the period.[6]

The procedure for the proof of wills described in a fourteenth-century provincial constitution and Lyndwood's comments upon it was as follows. The executors were to bring the will before the ecclesiastical judge and prove it with trustworthy witnesses. They were not to administer the dead man's goods before they had made an inventory of them, save in order to pay for the funeral. After the inventory had been produced, the judge could commit the administration to them. It was however only to be entrusted to those who

---

[5] Lyndwood, *Provinciale*, pp. 174-5; Kitching, 'Prerogative Court of Canterbury', pp. 191-5; 'Probate Jurisdiction of Cromwell', 102-6; Bowker, *Secular Clergy*, pp. 10-11; 'Supremacy and the Episcopate', 240-1. Fox played a prominent part in episcopal protests against the prerogative jurisdiction under Warham, and in his time a number of people of Winchester diocese who had been cited to prove wills claimed that the deceased had had goods and debts in a number of dioceses; see GLRO microfilm X 11, fos. 2ᵛ-3ᵛ, 8ᵛ-9, 11, 18ᵛ, 19, 92, 96; HRO CB 4, fos. 99ᵛ, 113ᵛ-14.

[6] See NNRO NCC will registers Robynson, fo. 113, Palgrave, fo. 149ᵛ, Godsalve, fo. 149, Grundisburgh, fo. 63, and above, pp. 31-2.

could give sufficient promise or pledge to render account of their administration when called upon to do so.[7]

How closely did the courts of the two dioceses follow the procedure outlined above? The probate certificates in the will registers throw little light on the question, since they usually tell us no more than that testaments were proved on given dates and that their execution was committed to the executors named in them, who were sworn in legal form. One Winchester deposition in a testamentary case does however describe the probate of one will in the archdeaconry some time in the early 1550s. The executrix brought the will to the archdeacon's registrar, accompanied by five witnesses. The registrar then read the will in the presence of the executrix and witnesses, after which he administered to them a solemn oath upon the gospels that the will was true and complete.[8]

The first feature of this description to note is that probate took place before a registrar, not a judge. Some of the worst abuses of testamentary administration in the diocese of Norwich in the second half of the century were to be blamed upon the greed and slackness of registrars.[9] A second point is that no mention is made of the production of an inventory. Grant of probate before the exhibition of inventories was probably common; indeed one wonders whether they were demanded at all in the case of the more meagre estates. It was obviously important for all concerned that more substantial estates should be properly inventoried, and the probate statute of 1529 dealt with the procedure in some detail. From 1558 onwards, lists survive of the inventories produced in the Norwich consistory court, and these lists suggest that they were filed in respect of most, possibly all, consistory wills. The same lists show that accounts were produced in only a small minority of cases; in 1561 (old style), for example, nearly 200 inventories were exhibited, fewer than thirty accounts.[10]

The procedure so far described was probate 'in common

[7] Lyndwood, *Provinciale*, pp. 174 (esp. n. h), 176–7.
[8] HRO CB 13, p. 77.
[9] See below, pp. 109–10.
[10] Sheehan, *Will in Medieval England*, p. 214; 21 Henry VIII, c. 5; NNRO INV 1(b), fos. 15–16.

form'. A probate in common form could subsequently be challenged, and this might have unfortunate consequences if the witnesses had died in the meanwhile.[11] A probate ' in solemn form of law' came as near as possible to giving a testament watertight protection and could only be reversed by appeal to a higher court. In solemn-form procedure the witnesses were examined upon the circumstances of the making of the will, and the judge made formal pronouncement upon its validity. All those interested in the estate, who might conceivably have objections to the will, were cited beforehand. A number of depositions apparently taken in the course of solemn-form probate survive in the court books, but despite its advantages, the majority of executors did not employ the solemn-form procedure.[12]

If a man died without making a will, the first step was to sequestrate his goods for their safe keeping if necessary until arrangements for the administration of the estate could be made. The power of sequestration was included in Winchester yeoman apparitors' patents. Custody was entrusted to the widows concerned, to proctors, apparitors and local clergy amongst others.[13] The administration of the intestate's estate was by virtue of a statute of 1357 to be granted to his next of kin. The statute of 1529 empowered the judge to commit it to the widow or the next of kin or both as seemed best to him. This act also directed him to take security for the faithful administration of the estate.[14] Administrators, like executors, were obliged to produce inventories. The estate was supposed to be divided into three equal parts between the widow, children, and pious uses. If the process of distribution presented problems, the administrators could seek an award from the judge. A number of these are set out in the Winchester court books, and in no case are pious uses

[11] Below, p. 109.
[12] Marchant, *Church under the Law*, pp. 88–91; NNRO ACT 7B, fo. 171; DEP 5B, fos. 188-9.
[13] HRO Reg. Fox, v, fo. 66ᵛ; CB 3, fos. 22ᵛ, 24ᵛ, 85ᵛ, 193-4; CB 5, fo. 25; GLRO microfilm X 11, fo. 97.
[14] 31 Edward III, st. 1, c. 11; 21 Henry VIII, c. 5.

referred to; it seems absolutely clear that the best recorded awards made no provision for them.[15]

The estates of those whose executors would not act were entrusted to administrators as in cases of intestacy. If a man named as executor was uncertain whether to assume responsibility or not, the judge could give him letters of collection which would enable him to take the measure of the dead man's assets before coming to a final decision. The collector would be bound to submit an inventory, but might refuse the onus of execution, and would be acquitted on handing over goods obtained. Excessive debts were sometimes the ground for refusal, and in such cases sums handed over were distributed among creditors warned to appear by proclamation.[16]

It seems likely that the great majority of recorded probates and grants of administration were sought without prompting by those concerned. An incalculable but probably large proportion of the population were too poor for it to be worth the courts' while to track down their meagre estates. Above the level of the poorest, however, there must always have been those who hoped that the estates under their control might escape the scrutiny of registrars and apparitors, and *ex officio* action was often necessary to enforce the jurisdiction of the courts. An interesting Winchester memorandum of spring 1572 tells us that '...John Colman of Rew in the parish of godshill died after Christmas [and] made a will [and] his wiff his executrix [and] the will is not warned in.'[17] A number of shorter, often cryptic, notes, apparently to the same effect, are scattered through the court books of both dioceses; sometimes they add that executors were administering estates without authority. The boundary between 'warning in' and prosecutions for unauthorized administration must have been a fine one, and the action taken depended very much on the discretion of individual registrars and judges. The numbers of testamentary prosecutions in the consistory court of Norwich

[15] Plucknett, *Concise History*, pp. 729-30; HRO CB 9, 10 Oct. 1551 (goods of Johanna Wynter); 14 May 1552 (goods of Avice Heath); CB 22, 6 Oct. 1565, *An ordre taken ... touching the goodes of Edward Wyle deceased ...*
[16] NNRO, NCC will register Haywarde, letter at beginning; ACT 6, fo. 162; ACT 7A, fo. 170v; ACT 7B, fo. 41v.
[17] HRO VB 11.

fluctuated markedly from year to year. Some years went by
with very few recorded prosecutions. 1534 on the other hand
apparently witnessed something of a drive against slack executors. Much of the work of enforcement probably went unrecorded in the court books; it was left, especially in the
second half of the sixteenth century, to the ubiquitous apparitors. At about the beginning of James I's reign, one of
them provoked a bitter complaint by citing executors to
prove a will the very morning after the testator's death, and
before his burial.[18]

Early in the period, fees were the most unpopular single
feature of testamentary administration. Their size was the
subject of complaint in parliament in 1529, when a new scale
was introduced by statute. Before 1529, probate fees had
supposedly been regulated by a provincial scale rather more
generous to the ordinary than that introduced by the statute.[19]
Unfortunately the records now surviving at Norwich and Winchester do not permit a comparison of the values of estates
and fees charged which would enable one to say whether the
early sixteenth-century judges of these dioceses observed the
provincial scale. But in Norwich archdeaconry, between 1525
and 1527, over 40 per cent of estates were held to be too
meagre for such fees to be levied from them at all. More irksome for the poor, however, than the probate fee due to the
ordinary was the 1s. 'acquittance' fee, due to the scribe,
which was payable even when an executor or administrator
was dismissed *in forma pauperis*.[20]

The other major complaint against ecclesiastical judges in
the testamentary field, made in the *Commons' Supplication
against the Ordinaries* of 1532, was that they delayed too
long before making grants of probate.[21] Lack of information
about dates of death hampers any investigation of this complaint. But we are usually told by the wills themselves when
they were witnessed, and by the probate certificates when

---

[18] NNRO ACT 5, fos. 32-7; Marchant, *Church under the Law*, p. 23; *Registrum Vagum*, i. 43.

[19] 21 Henry VIII, c. 5; Lyndwood, *Provinciale*, pp. 181-3.

[20] NNRO Norwich archdeaconry will register Randes, fos. 266-394 (190 wills).

[21] *Documents Illustrative of English Church History*, ed. H. Gee and W. J.
Hardy (1896), p. 149.

they were proved. Table 1[22] sets out the percentages of samples of fifty wills registered in the courts of the archdeaconries of Norfolk and Surrey and the consistory court at Norwich proved in given periods from the date of attestation or making.

TABLE 1

Court and date		Percentages proved in:		
		Less than 2 months	Less than a year	Over a year
Norfolk Archdeaconry	1515-17	54	88	12
	1570	62	94	6
Surrey Archdeaconry	1522-25	82	98	2
	1560	38	70	30
Norwich Consistory	1520-21	50	76	24
	1570	48	78	22

These figures suggest that at the level of the archdeaconry, where the smallest estates were handled, wills were usually proved fairly swiftly.[23] In the Norwich consistory court, which dealt with the wills of men of greater average wealth, probate (as was only to be expected) took rather longer than it did at the archdeaconry level, but even so, half the wills were proved in two months, over three quarters within a year. Some of the figures, especially those for Norfolk (1570) and Surrey (1522-5) point not to slowness in probate (the subject of complaint in the *Commons' Supplication* of 1532), but rather to excessive speed, something of which both Bishop Parkhurst of Norwich and his successor's chancellor, John Becon, complained in the 1570s.[24] It is hard to explain convincingly the comparatively long periods which elapsed between attestation and probate in the archdeaconry of Surrey at the beginning of Elizabeth's reign. It is possible, however, that the devastating epidemics of the later 1550s had encouraged an unusually high proportion of testators to make

[22] Based on NNRO NCC will registers Alblaster, Brygge; Norfolk archdeaconry registers 6 and 23 (first fifty wills in each of these four); GLRO DW/PA/7/2, fos. 164v-205v; DW/PA/7/6, fo. 253v to end.
[23] Cf. Bowker, 'Commons' Supplication against the Ordinaries', pp. 66-7.
[24] *Letter Book of Parkhurst*, 261-2; Strype, *Annals*, ii. pt. 2, 698-9, below, pp. 109-10.

their wills while still in health lest death catch them unprepared.

DISPUTES OVER AUTHORITY FOR ADMINISTRATION OF GOODS AND VALIDITY OF TESTAMENTS

There were two main types of suit concerned with testaments and administrations: those which had to do with the resolution of rival claims to administer estates and questions of validity, and those aimed at securing the proper execution of accepted testaments, the payment of legacies, for instance, or the rendering of accounts. It is important not to make the distinction between the two types too sharp, for a number of suits brought in both issues, validity and execution. But the majority of causes concerned with the estates of deceased persons may be classified in this way. Suits of the first type outnumbered those of the second in the two dioceses during our period. They arose in a number of ways. Prospective plaintiffs often wanted to discover by what authority men had taken goods into their hands. (A defendant might not be acting by virtue of a testament at all, but on the strength of a deed of gift; alternatively he might claim that he had not interfered with the goods.) Other plaintiffs wished to question the validity of testaments which were on the point of being proved or had already been proved in common form. If they did not have alternative documents to exhibit, or other serious grounds for impugning the testaments, production of witnesses might suffice to set their doubts at rest. Grants of letters of administration in prospect or already made also gave rise to disputes. Plaintiffs in such cases usually asserted that a testament had been made, or that they had as good a claim as the defendants or a better one to be granted letters of administration.[25] Such a claim might involve the examination of witnesses as to the relationship between the plaintiff and the deceased.

The most prominent issue in cases of the first main type, and the most difficult to resolve, was that of validity. Each

---

[25] See e.g. HRO CB 12, fo. 62; CB 18, 22 June, 15 July 1564, *Beale c. Beale and Beale*; CB 19, pp. 314, 316; CB 23, 31 May 1567, *Hall and Rumboll c. Rumboll*.

testament's validity depended upon its being adequately witnessed or written in the deceased's hand, upon his having the
right to make a testament and his being sane and free from
undue pressure when he made it, upon its being the last expression of his wishes, and upon the absence of fraudulent
alterations. Plaintiffs impugned testaments by pointing to the
absence of one or more of these prerequisites. Amongst the
depositions taken in this type of case are some of the most
vivid and sombre to be found in the court books. They tell of
animosities within the family and intrigues around the sick-
bed, of delirium and the agonies of death.

Two witnesses to the dead man's assent to the will were
necessary, or three if they were open to minor exceptions
such as that of friendship with the party producing them.
The judge had a fairly wide discretion in deciding whether exceptions were major or minor. Testimony of legatees was not
to be trusted in respect of their own legacies, though they
might be accepted as witnesses to the rest of the will.[26] A
properly witnessed will could be accepted for probate even if
it had not been written down in the deceased's lifetime. The
courts might be prepared to uphold such 'nuncupative' wills
even when they had been expressed with some informality a
long time before death.[27] In cases of this sort there was
sometimes a suspicion that the next of kin had suppressed a
will whose provisions were disadvantageous to them; in its
absence the testimony of the dead man's neighbours provided
the only evidence of his intentions. Of course this type of
case might present knotty problems which could best be
resolved by arbitration. This was the course taken in the
Norwich suit *Gunvile c. Cooke* (1550). Eleven witnesses described how a sickly young man, Edmund Cooke, had in a
series of conversations given details of the provisions of his
will, including the appointment of his master 'little Dick'
Gunvile as one of his executors in gratitude for the kindness
Gunvile had shown him. His kinsman Richard Cooke, a complete stranger to the parish, appeared at his burial, and

---

[26] Swinburne, *Testaments and Last Wills*, fos. 186–7.
[27] See e.g. *Bulwar c. Mychell*, NNRO DEP 7C, fos. 72–3; ACT 9, 16 Sept.
1561.

Edmund's will was apparently never found among his papers in his lodgings, as he had said it would be.[28]

A will could be accepted for probate, even if unwitnessed, provided that it was written in the testator's hand and found in his chest or among his papers. The custom of certain dioceses allowed the claim that it had been written by the deceased to be verified by its comparison with other instruments undoubtedly written by him and the testimony of those who knew his hand well.[29]

If one party to a case claimed that a dead man had not been capable of making a will, it was up to the judge to decide, on the basis of testimony, whether when the document had been drawn up the defunct had really had an 'earnest purpose' revealed by his concentration on points of drafting or his requesting by-standers to bear witness. If it could be shown that the dead man had only been able to give expression to the provisions of his 'will' at the prompting of those around him, the document might well be declared invalid.[30] Witnesses had as a matter of form to say whether the deceased had been of sound mind when his will had been declared. If there was doubt on this score, witnesses might remove it by showing that the dead man had been well in command of the situation. One testator had refused to reduce the price of a comb of oats; another, asked whether he heard his will when it was read over to him, had retorted that he heard it as well as the questioner, while a third had identified one witness and told another that she should have nothing.[31] If witnesses disagreed, those who testified to sanity were to be preferred, and the law took into account the possibility that the deceased had recovered from previous insanity or was enjoying a lucid interval. So it is not surprising that judges upheld a number of wills impugned on the ground of the testator's unsoundness of mind.[32]

[28] NNRO DEP 4B, fos. 35-8, 79-82; ACT 7A, fos. 10ᵛ, 15ᵛ, 47ᵛ.

[29] Swinburne, *Testaments and Last Wills*, fo. 191; NNRO DEP 4B, fos. 83ᵛ, 106; DEP 5A, fo. 265; DEP 6A, fos. 147ᵛ-8; HRO CB 19, p. 273.

[30] Swinburne, *Testaments and Last Wills*, fo. 261; HRO CB 12, fos. 24ᵛ-9, 35ᵛ.

[31] NNRO DEP 4A, fo. 282; DEP 5B, fo. 108; DEP 7B, fo. 29ᵛ.

[32] Swinburne, *Testaments and Last Wills*, fos. 36-9; NNRO DEP 4A, fos. 149ᵛ, 152-5; DEP 5B, fos. 10ᵛ-4, 30ᵛ-1, 32ᵛ-3, 37ᵛ-9; ACT 5, fo. 196; ACT 7A, fo. 245; ACT 7B, fo. 53; HRO CB 19, pp. 378-9; CB 24, fos. 12-9; CB 22, 13 Dec. 1566.

If more than one will had come to the notice of the court, the last to be made was to be upheld as a rule. A will could also be enlarged (and often substantially altered in the process) by means of properly attested codicils. But later wills and codicils could be challenged if witnesses were able to show that testators had been induced to make them by coercion or deceit. One unruly son wrung from his dying father the concession that he should have his shop for 40s. less than its likely selling price, a provision which the executor was understandably reluctant to include in the will he exhibited in court.[33] However, wills usually seem to have been redrafted or enlarged for good reasons, such as the insufficiency of goods to fulfil legacies earlier intended, and the desire to strengthen the hand of the widow against troublesome children.[34]

The question of the dead man's choice of executor was an important issue in a number of cases. Some testators changed their minds about previous nominees because of their untrustworthiness or indebtedness; one chose a fresh executor so as to prevent the same man's being executor and purchaser of his land.[35]

The issue of falsification of testaments seems to have arisen comparatively rarely. The frauds alleged in testamentary suits included unauthorised interlineations and erasures, insertion of names of witnesses who had not been present at the reading of the will, and the alteration of one will by a schoolmaster who had contrived to have the original, entrusted to him in order that he might make a fair copy of it, lost by his pupils.[36] But scribal errors and mistakes in drafting which had not been made in bad faith could be rectified by the production of witnesses. As Swinburne stressed, the judge's foremost task in cases of this nature was to discover what the

---

[33] Swinburne, *Testaments and Last Wills*, fos. 263-4; *Browne c. Browne*, NNRO DEP 5A, fos. 1, 103^v, 123-30, 272^v-3; DEP 5B, fos. 24-6; ACT 7A, fos. 135, 177^v-8; ACT 7B, fo. 126.

[34] NNRO DEP 6A, fos. 203, 261^v-2.

[35] NNRO DEP 3, fo. 350; DEP 4B, fos. 3-6; DEP 8, fo. 42^v.

[36] NNRO DEP 4, fos. 166^v, 378^v; DEP 4B, fo. 286^v; DEP 6A, fos. 120^v-1, 123^v-4; DEP 7B, fos. 23-5; DEP 7C, fo. 73; DEP 7E, fos. 12-14.

defunct's real intentions had been.[37] In achieving this goal he was allowed far more scope to consider circumstantial evidence than he was for instance in breach of contract cases.

In order to avoid the more obvious pitfalls encountered in drafting a will, testators or their families naturally sought technical advice. The depositions suggest that for most of our period the parish priest remained the most obvious source of such advice for the majority of people. His influence was strengthened by the common unwillingness to draw up a will before the onset of the terminal illness, which tended to bring together the making of testamentary dispositions and the last rites. The continuing influence of the clergy was recognized in the 1536 statute for the punishment of sturdy vagabonds and beggars and in the royal injunctions of 1547 which sought to use it to change testamentary habits in favour of the poor. Edward's reformation did much to reduce the standing of the clergy in the people's eyes, but the *Ordre for the Visitacion of the Sicke* in the 1552 Prayer Book still laid upon the minister the duty of reminding the sick man to dispose of his goods by will and declare his debts 'for discharging of his conscience and quietnesse of hys executours'.[38]

Depositions in testamentary suits sometimes show priests tactfully prompting parishioners to make wills. One urged a widow to do so in order to avoid strife amongst her children.[39] On the other hand we find one clergyman refusing to write a will, perhaps because he did not think the testator in a fit state to make one.[40] It is true that the clergy were not always so scrupulous (one incumbent wrote out a will which he had never heard the testator declare, even though he was still alive) and that their legal knowledge was not always entirely reliable.[41] Yet many depositions suggest that the local priest was a respected figure, believed to be impartial.[42]

---

[37] NNRO DEP 4A, fos. 343, 421; DEP 4B, fos. 12-15, 200; *Testaments and Last Wills*, fos. 190ᵛ-1.

[38] 27 Henry VIII, c. 25; *Visitation Articles and Injunctions*, ii. 127; *The First and Second Prayer Books of Edward VI* (Everyman edn. 1949), p. 419.

[39] NNRO DEP 6A, fo. 163; DEP 4B, fos. 122, 250ᵛ.

[40] NNRO DEP 4A, fos. 216-19.

[41] NNRO DEP 4A, fo. 154; DEP 6A, fos. 10ᵛ-1.

[42] DEP 3, fos. 205-8, 618.

and he was one of the people outside the immediate circle of family and friends most likely to be named overseer to keep a watch over the executors' discharge of their duties. On the whole it seems likely that the clergy's influence was salutary and that it helped to prevent manipulation and misinterpretation. Its decline during the period of the Reformation may have been one of the causes of the striking increase in testamentary litigation at this time.

THE EXECUTION OF THE TESTAMENT

Even if a testament had been approved as the valid expression of a man's last wishes as to the disposal of his property, the way to its fulfilment might be encumbered with various obstructions, some of which it was the responsibility of the church courts to remove.

Executors might be faced with difficulties in executing a testament because goods were in somebody else's possession. They could sue at the common law for debts or goods obtained, and though many of the testamentary causes which had been brought in the consistory court of Canterbury in the fifteenth century had apparently been concerned with the recovery of debts due by or to testators,[43] the courts of Norwich and Winchester heard hardly any such suits after 1520. Occasionally those who detained goods necessary for the execution of testaments were sued, but partly no doubt because of the increasingly hostile attitude of the common lawyers, very few such suits went as far as sentence or decree.[44] Many of those who held goods which executors sought to recover claimed that they did so by virtue of a gift made by a testator in his lifetime.[45] Such suits were usually dropped at an early stage. An attempt by an ecclesiastical judge to settle a case concerning an alleged gift *inter vivos* might well lay him open to the charge of encroachment upon secular

[43] Woodcock, *Medieval Ecclesiastical Courts*, p. 85.
[44] HRO CB 5, fos. 25ᵛ, 34ᵛ, 99; CB 22, 27 Apr. 1566, *OP c. Valver*; 15 June 1566, *Lockeye c. Frenisham*.
[45] NNRO ACT 3B, fo. 201ᵛ; ACT 4A, fo. 194ᵛ; ACT 11, 5 Mar. 1568, *Gase c. Gase and Jeye*; 2 June 1568, *Bradie c. Bradye*; HRO CB 3, fos. 54, 131ᵛ-2; CB 6, p. 135; CB 12, fo. 51ᵛ.

jurisdiction, especially if, as was sometimes the case, defendants exhibited formal deeds of gift.

Most of the cases concerned with the execution of testaments which came before the church courts in our period arose from the real or supposed misdeeds or negligence of executors. Suits for unpaid legacies formed the biggest category. Executors were brought to court both by the temptations to which they had succumbed and the difficulties they had failed to foresee. There seems to have been a widespread feeling that an executor should profit from the discharge of his responsibilities, and some men were evidently determined to do so even if this meant taking illicit bites at the estate. The sensible testator provided for the reasonable reward of his executors. Swinburne thought that the residue, which was supposed to be distributed to pious uses, was generally allowed to the executors in practice even when it was not bequeathed to them, on the pretext that they might need it to cover 'unknown' debts of the testator's which might later come to their notice.[46]

Judicial acceptance of inventory and account provided the executor and administrator with their most important safeguards if the estate turned out to be insufficient to fulfil the will. Interested parties were entitled to demand inventory or account if they had not already been produced and to impugn those submitted. Suits for unpaid legacies often involved the production of either or both at some stage in the proceedings. If he failed to make an inventory, the executor could be held responsible for the payment of all legacies, whether or not there were sufficient goods.[47] Inventories were challenged in court either because executors had omitted debts or even goods (which in one case had been secreted by the widow in neighbours' houses till after the inventory had been drawn up) or because valuers had underpriced the goods.[48] Those exhibiting inventories in court at the instance of parties were not allowed to add to them as were those who produced

[46] Swinburne, *Testaments and Last Wills*, fo. 235; NNRO DEP 5B, fo. 181.
[47] Swinburne, *Testaments and Last Wills*, fos. 220ᵛ-1; Lyndwood, *Provinciale*, p. 176, n. p.
[48] HRO CB 18, 3, 10, 24 July, 2 Oct. 1563, *OP c. Wilmott*; NNRO DEP 6A, fo. 22ᵛ; DEP 7C, fos. 46–7, 60, 79–80. DEP 7D, fos. 40ᵛ-1, 82ᵛ-3.

them in the normal course of execution. It was understandable that one Norwich chancellor's neglect of this rule, so necessary to discourage fraudulent omissions, should have provoked strong protests in a case he heard in 1562-3.[49] When the executor rendered account he had to set out such things as court fees, funeral expenses, and debts which he had been obliged to pay before handing over legacies, and claims in respect of such items were sometimes questioned.[50]

Insufficiency of goods was the most important but not the only reason advanced for the non-payment of legacies. They were also withheld in a number of cases because legatees had failed to satisfy stipulations upon whose observance testators had made payment conditional, such as marriage in accordance with their wishes.[51] Executors' desire for a sufficient acquittance sometimes held up the payment of legacies. In such cases judges had to insist that legacies be paid first, but after payment they would order acquittances to be made out. An executor might also sue for an acquittance in a *negotium acquietancie*.[52]

Children's minorities gave rise to much litigation. They gave unscrupulous executors opportunities to exploit the estates and even the persons of minors, and their accounts might well be difficult to challenge later on.[53] Payments of legacies were sometimes deferred because of alleged doubts as to whether legatees had reached the age stipulated by testators, doubts which parish registers were helping to resolve more speedily by the end of our period.[54] A minor could neither sue for legacies himself nor acquit the executor upon receipt, so that the latter ran the risk of being sued if he

[49] Conset, *Practice*, p. 290; *Allen c. Myhell*, NNRO ACT 10, 8 Dec. 1562, 23 Mar., 5, 6 May 1563.
[50] NNRO DEP 7D, fo. 43; DEP 12, fo. 68.
[51] NNRO DEP 6A, fos. 46ᵛ, 66; DEP 12, fo. 149; HRO CB 12, fo. 72.
[52] *Tuddenham c. Rudd and Tuddenham*, NNRO DEP 7E, fo. 42; ACT 9, 2 June 1562; *Leman c. Rokewoode*, NNRO DEP 5B, fo. 124; ACT 7B, fos. 81, 183; *Boyton c. Goodwyn*, NNRO ACT 11, 6 Oct. 1569; HRO CB 22, 9 Feb., 6 Apr. 1566, *Knight c. Brough;* CB 18, 10 July 1563, *OP c. Foster.*
[53] NNRO DEP 6A, fos. 151ᵛ, 201; DEP 12, fo. 68; *Davye c. Davye and Sympson*, NNRO DEP 7C, fo. 55; DEP 7D, fos. 100, 110ᵛ-11; DEP 7E, fos. 38-9; ACT 9, 2 Dec. 1561, 28 July 1562.
[54] HRO CB 19, p. 348; NNRO ACT 11, 9 June 1568, *Fitlinge c. Spendlove*; DEP 11B, 18 Jan. 1570, *Burton c. Linsted.*

handed legacies over to a minor's representative, as were one Hampshire couple who trusted a legatee's father with what was due to him. They had followed the appropriate procedure of taking from the father a bond to save them harmless, but this failed to protect them, and they lost their case.[55]

Suits in the interests of minors were undertaken by *curatores ad lites*, usually the next of kin or the guardian or tutor appointed by the testator.[56] When a man died without making provisions for a minority, the ecclesiastical judge might play a big part in ensuring that adequate arrangements for guardianship were made. In 1566, for instance, a suit by the next of kin of a Hampshire orphan girl ended in a court order (to which they agreed) entrusting her to a priest of Southampton who undertook to provide for her education and to prevent her contracting marriage without the consent of her friends and next of kin.[57] When a guardian's conduct had given rise to justifiable suspicions, it was up to the executors or overseers to seek the termination of his authority from the judge.[58]

THE UNDERLYING CAUSES OF TESTAMENTARY LITIGATION AND THE EFFECTIVENESS OF THE COURTS

Conflict amongst the members of testators' immediate families and between immediate families and legatees or executors outside them, probably lay at the root of most testamentary litigation. Unfortunately the court records throw all too little direct light on the underlying causes of disputes. Depositions very often describe the making of the will and the last hours of the testator's life in the most vivid detail, but they frequently say very little about the motives and attitudes of those who surrounded the deathbed. In a large number of cases, moreover, they were not taken. It is therefore impossible to pinpoint the reasons for the majority of suits in terms which would satisfy a sociologist.

---

[55] *Byrde c. Foster and Foster*, HRO CB 6, pp. 369–71; CB 8, 4 Nov. 1542; cf. CB 17, pp. 115–16; Clarke, *Praxis*, p. 287.

[56] Clarke, *Praxis*, pp. 283–5.

[57] HRO CB 22, 27 Apr. 1566, *OP (Fielder) c. Bannyster and Warner*.

[58] Ibid., 12 Oct. 1566, *OP (Hooker and Turneham) c. Gibbes and Gibbes*; 9 Nov. 1566, *OP (Hacker) c. Andrewes and Hobbes*; 23 Nov. 1566, *OP (Searle and Searle) c. Pratt*.

Clearly the widow's position was often a very difficult one; the pressures and temptations to which she was subjected gave rise to much litigation. A bill sent to the chancellor of Winchester diocese in 1539 describes in stark terms the sort of situation which might arise from a widow's remarriage.

Instruccions for master chaunceler.

John gambylfelde in his dethe bed beqweth to rycharde hys sonn x$^{li.}$ Item to his other sonn John v markes and to hys iii dowghters xv markes to be egally devyded and if it sholde happe any of the seyde chyldryn to dye then that porcyon to remayne to the survyvers etc. Of the whiche v chyldryn there is no mo left alyve saff only elyzabeth his dowghter to whome the hole legatyes doth remayne by hyr fathers last wyll. The seyde John gambylfelde made his wyfe whose name was Jone and mother to the seyde chyldryn hys hole excecutryx & she provyd hys testament and take [*sic*] vppon hyr to fulfyl the legacyes. This woman afterwarde was maryed to on William Smyth, to the which William all theese goodes came, and now wyl he not pay i^d to me the seyde elyzabeth, having no thinge to help my self with but only my fathers beqwest beseching your mastershyp in the wey of pytte to helpe me your poore bedmaydyn or els am I but as a frenles gerle lyke to be utterly cast away.[59]

Elizabeth's 'instruccions' are worth setting out in full both because they give a clear description of a common predicament and because they are (in my experience) unique, throwing a lone shaft of light on what may have been for poor people a common mode of initiation of suit. Perhaps there was more in this case than meets the eye; but that situations very similar to the one here described very often gave rise to litigation is indicated both by the more oblique allusions of numerous depositions and by the prominence of remarried widows and their new husbands among the defendants in testamentary causes. Even if the widow sincerely mourned her husband and found no cause for resentment in the provisions made for her, her choice of a new partner might well pose a threat to the effective execution of her husband's testament. It is clear from wills and depositions that testators were often inspired with foreboding by the prospect of their widows' remarriages, and that testamentary disputes sometimes grew out of longstanding mistrust between husband

[59] HRO CB 7, 7 June 1539.

and wife. Many wills included clauses providing that widows should lose intended benefits if they remarried. One man of Norwich diocese urged the neighbour who wrote his will to 'make yt so suer as his wief should take no benefyt by the same', and when another became convinced that he would shortly die, he told his wife that '... if I wist thou wouldest not do honestly for me, I would make all the town privey of that I have.'[60]

Some trouble arose from what was felt to be testators' unfair treatment of individual members of their families. At least two dying fathers expressed resentment at their sons' failure to appear at the bedside, and penalized them in their wills.[61] Other testators were described as making no provision for children whom they thought sufficiently well off already.[62] The unruliness of their children worried a number of testators, and provisions to strengthen the position of the widow or the overseers, or to deter children from quarrelling or going to law (difficult to enforce though these last must have been), were sometimes described.[63]

Attempts by the immediate families of the dead to suppress wills which they considered unduly favourable to those outside their circle were probably responsible for much litigation. The appointment of an executor from outside the family's ranks (sensible though it might appear in view of the likely consequences of the sorts of conflict within it described above) or the bequest of a valuable legacy to an old friend might tempt those around the deathbed to conceal evidence of the deceased's intentions so far as possible. It is clear, however, that few disputes arose from men's complete neglect of their kindred in favour of people not related to them. Indeed testators responsible for such dispositions were nearly all unmarried men with no kindred in the first degree, or men who claimed to have made adequate provision for their relations during their lives.[64]

[60] NNRO DEP 7E, fos. 85–8; DEP 3, fo. 210v.
[61] NNRO DEP 5B, fos. 200–1; DEP 8, fos. 65–6.
[62] NNRO DEP 4B, fo. 99^v; DEP 6A, fos. 75^v–6.
[63] NNRO DEP 4A, fo. 234; DEP 4B, fos. 122–3; DEP 7C, fo. 75; DEP 7E, fos. 18^v–19.
[64] See e.g. HRO CB 19, p. 329.

There was a striking increase in the number of testamentary suits heard in the consistory courts of both Norwich and Winchester during our period.[65] How is one to explain this development? It is generally agreed that the population increased rapidly during the sixteenth century, and at least some sections of it grew more prosperous. Was the great increase in litigation due simply to the fact that more wills were being made? The fact that litigation reached a peak in the Norwich consistory during the early 1560s, not long after the high mortality and abnormally intense testamentary activity of the late 1550s, makes such a hypothesis superficially attractive, but the lack of correspondence between the numbers of wills made and the amount of testamentary litigation over a longer span of time shows that other factors were at work. The average number of wills proved each year in the consistory court of Norwich in the mid-thirties was about 140; by the late forties it had sunk to just over 120; in the early fifties it rose sharply to about 180. Between these same periods the average numbers of testamentary suits brought each year rose steadily — from 12 to 19 to 29.

Was the increase due to an exacerbation of the conflicts which lay at the roots of litigation? At first sight this seems an attractive hypothesis. Perhaps the development of legal opinion favouring the individual's testamentary freedom, and the decline of customary limitations upon it enabled testators to make dispositions which led to litigation because their families felt them to be inappropriate or unjust. Unfortunately no substantial support for such a hypothesis can be found in court depositions. Family quarrels and suspicions lay at the root of much if not most testamentary litigation, but there is barely any evidence in the records of a wider conflict between testators' dispositions and accepted conventions. In any case, the growth of testamentary freedom was a very gradual process. It cannot be invoked in explanation of an extremely rapid short term development such as the growth of testamentary litigation in the mid-sixteenth century. In one respect of course our period saw an important extension of the testator's freedom: the statute of wills of 1540 (32 Henry VIII,

---

[65] See appendix 2.

c. 1) gave a large number of landholders greater freedom to devise their lands by will. Strictly speaking, the church courts could neither demand the registration of wills of land nor settle disputes relating to land. The possibility remains that a sizeable number of suits over wills disposing of lands came before them nevertheless. Certainly Bishop Parkhurst wrote that when testaments were challenged in his diocese a long time after they had been proved 'such as hold landes and goodes by the testamentes are clene dischardged thereof, to the great vndoing of manye',[66] as though this were a common occurrence. Did the statute of wills indirectly encourage testamentary litigation by increasing the prizes at stake? Without a much more thorough investigation of its effects upon the small and middling landholders whose wills were likely to be proved in the diocesan courts than historians have yet undertaken it is impossible to say.

Declining respect for the church courts, their own laxity in the field of probate administration, and procedural changes in the handling of cases probably played the biggest part in the growth of testamentary litigation. Strong testimony on the first two was given by Bishop Parkhurst and by John Becon, who became chancellor of Norwich diocese in 1575. Parkhurst singled out for condemnation as a major abuse the 'vngodlye practise' used in his diocese 'of late time' of impugning testaments proved twenty or thirty years before. Executors often found themselves unable to prove the testaments thus challenged because witnesses had died or forgotten their contents. Both men criticized over-hasty grants of probate particularly strongly. The greed of registrars, Becon alleged, had led them to approve wills without examining the circumstances, and even to accept the allegations of proctors for the executors. The fact that they had not themselves had to take an oath had emboldened men to forge or suppress wills. Parkhurst put first of a long list of abuses committed by registrars grants of administration to one executor alone, who 'being more subtill then the other, getteth the testament, and streightway (yea sometymes before the testatour be buryed) cometh to the regester ...' The same readiness to

<hr>

[66] *Letter Book of Parkhurst*, 263.

grant without due enquiry letters of administration and collection had frustrated valid dispositions and given rise to much unnecessary litigation.[67]

Probate was already being granted quickly, perhaps too quickly, before 1532, when the *Commons' Supplication* complained of long delays.[68] The atmosphere in the following years was hardly favourable to any attempt to tighten up supervision of the process of administration. Successive blows to the jurisdiction of the church and its moral authority may well have encouraged the grossly contemptuous actions of which Parkhurst and Becon complained. The internal evidence of the act books of the 1560s lends weight to one of Parkhurst's major criticisms. By 1569 many of the testaments disputed in litigation at Norwich whose dates of probate are known had been proved some years before the initiation of suit. In some cases attempts were clearly made to claim that people whose wills had long ago been registered had died intestate.[69] Some of this litigation may have been collusive, aimed at depriving third parties of their dues. This was openly alleged in 1567 in the course of one suit before the Norwich consistory court when a woman was accused of suing her mother, executrix of her late father's testament, in order to disprove it and thus defraud a legatee. The testator had died about nine years before, and all his witnesses had subsequently died too.[70] The Norwich records of these years hint at other abuses. A suspiciously large number of defendants claimed, when challenged to show the authority by which they administered goods, to have neither goods nor authority.[71] A third sinister development was the increase in the number of defendants who claimed to hold goods of the deceased (in some cases all his possessions) by virtue of a deed of gift. This development posed a serious threat to ecclesiastical jurisdiction. Such claims were much rarer at

---

[67] Ibid. 261–3; Strype, *Annals*, ii, pt. 2, 698–9.

[68] Above, p. 96.

[69] NNRO DEP 11B, 18 Jan 1570, *OP (Daynes) c. Raven and Browne;* NCC will register Cowlles, fo. 377.

[70] NNRO ACT 11, 4 Feb., 23 Apr. 1567, *Warner c. Poynter.*

[71] Ibid. (all cases 1568), 13 July, *Allen and Braye c. Olyvere and Olyvere;* 16 Nov. *OP (Easton) c. Fenne; Feser c. Guibon, Cribbes;* 23 Mar. *Lacye c. Welles.*

Winchester, and at least one case there in which the defendant exhibited *quandam donacionem* ended in a condemnatory sentence.[72] No contemporary criticisms of Winchester probate administration comparable with those made at Norwich have survived. But probate administration here was certainly not free of blemishes, and a Winchester case of 1567 provides one of the most striking instances of laxity in this field. A woman was alleged to have obtained letters of administration in her husband's lifetime, and her failure to appear in court, followed by prompt revocation of the grant, suggest that the allegation was well founded. Disquieting evidence of carelessness was produced in a number of other suits.[73]

The growth in the number of suits between parties at Winchester sprang in part from an apparent procedural change. In the 1520s, judges undertook many suits concerned with testaments and their execution *ex officio mero* or *ex officio promoto*.[74] At the beginning of Elizabeth's reign, many testamentary cases promoted by individuals were still recorded in the office act books of the consistory court. In the next few years, however, a change of attitude seems to have taken place. For some time there was considerable doubt as to whether cases of this sort should be considered as matters of instance or matters of office. A number of cases were entered at different stages of their course through the court in both instance and office act books.[75] By about 1566, however, it is clear that most testamentary cases initiated in the interest of individuals, i.e. those which were not primarily concerned with securing probate fees for the courts, were being recorded in the instance act book, and there was a decline in the use of the procedure *ex officio promoto*. It is difficult to explain this procedural change satisfactorily, but it may have been due to some extent to a feeling on Bishop Horne's part that judges should not concern themselves *ex officio* with contentious cases at a time when huge correctional

---

[72] HRO CB 22, 3 Nov., 15 Dec. 1565, *Wheteland c. Wheteland*.
[73] HRO CB 23, 5 Oct. 1567, *OP (Bennett) c. Egerton*; cf. CB 11, 16 July 1558, *Hide c. Hyde*; CB 19, pp. 314, 316; CB 22, 31 May 1567, *Hall and Rumboll c. Rumboll*.
[74] Above, p. 38.
[75] eg. *OP (Foster) c. Foster*, HRO CB 17, p. 22; CB 18, 10 July 1563.

tasks in the pastoral field demanded their attention. This is surmise. What is certain is that the scribes and proctors would have encouraged any change which put the burden of initiating suits more firmly and unequivocally on the shoulders of parties.

How effectively did the courts handle testamentary suits once initiated? The act books leave us in the dark as to the outcome of many suits. This did not necessarily mean that the plaintiffs concerned had failed to obtain satisfaction; a number of these cases may have been settled privately, especially when plaintiffs were satisfied that the validity of wills or the insufficiency of estates had been established by witnesses. Peaceful settlement by compromise and arbitration under the auspices of the courts was encouraged, and peaceful conclusions were commoner than sentences and decrees in testamentary causes over the period as a whole. As in other types of case, Winchester judges were readier than their Norwich colleagues to give informal orders and decrees.

In suits concerning the validity of wills (always the commoner type of testamentary cause both at Norwich and Winchester), the great majority of known sentences were given for parties who appear to have been defending wills against attempts to impugn or ignore them. Normally these parties were defendants; occasionally they were plaintiffs seeking the revocation of letters of administration. Judges were clearly reluctant to give sentences against wills. Surviving depositions suggest that when they did so it was usually because the 'will' in question had been made or substantially altered when its supposed author had been coerced or incapable of approving it.[76] In cases concerned with the execution of testaments, with inventories, accounts, and the payment of legacies, the majority of known sentences were given for plaintiffs. It was hard for a defendant to win such a case unless he could show clearly that the goods had been insufficient for the execution of the testament.[77] So far as one can see the sentences given were sensible and equitable.

---

[76] CB 12, fos. 24ᵛ-9, 35ᵛ.
[77] e.g. *Emerye c. Otte*, NNRO ACT 9, 3 Dec. 1560, 3 June 1561; DEP 7C, fo. 25.

Whether or not they were obeyed is a different question on which the records of the courts throw no light. There is no evidence in the records of the two dioceses that the common law courts were actively hampering the work of ecclesiastical judges in our period. Only one prohibition is known to have been issued, in a cause concerning a will of lands.[78] Of course the church courts could only avoid conflict by keeping within the already narrowed confines of their jurisdiction. As we have seen, they seem practically to have ceased to entertain suits for debts owed to testators by the 1520s.[79] The probate statute of 1529 stated clearly that the proceeds of land sales were not to be included amongst the goods of the deceased, which made it very doubtful whether the church courts could entertain suits for legacies payable out of such proceeds. Gifts *inter vivos* fell within the sphere of the lay courts, and in the 1560s Norwich chancellors steered clear of possible conflict by not questioning deeds of gift.

Existing limitations on ecclesiastical jurisdiction must often have prevented judges from acting to ensure the fulfilment of wills. Many litigants had to turn to the court of Chancery in order to overcome the difficulties posed by these limitations. In the reign of Elizabeth I Chancery was on the whole, despite some encroachment on their work, a mainstay of the testamentary jurisdiction of the church courts, to whose activities its own were largely complementary.[80] An analysis of the lists of chancery proceedings originating in Norfolk and Suffolk between 1553 and 1555 serves to illustrate the complementary role of the court not long after the middle of our period. Over eighty suits in the court appear to have been concerned with problems connected with inheritance and the disposal of dead men's property. Nearly sixty of these had to do with 'lands of the deceased', with which church courts had no power to deal. About twelve cases concerned the detention of goods or copydeeds from executor or heir, nine debts to or from executors. Only three concerned

[78] NNRO ACT 12, 20 Apr. 1570, *Annott c. Symkins and Depden.*
[79] Above, p. 102.
[80] W. J. Jones, *The Elizabethan Court of Chancery* (Oxford, 1967), pp. 400–17, esp. pp. 403–8, 414–15, 417.

legacies, and only one suit previously heard by the chancellor of Norwich (in which the plaintiffs alleged forgery of a will) seems in this period to have come into Chancery.[81] These figures strengthen one's impression that Chancery was not at this stage dealing with suits which the church courts were competent to settle and that the boundaries of the latters' jurisdiction in matters testamentary were (for the time being at least) fairly clear.

CONCLUSIONS

The efficiency of probate administration during the period of the Reformation is difficult to assess because the quality of the surviving evidence varies so markedly from diocese to diocese. At London, as at Norwich and Winchester, probate certificates are meagre and uninformative, while at Canterbury they are a good deal fuller and usually contain notes of the exhibition of inventories, the value of the goods, and the fees charged.[82] We may be fairly sure that the church courts made vigorous efforts during and beyond the Reformation period to secure the probate of wills. But they may not always have insisted on the production of inventories in the case of smaller estates, and accounts were, to judge by surviving records, rarely produced save when interested parties sought them in instance or promoted office suits.[83]

In 1532 the *Commons' Supplication* criticized probate administration for both excessive fees and tardiness. Practice with regard to fees varied from diocese to diocese on the eve of the Reformation: in the archdeaconry of Canterbury, the long-established provincial scale was observed, while in the diocese of Lincoln there is some evidence that it was not. In the archdeaconry of Buckingham, as in that of Norwich, a large proportion of small estates paid no fees to the ordinary. Yet all executors, in the diocese of Rochester as in that of

---

[81] For the last four cases referred to, see *List of Early Chancery Proceedings*, x (PRO Lists and Indexes, 55, 1936), 1330/29, 1341/41-2, 1373/54-7, 1368/3-6; NNRO DEP 5B, fos. 270ᵛ-2, 283ᵛ-7.

[82] Woodcock, *Medieval Ecclesiastical Courts*, p. 72; *London Consistory Court Wills, 1492-1547*, ed. I. Darlington (London Record Soc. xii, 1967), xv-xvi.

[83] Cf. for a slightly later period, *Act Book of the Archdeacon of Taunton*, ed. Jenkins, and *The Archdeacon's Court*, ed. Brinkworth.

Norwich, had to pay a fee of 1*s.* to the scribe which clearly weighed heaviest on the poor. Ecclesiastical lawyers may also have compensated themselves for the stabilization of fees enforced in 1529 by increasing incidental fees which the statute did not touch, as has recently been suggested in a study of the prerogative court of Canterbury.[84]

The other complaint regarding probate made in the *Commons' Supplication* was probably a good deal less well founded. Whatever the delays attendant upon the probate of wills disposing of the estates of the wealthy, it seems likely that most wills dealing with small or middling estates were proved very quickly. Evidence on this point from the dioceses of Lincoln, London, and Chichester tallies with the figures from Norfolk and Surrey. During the episcopate of Bishop Sherburne of Chichester, over 80 per cent of wills were proved within three months of being written.[85]

During and after the Reformation there was a great increase in testamentary litigation in the dioceses of York and Chester as well as in those of Norwich and Winchester.[86] The reasons for this development probably varied from diocese to diocese. At Winchester an important procedural change was partly responsible for it. But declining respect for the courts, coupled with increasing slackness on the part of their officials, may have been largely to blame. In the same decade that Parkhurst and Becon were listing the shortcomings of Norwich registrars in probate matters, Edmund Grindal was collecting testimony about abuses in the prerogative court of Canterbury, the highest court of probate in the land. It was suggested to him that new rules were needed to prevent too hasty grants of administration, the making of more than one grant of administration concerning the same estate, and commission of the execution of wills to one of the executors in the absence

---

[84] Bowker, 'The Commons' Supplication against the Ordinaries', 69; Kitching, 'The Prerogative Court of Canterbury, pp. 208-9.

[85] Bowker, op. cit. 66-7; Lander, 'Church Courts and the Reformation', p. 226; *London Consistory Court Wills*, xv; above, p. 96.

[86] Marchant, *Church under the Law*, p. 110; Haigh, *Reformation and Resistance*, p. 227n.

of the others. In 1587 Whitgift set about remedying some of these shortcomings in a new set of regulations.[87]

The testamentary jurisdiction of the sixteenth-century church courts was subject to important limitations, but in playing their part in ascertaining and enforcing the wishes of the deceased, they were still performing an important task, and on the whole they did not fulfil it too badly. They were not supposed to interfere in any way with real estate, and they had practically ceased to have anything to do with the recovery of debts due to testators. But the assessment of the validity of wills still belonged to them, and as we have seen this could be a complex task if coercion or unsoundness of mind were alleged, or if a written will could not be produced.[88] The division of intestates' estates, the scrutiny of inventories and accounts, the resolution of the problems which arose from the dishonesty, incompetence, or misfortune of executors, and the determination whether or how certain legacies should be paid: all these were primarily the responsibility of the ecclesiastical judge. Before the century was out, the common lawyers were to commence fresh inroads on this area of ecclesiastical jurisdiction; but during and immediately after the Reformation there were as yet few signs that this would happen.

[87] Strype, *Grindal*, pp. 304-5; Kitching, 'Prerogative Court of Canterbury', p. 207; above, pp. 109-12.
[88] Above pp. 98-9.

5

TITHE DISPUTES

In the last two chapters we have been concerned with the courts' regulation of relationships between men and women and their supervision of the discharge of important family and social obligations. We now move to aspects of their work much more intimately connected with the institutional life of the church itself. In this sphere it was their responsibility to see discharged three main duties which constitute the central themes of the four chapters which follow. The first of these duties was that of all Christian people to contribute towards the material needs of the church by helping to support its clergy and maintain its buildings and their contents. The second was that of the clergy to provide their people with an adequate ministry of word, example, prayer, and sacraments. The third and last, the most important of all, was the duty of all Christian people to believe what the church taught on all matters necessary to salvation, and to take part in all its prescribed observances and common worship.

The people's obligation to contribute to the material needs of the church was founded on a number of scriptural texts. It was implied in places in the New Testament,[1] but most fully stated in Deuteronomy 14, where it was laid down that the children of Israel were to tithe their arable produce and young animals. These tithes were partly to be consumed by individual worshippers in the holy place, partly to be given to the Levites and the fatherless and widows. The arrangements made in the early Christian church were clearly related

[1] Matthew 10:10, 23:23; 1 Corinthians 9:7.

to these. The offerings of the people were divided into four, a quarter going to the bishop, a quarter to the local clergy, a quarter to the upkeep of the church, and a quarter to the relief of the poor. Later, the payment to the clergy of a tithe of agricultural produce and the profits of trade and industry became the standard aimed at in ecclesiastical legislation. The clergy's duty to contribute from tithes received towards the needs of the poor and church fabrics was recognized, but, as we shall see, a large share of the burden was placed on lay shoulders. In fact the clergy never received the full tithe envisaged in ecclesiastical legislation, on account of practical difficulties of assessment and collection and (in England) the insistence of the king's courts that a number of commodities were not tithable.

The law made a basic distinction between 'personal' and 'predial' tithes. 'Personal' tithes were supposed to be paid of their incomes by wage- and salary-earners, craftsmen and merchants, after expenses had been deducted. 'Predial' tithes were due of such things as corn which were products of the earth. Schemes of division usually include a third category of 'mixed' tithes, embracing wool, cheese and milk, and the young of animals. All these were the products of animals, not directly of the earth itself. But the canon law made no distinction as to manner of payment between predial and mixed tithes. No expenses were to be deducted in either case.[2]

Agriculture formed the basis of early medieval society. Its yields, especially those of arable cultivation, were visible and comparatively easy to tithe. But the largely invisible profits of steadily growing industry and commerce could not be tithed efficiently without a far more elaborate machinery of supervision than the church had at its disposal. It conceded that expenses might be deducted before payment of such tithes, and in practice received much less even than a tenth of clear profits. The mixed tithes of animal husbandry, especially those of perishable dairy products, gave rise to problems of

[2] Lyndwood, *Provinciale*, pp. 195-6, 200-1; E. Coke, *The Second Part of the Institutes* (1669), p. 649; Burn, *Ecclesiastical Law*, ii. 374-5; J. E. C. Hill, *Economic Problems of the Church from Archbishop Whitgift to the Long Parliament* (Oxford, 1956), p. 78; C. St. German, *Doctor and Student*, ed. T. F. T. Plucknett and J. L. Barton (Selden Soc. xci, 1974), 305.

collection which often led to the establishment of tithing customs yielding less than a true tenth but accepted for the sake of harmony. In theory the canon law would not accept any tithing custom which yielded less than a true tenth of a given product. Grain tithes, which were the easiest to assess, bore heaviest on the peasant, for whereas the common law had by our period established the exemption from tithe of much pasture,[3] the arable cultivator was not allowed to deduct the share of his product claimed by rent and seed corn before tithing.

The majority of lawsuits concerning tithe came before the ecclesiastical courts for settlement up to and beyond our period. Most causes had to do with the rate or manner of payment, or the amount due.

The system of tithes may seem to us oppressive and riddled with anomalies. Yet to most members of a predominantly rural society accustomed to seeing religion in material terms, the services thus paid for were well worth the price. The tithe of their produce sustained those who performed the potent rites so vitally important to every community. Many wealthy benefices, however, were habitually held by pluralists who rarely visited their parishes. Others had been appropriated to monastic houses. This meant that the most valuable tithes, in particular those of grain, went not to the vicar or chaplain actually responsible for saying services in the parish church, but to a remote proprietor. The connection between proprietorial rights and the spiritual welfare of the parishes in question was still further weakened when at the Reformation the monastic tithes passed into lay hands.

The acquisition by the laity of a large share of 'spiritual' income was only one of the changes which made the Reformation a crucial phase in the history of English tithes. The campaign against the church and the divestment by Protestant regimes of what were in the eyes of the mass of the people quasi-miraculous priestly powers gravely damaged popular respect for the clergy. In 1548, auricular confession, in which contact between priest and parishioner was closest, the former's opportunity for the exercise of influence greatest,

[3] N. Adams, 'The Judicial Conflict over Tithes', *EHR* lii (1937), 18-19.

ceased to be obligatory. These changes coincided with the passage of acts of parliament which, though largely designed to protect tithe-owners' interests, were soon to be interpreted by the common lawyers in a sense unfavourable to the church courts, hitherto the most important agencies for the enforcement of the payment of tithes by the recalcitrant. All these changes came at a time when rising rents and prices and periods of severe dearth were in any case likely to sour relations between those who paid tithes and those who received them.

The payment of tithes was regulated by the ecclesiastical law, and in particular by provincial legislation, subject to the limitations imposed by the common law courts, statute and custom. These affected both the types of case which the ecclesiastical courts might try and the range of commodities liable to tithe. By means of prohibitions the king's judges had long prevented the spiritual courts from entertaining suits which related to tithe amounting to a quarter of the value of the benefice or more, to tithe already separated from the other nine parts (unless the protagonists were clergy), or to arrears due to the tithe-owner by somebody who had bought or leased tithes from him.[4]

In the thirteenth and fourteenth centuries there had been prolonged and sometimes acrimonious disagreement between the king's judges and the Commons on the one hand, and the ecclesiastical judges on the other, over the tithability of minerals, pastures, wild animals, new mills, and cut wood. The exemption of timber of the age of twenty years or more had been laid down in a statute of 1371. Writing early in the seventeenth century, Sir Edward Coke declared that certain other products were also exempt from tithe, including after pasture and the rakings of corn fields.[5]

During the Reformation, a number of important statutes relating to tithe were passed. The preamble of the 1536 *Acte conteyning an Order for Tithes thorowe the Realme* deplored widespread attempts to withhold tithe and unprecedented contempt of the ecclesiastical courts.[6] It ordered that all

[4] Ibid., pp. 6-12.
[5] Ibid., pp. 18-22; 45 Edward III, c. 3; Coke, *Second Part*, pp. 651-2.
[6] 27 Henry VIII, c. 20.

subjects should pay tithes according to the laws of the church
'and after the laudable uses and customs of the Parish, or
other place' where they lived. It enabled the ecclesiastical
judges to seek the aid of the council or justices of the peace
in case of contempt. Four years later an act concerning the
payment of tithes and offerings was passed.[7] This too complained of the withholding of tithes, and alleged that a
number of tithe-payers had been 'the more encouraged there-
to' by the fact that lay owners or lessees of ecclesiastical
benefices could not sue for tithes in the ecclesiastical courts.
This act empowered them to do so, and gave authority to
two justices of the *quorum* to imprison any defendant who
still refused to pay his tithe after a condemnatory sentence in
the ecclesiastical court. A clause of the statute provided explicitly that nothing in it was to be interpreted to the derogation of ecclesiastical jurisdiction. In the passage of the act
which insisted that tithes be paid there was however a small
but significant modification of the wording used in 1536.
Tithes were to be set out 'according to the lawful Customs
and Usages of the Parishes and places where such Tithes ... be
due ...' No mention was made of the laws of the church.

In 1549 was passed the lengthiest of all the tithe statutes
of the Reformation period.[8] In one important respect it
clarified the provisions of its predecessor. According to the
ecclesiastical law, prescriptive right was conferred by forty
years' possession. The act of 1549 laid down that predial
and personal tithes should at any time be paid as they had
been paid during the preceding forty years, and this provision
was probably intended to cover mixed tithes as well. This
statute also laid down that the personal oath was no longer to
be used to ascertain men's liability to personal tithes, and
exempted common day-labourers from paying them. It also
exempted the crops on formerly barren lands newly brought
into cultivation from tithe for the first seven years, though
this clause was to be so narrowly interpreted as to confer
little practical benefit on the tithe payer. It also prohibited
tithe-owners from suing for tithes of lands exempted by
privilege, prescription, or composition real. On the other

[7] 32 Henry VIII, c. 7.   [8] 2 & 3 Edward VI, c. 13.

hand, it insisted on the true payment of tithes due, and laid down penalties of treble the value or double the value plus costs for carrying away predial products before they had been properly tithed.

Two of the main aims of these statutes were probably to enforce the payment of tithe of agricultural products and to give much-needed support to the ecclesiastical courts at a time when their authority had been seriously impaired. The most important long-term consequences of the statutes of 1540 and 1549 were however quite different. In the first place, they made it much more difficult for tithe owners to alter long-established customary payments which had ceased to yield a true tenth of a given product. This was particularly damaging in a period of sharp price rises. Secondly, they opened the way to wider interference with the church courts' work on the part of lay judges. The common lawyer Christopher St. German, writing on the eve of the Reformation, held that no prohibition would lie in a case in which an ecclesiastical judge disallowed a defendant's claim to pay less than a true tenth by virtue of prescription or composition.[9] But after the legislation of 1540 and 1549 these were fully supported by statute, and defendants who could plausibly claim that they were threatened by ecclesiastical judges could now seek prohibitions. Elsewhere in the 1549 act other grounds for seeking prohibitions were to be found.

TITHES AND THE DIFFICULTIES TO WHICH THEIR ASSESSMENT AND COLLECTION GAVE RISE

Nearly all the evidence in the court records examined relates to tithes of agricultural produce. It will however be convenient first of all to dispose of the problems connected with personal tithes and related dues. The *Valor Ecclesiasticus* reveals that personal tithes still made up an important proportion of the value of many benefices. There were big local variations in their value and importance. Generally, the clearest evidence of their survival came from towns. They were widely paid, too, in rural north-west Norfolk; here their

---

[9] St. German, *Doctor and Student*, lx, 312-14.

value differed sharply between one country parish and the next in a fashion too striking to be attributable to differences in population. The *Valor* tells us little of how they were assessed.[10] What small evidence there is of attempts to tithe personal gains in the two sets of court records examined comes from the diocese of Norwich. Here at least three suits took place in the period up to 1549.[11] The outcomes of two of these cases were not recorded; in the other one, the defendant was dismissed after answering upon his oath, presumably because it had proved impossible to produce witnesses who could testify adequately to the extent of his gains. After the passage of the statute of 1549 which took away the oath imposed upon the defendant as a means of ascertaining men's liability to pay personal tithes, there seem to have been hardly any suits of this type. In view of the fact that they had already been rare beforehand, it would be rash to jump to the conclusion that the act had any very drastic effect on tithe owners' willingness to sue. In 1552 Nicholas Smyth, a rich mercer of Halesworth (Suffolk) was sued by the farmer of the benefice for personal and other tithes. Smyth, who answered 'by his honestie and fidelite, and not by vertue of his othe', claimed evasively that he did not know what his gains had been, but that nevertheless he had 'dyscharged his conscience' in so far as his personal tithes were concerned. The witnesses testified that he was very rich, but all agreed that personal tithes had not been paid in the parish for many years.[12]

Personal tithes are not always easy to distinguish from offerings or oblations, whose continued payment, in accordance with the practice of the previous four years, was laid down in the statute of 1549. These oblations were supposed to be paid on four offering days during the year, or in a lump sum at Easter. In the *Valor Ecclesiasticus* offerings were often bracketed together with personal tithes.[13] Sometimes

[10] A. G. Little, 'Personal Tithes', *EHR* lx (1945), 85–8; *Valor Ecclesiasticus*, vi. i–v, valuation of benefices in Heacham deanery in diocese of Norwich. Nearly all the separate entries relating to personal tithes appear under vicarages.
[11] NNRO DEP 3, fos. 12, 94ᵛ; ACT 6, fo. 81ᵛ.
[12] NNRO DEP 5B, fos. 100(ii)ᵛ, 178–81.
[13] Little, 'Personal Tithes', 85.

the two types of due were covered by the same payment. In the city of London a proportion of the rent of the house occupied by the tithe-payer was given in lieu of certain offerings made on Sundays and some holy days. The clergy vigorously opposed the idea that this payment covered personal tithes, but the dispute was finally settled in the citizens' favour by a decree of 1546.[14] In the diocese of Winchester there were a number of cases concerning the payment of a proportion of the rent of houses in Winchester and Southampton between 1526 and 1547. This due was often referred to as an *oblatio dominicalis*. The meaning of this latter phrase is revealed by the testimony of certain inhabitants of the Soke in Winchester, who explained that for each pound of annual rent they paid 1*d*. every Sunday.[15]

Oblations of 2*d*. to 4*d*., distinct from whatever personal tithes may have been paid and usually due at Easter or the dedication feast, are mentioned in both the Norwich and the Winchester records. In certain north Norfolk parishes in the sheep-corn area the Easter offering was paid by each parishioner using a plough and was known as 'plough silver' or 'paschall money'. Offerings paid by individual parishioners were usually small, but collectively they formed a very important part of the income of many incumbents, especially vicars. Payments had also to be made to the clergy officiating at marriages, christenings, churchings of women, and burials, but few references to these dues appear in the surviving court records.[16]

Another due, exacted from parishioners' goods after death, the mortuary, should be considered here since it was meant

[14] J. A. F. Thomson, 'Tithe Disputes in Later Medieval London', *EHR* lxxviii (1963), 17; 37 Henry VIII, c. 12; Little, 'Personal Tithes', 76-8, which shows that a personal tithe was still levied in the Surrey suburbs.
[15] HRO CB 5, fo. 48; CB 7, 9 Nov. 1538, 16 Jan. 1539, *OP (Laurence) c. White*; two loose statements about the payment of tithes in the Soke at Winchester; ibid., 20 May 1542, *OP (Browne) c. Stone*; CB 8, 26 Oct., 3 Nov. 1543, *Barker c. Greffyn and Hodson*; 23 July 1547, *Newton c. Wakelinge*; CB 6, pp. 473-7, 481-2.
[16] NNRO DEP 5A, fos. 14, 40V-2, 167; DEP 5B, fos. 122, 253V-6; ACT 10, 6 June 1564, *Farmer of Dennington c. Godbold*; DEP 11B, 7 Dec. 1569, *Farmer of Bacton c. Stephens*; HRO CB 2, fo. 58V; CB 3, fo. 135V; CB 4, fo. 87V; CB 19, pp. 219-20; VB 3, p. 139; see also Burn, *Ecclesiastical Law*, ii. 101; *Valor Ecclesiasticus*, vi. i-v.

to be a recompense for personal tithes which parishioners had
by oversight omitted to pay. According to a constitution of
Simon Langham (1366-8), the second-best beast of every
parishioner who possessed three animals was to be paid. The
mortuaries act of 1529 laid down a scale of maximum payments related to the value of the deceased's moveables. No
mortuary was in future to be paid of the estates of those who
died with goods worth less than 10 marks.[17]

At least six cases concerning mortuaries came before the
Norwich consistory court between 1519 and 1529.[18] In three
of these cases it is clear that the mortuary claimed was an
animal, or, failing an animal, a garment or jewel. The exaction
of mortuaries from the estates of people who were not
normally resident in the parishes where they died was one of
the abuses complained of in the mortuaries statute, so it is
significant that the deceased whose goods were involved in
two of these cases had been people of disputed domicile. A
Star Chamber bill dating from the period immediately following the passage of the act complained that the parson of
Haverhill (Suffolk) had not allowed a stranger's friends to
take away his body until a mortuary had been paid,
'p[re]sumptuously saying that the kyng had made that acte
w[it]t[h]out the concent of hys clerge ...'[19] At least five
more mortuary cases took place at Norwich between 1548
and the end of the period. But an animal was no longer
referred to; the main matters at issue were the value of the
goods and the amount of money to be paid.[20] The act of
1529 seems therefore to have put an end to attempts by the
clergy of Norwich diocese to levy mortuaries in kind. A
number of suits were brought at Winchester both before and
after the passage of the act, but there is nothing in the records

[17] Lyndwood, *Provinciale*, pp. 19-22, 196; 21 Henry VIII, c. 6.
[18] NNRO ACT 3A, fo. 109ᵛ; ACT 3B, fo. 200; ACT 4A, fo. 106; DEP 3,
fos. 37ᵛ, 323, 324-5, 384-5, 606, 616.
[19] PRO Star Chamber 2/31/61.
[20] NNRO ACT 6, fo. 197; DEP 7C, fo. 54; DEP 7D, fo. 56; DEP 9, fo. 190;
ACT 11, 23 Apr. 1567, *Alforde c. Westbrook.*

of most of these cases to show what was being sought from defendants.[21]

We may now turn to the tithes of the produce of the earth and of animals with which the overwhelming majority of church court suits were concerned. The law of the church laid down that a true tenth was to be paid of these products. Three main questions have to be answered in connection with each of these tithes. Did its collection in kind pose any special problems? Were customary payments accepted in lieu of it? And lastly, did the product concerned normally escape tithing because protected by customary or common law exemptions? The second of these questions is not always easy to answer because it can be hard to distinguish between customary dues and money payments according to current value accepted by tithe owners for the sake of convenience on what was intended to be a temporary basis, for there was an insidious tendency for the latter to turn into the former which was doubly threatening to the tithe-owner in a period of inflation and thus especially likely to give rise to litigation.

For the sake of convenience, the tithable products which gave rise to litigation may be examined in the following order: grains, milled corn, hay, pasture, the young of animals and their other products, fish, wood, new crops, garden produce, minerals, and bricks.

Tithes of grain were often the most valuable. The commonest complaint against parishioners in respect of these tithes was that they had failed to pay a true tenth, either by leaving no tithe at all on part of the field, or (more commonly) by leaving fewer sheaves than one in ten.[22] In some places difficulties arose in the course of tithing the 'rakings' left after the main crop had been harvested, the amount of which would depend on the care with which the main operation had been carried out. Coke was to cite a common-law ruling that rakings were exempt from tithe unless the first reaping had been carried out in such a way as to defraud the tithe-owner

[21] HRO CB 2, fos. 20, 125; CB 3, fos. 31ᵛ, 65; CB 5, fos. 60, 81; CB 11, 9 July 1558, *Mothe c. Knyght*; 22 Apr. 1559, *Audrye c. Lawrens*; 27 May 1559, *Wright c. Miller*; 30 Mar. 1560, *Willyamson c. Erle*; CB 14, 22 Nov. 1561, *Cockerell c. Roke*; CB 24, fos. 473-4. In the last case, the plaintiff sought a money payment.
[22] NNRO DEP 5A, fos. 38ᵛ-9, 45, 93, 205.

of his share.[23] But only once did a claim that parishioners should not have to pay a full tenth of the main crop find its way into the court records. This happened in 1528 when a Hampshire man got into trouble for telling his neighbours that allowance should be made for seed corn (which might take a fifth of the crop) before tithe was paid.[24]

No customary payments in lieu of tithes of grain were ever claimed in court, though some personal compositions entered into by individual tithe payers were said to cover them.[25] A much more important source of disputes was the provision of the act of 1549 that improved heath and barren land should pay the tithe previously levied from it, if any, and not tithe of corn or hay, for seven years after the improvement.[26] The influence of the statute in encouraging people to convert land to arable was probably reinforced by a series of poor harvests between 1549 and 1551. Within the diocese of Norwich most of the recorded disputes started in two fairly well defined areas. In the first, the stretch of Norfolk between Norwich and Cromer, a fairly heavily settled area partly dependent upon the worsted weaving industry, parishioners began to cultivate parcels of waste or pasture, most of them small, in order to satisfy their needs.[27] A smaller cluster of disputes started in Suffolk, on the eastern fringe of the wood-pasture region. Here, on the edge of an area already increasingly dependent upon the sheep-corn region for much of its grain, the sharp dislocation of supplies by dearth seems to have encouraged the conversion of rather more sizeable pieces of land.[28] In two of these cases, areas of 28 and 40 acres were involved, the former cleared of woodland in the three years up to 1553. Not a single sentence appears to have been given for a defendant in these cases concerning newly converted ground, perhaps because the word 'barren' was already being

[23] NNRO DEP 4A, fos. 241-8; DEP 5A, fo. 120; DEP 5B, fo. 9ᵛ; Coke, *Second Part*, p. 652.

[24] HRO VB 3, p. 249.

[25] NNRO DEP 5A, fo. 17ᵛ; HRO CB 19, pp. 368-9.

[26] 2 & 3 Edward VI, c. 13.

[27] NNRO DEP 5A, fos. 26, 76ᵛ, 98-100, 142, 278ᵛ-9; DEP 5B, fos. 16, 27, 46, 72-4, 242-3, 252ᵛ, 304-5.

[28] NNRO DEP 5B, fos. 215, 311ᵛ-12; DEP 6A, fo. 67.

interpreted in an extremely narrow sense, as was certainly to be the case later on.[29] Some plaintiffs were able to show that the ground in question had once been sown, as could be seen by the ridge and furrow on the ground or from documentary evidence.[30]

When grain was ground at the mill, the miller took a proportion in mulcture. According to the canon law, a predial tithe should be paid of it. Lyndwood thought that a full tenth of the mulcture should be paid, though he conceded that the tithe owner might if he preferred take his tithe 'according to the farm', that is, presumably, a tenth of the rent of the mill.[31] The rent seems to have been the basis of the claims made by the majority of plaintiffs. This was not always the case. In 1545 a South Hampshire mill owner could claim that by virtue of a composition he had arranged between his tenant and the incumbent 'master parson hath hadd more profit by the mille then I haue hadd this vii yeres.'[32] In one case the miller gave in his personal answers an estimate of his income from the mill after deduction of expenses.[33] Occasionally the question of the quantity of grain milled arose.[34] On their side, defendants often appear to have claimed that they should pay only what had previously been paid, in the hope that long-established payments would become customary.[35]

Hay could be tithed by the load or the cock, depending on the individual's meadow holding. One Basingstoke dispute of 1527 arose from the tithe-payer's leaving his hay on the ground in 'swarfes' instead of making it into cocks, so that it had been ruined by wet.[36] Provincial legislation had laid

---

[29] J. Godolphin, *Repertorium Canonicum, or An Abridgement of the Eccleasitical Laws* (1680), pp. 387-9; Sir S. Degge, *The Parson's Counsellor, with the Law of Tithes or Tithing* (1676), pp. 223-5.

[30] NNRO DEP 5B, fos. 46, 73; DEP 6A, fo. 109^v.

[31] Lyndwood, *Provinciale*, p. 195, n. c.

[32] HRO CB 8, loose letter from John Milles, 14 May 1545.

[33] NNRO DEP 5A, fo. 189.

[34] HRO CB 5, fo. 117; CB 6, p. 422; CB 8, 10 Dec. 1541, *Winchester College c. Danyell*; NNRO DEP 4B, fo. 114.

[35] NNRO DEP 4A, fo. 83; DEP 6A, fo. 49; DEP 9, fos. 31, 38, 39; DEP 12, fo. 128.

[36] HRO CB 3, fo. 111.

down that tithe be paid of even the smallest patches of hay, but only one or two disputes over hay grown on the ollands or headlands of the arable fields were recorded.[37] Tithes of hay were amongst those most commonly commuted for a quasi-customary payment, probably because of the smallness of most men's portions of meadow. The recorded payments ranged from 2d. to 5d. per acre, and some of them were clearly becoming inadequate.[38]

The church had attempted to tithe all kinds of pasture, but this attempt had foundered on the stubborn insistence of the common law that tithes of pasture should only be paid if the tithe owner derived no other benefit from the animals (which he did not, if, for instance they were cattle which were being fattened in the parish before being driven on to be sold elsewhere). There seem to have been no clear general rules determining whether the owner or the lessee of the ground should be responsible for payment, or laying down how the tithe (which clearly could not be paid in kind) was to be assessed — whether on the basis of the estimated consumption of the animals known to have grazed the land, or the rent paid for the grazing.[39] Efforts to decide responsibility for payment and the basis of assessment were bedevilled by rights reserved by lessors, by leases lasting less than a year, by long leases (normally incorporating high entry fines, so that the yearly rent bore little relation to the value of the grazing), and by the frequent pasturing of different sorts of beast on the same ground.[40] Most of the depositions clearly relate to leased pasture, not common pasture, for which, it was in one case explicitly claimed, no tithe was due.[41]

Nearly all the evidence relating to the tithing of pasture comes from East Anglia. Although there are several references in the Winchester records to tithes of pannage, levied in the

[37] Lyndwood, *Provinciale*, pp. 192-3; NNRO DEP 5A, fo. 144; DEP 5B, fo. 105.
[38] NNRO DEP 4B, fo. 120; DEP 5A, fos. 12, 14; DEP 6A, fo. 71ᵛ.
[39] Lyndwood, *Provinciale*, p. 195; Coke, *Second Part*, p. 651; Godolphin, *Repertorium*, pp. 384-5, 413, 428; Degge, *Parson's Counsellor*, pp. 165-8.
[40] NNRO DEP 5B, fos. 9, 29ᵛ, 101, 254; DEP 7D, fos. 95-8, 109; DEP 12, fos. 159, 175ᵛ-6.
[41] NNRO DEP 5B, fo. 54.

wooded areas of Hampshire, tithes of pasture were much less often mentioned, and in one case in which they were clearly at issue, the defendant refused to pay them, claiming that he was not bound by law to do so.[42]

Tithes of pasture were amongst the most difficult to levy, and were a very important source of disputes. By the time of the Civil War, so it was to be claimed, the twentieth part of the value of the feeding was commonly accepted.[43]

Tithes were paid both of the young of animals and of certain other animal products. These were known as 'mixed' tithes because they were not directly products of the earth, but of animals nourished by the earth. But the same general rules applied to them as to things subject to a predial tithe.

The tithing of young animals such as calves and piglets which were often reared in numbers less than ten gave rise to a particularly large number of disputes. If a parishioner had more than six young animals but fewer than ten the tithe-owner was to take one or its value, returing ½d. to the parishioner for each animal by which the number fell short of ten. If however the parishioner had fewer than seven young, the tithe-owner was to take ½d. for each animal, or alternatively wait until the number of young was large enough for him to take one. If he chose the latter course, the tithe-owner was to be rewarded for his patience by being allowed to choose the second- or third-best animal.[44] 'Driving forward' was obviously to the advantage of the tithe-owner (and in some places it was said to be customary) but it could cause ill will, exacerbated by the difficulty involved in keeping track of the young from year to year.[45] An additional complication might arise if some of the young were sold. Thus one Hampshire defendant who had weaned three of his six calves and sold the remainder paid ½d. each for those he had weaned and a tenth of the price of those he had sold.[46] In some places a fixed sum was said to be payable for each young animal, irrespective of the total number born. One

[42] HRO CB 5, fo. 142; cf. CB 4, fo. 181.
[43] Degge, *Parson's Counsellor*, p. 165.
[44] Lyndwood, *Provinciale*, p. 193.
[45] NNRO DEP 5B, fo. 10; DEP 4B, fo. 41ᵛ; HRO CB 2, fo. 73ᵛ.
[46] HRO CB 20, 8 Nov. 1564, *Tayntor c. Hooker*; cf. CB 19, pp. 242–3.

man of Shouldham (Norfolk) claimed that he should continue to pay 1*d*. for each foal even though he had had twenty-seven between 1548 and 1550. But witnesses revealed that no parishioner had ever had so many before, so that no 'custom' could have been established to deal with the problem involved, and he lost his case.[47]

Provincial legislation had laid down that tithes were to be paid of the milk and cheese of all animals. Only once, however, in a Winchester case, has a clear reference to the payment of a tithe of ewe's milk been encountered.[48] Nearly all cases were concerned with the tithes of cows' milk and cheese. The variety of customs governing their payment was particularly wide. In some places milk was paid, in others cheese. The tithing of either milk or cheese throughout the period of production clearly posed severe problems, and in East Anglia the milk or cheese produced in a given period was often levied — the cheese made in the fortnight after 14 September in one place, or the milk produced by a herd in nine nights and nine mornings in another. At Swaffham (Norfolk), there was partial commutation; the alleged custom was to pay 1*d*. for each cow and the milk of three days at Whitsun.[49] Fixed money payments in lieu of milk had clearly become widespread by the middle of the sixteenth century; they varied greatly from parish to parish. Some of these payments were to become established as unalterable customs, as eighteenth-century glebe terriers show. The variety in customary rates no doubt resulted from the fact that some clergymen were readier than others to make a stand for what they conceived to be their rights, and in the last resort to go to law in defence of them; such readiness would in turn depend upon their ability to bear the costs of litigation and the importance of milk products in the local economy.[50]

Wool seems to have been tithed in a straightforward manner

[47] NNRO DEP 5A, fo. 198ᵛ; ACT 7B, fo. 92.
[48] HRO CB 28, 29 May 1568, *Dickenson c. Scut.*
[49] NNRO DEP 4B, fo. 113; DEP 5A, fo. 30; DEP 5B, fo. 10; DEP 7E, fos. 39, 57, 61; DEP 8, fos. 29, 105-6, 111-12; HRO CB 13, pp. 53-5, 80-1.
[50] HRO CB 19, pp. 276-81, 299; NNRO DEP 5A, fo. 145; DEP 5B, fos. 112ᵛ, 163; DEP 9, fo. 210; DEP 12, fo. 161; glebe terriers for E. Dereham, 1735, Blickling, 1706.

either in kind or (commonly) in money according to the value of the current crop. The method of tithing in itself gave rise to few disputes when the issue was not complicated by such matters as inter-parochial grazing rights. In Hampshire and the Isle of Wight, however, some bitter quarrels were generated by tithe owners' desire to levy a tithe of the 'lockes' of wool, that is the shortest wool left on the legs and body of the sheep after the removal of the fleece. By Coke's day, such wool was held to be exempt from tithe. Winchester judges of our period insisted on payment, though in at least one case it was claimed that such a tithe had never been paid in the parish before.[51]

Wild beasts and fish of the sea and common rivers had long been held by the common lawyers to be exempt from tithe unless subject to special local custom. Such a custom was in operation on the East Anglian coast, and its implementation occasionally caused disputes. It is clear that although the tithe might bear some relation to the size of the catch, a true tenth was not paid. At Aldeburgh (Suffolk) in 1559, according to a defendant, half a dole was paid on a catch of between thirty-six and sixty doles, while at Yarmouth, so it was claimed shortly afterwards, a dole was put aside for 'Christ and the haven', and of the half-dole due to Christ, half went to the parson of Yarmouth, half to the clergy of the parishes where those mariners who dwelt outside the town were domiciled.[52]

Wood was tithable if, when lopped, it would grow again from the same trunk or stem. A statute of 1371 had established that timber twenty years old was exempt from paying tithe, and this was a common pretext for non-payment. Another was that the wood in question had not been sold but had been used for fencing or burnt on the hearth; the common lawyers held that wood used in these ways was also exempt. But for burnt wood a separate payment might nevertheless be due by local custom.[53]

[51] HRO VB 1, fos. 4, 14, 20ᵛ, 46ᵛ, 54ᵛ; VB 3, p. 24; CB 4, fo. 83; Coke, *Second Part*, p. 652.

[52] NNRO DEP 4B, fo. 269; DEP 7E, fo. 32ᵛ; DEP 8, fo. 45.

[53] Lyndwood, *Provinciale*, p. 190; 45 Edward III, c. 3; Coke, *Second Part*, p. 652; HRO CB 6, p. 140; CB 7, 24 Oct. 1539, *R. Dowlyng*; CB 8, 20 Oct. 1543, *Wardroppe c. Whytinge*; CB 19, p. 313; NNRO DEP 5A, fos. 23, 69ᵛ, 141ᵛ; DEP 5B, fos. 31ᵛ, 164, 199ᵛ; DEP 6A, fos. 49ᵛ, 112; DEP 4A, fos. 79-80.

During our period the cultivation of certain crops was either introduced from abroad or very greatly extended; these included such crops as hemp, mustard, and rapeseed, which were occasionally mentioned in depositions. The main problem in connection with these crops was not their tithability but the question of their allocation to rector or vicar. Thus at Islington (Norfolk) an agreement between rector and vicar on the division of tithes of grain broke down over rapeseed in 1556. Ultimately, the tithes of many of these new crops were by a series of common law decisions to be declared 'small', i.e. payable to vicars.[54]

Gardens presented a sizeable tithing problem because they contained tiny quantities of a large number of crops. They seem often to have been covered by a lump payment known as 'porte' in Norwich diocese. The Winchester court books do not reveal the existence of a generally accepted custom, though some clergy certainly tried to levy tithes of gardens. In the Soke at Winchester, there was some controversy as to whether the *dominica oblatio*, a portion of their house rent paid by parishioners, covered the tithes of their gardens too. In at least one rural parish defendants had to agree to pay tithes of certain individual garden crops.[55]

According to the canon law minerals (including such things as bricks and tiles) were subject to tithe. But in the eyes of the common law the fact that they did not grow again from year to year was sufficient to exempt them from tithe unless there was a contrary local custom. Tithes of bricks were however sued for in the diocese of Norwich, tithes of salt in the diocese of Winchester.[56]

The majority of tithe disputes were caused by failure to pay the right amount of tithe, or by disagreements over the rate or manner of payment. In a large minority of cases,

[54] NNRO DEP 4B, fos. 41ᵛ, 88; DEP 5A, fos. 17, 20ᵛ, 131; DEP 5B, fos. 8ᵛ, 85; DEP 6A, fos. 77, 107ᵛ-8; DEP 12, fos. 84ᵛ-6; Hill, *Economic Problems*, pp. 82-3.
[55] NNRO DEP 5B, fo. 85ᵛ; DEP 7D, fos. 6ᵛ, 16ᵛ; DEP 12, fos. 84ᵛ-6; HRO CB 7, loose statements of *c.* 1539 concerning garden tithes within the Soke; 25 Feb. 1541, *M. Whithed*; CB 8, 24 July 1546, *Vicar of Kingsclere c. Nayshe, Furber*.
[56] Adams, 'Judicial Conflict', 18; NNRO DEP 5B, fo. 162ᵛ; DEP 6A, fo. 9; HRO CB 8, 9 Dec. 1542, *Kykisley c. Rolf*.

however, the main difficulty was to decide by whom or to whom tithe should be paid. In a number of suits the fact that the tithe-payer was the defendant served only to obscure the real issue: the inability of two competing tithe-owners to reach agreement.

The tithing of wool and lambs was particularly likely to give rise to disputes of this kind, because sheep were often driven from one parish to another to sleep, to winter, to lamb, or to be shorn. The provisions of the provincial legislation were on the face of it straightforward. The tithe payable was to be divided among the various parishes according to the proportion of time spent by the sheep in each. More tithe was to be paid to the incumbent of the parish where the sheep pastured than to the incumbent of the one in which they slept. Sojourns amounting to a total of less than thirty days in the year were not to count.[57] The depositions show how difficult these rules were to apply in practice because witnesses were uncertain, or gave conflicting evidence, as to which parish sheep had come from, how long they had spent there, what proportion of the lambs had been born in each parish. These problems were made still more complex by the existence of local customs, by the fact that more than two parishioners were often involved, and by the existence of pastures common to two or more parishes.[58]

Sometimes the clergy tackled problems like these by coming to agreements amongst themselves.[59] Arrangements made in this way could not bind the successors of the men who had made them, but in order to terminate them it was frequently necèssary to go to law. That such an agreement could easily become unsatisfactory is well illustrated by the circumstances of a suit undertaken in 1551 by the vicar of Banham (Norfolk) against three men of Tibenham who had sheep pasturing in his parish. At this time he received 1s. a year from the vicar of Tibenham for each of the latter's

---

[57] Lyndwood, *Provinciale*, pp. 197-8; for clarification of the somewhat obscure wording of the constitution, see esp. p. 197 n. t, 198, n. z.

[58] NNRO DEP 5A, fos. 45-8, 100-3; DEP 9, fos. 162, 179; HRO VB 1, fo. 20ᵛ; CB 9, 9 Nov. 1548, *W. Wordlyche*.

[59] Lyndwood, *Provinciale*, p. 192, n. f; (Anon.), *Tithes and Oblations according to the Lawes established in the Church of England* (1595), p. 55.

parishioners who had sheep pasturing in Banham. As these three had each had large numbers of sheep grazing in Banham for much of the year, his dissatisfaction with the agreement is understandable. There was a danger that if such an arrangement survived for forty years it might become an established custom. This the vicar of Kenninghall (Norfolk) strove to avert in 1553 when he terminated an arrangement governing the payment of tithes of wool into which he had entered with the incumbent of the neighbouring parish of Garboldisham. The fixed sums it yielded him had become inadequate. It was for this reason, too, that in 1550 the vicar of Wiggenhall St. Mary in the Norfolk Marshland, where men often had great numbers of animals pasturing in other parishes, utterly denied the existence of a *custom* regulating inter-parochial tithe payments; they had, he claimed, always been made in a manner to which all the clergy concerned could agree.[60]

Uncertainty as to which tithe owner had the right to receive the tithes of a given piece of ground gave rise to some of the most involved disputes recorded in the court books. Sometimes the course of the parish boundary was itself disputed. The existence of chapels which lacked parochial status led to disagreements over the apportionment of tithe either between the chapel and the mother church or between two neighbouring parish churches. But suits of this type were rare.[61]

Certain lands were held to be either altogether exempt from tithe or liable to pay only a token sum or object in lieu of it. Large numbers of former monastic estates were exempted from tithe by statute in 1539, and erstwhile possession by a religious house was claimed as a reason for non-payment of tithes by some defendants. Others claimed that by virtue of long-established compositions they were bound to make only a token payment for the tithes of lands they occupied. One such defendant farmed a former monastic grange. Others occupied parks, and it is clear in at least two of these cases that former parkland had been brought under

[60] NNRO DEP 5A, fos. 92, 121ᵛ-2, 163-5; DEP 5B, fos. 281ᵛ-2.
[61] NNRO DEP 3, fos. 101ᵛ-5, 138ᵛ-45; DEP 6A, fos. 48ᵛ-9, 56, 62; DEP 8, fos. 43, 68-75, 79ᵛ-86, 91-3; HRO CB 19, pp. 246-7, 281-7, 303-5, 312, 348-9.

cultivation and was yielding a greatly increased profit to the
occupier. Under these circumstances former agreements
might well be held to have lapsed, and both sentences went
against the defendants concerned.[62]

THE COURSE OF SUITS

Tithe-owners confronted with refusal to meet their full claims
very often tried to reach agreement with tithe payers before
resorting to the ecclesiastical court. Since, as we have seen,
the principle of tithe payment was not itself at issue in the
great majority of tithe disputes, there was usually some room
for manoeuvre.

We catch frequent glimpses of the process of bargaining in
the Norwich records. In about 1554 the servants of the farmer
of Thurgarton (Norfolk) 'made a business' about the tithe of
a field of wheat; upon the addition of three more sheaves
their master appeared to be satisfied. Our regret that the
rector of Badingham (Suffolk) went to law with a parishioner
in the summer of 1556 is the sharper on account of a neighbour's testimony that they had once agreed 'within one
groat'.[63]

Offers might be made before 'diverse of the honestie of the
parysshe'. At Letton (Norfolk), in 1518, the greater part of
the parishioners were present when one of their number accounted for the tithe of a close. The community was ever
watchful, and neighbours might offer to intervene and 'have
the matter in hearing'. The outcome of a disagreement over
tithe might well be of the greatest importance to other parishioners, who all stood to lose if the tithe owner succeeded
in establishing his right to an unpopular due by means of a
test case. In 1551, when the rector of Combs (Suffolk) was
suing certain poor men for the tithe of cheese in kind, the
defendants' proctor produced an instrument under the seals
of thirty-four past and present inhabitants of the parish who

[62] W. Easterby, *The History of the Law of Tithes in England* (Cambridge,
1888), pp. 97–100; NNRO DEP 5A, fos. 48ᵛ–53; DEP 6A, fos. 14–16, 56, 62;
DEP 7E, fos. 36, 72, 82; DEP 8, fos. 150, 165; DEP 12, fo. 107; ACT 10, 23 Mar.
1563, *Rector of Gressenhall c. Harwarde*; HRO CB 12, fos. 36, 43ᵛ; CB 14, 14
Nov. 1562, *Jefferye c. Dawterye*.
[63] NNRO DEP 4B, fo. 118ᵛ; DEP 6A, fo. 55ᵛ.

testified that it had never been paid. This exceptional common action may have played an important part in persuading the parson to end the case by agreement.[64]

Clergy might in their efforts to settle a dispute seek the aid of their colleagues from neighbouring parishes when they assembled for one of the archdeaconry visitations or inquisitions. At Easter 1551 the rector of Brisley (Norfolk) desired two of his fellow clergy to 'take in compromise' a dispute between himself and his parishioner John Johnson. They made their award after charging the parties on their oaths to abide by their decision. Johnson had been unwilling to pay the rector 4d. for plough money, but he entrusted this sum to the incumbent of Horningtoft, who agreed to pay it to the rector of Brisley when the latter had received it of four other 'honest and substantial men'.[65]

The reception accorded to parties after they had failed to resolve their differences and resorted to the courts appears to have differed from diocese to diocese. In Norwich diocese, withholding of tithes does not seem to have been regarded in our period as a matter which could normally be dealt with by means of *ex officio* proceedings, though there is some evidence that it had been so regarded in earlier years.[66] But in Winchester diocese those who refused to pay tithe often faced correctional proceedings in the 1520s both in the consistory court and during visitations. By this method cases were dispatched speedily and informally, greatly to the tithe-owner's advantage. Parishioners were commonly charged to say whether or not they had paid certain tithes. If they answered that they had not done so, they would be commanded to show cause why they should not be compelled to do so by ecclesiastical censures. The whole onus of contesting the obligation to pay was thus placed on them at short notice. Instance machinery worked much more slowly; it gave parties time for reflection and renewed efforts at compromise, and it also gave defendants and their proctors

---

[64] NNRO DEP 3, fo. 99; DEP 5A, fos. 153v-4; DEP 5B, fo. 105; DEP 6A, fo. 179v; ACT 7A, fo. 250; cf. HRO CB 4, fo. 70v.
[65] NNRO DEP 5B, fos. 122, 160.
[66] Oxford, Bodleian Library Tanner MS. 100, fo. 40v.

more opportunities to marshal their own case. The briskness of the Winchester disciplinary procedure is well illustrated by an incident which occurred during the episcopal visitation of 1517. Seven men admitted that they had not paid the vicar of Carisbrooke the tithe of the 'lockes' of wool. One of them, William Whitsede, said that neither he nor his father had ever paid such tithes, and that they were not customary in his parish. The judge immediately pronounced the custom unreasonable and unlawful, and asked Whitsede whether he would pay the tithe. The latter answered staunchly that he would do not otherwise than his neighbours, whether he went to heaven or hell, whereupon he was declared to have incurred excommunication.[67] Nothing like this is to be encountered in the Norwich records. In this respect, as in others, the Reformation brought about a big change at Winchester. The old *ex officio* method of tackling tithe cases went out of use, and the number of suits between parties in the consistory court greatly increased from about 1540 onwards. For some time after this, however, many cases in the consistory court were treated as though the judges found it hard not to think of them as disciplinary. After their personal answers, many defendants were simply warned to satisfy plaintiffs. One defendant was told, almost as if it were the result of an afterthought, to certify the court whether he wished to yield or to contest the case.[68] Not till the 1560s were full instance formalities almost invariably observed.

In very many cases, bargaining probably began or was resumed soon after the citation had been served. Peaceful conclusions were common in both consistory courts. Settlements might be achieved by the parties or their chosen representatives, by arbiters to whom the judge had committed the hearing of the case, or by the judge himself. Unfortunately, even when the court records tell us that parties reached agreement, the terms of the settlements are very rarely to be found. No awards upholding defendants' claims have been found, but it is clear that plaintiffs sometimes gave

[67] HRO VB 1, fos. 14, 15ᵛ–6.
[68] HRO CB 8, 19 Nov. 1541, *Denys c. Palmes*; cf. ibid. 21 May, *Bently c. Tanner, Crafford c. Stepe*.

ground. In 1550 the chancellor of Norwich helped by his personal mediation to bring about an agreement by which the vicar of Barton (Suffolk) was to receive a fixed lump sum each year from one of his parishioners for all the latter's tithes although this was a time of sharply rising prices.[69] Two Norwich plaintiffs accepted sums smaller by about a third in one case, by a quarter in the other, than those they had originally claimed. In a Winchester case of 1542, the judge simply split the difference between what the plaintiff claimed and the defendant confessed he owed.[70]

It was probably common practice to ensure parties' observance of the terms of awards by taking their oaths, or even bonds.[71] Once accepted, an *arbitrium* of this sort would be held to bar further action by the plaintiff to gain through the court terms more favourable to himself. Thus in 1547 a Hampshire priest concluded a letter describing his success in bringing about an agreement between the curate of Subberton and one of his parishioners by telling the judge that '... yf eny action be enterd before yower masterschyp for eny suche dewte ye maye at yower plesure relese hyt consyderyng the agremente fully made betwene them ...'[72]

Court proctors and scribes were often named as arbiters in tithe causes by judges, though usually in conjunction with partners from outside diocesan administration. Local gentlemen and clergy formed the biggest groups amongst the arbiters. Although non-gentle fellow parishioners of defendants often intervened to help settle disputes before they came to court, it very rarely happened that judges referred cases back to them. This happened in two Norwich suits of 1537-8, but the judge's exceptional action in these cases was perhaps due in large part to the unusual weakness of diocesan government at this time.[73]

[69] NNRO ACT 7A, fo. 60ᵛ.
[70] Ibid., f. 164ᵛ; DEP 5A, fos. 60ᵛ-1; HRO CB 7, 10 Oct. 1539, *OP (Knottes) c. Cuffley*; CB 8, 9 Dec. 1542, *Rector of E. Meon c. Roche*.
[71] Oxford, Bodleian Library Rawlinson MS. C 432, fos. 8-9; NNRO ACT 5, fo. 259.
[72] HRO CB 8, loose letter no. 2.
[73] Ibid., loc. cit. and no. 4; CB 5, fo. 53; CB 13, pp. 147-8; NNRO ACT 5, fos. 100ᵛ, 115ᵛ, 194ᵛ, 259; ACT 6, fo. 79; ACT 7B, fo. 92; ACT 8, fo. 215ᵛ; above, p. 22.

Tithe causes tended to last longer than other types of suit and were probably the most expensive to pursue. The numbers of witnesses produced were often very large, and they frequently included old men, produced to testify on such matters as parish boundaries and long-established customs, who sometimes had to be examined by commission in their own parishes because they were too decrepit to travel. Exceptions against tithe-owners' witnesses, often on the grounds of dependence upon them, seem to have been particularly numerous. Documents were often exhibited, including incumbents' tithe-books, manorial surveys, charters, abbey rentals, bishops' registers, and indentures of leases. The likely length and costs of suit must have provided parties with powerful incentives to come to peaceful agreement.[74]

Few of those defendants who fought to the finish won their cases. Over 80 per cent of the sentences found in the records of the two dioceses were given for plaintiffs. The issues upon which sentences were given in tithe cases are often particularly difficult to isolate, since many different kinds of tithe were often included in the same libel and custom and the value of tithe might be at issue in the same suit. In a minority of those cases which proceeded as far as sentence we can nevertheless single out the most important issues fairly confidently.

Plaintiffs usually seem to have been successful in cases in which the issues were the correct method of tithing grain and the amount due.[75] A number of sentences appear to have condemned fixed money payments for milk and cheese. In one of these cases an unusual entry in the court book makes it clear that the defence was invoking parochial custom.[76] Since these cases followed the legislation decreeing that tithes be paid according to custom,[77] the judges concerned must

---

[74] NNRO ACT 4A, fos. 115ᵛ, 261ᵛ; DEP 5A, fos. 222ᵛ-6, 191ᵛ; ACT 7A, fo. 149; HRO CB 22, 6 July 1566, *More c. Barckley*; 5 July 1567, *Ughtred c. Person et al.*

[75] But see *Bayley c. Barnard*, HRO CB 19, pp. 27-8, 43, 47-9, 82-4; CB 20, 10 Mar., 23 June 1565; *Reynoldes c. Juniper*, HRO CB 19, pp. 250, 294-6, 316-9, 331-3, 337-8; CB 22, 16 Nov. 1566.

[76] NNRO ACT 10, 16 May, 6 June 1564, *Rector of Massingham c. Anderson and Jecler*.

[77] Above, pp. 121-2.

have decided that witnesses for the defence had failed to prove that a contested manner of payment had achieved customary status. Some other tithes, such as those of pasture and mills, were either impossible or difficult to pay in kind.[78] Sentences given in cases in which the bases of assessment of these types of tithe were in question were nearly always condemnatory.

Defendants were successful in a number of suits whose root causes were the rival claims of different tithe owners or uncertainty as to how tithes should be divided when animals had been pasturing in different parishes.[79] Plaintiffs also lost some cases which arose from their attempts to challenge exemptions of monastic land and to tithe wood over twenty years old or the catches of fishermen fishing waters held to belong to the king.[80]

Defendants rarely won cases concerning the rate of tithes or their manner of payment, which probably made up the great majority of those dealt with by the courts. It is hardly surprising, therefore, that a proposal of 1536 to set up a special court to hear tithe causes should have been justified by reference to the notorious partiality of the church courts in such cases.[81] Nevertheless, analysis of the sentences given in tithe cases can by itself give a quite erroneous impression of the courts' work. The causes which were abandoned or peacefully settled greatly outnumbered those in which sentences were given.[82] The effects of peaceful settlements

---

[78] Above, pp. 128-30.

[79] *Aprice c. Willmot*, HRO CB 30, 23 July 1569, 14 Jan. 1570; *Milton c. Chater*, HRO CB 24, p. 241; CB 28, 8 May 1568; *Reniger c. Steere*, HRO CB 24, p. 335; CB 28, 31 July 1568; *Vicar of Fressingfield c. Aldous, Barbor, Wulnaugh*, NNRO DEP 8, fos. 29-37; ACT 10, 8 Dec. 1562; *Farmer of Barningham Rectory c. Mylborn and Chosell*, NNRO DEP 9, fos. 83ᵛ-4; ACT 10, 7 Dec. 1563.

[80] *Hopton c. Aldred and Sturges*, NNRO DEP 5A, fos. 48-53; ACT 7A, fos. 9ᵛ, 181; *Ladd c. Crane, Harryson, Annott*, NNRO DEP 9, fos. 25, 27, 83; ACT 10, 10 Dec. 1563, 8 Feb. 1564 (cf. HRO CB 12, fos. 36, 43ᵛ for a judge's refusal to proceed when he heard that a monastic exemption was at issue); *Rector of Redenhall c. Allen*, NNRO DEP 7C, fos. 87-8; ACT 9, 22 Oct. 1561; *Rector of Barnham Broom c. Clerke*, NNRO DEP 8, fo. 146; ACT 10, 29 Oct. 1563, 8 Feb. 1564; *Rector of Stokesby c. Nele*, NNRO DEP 9, fos. 86, 105; ACT 10, 8 Dec. 1563.

[81] *LP* xi. 106.

[82] Below, appendix 2.

cannot be assessed since we know nothing of the terms of the overwhelming majority of them. It is impossible to say how much ground plaintiffs agreed to concede.

The numbers of litigants who, dissatisfied with the handling of tithe causes by the church courts, invoked the aid of the common-law judges by requesting writs of prohibition, increased very rapidly in the closing years of the sixteenth century. In our period, however prohibitions did not as yet pose a serious threat to the efficiency of the courts of the two dioceses. Tithe causes heard in the Norwich consistory court were affected by four prohibitions issued between 1552 and 1554 and by a further nine at least in the 1560s.[83] Since the act books contain no direct statements on the point, one can only suggest, on the basis of the evidence provided by depositions (often lacking) why prohibitions were issued in given cases. They show that amongst the issues raised in the twelve cases in question were the tithability of wood, common pasture, and ground newly converted to arable, and the validity of compositions and allegedly customary payments by virtue of which less than a true tenth was paid. These issues had been covered by judicial decisions of the fourteenth century and by the statutes of 1371, 1540, and 1549.[84] Those who sought the prohibitions presumably suggested that judges had contravened previous decisions or statutes in entertaining these cases. Since some of them at least were resumed later, it is clear that the common-law judges did not always feel that the suggestions were valid, and that they granted 'consultations' enabling the ecclesiastical

---

[83] The Norwich causes in which prohibitions were granted were as follows: *Chaunte c. Warde*, DEP 5B, fo. 68; ACT 7B, fo. 114ᵛ; *Denton c. Smith*, DEP 5A, fo. 67; ACT 7B, fo. 202ᵛ; *Buckley c. Chamberlayn*, DEP 5A, fos. 192-3, 281; DEP 5B, fos. 22ᵛ-3; ACT 7B, fo. 250; *Davye c. Houghton*, DEP 5B, fos. 28-9; ACT 8, fo. 120ᵛ; *Proprietor of Aslacton c. Wright*, DEP 9, fo. 154; ACT 10, 6 July 1563; *Rector of Gaywood c. Gresham*, DEP 8, fos. 8ᵛ-9, 90; ACT 10, 7 Oct. 1562; *Rector of Sotherton c. Barrett and Wulnaugh*, DEP 8, fo. 153; ACT 10, 2 Mar. 1563; *Farmer of Attleborough c. Neve*, ACT 11, 10 Feb. 1568; *Farmer of Tibenham c. Underwood*, ibid. 10 Feb. 1568; *Vicar of Flixton c. Cooke*, ibid. 7 Dec. 1568; *Farmer of Wingfield c. Warner*, ibid. 8 Feb. 1569; *Rector of Bixton c. Jackson*, ibid. 11 Mar. 1569; DEP 12, fo. 73; *Farmer of Bricett c. Martine*, ACT 11, 21 June 1569.

[84] Above, pp. 120-2.

judges to proceed.[85] Prohibitions had begun to interfere with the work of the Norwich consistory court before the end of our period. But this interference was not yet serious. Not till 1568 were as many as three prohibitions granted in a single year, a year in which at least fifty-eight tithe suits came before the consistory court and probably many more. No prohibitions in tithe causes were mentioned in the Winchester court books before the 1560s, when at least four were sought, three of them in order to thwart attempts to tithe wood and the produce of monastic land.[86] The threat posed by prohibitions, which were within thirty years to menace the continued independence and efficiency of the church courts, was not in the early years of Elizabeth's reign a serious one.

WHO WERE THE PLAINTIFFS?

Tithe-owners of all three categories (proprietors, incumbent rectors, and vicars) were to be found amongst the plaintiffs in both dioceses, as can be seen from Table 2. Benefices of each type were leased to farmers. Appropriated rectories became impropriated when they passed to laymen.

TABLE 2
Benefices involved in tithe litigation:
percentages in each category[87]

Archdeaconry	Appropriated rectories	Rectories	Vicarages
Norwich	23½	60	16½
Winchester	21	47	32

To what extent did the percentages in this table correspond with the numbers of benefices held by tithe-owners of each class? Unfortunately the precise numbers of benefices held by proprietors (corporate or lay) are hard to calculate. The information concerning appropriated rectories given by the

[85] NNRO ACT 8, fos. 67, 110[v], 205[v].
[86] HRO CB 20, 3 Feb. 1565, *Jefferey c. Dawtry*; CB 22, 6 Oct. 1565, *Slater c. Wolgar*; 1 Feb. 1566, *Rector of Sherborne St. John c. Pexall*; CB 28, 11 Dec. 1568, *Kindge c. Edmundes*.
[87] This table refers to litigation in the consistory courts, and is based on the same sample years as appendices 1 and 2.

Valor Ecclesiasticus varies greatly in fulness from diocese to diocese and deanery to deanery. But in both dioceses there were a number of appropriated churches in which no vicarages had been established, and appropriated rectories almost certainly outnumbered vicarages. Norwich and Winchester records do not, however, lend support to the idea that the great upsurge in litigation which took place in the second half of the period was to a large extent due to the efforts of new lay proprietors to enhance the value of tithe. This may have been the case in the diocese of York,[88] but in these archdeaconries the great majority of litigants during our period were incumbent clergy and their farmers.

The incumbent rectors bulk largest in the table. In the archdeaconry of Norwich there were in the mid-1530s nearly three times as many rectories as vicarages (221 compared with 76), in the archdeaconry of Winchester nearly twice as many (150 compared with 77).[89] But Table 2 reveals a clear difference between the patterns of litigation in the two archdeaconries which it covers. In the archdeaconry of Norwich the vicars initiated less litigation than their share of the benefices might have led one to expect, while in the archdeaconry of Winchester the reverse was true. The Norwich figures do not surprise, since the average vicarage was poorer than the average rectory, and rectors were as a class rather better able to bear the costs of litigation than were vicars. In order to explain the divergence between the patterns of litigation in the two dioceses one must turn to a procedural difference between the two consistory courts. In the Norwich consistory court tithe disputes were during our period regarded as matters of instance. Winchester judges, who had earlier tended to regard the withholding of tithe as a matter for correction, often handled cases of this type as late as the 1540s in a relatively informal and summary manner which probably gave encouragement to go to law to quite small fry amongst the clergy, who might otherwise have faced the prospect of a costly suit with some trepidation. But by the 1560s

---

[88] Purvis, *Select Causes in Tithe*, viii.

[89] These figures come from *Valor Ecclesiasticus*, iii (sections dealing with the archdeaconry of Norwich) and *Reg. Gardiner et Poynet*, 156-68.

tithe disputes were usually regarded as matters to be settled
by instance procedures. The result was a sharp decline in the
proportion of plaintiffs who were vicars. Whereas before
1560 the rectors who sued for tithe had barely outnumbered
the vicars, in the 1560s the ratio of rectors to vicars amongst
the litigants rose to 5:3.

In the second half of our period a substantial proportion
of tithe litigation was initiated not by incumbents themselves
but by their farmers. The leasing of benefices, although fairly
common beforehand, may well have been on the increase
during the period of the Reformation. The religious and social
unrest of the time, sharp increases in agricultural prices, and
certain provisions of the tithes statute of 1549 almost
certainly increased the difficulties of tithe collection. Many a
clergyman must have been glad to leave the organization of
labour, the assessment of tithe and the endless badgering of
the unwilling to a man who knew the district and its farming
methods better than he did. Other clergymen were compelled by patrons to lease their benefices to them or their
nominees on favourable terms as a condition of presentation.[90]
A lay farmer might well adopt a more businesslike approach
to tithe collection than a man who had to combine it with
the discharge of pastoral responsibilities, and it is significant
that Kett's rebels should have demanded that gentlemen be
forbidden to farm benefices.[91] In some ways the men who
were of all best placed to exploit leases of benefices to the
full were members of the diocesan administration. In February
1543 the parson of Steventon (Hants) granted to his farmer
John Cooke (probably the Winchester diocesan registrar) all
manner of tithes and oblations due to him from Richard
Pexall, member of a powerful local family, for the five years
since he had become parson.[92] Faced with an obstreperous
parishioner, this incumbent very wisely handed over the
responsibility for squeezing arrears out of him to a man who
was perhaps well placed to influence the course of prosecution

[90] See below, pp. 193–4.
[91] *English Economic History, Select Documents*, ed. A. E. Bland, P. A. Brown
and R. H. Tawney (1914), p. 250.
[92] HRO CB 6, pp. 406–10.

in the consistory court. Three years before this, laymen had
for the first time been explicitly empowered to sue for tithes
by the statute 32 Henry VIII, c. 7. This act was of course of
the greatest use to the new lay proprietors of monastic benefices, but it also benefited farmers of benefices, and the
latter soon began to initiate suits in the church courts in
rapidly increasing numbers.

TRENDS IN LITIGATION AND THEIR BACKGROUND

Between the 1520s and the 1560s there were in the Norwich
and Winchester consistory courts respectively five- and ten-
fold increases in identifiable tithe litigation.[93] The scale of
the Winchester increase is somewhat misleading because as we
have seen Winchester judges still saw subtraction of tithes as a
matter normally to be dealt with by means of *ex officio* proceedings in the early years of our period. Many withholders
of tithe, therefore, never appeared as parties to instance cases
in the consistory court. Nevertheless, the expansion of litigation was striking enough. When one considers the figures in
the light of the general weakening of the church's economic
position between the 1530s and Elizabeth's accession and the
sharp knock which the Edwardian Reformation gave the
standing of the parochial clergy (who constituted the majority
of plaintiffs), it seems likely that tithe owners were on the
whole acting defensively in resorting to the courts. In other
words, the proliferation of tithe suits was one more symptom
of the declining authority of the church. The fact that the
statute of 1536[94] complained of unprecedented boldness in
the withholding of tithe tends to support this suggestion. But
we must not forget that tithe-payers suffered too in a period
which saw rapid population increase, sharply raised rents, and
some of the worst harvests of the sixteenth century. Failure
to pay tithe must often have been due rather to hardship
than to a conscious determination to exploit the clergy's
weakened position, though both were doubtless at work in
many cases.

Litigation in the church courts shrank to a mere trickle in

---

[93] See appendix 2.   [94] 27 Henry VIII, c. 20.

the middle years of the 1530s. King Henry's increasingly clear wish to retain the courts in their existing shape and with most of their old jurisdiction soon encouraged would-be plaintiffs to return to them. Tithe litigation in particular was stimulated by the statutes of 1536, 1540, and 1549.[95] The first two encouraged tithe-owners to seek the courts' help in maintaining their rights and extended the right to sue for tithes to laymen: those of 1540 and 1549, by insisting that tithes be paid according to custom (which might yield very much less than the true tenth demanded by the canon law), encouraged defendants to resist attempts to bring into line with current prices payments which in their eyes enjoyed customary status. At Norwich, the number of tithe-owners seeking redress in the consistory court rose very sharply in the year which followed the passage of the act of 1536. At Winchester, there was a striking growth in the number of tithe causes between the 1520s and the 1540s. It was in the second half of the period, however, that the biggest increases in litigation took place.[96] At Norwich, the great burst of judicial activity which marked the early 1550s, the period immediately following the downfall of the hopelessly in-effectual Bishop Rugge[97] and the arrival of his successor's chancellor, manifested itself most clearly in the field of tithe litigation. The year 1549 had seen both the passage of the great tithes act already so often referred to and the production of the demands of the rebels led by Kett, who called amongst other things for the commutation of tithes into money payments.[98]

Economic developments sharpened the conflict and were reflected in the changing pattern of commodities sued for. The dramatic price rise and severe dearths of mid-Tudor England left their mark on Norwich tithe litigation. Whereas in relatively 'normal' times pasture tithes, which were intrinsically the most difficult to assess not surprisingly caused the most litigation, rapidly worsening inflation in the 1540s

---

[95] Above, pp. 120-2.
[96] Below, appendix 1.
[97] Above, p. 22.
[98] *English Economic History Documents*, p. 249.

increased the number and proportion of suits over tithes of milk, cheese, hay, and other commodities for which customary or quasi-customary payments were widely made. Dearth in 1549-51, the terrible famine of 1556 and to a lesser extent the provisions of the 1549 statute relating to barren lands pushed up the number of disputes over tithes of grain.[99]

CONCLUSION

Nearly thirty years ago, in her important study of the clergy of the south-west Midlands between the Reformation and the Civil War, Dr. D. M. Barratt drew attention to the number and fierceness of disputes over means of tithing animal products which yielded less than a true tenth.[100] Such disputes were also very important in Norwich and Winchester dioceses in the period of the Reformation, though in the former diocese, before 1540 and after 1560, tithes of pasture, which presented unique assessment problems, were an even more potent source of conflict. The Norwich and Winchester evidence lands weight to another of Dr. Barratt's main findings — that tithes of grain were not commuted into cash payments in the sixteenth century. This is not to say that they did not give rise to litigation, however. They clearly did, and years of dearth stimulated tithe disputes in the diocese of Lichfield in the early seventeenth century just as they did in that of Norwich in the mid-sixteenth.[101] The paucity of Norwich and Winchester suits for personal tithes, both before and after the statute of 1549, suggests that the clergy of the two dioceses had practically given up trying to get a true tenth of the gains of labourers, craftsmen, and traders before our period. It seems probable that in this respect the act of 1549 merely set the seal upon accomplished fact.[102]

It was the better-off incumbents and their farmers who were readiest to pursue tithe causes at Norwich during our

[99] Houlbrooke, 'Church Courts and People', p. 402.

[100] D. M. Barratt, 'The Conditions of the English Parish Clergy from the Reformation to 1660' (Oxford Univ. D.Phil. thesis, 1949), ch. 6.

[101] M. R. O'Day, 'Clerical Patronage and Recruitment in England in the Elizabethan and Early Stuart Periods, with special reference to the Diocese of Coventry and Lichfield' (London Univ. Ph.D. thesis, 1972), p. 339.

[102] Above, pp. 122-3.

period. At Winchester vicars became much less prominent as litigants during the course of the Reformation as judges came to accept that those who withheld tithes must be sued with full instance formalities, which made litigation a much more daunting prospect for poorer incumbents.[103] Christopher Hill demonstrated in his study of the economic problems of the church that the gap between the incomes of richer and poorer clergy widened in a remarkable fashion during the century following the Reformation.[104] Hardest hit by what were claimed to be customary methods of paying tithes on 'mixed' products (which often formed the backbone of their income), vicars were also less able than the majority of rectors or their farmers to bear the costs of suits which might check the process of erosion. One is careful to refer to 'rectors *and their farmers*'. Christopher Hill stressed that the leasing of the better clerical benefices to laymen became very widespread during the later sixteenth century.[105] The records of tithe litigation at Norwich provide added evidence of the truth of this assertion. After the statute of 1540 there was a dramatic increase in the proportion of tithe suits initiated there by laymen, as there was also at Chester.[106]

Norwich and Winchester were not the only dioceses to experience a great increase in tithe litigation in the period of the Reformation. At York the number of tithe suits known to have been dealt with between 1540 and 1560 was four times larger than the number heard during the previous forty years. By 1601-2 the number of suits introduced into the consistory court in a year was to be ten times as great as in 1561-2.[107] Historians have already suggested some reasons for the great increase in tithe litigation during the sixteenth century. Christopher Hill in particular stressed the importance of the statute of 1549 and the rise in prices.[108] The acts of 1540 and 1549 firmly established custom as the yardstick by

---

[103] Above, pp. 143-5.
[104] Hill, *Economic Problems*, pp. 108-13.
[105] Ibid., pp. 114-17.
[106] Haigh, *Reformation and Resistance*, pp. 58-9, 61.
[107] *Select Sixteenth Century Causes in Tithe from the York Diocesan Registry*, ed. J. S. Purvis (Yorks. Arch. Soc. Record Ser. cxiv, 1949), viii; Marchant, *Church under the Law*, p. 62.
[108] Hill, *Economic Problems*, pp. 90-1, 96.

which liability to tithe was to be assessed, and thus made it
much more difficult for clergy to keep the scale of payments
in line with current prices. The sharp rise in prices in the
1540s and 1550s and the poor to bad harvests of 1549 to
1551 and 1555-6, coming soon after the act of 1549, brought
a veritable explosion of litigation. There were short term fluctuations in its volume. At both Norwich and Chester, for
example, the numbers of tithe suits heard dropped in the first
half of the 1550s.[109] The time at which this development
began was not exactly the same in both dioceses, but it is
hard not to connect it in both cases with a short run of better
harvests and a temporary slackening in the speed of the price
rise.

Even after the legislation of the 1540s it remained very difficult for defendants to win tithe cases at either Norwich or
Winchester. But this does not mean that the ecclesiastical
judges ignored the acts of 1540 and 1549. The fact that
Winchester judges began to change their method of handling
tithe cases so markedly in the 1540s[110] points in the opposite
direction. We know next to nothing of the terms concluded
by those many litigants whose causes were terminated by
peaceful agreement. Without such knowledge no definitive
judgement on the effectiveness of the courts in handling tithe
disputes in the period of the Reformation is possible.

[109] Haigh, *Reformation and Resistance*, p. 152.
[110] Above, pp. 137-8.

6

PAROCHIAL FINANCES AND THE MAINTENANCE OF THE PARISH CHURCH AND ITS CONTENTS

From the early days of the Christian church, portions of ecclesiastical revenues were supposed to be allotted to the
church fabric and the poor. In our period these burdens were
shared by clergy and laity.[1] The responsibility for the upkeep
of the parish church was divided between the parishioners,
whose duty it was to look after the nave and churchyard, and
the rector, who had to take care of the chancel. Parishioners
paid for the bread and wine used in the celebration of the
eucharist, for lights, and for the ornaments, books, and other
equipment needed in the church. (After the Reformation, the
rector had to help pay for certain books.) Both incumbent
and parishioners were bound to support the poor of their
parishes. This obligation was restated and more closely defined
in royal injunctions and in statutes in the period of the Reformation. The parishioners had also to pay for the services of
certain humble parochial officials. It lay with the church
courts in particular to see that these various responsibilities
were discharged, and to resolve disputes which arose out of
them.

The weighty responsibility of managing lay contributions
to parochial funds rested on the shoulders of the churchwardens. They were supposed to be elected each year and to

---

[1] Lyndwood, *Provinciale*, pp. 132-4, 251-3; B. Tierney, *Medieval Poor Law: a
Sketch of Canonical Theory and its Application in England* (Berkeley and Los
Angeles, 1959), pp. 69-79; *Visitation Articles and Injunctions*, ii. 10-11, 35-6,
117-19, 121-2, 127-8.

render account before the end of their term. The position was not one eagerly sought after. It was usually held by farmers or craftsmen, only rarely by gentlemen. The other parishioners were often happy to see the same men continue in office beyond their year. In Hampshire a two year term was customary; longer ones were not uncommon, and Bishop Parkhurst of Norwich found it necessary to draw a neglectful commissary's attention to the fact that one Norfolk man had served for nine years.[2] On the whole the system seems to have worked well, but churchwardens were sometimes brought before the courts for peculation, incompetence, or failure to render accounts for several years. Here, their accounts could be challenged, and as the result of one such suit in the Norwich consistory court (1561) a churchwarden who amongst his other misdemeanours had allegedly claimed over seven times as much for certain repairs as they had cost him was ordered to pay the substantial sum of £6 6s. 8d.[3]

The churchwardens raised the money needed to discharge parishioners' responsibilities in a number of ways. Many expenses were met with the help of church property. In Hampshire the animals belonging to the parish were often the chief source of income.[4] At Stoke Charity two-thirds of the churchwardens' regular income came from the parish flock in the 1540s, nearly all of it forty years later. Some parishes kept the animals under communal management, others leased them out to individuals. Rents payable for such animals were the subject of a large number of court proceedings early in the period. During the visitation of 1527 and the following year, cases of failure to pay were reported from thirteen parishes in the archdeaconry of Winchester. In some cases the rent had not been paid for between five and twelve years. The number of animals involved could be quite large: twenty-seven in one case, forty-two in another. The biggest sum said

[2] *Synodalia: A Collection of Articles of Religion, Canons and Proceedings of Convocations*, ed. E. Cardwell (Oxford, 1842), i. 122; *Hants Churchwardens' Accounts*, xii–xiv; *Letter Book of Parkhurst*, 259.
[3] NNRO AI (1550), Gunthorpe; NAGB 2A (1564), Marsham; *Brantham churchwardens c. Scryvener*, ACT 9, 22 Apr., 28 July 1562; ACT 10, 5 May 1563; DEP 7E, fo. 23; HRO VB 10, fos. 17, 50ᵛ, 48ᵛ.
[4] *Hants Churchwardens' Accounts*, xxv–xxix.

to be due was just under 25s.[5] Other sources of parochial income less often referred to were small pieces of land and houses. In one instance, however, a Winchester judge refused to hear a dispute about a house given to the church because he held that it belonged to the secular court.[6] Suits over the rent of animals were far less common after the Reformation than they had been before, and this was perhaps due to a growing reluctance on the part of ecclesiastical judges to entertain any sort of plea of debt.

Money was sometimes raised by the sale of assets. If we are to believe Stephen Gardiner, some of the ornaments were often sold to meet emergency expenditure even before the Reformation.[7] In the years of uncertainty between 1536, when wholesale confiscation of ornaments was first rumoured, and 1553, when it was actually carried out, large amounts of church goods were sold to meet the costs of new equipment, church repairs and (in some cases) road maintenance and poor relief. In the diocese of Winchester, churchwardens admitted to royal commissioners in 1552 sales of ornaments, especially second chalices, censers, and paxes, which had brought in sums of up to nearly £70 in the previous three years. In Suffolk a similar situation stood revealed.[8] Even after the Reformation, when stocks of ornaments had been much depleted, they were still occasionally sold to meet parochial needs. In 1565 the churchwardens of Stockbridge (Hants) sued in the consistory court at Winchester certain parishioners who had spent £3 7s. 1d. 'made of the chalice' on a Chancery suit to gain a fair, market, and parliamentary representation for the town. The defendants said they hoped to be able to pay it back in a term or two, but two and a half years later the sum had still not been paid in full.[9]

Penalties exacted from offenders could help to balance the

[5] HRO CB 4, fos. 106ᵛ, 119, 138; VB 3, p. 33.
[6] *Hants Churchwardens' Accounts*, xvi; HRO CB 10, 4 July 1556, Southampton St. Lawrence.
[7] *Letters of Stephen Gardiner*, p. 257.
[8] A. G. Dickens, *The English Reformation* (1964), pp. 254–5; W. K. Jordan, *Edward VI: The Threshold of Power* (1970), pp. 386–401; *VCH Hants*, ii. 69; *VCH Suffolk*, ii. 33–4.
[9] HRO CB 20, 5 May 1565; CB 22, 24 Nov. 1565; CB 27, p. 9.

parochial budget. In lieu of penance people were sometimes told to purchase quite expensive items of equipment.[10] From 1559 onwards, fines for absence from church were supposed to be levied by the churchwardens to the use of the poor, though the court books do not reveal how regularly they were exacted in practice. Bishop Parkhurst of Norwich later complained that his commissary in Norfolk archdeaconry failed to see that they were paid.[11] Church ales seem to have been an important source of income in Hampshire parishes, but the courts had little to do with them save indirectly when the less fortunate consequences of the convivial abandonment of conventional restraints were brought to their notice.

At the beginning of our period, parishioners could be relied upon to meet a large part of the parish's needs by means of gifts and bequests. The gilds, whose primary purpose was to ease their members' lot in the next world, were also channels through which benefactions flowed to the maintenance of fabric and ornaments. Parishioners very often left quite sizeable legacies to parochial uses, including roads, and proceedings concerned with sums bequeathed continued to be quite common right through the period.[12] But the changes of the Reformation discouraged parishioners from leaving money towards the maintenance and adornment of their churches. The decline in the number of such gifts and bequests, the confiscation of gild stocks by the Edwardian government, and the growing problem of poverty, made it increasingly necessary to raise money by means of compulsory dues or rates. The court books throw little light on the method of assessment, but the size of individuals' contributions probably depended upon the amount of land held in the parish. Rates were levied to pay the wages of the parish clerk, to meet the cost of poor relief, and to maintain and equip the church.

The wages of the parish clerk, under which name funds were sometimes raised for other purposes, seem to have been

[10] See e.g. HRO CB 4, fo. 136v.

[11] 1 Elizabeth I, c. 2; *Letter Book of Parkhurst*, 259.

[12] HRO CB 4, fo. 106; VB 10, fo. 46; NNRO DEP 4A, fo. 355; AI (1550), Islington, North and South Wotton, Sandringham, Tilney, Wiggenhall German.

the earliest object of regular contributions by parishioners. They were the subject of many petty disputes in both dioceses, and gave rise to more proceedings before the commissary in the archdeaconry of Norwich than did any other item on the parochial budget.[13]

A statute of 1536 provided for the appointment of parish collectors for the poor and the establishment of parish poor boxes, and instructed the clergy to urge their parishioners to help the destitute. Another, of 1552, empowered the bishop to send for those who refused to contribute 'and so take order according to his discretion.' One of the few remaining examples of a collectors' book begun in accordance with the provisions of the act was kept in the parish of St. Saviour's, Southwark. It was however an act of 1563, which ordered householders able to contribute to do so, and empowered the bishop to bind the recalcitrant to appear before the justices, which led to the first prominent burst of presentments in the Norwich archdeaconry court. Towards the end of our period this court played a part in the enforcement of poor rate payments even in the city of Norwich, where the municipal authorities had long been aware of the problems posed by urban destitution.[14]

Fabric rates caused disputes in a number of parishes in Norwich archdeaconry in the 1560s. Contributions had also to be levied towards the cost of new equipment under both Mary and Elizabeth. In 1556 the churchwardens of Lambeth (Surrey) entered a list of sums ranging from 4d. to 20s. received from thirty-nine people 'sessyd to the forniture of our Churche by the commaundment of the kynges and quenes Commissioners ...'[15]

Proprietors' and incumbents' obligations to contribute

[13] See e.g. NNRO AI (1549), Alderford, Babingley, Briningham, Hempstead, Terrington, Thetford St. Nicholas, Thurning, Walsingham Parva, Wighton, Wiveton; HRO VB 3, p. 11; CB 4, fos. 11, 123v, 130v, 137; VB 10, fo. 18.

[14] 27 Henry VIII, c. 25; 5 & 6 Edward VI, c. 2; 5 Elizabeth I, c. 3; I. Darlington, 'The Reformation in Southwark', *Proceedings of the Huguenot Soc. of London*, xix (1955), 73: NNRO NAGB 2A (1560), Wiggenhall Mary; (1563), Edgefield, Wells, Stokesby; (1568) Norwich St. Julians's, original presentment.

[15] NNRO NAAB 2 (1567), Glamford, Hempstead, Hindringham, Houghton; *Lambeth Churchwardens' Accounts*, i, ed. C. Drew (Surrey Record Society, xviii, 1941), 69.

towards poor relief and fabric maintenance were set out more
clearly than hitherto in injunctions and statutes. The canon
law had formerly laid down that one quarter of ecclesiastical
incomes should go to the poor. The duty of non-residents in
particular to contribute to the relief of the poor of their
parishes had been underlined by a provincial constitution of
1281; a statute of 1391 had insisted that the poor be provided
for in all appropriations of benefices.[16] Few proceedings
against those who neglected this duty have been found in the
early sixteenth-century records of either diocese. But in 1527
the proctor for the proprietors of Newton Valence (Hants)
was ordered to say why they should not be compelled to
make distribution amongst the poor, and the judge later
sequestrated 20s. for the purpose which he entrusted to a
neighbouring vicar.[17] The royal injunctions of 1536 laid
down that non-resident clergy with an income of £20 from
their benefices should bestow the fortieth part upon the
poor, and the royal articles of 1547 asked whether residents
kept hospitality on their cures.[18] According to returns
demanded by Matthew Parker, hospitality was neglected on a
substantial minority of the benefices in both Norwich and
Winchester archdeaconries in 1561-2.[19] Nearly three-quarters
of the reported cases of neglect were associated with non-
residence or pluralism. After 1536 incumbents were presented
on this score more frequently than before the Reformation,
but with little perceptible effect. In the 1560s (a decade comparatively well covered by its surviving records) some seventeen
incumbents beneficed in the archdeaconry of Norwich are
known to have been presented for their neglect of hospitality,
but hardly any of these presentments were followed by further

[16] Lyndwood, *Provinciale*, pp. 132-3, 153, n. h; 15 Richard II, c. 6.
[17] HRO VB 3, p. 20; CB 4, fo. 82^V. During next year's visitation the rector of
Dogmersfield was warned to reside on his benefice and to keep hospitality; VB 3,
p. 227.
[18] *Visitation Articles and Injunctions*, ii. 10, 106.
[19] Cambridge, Corpus Christi College MS. 97, fos. 198-210; A. W. Goodman,
'The Cathedral Church and the Archdeaconry of Winchester in 1562', *Papers and
Proceedings of the Hants. Field Club and Arch. Soc.*, xiv (1940), 63-85. The pro-
portions were a third in the archdeaconry of Norwich, a quarter in that of Winchester.

action.[20] The names of four men were noted in the court book after the episcopal visitation of Winchester archdeaconry in 1551. One of them was dismissed when his proctor claimed that he was not bound to distribute the fortieth part because his income was less than £20, and there is no evidence of effective action in the other three cases. Only two names were noted after the visitation of the archdeaconry of Surrey in 1567.[21]

The responsibility for the maintenance of most chancels had long rested with rectors and proprietors. The royal injunctions of 1536 laid down that an incumbent or proprietor must if need be devote one-fifth of his income from a given benefice to this purpose. Those of 1547 provided that the rector or proprietor must bear half the cost of purchasing the English Bible and the *Paraphrases* of Erasmus in each parish.[22] What the court books tell us about the state of fabrics will be discussed shortly, and it will be convenient to postpone till then an assessment of the measures taken to ensure the discharge of rectorial responsibilities in this respect. Presentments that the Bible and the *Paraphrases* were lacking very seldom specify whether parishioners or incumbent were to blame, though in the archdeaconry of Norwich some parishes complained in Edward's reign of the failure of parsons or proprietors to pay their part.[23]

The fulness and number of the entries relating to fabrics and furnishings varied so much from year to year and from one jurisdiction to another that it is impossible to use them to attempt an accurate comparison of developments in different dioceses over a period of time. In the archdeaconry of Norwich, for instance, there was in the second half of the period an increase in recorded presentments relating to fabric defects so marked as to suggest a change in scribal practice or

[20] For three early Hants cases, see HRO CB 7, 17 Oct. 1539, *rector of Buriton*; 12 Nov. 1540, *rector of Over Wallop*; 14 Jan. 1541, *rector of Compton*. Norwich archdeaconry figure based on surviving records of commissaries' inquisitions in NNRO NAAB 1, 2, NAGB 2A.

[21] HRO CB 9, (16 Oct.?) 1551, *A. Barker, G. Toly, R. Legg*; 7 Dec., *R. Francis*; VB 10, fos. 42v, 53.

[22] *Visitation Articles and Injunctions*, ii. 11, 117-18.

[23] NNRO AI (1550), Thornage, Toftrees, Great Ryburgh, Haveringland.

visitatorial priorities.[24] But no visitation records of our period from either diocese give so detailed a picture of defects in the fabrics and contents of churches as do the surviving *acta* of a visitation of the archdeaconry of Leicester carried out in 1516.[25] Those responsible for this record clearly devoted special attention to the state of churches and chapels, and it contains very few of the usual entries relating to sexual lapses. There is no surviving evidence that the churches of the Winchester or Norwich dioceses were subjected to such a searching inquisition during the Reformation period.

During these decades the problems presented by the maintenance of churches differed both in nature and scale from those involved in their equipment, and it will therefore be convenient to deal with them separately here. The courts still continued to try to ensure that fabrics were properly looked after as they had done throughout the later middle ages, but they had to supervise the purchase of a number of new books and items of church furniture.

Many lists of presentments of dilapidations share common features. Reported defects in churchyard enclosures very often outnumbered those in the body of the church. Parochial representatives may perhaps have presented these trivial defects so often because they wanted to make their bills look slightly more impressive whilst at the same time avoiding mention of more serious matters. Church repairs were usually the responsibility of the whole parish and might entail the levy of a rate. The responsibility for maintaining the churchyard wall was often apportioned amongst the parishioners, to each of whom a given stretch of wall was allotted.[26] Repairs were thus burdens on individuals rather than the community as a whole, though the obligation might be disputed. Defects in chancels nearly always outnumbered those in rectories and vicarages, either because the former were more apparent to

[24] See appendix 3.

[25] A. P. More, 'Proceedings of the Ecclesiastical Courts in the Archdeaconry of Leicester, 1516-35', *Associated Architectural Societies' Reports and Papers*, xxviii (1905-6).

[26] HRO CB 4, fo. 119[v]; H. E. Malden, 'Abinger Registers. Churchyard Fencing and Lease of Ground for a Pew', *Surrey Arch. Collections*, xxx (1917), 106-9; cf. Bowker, *Secular Clergy*, pp. 130-1.

churchwardens and questmen, or because the clergy took greater care of the houses in which they or their deputies lived than of the chancels in which they officiated. Most houses were probably relatively easy to maintain at this date. Reports that outhouses on the glebe needed repair were rarely entered. Bishop Parkhurst of Norwich, in his visitation of 1569, appears to have paid quite unusually close attention to the state of houses and outbuildings, and on this occasion, for once, recorded reports that they were in disrepair outnumbered entries relating to chancels.[27]

In a number of visitations and inquisitions more chancels than naves were said to need repair, though this was not always the case, and the entries made as a result of the diocesan visitation of the archdeaconry of Winchester in 1527 form a striking exception to this generalisation.[28] The reasons for the relative abundance of such reports are not clear. The maintenance of the body of the church cost more than did that of the chancel, but the former load was of course spread over many more shoulders than was the latter, and adequate church repairs and maintenance no doubt took in most cases a bigger proportion of the rector's income than of that of the parish as a whole. The increased burdens imposed on the clergy during the Reformation made it more difficult for them to maintain their chancels in adequate repair, and this fact no doubt helps to explain why there was a substantial increase in the number of complaints about the disrepair of chancels between the eve of the Reformation and the middle of Edward's reign in both dioceses.[29] In 1551 the rector of Headbourne Worthy (Hants) claimed that he was not bound to repair his chancel roof because he was still paying first-fruits, and he was no doubt only one of many clergy who were finding it hard to make ends meet.[30]

A monition to carry out repairs by a given date was the

[27] NNRO VIS 1 (1569), *passim*.
[28] HRO VB 3, pp. 1–129.
[29] Known defects in chancels in archdeaconry of Norwich: 1532-3 (surviving material covers nearly two-thirds of the archdeaconry) 4; 1550, 24. In archdeaconry of Winchester: 1527, 20; 1551, 30 (NNRO AI (1532, 1550); HRO VB 3, CB 4, CB 9).
[30] CB 9 (16 Oct.?) 1551, *Mr. Dyrrecke.*

usual method of dealing with dilapidations, backed if necessary by an appropriate sanction. In many cases no minutes of action taken were entered in the record. Very few original certificates of repair survive. One that does inspires no confidence: it was sent by the vicar of Briston (Norfolk) to the archdeacon, probably in 1568, and it is a bare statement that 'I have Amendyd the state of my vyckarage',[31] without any corroborative testimony. He begged to be spared appearance at the forthcoming session of the commissary's court. If such certificates were commonly accepted, it is easy to imagine that dilapidations could escape serious attention for many years.

Churchwardens were fairly frequently warned to carry out repairs or provide equipment on pain of a fine (sometimes as high as £1) which was presumably intended to be devoted to repairs. But such fines seem to have been levied very rarely in practice.[32]

The threat of a fine was sometimes employed against the clergy too, but in their case sequestration of the fruits was a more formidable alternative. This sanction was not however available to all judges. Archdeacons were in theory debarred from using it,[33] and the commissaries in the archdeaconry of Norwich very rarely did in our period. In view of the relative infrequency of episcopal visitations in this diocese,[34] this imposed a serious handicap on efforts to ensure adequate standards of fabric maintenance. Five out of thirty-six Norwich sequestrations recorded between October 1512 and April 1516 were ordered for this purpose.[35] In one case in which sequestration was at last ordered after the episcopal visitation of 1537, the dilapidations, for which vicar and proprietor blamed each other, had been repeatedly presented, till the church was reported to be in danger of collapse if something was not done.[36] In the diocese of Winchester

[31] NNRO NAAB 2 (1567-69).
[32] HRO VB 2, fos. 29, 30; VB 3, pp. 21, 23, 30, 36; NNRO AI (1549), Holt, Congham, Gayton, Gayton Thorpe.
[33] Lyndwood, *Provinciale*, p. 254, n. r; *Registrum Vagum*, i. 34.
[34] Above, p. 29.
[35] NNRO SUN 1(b), fos. 2-37.
[36] NNRO ACT 5, fos. 218-19.

sequestration orders were made more frequently, but their use grew rarer during the Reformation. At least six sequestration orders were issued on account of dilapidations during the visitation of the archdeaconry of Winchester in 1527 (all of them against proprietors), but apparently only one after the visitation of 1551.[37]

A negligent clergyman or his executors could be sued by his successor on account of dilapidations even if he had escaped presentment during his tenure of the benefice. Such suits were rare, however, for good reasons. The incoming clergyman was supposed to prove the extent of dilapidations by means of the expert testimony of witnesses from each craft which would be concerned in repair work.[38] At the time of his induction, some months would already have elapsed since his predecessor's departure or demise, and the longer he put off recourse to the court, the easier he would make it for his predecessor to contest liability, though the period following his induction was the one in which he could least afford to go to law. Fresh difficulties might well arise in course of suit. In one case, estimates of the probable cost of repairing a barn ranged from £13 to £20, while another case was complicated by widely differing estimates of the value of the benefice in question.[39] Not surprisingly, clergy were sometimes strongly tempted to settle for what they could get from their predecessors without recourse to law but such sums could be utterly inadequate. A former rector of South Elmham admitted in 1567 when sued for dilapidations that he had received £6 from *his* predecessor to cover the cost of repairs, but claimed that £30 or £40 would still have been insufficient, and asserted that he had spent £20 more than his net income from the benefice upon repairs.[40] Two incumbents of Edgefield (Norfolk) where dilapidations were intermittently complained of between 1551 and 1567 came to peaceful agreements with their predecessors, but as

---

[37] HRO VB 3, pp. 5, 16, 17, 18, 35, 95; CB 9, 7 Dec. 1551, *J. Wygge.*
[38] Lyndwood, *Provinciale*, p. 254, esp. n. e; Conset, *Practice*, pp. 363-5.
[39] NNRO DEP 4B, fos. 51-2; DEP 6A, fos. 175ᵛ-6; DEP 9, fos. 40, 45, 132-4.
[40] NNRO DEP 12, fos. 58-66, 70; ACT 11, 6 Oct. 1568.

the trouble continued, neither agreement can be regarded as
satisfactory.[41]

Certain other procedures available to the courts for tackling the poverty which often lay at the roots of dilapidation
were in these dioceses seldom used in practice. Ordinaries
could revise terms of appropriation of inadequately endowed
vicarages, but suits for augmentation were rare. They could
order unions of impoverished benefices with the consent of
interested parties, but, not surprisingly, this was often hard
to get, and such unions were infrequent.[42] The bishops of
Norwich could order personal unions of benefices during the
lives of incumbents, and poverty and dilapidations were
amongst the reasons advanced for such unions. But bishops
used this power comparatively infrequently until they were
compelled to do so by the very grave shortage of clergy which
developed after the middle of the sixteenth century, and dilapidations certainly continued after union in some cases.[43]

The transfer of ecclesiastical property into lay hands by
means of impropriation and lease doubtless made it harder to
apply some of the traditional remedies for dilapidations.
When it came to getting repairs carried out or securing the
augmentation of a vicarage, lay impropriators were probably
less ready to comply with the orders of ecclesiastical judges
than their monastic predecessors had been. Christopher Hill
suggests that at a slightly later period they were apt to ob-
struct proceedings by seeking the aid of the common law
courts. One of the complaints against Stephen Nevinson,
Parkhurst's third chancellor, shows the way the wind was
blowing. He was charged with granting a sequestration of a
benefice in lease 'whereby my Lord bisshop is not without
danger of praemunire.' If this was indeed the case, judges
must have been increasingly wary of using what had previously been the most useful weapon against dilapidation.[44]

[41] NNRO AI (1550 and 1551); NAAB 2 (1567-9); DEP 7C, fos. 29, 50, 56;
ACT 9, 16 Sept. 1561.

[42] For one such case, see HRO CB 4, fos. 165, 171.

[43] *Registrum Vagum*, i. 56-60; NNRO NAGB 2A (1564), Hevingham; (1565),
Brundall, Felthorpe; VIS 1 (1569), fo. 19.

[44] More, 'Proceedings in Leicester Archdeaconry', 124-5; Hill, *Economic
Problems*, pp. 134-5, 143-4, 149; PRO E 135/25/35.

A common standard of fabric maintenance was impossible to impose. The poor parish no doubt had to put up with damp and draughts which its richer neighbour would not tolerate. The task of ensuring that parishes possessed all that was necessary for the conduct of services was more clearly defined, for official requirements were precisely laid down in constitutions, statutes, and injunctions. Even before the Reformation, when liturgical requirements, long established, were well known, many presentments were made about of equipment defective or lacking: in about one in seven of the churches visited in the archdeaconry of Winchester in 1527, for instance.[45] After the break with Rome, the courts played a considerable part in communicating to the parishes knowledge of the changing requirements of the Reformation period.

A series of major changes began in 1536. In that year, the provision of a poor box was required by statute. In 1538, the second royal injunctions ordered the purchase of English Bibles and the keeping of parish registers. The Edwardian injunctions of 1547 ordered that copies of the *Paraphrases* of Erasmus upon the Gospels be bought, that pulpits be set up, and that homilies be read on Sundays when there was no sermon.[46] Council mandates of 1548 and 1550 and a statute of the latter year ordered the destruction of images, altars and Catholic service books, and the confiscation of most of the vestments and ornaments which had not already been sold or entrusted to safe keeping was set on foot in 1553.[47] The acts of uniformity passed in 1549 and 1552 ordered the use of new Prayer Books.[48] In Mary's reign the apparatus of Catholic worship had to be restored,[49] and though much had survived, the restoration entailed further heavy expenditure in most parishes. After Protestantism had been restored by

[45] HRO VB 3, pp. 5-124.
[46] 27 Henry VIII, c. 25; *Visitation Articles and Injunctions*, ii. 35-6, 39-40, 117-18, 126, 128-9.
[47] *Documentary Annals of the Reformed Church of England, 1546-1716*, ed. E. Cardwell (Oxford, 1844), i. 47-9, 100-2; 3 & 4 Edward VI, c. 10; Jordan, *Threshold of Power*, pp. 390-1.
[48] 2 & 3 Edward VI, c. 1; 5 & 6 Edward VI, c. 1.
[49] *Documentary Annals*, i. 126-7.

the Elizabethan act of uniformity of 1559, the Queen's injunctions laid down that the Bible and *Paraphrases* were again
to be provided, the *Homilies* again read by the clergy.[50] The
royal visitors who initiated the enforcement of the injunctions
also inquired whether all relics of popery had been removed
and demanded inventories of church goods.[51] Much of the
work of enforcement was perforce left to local courts; two
further measures carried out (unevenly) in the early years of
the Queen's reign were the destruction of rood lofts and the
conversion of chalices into communion cups. Other directives
were issued in the eventful decades that followed Henry's
break with Rome; but these were the most important stages
in the process of physical change in English churches.

The speed with which successive official mandates were
obeyed has never been systematically investigated on a large
scale. Churchwardens' accounts would be one essential source
for such an investigation, but relatively few survive, many
even of these marred by gaps and slack accounting. Church
court records seldom remain in sufficiently long unbroken
series to throw much light on the work of enforcement. But
study of the Norwich archdeaconry court books which cover
the years 1548-51 shows that even when a run of such books
survives for a crucial period, it leaves many questions un-
answered. To begin with, these books contain few references
to the most crucial change of all — the introduction of the
first Edwardian Prayer Book of 1549. The act of uniformity
placed the burden of enforcement in the first instance on the
shoulders of the justices of oyer and terminer and assize, with
whom bishops might 'at their pleasure' associate themselves.
Almost as if as the result of an afterthought, the act's penultimate proviso gave the ecclesiastical courts full power to
inquire of offences against it and to punish the same. In fact
it looks very much as though proceedings against those who
failed to use the Prayer Book must have been left to the lay
justices in the archdeaconry of Norwich.[52]

---

[50] *Visitation Articles and Injunctions*, iii. 10-11.

[51] Ibid. 2; Bayne, 'Visitation of the Province of Canterbury', 660-4.

[52] Thomas Brigges, rector of Eccles by Wilby, came to the notice of the justices
for his alleged celebration of services according to the Sarum use: NNRO Norfolk
sessions rolls, 1549.

Whatever the role of ecclesiastical courts in enforcing acts of uniformity, it was clearly their responsibility to see that royal injunctions were observed. Yet there are in the Norwich archdeaconry court books covering the years of the Edwardian Reformation very few references to the *Homilies* whose use was ordered in 1547, so that it is impossible to say how widespread their purchase was.[53] It is however clear that the purchase of the first part of the *Paraphrases* which appeared in January 1548 was fairly widely enforced. Between 1548 and 1551 failure to purchase the *Paraphrases* was reported in nearly half the parishes of the archdeaconry, and one in six of them attracted the commissary's attention on this score two years running. Enforcement was carried on evenly throughout the archdeaconry, save possibly in the extreme west — the remotest part. The records give the impression that the commissary's court was at its most efficient in enforcing the purchase of the *Paraphrases*. But this was one of the least important aspects of the Edwardian Reformation.[54]

The courts were also continuing under Edward to require the implementation of injunctions issued before 1547: a number of presentments relating to poor boxes, parish registers and Bibles were made in both dioceses. Surviving churchwardens' accounts confirm that the speed of compliance varied very much from place to place. No other enforcement agency was as well placed as the church courts to maintain a relatively gentle but steady pressure upon the laggards.

The court books contain comparatively little evidence of the destructive work of the Edwardian Reformation. Images of tabernacles were reported not to have been destroyed in some parishes.[55] Altars seem to have been removed fairly quickly. Bishop Thirlby claimed that most of the work had been done by the metropolitical visitors during the vacancy

---

[53] They were said to be lacking at Themelthorpe in 1548: see NNRO AI (1548), additional notes at the end of the inquisition.

[54] On *Paraphrases*, see helpful article by E. J. Devereux, 'The Publication of the English *Paraphrases* of Erasmus', *Bulletin of the John Rylands Library*, li (1968-9). It appears from this that all the Norwich entries almost certainly referred to the first volume; the purchase of the second does not seem to have been properly enforced; see ibid., pp. 359, 365. See also *Hants Churchwardens' Accounts*, p. lviii.

[55] NNRO AI (1548), Themelthorpe, Litcham, Scottow.

of the see in 1550, and few presentments concerned with their non-removal were made in Norwich archdeaconry in 1550-1.[56] All three Hampshire churchwardens' accounts covering the years in question record the setting up of communion tables under 1551 or 1552.[57] Chancellor Fuller of Norwich presided over a public holocaust of books in August 1550,[58] but no doubt their destruction was one of the more difficult measures to carry through thoroughly, because of the ease with which they could be taken away and hidden. Few later presentments relating to them appear to have been made.

Most of the evidence relating to the Marian re-equipment of the churches of the two dioceses has been lost. Changes in the Norwich city churches were enforced in the consistory court. St. Andrew's parish, perhaps because of its known radical sympathies, was singled out for a separate monition in December 1554. The churchwardens of seventeen other parishes were summoned to appear on the following 8 February, when those who came were asked whether they had provided the necessary ornaments and obliterated the scriptural texts painted on their walls in the preceding reign. Only five parishes, including the wealthy one of St. Peter Mancroft, were able to report that they had all the necessary equipment. The churchwardens of the poor parish of All Saints, Ber St., reported that their church lacked ornaments and that texts had never been painted on its walls. Bishop Hopton's abiding concern that all scriptural texts should be obliterated from the walls of churches is apparent from rough notes in visitation books of 1555 and 1556. Some of these notes refer to parishes such as Stoke Nayland and Bergholt which were famous for their early adherence to Protestantism.[59] A visitation carried out in September 1555 revealed that twenty-five parishes in Winchester archdeaconry lacked some items, but this figure is misleading, since it is clear that other parishes

[56] Above, p. 35; Hughes, *Reformation in England*, ii. 120n; NNRO AI (1550), Wiggenhall Mary; (1551), Beetley, Letheringsett, Longham, Wells.
[57] *Hants Churchwardens' Accounts*, pp. 39-40, 79, 116.
[58] NNRO ACT 7A, fos. 22v-3.
[59] NNRO ACT 8, fos. 177v, 203-4; VIS 1 (1555), fos. 54, 95, 96, 97v; (1556), Bergholt.

covered by the visitation were not fully re-equipped some time after this.[60] A much more reliable indication of the likely state of affairs is provided by the record of a visitation of the diocese of Canterbury carried out in 1557. Hardly any of the churches visited had a complete set of vestments; about a quarter lacked some liturgical books, or a cross for the altar; nearly a fifth the altar itself, the candlesticks to stand upon it, a decent receptacle for the reserved sacrament, and a holy-water stoup.[61]

Slowness in compliance was doubtless due less to dissaffection than to the straitness of parochial finances, the reluctance of wardens to spend money when the settlement might not last very long, and difficulties encountered in recovering church goods from private hands. On this last the court records throw some light. For neither of our dioceses is the information as full as it is for that of Salisbury, where the metropolitical visitation of 1556 revealed very widespread detention of church goods by parishioners.[62] But seven suits probably concerned with the recovery of church goods came before the Norwich consistory court in 1555; nine cases, nearly all concerned with liturgical books, vestments, and ornaments, came before the Winchester consistory court in three months in the summer of 1556.[63] Very many more cases were probably dealt with more informally in the archdeaconry courts. One suit for the recovery of a tabernacle was being heard at Winchester a few days before Mary's death.[64]

The only portion of the official record of the royal visitation of the southern province in 1559 known to have survived, that which covers the eastern dioceses, says next to nothing of the work of removal and re-equipment; we learn from other sources that commissioners ordered the destruction

[60] HRO VB 8. Cf. suits for recovery of church goods in June–Sept. 1556, in CB 10, and *Hants Churchwardens' Accounts*, pp. 42–3, 82–4, 173–4.
[61] *Archdeacon Harpsfield's Visitation, 1557*, ed. L. E. Whatmore (Catholic Record Soc., xlv–xlvi, 1950–1); findings conveniently summarized in Hughes, *Reformation in England*, ii. 236–7.
[62] *VCH Wilts.* iii. 31.
[63] NNRO ACT 8, fos. 197, 250, 260ᵛ, 274, 278, 309ᵛ, 317; cf. DEP 6A, fos. 19ᵛ–21, 129, 149ᵛ–51; HRO CB 10, 3 June, 4, 6, 18, 24 July, 1, 22 Aug. 1556.
[64] HRO CB 12, fo. 13ᵛ.

of images, rood lofts, mass books, and ornaments.[65] The long intervals which elapsed in many cases before the arrival of the first Elizabethan bishops left the responsibility for following up the commissioners' work to diocesan courts largely staffed by conservatives. But it is clear that the commissary's court in the archdeaconry of Norwich was active in enforcing at least the negative aspects of the Elizabethan settlement in 1560. The destruction of Latin books and surviving holy-water stoups was certified by several questmen. By this stage the main attack was evidently focused on the rood loft, the most prominent and contentious surviving symbol of the old order. A large majority of the parishes covered by what survives of the record of the inquisitions of 1560 apparently certified that they had destroyed their lofts, and in subsequent inquisitions the removal of the last traces, such as the doors which had given access to the lofts, and the beams which had supported them, was reported. Yet this drive was not recorded in the 1560 act book of the sister archdeaconry of Norfolk, a fact which illustrates both the extent to which scribal practice could vary even within the same diocese and the pitfalls which await those who seek to use the court records to chart the progress of the official Reformation.[66] Lofts did not always come down easily; in 1561 a Norwich man of reforming sympathies told another inhabitant of the city that the loft would come down in the latter's parish despite its many 'Rebels' hearts'; a popish clique prevented the destruction of the loft in the church of St. Gregory's until at least 1573.[67] Despite the fact that the church of Lambeth lay under the eye of the Archbishop himself, it was not till 1570 that the churchwardens of the parish recorded

[65] PRO PROB 34/1, fos. 76ᵛ, 117ᵛ, 126; Bayne, 'Visitation of the Province of Canterbury', 652-3, 676-7.

[66] NNRO NAGB 2A (1560), *passim* (the entries are however even more untidy and illegible than usual, so that one cannot always be sure whether a particular note refers to the destruction of a rood loft or not); (1563), Cley, Holkham, Houghton, Wighton; Norfolk archdeaconry act book 1.

[67] *Depositions taken before the Mayor and Aldermen of Norwich, 1549-1567*, ed. W. Rye (Norwich, 1905), pp. 65-6; *Letter Book of Parkhurst*, 212. For some Winchester presentments, see HRO CB 17, p. 49; CB 31, fo. 140; CB 35, fos. 25, 47, 56.

the taking down of their rood loft.[68] It is clear, too, that it was a long time before all other 'monuments of superstition' were destroyed; presentments concerning the survival of images and books in particular continued to be made in both dioceses throughout the 1560s.[69] Such entries bulk rather larger in the Winchester than in the Norwich records, either because of the greater conservatism of the first diocese, or because of the greater vigour of Horne. Of the latter there can be no doubt. The flavour of an encounter with the bishop of Winchester is admirably conveyed by the record of an exchange between him and the churchwardens of Andover in 1564. Apparently the churchwardens had failed to build a suitable rostrum in the nave for the minister to stand on; they had done their best, but the 'maisters of the town' were unwilling to contribute, and the church stock was insufficient to meet the cost.

Tunc dominus monuit et iniunxit eis To sele ther vestamentes and albes, ther sensors and such other trashe, to make monnye on, and if that will not serve, to levey so moche as dothe lack vppon the parishioners heades equallye and accordinge to ther discreassions, and those that doth refuse to pay, to certifye ther names unto hym, And to buyld up the same fytt place ... before Satterday next cum thre wekes.[70]

As in Edward's reign, the church courts were responsible for making sure that the *Homilies* (a second volume of which was published in 1563) were read, and that the Bible and *Paraphrases* were purchased. A number of presentments that one or more of these books were lacking were made in all the Norwich archdeaconry inquisitions of the 1560s.

Subsequent mandates added little to the requirements of 1559. In 1561 Elizabeth ordered that copies of the ten commandments be displayed in all churches, that communion tables have on them a 'fair linen cloth, with some covering of silk, buckram or other such like', and that copies of parish register entries be delivered annually to diocesan registrars.[71]

---

[68] *Lambeth Churchwardens' Accounts*, i. 104.
[69] See e.g. HRO CB 35, fos. 27, 28ᵛ, 47, 56ᵛ, 91, 227, 237ᵛ, 242ᵛ, 254ᵛ, 314ᵛ.
[70] HRO CB 17, p. 101.
[71] *Correspondence of Parker*, 132-4, Cardwell, *Documentary Annals*, i. 296; *Visitation Articles and Injunctions*, iii. 109-10.

The table of ten commandments was occasionally referred to in the court books.[72] The order touching the covering of communion tables seems to have conflicted with an injunction given by Parkhurst in his primary visitation of 1561 which ordered that communion tables should not be decked like altars. The discrepancy between the two mandates perhaps helps to explain why there was in Norwich diocese after the metropolitical visitation of 1567 a spate of presentments relating to communion tables and their coverings.[73] The submission of register copies has left few traces in the court books of either diocese, but in 1563 all those churchwardens who had failed to appear in the Winchester consistory court to exhibit such copies after being cited to do so were excommunicated.[74]

During the 1560s it was decided that all chalices should be converted into communion cups.[75] Convocation failed to agree on this measure in 1563, and it was carried out in different dioceses at different times. In Winchester diocese, an order for conversion seems to have been given some time in 1567, and the court books of the following year contain scores of reports of implementation.[76] Parker's commissaries asked when they visited Norwich diocese in 1567 whether or not the clergy used decent communion cups, and about 275 of the surviving Norfolk cups date from 1567-8. Most of the presentments made after the metropolitical visitation related to the provision of a cover for the cup, usually fashioned out

---

[72] e.g. NNRO NAAB 2 (1567), Westwinch.

[73] W. P. Haugaard, *Elizabeth and the English Reformation* (Cambridge, 1968), p. 150. In many places, so it was noted, 'mensa dominica indecora est', e.g. NNRO NAAB 2 (1567), Gunthorpe, Briningham; in others simply that 'deest mensa dominica', e.g. NAAB 1 (1567), Ringland, Thurning, Bawdeswell. These latter parishes had perhaps never replaced their altars.

[74] HRO CB 16, fo. 74, precise date uncertain; cf. CB 25, 18 Jan. 1566.

[75] The main reasons for conversion were the association of the chalice with the mass and its inadequate size. The form was changed; 'instead of being a shallow wide bowl, it was elongated into the form of an inverted truncated cone, slightly bell-shaped.' (J. C. Cox and A. Harvey, *English Church Furniture* (1907), p. 35.)

[76] *Visitation Articles and Injunctions*, iii. 155n; HRO CB 27, pp. 68ᵛ-95ᵛ; CB 29, fos. 1ᵛ, 2, 3, 7, 22ᵛ, 23, 32ᵛ, 33ᵛ, 34, 39-46ᵛ, 60-72ᵛ, 77, 79, 89-95ᵛ.

of the old paten, rather than to the cup itself.[77] In some dioceses, such as London, the great change was carried out earlier than in our two dioceses; in others, such as Lincoln and Salisbury, it did not occur for another few years.[78]

CONCLUSION

In the areas of activity covered by this chapter the church courts almost certainly came to bulk larger in parishioners' lives during the Reformation than they had done before. Many of the directives issued in this period of rapid religious change had to be enforced by the courts. They had too to support with their sanctions the levy of parochial rates for a whole variety of purposes which grew much more important after confiscation of parochial endowments had discouraged parishioners' voluntary contributions. During the Reformation, then, local communities were probably subjected to more badgering by the church courts than previously they had been, and this cannot have made the courts more popular.

Some of the pressure was probably fairly effective. Of course the rate of progress varied from area to area, and officials of conservative outlook could themselves hinder the implementation of official programmes by deliberate neglect or by concentration on the trivial at the expense of the important. Bishop Downham of Chester, for instance, ordered the destruction of images, altars, and roodlofts only in 1564, and in many places they survived far longer than this. As late as 1604 there were many churches in this diocese without *Homilies*.[79] Nevertheless, no other organisation was as well adapted as the church courts to the task of enforcing the purchase of books or equipment, both by adequate publication of official requirements and the maintenance of steady pressure on the unwilling over a period of years.

On the other hand the evidence of the court books on

---

[77] *Visitation Articles and Injunctions*, iii. 199; N. Pevsner, *The Buildings of England: North-East Norfolk and Norwich* (Harmondsworth, 1962), pp. 55-6. I have noticed some thirty-nine presentments in NNRO NAAB 1, 2, NAGB 2A, and VIS 1 (1569) relating to churches in Norwich archdeaconry.

[78] Emmison, *Morals and the Church Courts*, pp. 256-7; G. A. J. Hodgett, *Tudor Lincolnshire* (Lincoln, 1975), pp. 171-2; *VCH Wilts*. iii. 32n.

[79] Haigh, *Reformation and Resistance*, pp. 219-20, 244.

both the state of fabrics and the action taken to deal with dilapidations is all too often extremely vague. The level of efficiency varied markedly from decade to decade. In the archdeaconry of Norwich, for instance, recorded minutes of presentments became more numerous and specific in the 1550s and 1560s. 'Drives' to improve standards of fabric maintenance took place in Lancashire in Mary's reign and in Essex in the mid-1570s.[80] But on the whole it cannot be said that the action taken by the courts was obviously efficacious. Judges appear to have been loath to employ the most effective sanctions at their disposal. In this period of upheaval their role was confined for the most part to putting extra weight behind the efforts of those in the parishes who wanted to get things done. Their means of coping with the results of poverty, impressive on paper, were inadequate in practice. The wilfully negligent could all too often put off effective action till it was too late to bring them to book.

[80] Ibid., pp. 202-3; Emmison, *Morals and the Church Courts*, p. 250.

7

THE SECULAR CLERGY AND THE COURTS

The supervision of the secular clergy by the church courts had as its aim the maintenance of adequate standards in both the cure of souls and in the clergy's personal lives and demeanour, or what might be called the ministry of example. Both before the Reformation and after it, the clergy were bound to pray for and with their people, to expound the faith to them, and to minister the sacraments. In their personal behaviour they were supposed to maintain chastity and sobriety in both dress and demeanour.

The Reformation, by lessening the importance of the clergyman's role as dispenser of sacraments, and by placing more emphasis on his duty to expound the Word of God, greatly altered accepted notions of what constituted an adequate standard of cure. But the conservatism or ignorance of the majority of the clergy, together with a serious shortage of suitable ordinands, prevented the fulfilment of the reformers' pastoral aims for many years. There was some open resistance to doctrinal change amongst the clergy, but this was small in scale compared with apathy, absenteeism, and the covert maintenance of old ideas and practices.

The clergy were supervised, and, when necessary, corrected, in the archidiaconal and diocesan courts and by means of episcopal visitations. Clerical faults were probably punished in the bishop's court of audience, too, if he had one; he might alternatively choose to deal with certain offenders by means of personal interview.[1] Diocesan synods of the clergy

---

[1] HRO CB 3, fos. 68ᵛ, 148ᵛ; CB 17, pp. 94-5; NNRO DEP 6A, fo. 192.

may also have had correctional functions.[2] Some of this disciplinary work was probably never recorded, and a sizeable proportion of the records which once existed has perished. It is, therefore, difficult if not impossible to describe fully the supervision of the clergy by the diocesan authorities in the period of the Reformation.

Our picture of the courts' work in this field is distorted not only by the loss of records but also by the fact that surviving records sometimes mislead us by telling us more about the faults of certain sections of the clergy than those of others. Within the ranks of the clergy three major types may be discerned, each of which presented diocesan authorities with different disciplinary problems.[3] First there were the richer beneficed clergy, many of them non-resident because they were pluralists, perhaps also busy in episcopal, noble or royal service. The second class included the bulk of the middling to poor beneficed clergy. Below them in turn came the unbeneficed stipendiaries, the clerical proletariat, probably the most rootless and mobile section of the clerical population. It was probably the first and third groups which, for different reasons, were least amenable to discipline. The second group had most to lose by annoying parishioners or diocesan authorities, and parochial representatives might for their part feel that presentments of members of this group were the ones most likely to lead to solid results.[4]

The courts employed a very wide range of censures and penalties in dealing with erring clergy. Excommunication and penance were used against them as against the laity. Penance was the standard punishment for proven moral failings. Other disciplinary weapons used against the clergy were suspension from office, sequestration of the fruits of the benefice, and deprivation. Temporary suspension from office was a flexible disciplinary instrument employed against both incumbents and the unbeneficed. It could be used not only to bring the

[2] NNRO ACT 4B, fo. 134ᵛ; ACT 5, fo. 72; above, p. 30.
[3] Cf. M. L. Zell, 'The Personnel of the Clergy in Kent, in the Reformation Period', *EHR* lxxxix (1974), 513-15.
[4] But correctional records do not conform to a standard pattern in this respect. The majority of the clergy of Winchester archdeaconry noted in 1527-8 as suspected of incontinence were unbeneficed.

contumacious to heel, but also to provide the insuffient with an incentive to improve their qualifications or efficiency.[5]

Sequestration of the fruits was a fairly commonly used sanction. A surviving register at Norwich shows that at least thirty-six orders were made by the diocesan authorities between October 1512 and April 1516, twenty of them for neglect of the cure, four for neglect and dilapidations, one for dilapidations.[6] During the visitation of Winchester archdeaconry in 1527 at least twenty-one sequestration orders were made or referred to as being already in force.[7] Amongst the reasons for them were dilapidations, non-residence, and failure to provide a curate. Sequestration was also, at Winchester, the standard penalty for failure to appear in the episcopal visitation. But sequestration orders were not always immediately effective. The incumbent of Sparsholt (Hants) confessed in 1528 that he had not appeared in the 1526 visitation either in person or by proxy, and that, subsequently hearing of the sequestration of the fruits of his benefice from the diocesan registrar, he had ignored it, thus incurring *ipso facto* excommunication.[8]

Errant curates were often forbidden to serve in a given diocese henceforth, but deprivation was very rarely used before the Reformation, as Mr. Heath has already pointed out in his study of the parish clergy. In Norwich diocese between 1503 and 1528, and in Winchester diocese between 1531 and 1550 little more than 1 per cent of the vacancies whose causes are known were due to deprivation.[9] It was the proud boast of Fox of Winchester, towards the end of his life, that he had never deprived a man in any diocese he had been in.[10] The weapon was reserved for use in exceptional cases such as that of the rector of Ridlington (Norfolk) whose actions brought him before the consistory court in

[5] NNRO ACT 3B, fo. 16; ACT 4B, fo. 24.
[6] NNRO SUN 1(b), fos. 2-37; but see above, p. 160.
[7] HRO VB 3, pp. 5, 7, 16, 17, 18, 35, 56, 65, 77, 81, 82, 84, 95, 99, 100, 102, 105, 107, 114, 115, 119.
[8] HRO CB 4, fos. 175ᵛ-6.
[9] HRO VB 1, fos. 21, 45, 65; VB 3, pp. 113, 223: CB 4, fo. 86ᵛ; P. Heath, *The English Parish Clergy on the Eve of the Reformation* (1969), p. 114; *Reg. Gardiner et Poynet*, xxxii.
[10] *Letters of Fox*, p. 151.

1522. He was said to have burnt the timbers of his chancel, wasted the goods of the church in secular business, and thrown stones at his parishioners. Even he appears to have been given a chance to resign, for a form of resignation was entered in the deposition book.[11] Only the bishop and his chancellor could impose this severe penalty. Deprivation did not belong to the archdeacon by canon law, and it was (we are told) never delegated to the commissaries of the bishops of Norwich.[12]

Deprivation was first used on a large scale in the drive against the married clergy which began in 1554. This marked a sharp break with medieval practice. Another upheaval followed Elizabeth's accession. In 1559 the royal visitors restored to their benefices a number of those deprived for marriage under Mary, and deprived of their livings those who refused the oath of supremacy. The first generation of Elizabethan bishops used deprivation more frequently than their predecessors had done before 1554. Most of those who suffered the loss of their livings at this time were probably being punished for neglect of their cures; in many cases covert opposition to the new regime lay behind this neglect.

Judges sometimes imprisoned members of the clergy. They were empowered by a statute of 1485 to confine the incontinent, but the court books suggest that this power was rarely used.[13] In 1527 one priest of the Isle of Wight was imprisoned for celebrating mass despite his excommunication.[14] Until 1576 the bishops' prisons also sheltered criminous clerks, convicted before the king's judges, who might if they were not 'notorious offenders' be admitted to compurgation in due course. The test of clerical status was literacy. The best recent study of the working of the compurgation system up to the 1540s has been written by Mr. Heath, drawing heavily on information contained in York and Lincoln episcopal registers. He shows that it was not the 'professional clergy' who were the major beneficiaries of the system; they were

---

[11] NNRO DEP 3, fos. 226ᵛ-8, 309ᵛ; ACT 4A, fos. 99ᵛ-100.

[12] Gibson, *Codex Juris*, ii. 1068; *Registrum Vagum*, i. 34.

[13] 1 Henry VII, c. 4; Storey, *Diocesan Administration*, p. 29; NNRO ACT 3B, fo. 218; ACT 5, fo. 233.

[14] HRO CB 4, fos. 73, 74ᵛ.

greatly outnumbered by 'clerks who were in effect laymen', and such people continued to claim benefit of clergy in large numbers even after an act was passed in 1532 which in theory limited the privilege to those in major orders. Heath also found a remarkable duplication of names on lists of compurgators, suggesting that many of them could not have known personally the clerks concerned. Proclamations were made so that objectors might appear, but they very seldom did so. A register of compurgations survives at Norwich which covers the period 1528 to 1563, with a gap between 1544 and 1555. Sixty-nine individuals were admitted to purgation between 1528 and 1544, ninety-four between 1555 and 1563. The majority had been convicted of theft, some of homicide. Unfortunately indications of occupation or status are very seldom given in these lists, but there is nothing to show that more than a tiny minority were what Heath has called 'professional clergy'; if not, it is clear that the abolition of minor orders had no more effect on the working of the system than the act of 1532, which one also infers from the increase in the numbers of those admitted to purgation after 1550. At Norwich, as at York, there was very considerable duplication of names amongst the lists of compurgators, and large numbers of potential objectors failed to appear. The operation of this procedure must have provided a sorry spectacle, and the final severance of their connection with this hoariest of anomalies was one of the achievements of the Reformation for which ecclesiastical judges had most cause to be grateful.[15]

SEXUAL DISCIPLINE AND CLERICAL MARRIAGE

Becoming conduct on the part of the clergy (which it was the courts' duty to enforce) included the avoidance of excess or unseemliness in dress, drink and pastimes. But above all it meant chastity.

In the first part of our period, proceedings for sexual misconduct were the most numerous of those undertaken against the clergy by the church courts. No other accusation against

---

[15] Heath, *English Parish Clergy*, pp. 119-33; Plucknett, *Concise History*, pp. 439-41; NNRO CON 1.

the clergy was so frequently bandied about among the laity as was that of incontinence, and no other did so much to lower their reputation among the broad mass of the people. Mr. Heath and Mrs. Bowker have recently examined the scale of the problem and the effectiveness of measures taken to tackle it, and they agree, broadly, in concluding that the problem was a *comparatively* small-scale one. Mrs. Bowker shows that the incumbents of some 10 per cent of the parishes of Lincoln diocese visited between 1514 and 1521 came under suspicion in connection with women, but that only 0·7 per cent were 'proven immoral'; Mr. Heath shows that within the jurisdiction of the dean and chapter of York, covering an area which fluctuated in size between fifty and eighty-six parishes, 1·5 certain or possible offenders were reported in an average year between 1453 and 1491. The two scholars differ in their assessments of the effectiveness of the available means of tackling the problem. Mr. Heath's careful analysis leads him to the conclusion that purgation worked satisfactorily in the case of the clergy, that the imposition of penance (an impressive weapon, in his view) was 'responsible and prudent' and that there was very little backsliding. Mrs. Bowker's judgement is that there is 'a note of defeat in the records over this problem'.[16]

In Winchester diocese most errant clergy were dealt with in the course of visitations and in subsequent consistory court correctional proceedings, in Norwich diocese in the consistory and archdeaconry courts. Unfortunately very few years before the middle of our period are covered by a range of correctional records which is anywhere near complete, so that it is difficult to assess the extent of clerical incontinence in the two dioceses with which we are concerned or the effectiveness of the measures taken to deal with it. In 1527–8, eleven clergy of the archdeaconry of Winchester (which contained about 230 parishes) came to the notice of the authorities during the visitation and subsequent correctional proceedings. In 1538 proceedings were initiated in the consistory or archdeaconry court against eight clergy of some 200 parishes (all

---

[16] Heath, *English Parish Clergy*, pp. 115–19; Bowker, *Secular Clergy*, pp. 116–21.

that are covered by surviving records) of the archdeaconry of Norwich.[17] Few of the charges were proved, and the numbers involved seem small, especially when one bears in mind the fact that most parishes contained more than one priest, some many more.

The Norwich consistory court seems to have ceased to deal with immoral clergy in the 1540s, possibly because priestly incontinence had been made by the act of six articles of 1539 a statutory offence carrying penalties far more ferocious than those the church courts were able to inflict. The act's repeal in 1547, followed by the legalisation of clerical marriage, created a completely new situation. How effectively did the courts deal with suspected offenders before 1539? Tabulation of the results of proceedings suggests that the level of efficiency varied from court to court. In the archdeaconry of Norwich the proportion of cases with unknown outcomes was very large. If the commissary in the archdeaconry was indeed as slack in following up cases as this sample suggests,

TABLE 3

Results of proceedings against incontinent clergy

	Winchester 1527-8	Norwich consistory 1519-24, 1534-8	Norwich archdeaconry 1532-3, 1538
?	2	11	8
Cleared themselves	4	6	1
Assigned penance	2	7	1
		(1 commuted)	
Granted letter of correction		2	1
Short confinement		2	
Dismissal with warning	1	3	
Warned not to serve in diocese	2		
Dead			1
Total	11	31	12

[17] These figures are based on NNRO AI (1538), Beeston, Billingford, Breccles, Ingworth, Saxlingham; ACT 5, fos. 226, 236^v-7, 243; HRO VB 3, pp. 19, 90, 110; CB 4, fos. 84, 95^v, 97, 98^v, 100, 110^v, 118, 127^v, 130^v, 147, 148, 149, 152, 161, 166.

it is easy to understand why there should have been some backsliding amongst those proceeded against.[18] It is possible that the commissary referred cases to higher authorities, but there is no evidence that this was a routine practice.[19] The proportion of cases with unknown outcomes was smallest in Winchester diocese, where co-ordination of correctional proceedings was most effective.[20] In both diocesan and archdeaconry courts some clergy were dismissed on their own word or oath or without producing the full number of compurgators. Of those found guilty some were simply warned not to serve in the diocese or had their penance commuted. The records of proceedings to curb clerical incontinence in these two dioceses do not inspire a great deal of confidence. If incontinence was indeed as rare among the clergy on the eve of the Edwardian Reformation as court presentments and subsequent proceedings suggest, this was probably due (in these dioceses, at any rate) more to the clergy's sense of responsibility or at least knowledge that inchastity would destroy the respect of their flocks, than to fear of the sanctions at the disposal of the church courts.

In England, as elsewhere, the Reformation brought to an end the attempt to maintain clerical celibacy. The continental Protestant reformers upheld clerical marriage, and, probably under the influence of their teaching, some English priests braved the penalties laid down by the law before the act of 1549 which permitted English clergymen to take wives for the first time since the twelfth century.[21] Two incumbents, George Fenne of Debenham (Suffolk) and John Palmys of Bentworth (Hants) were deprived for their *de facto* marriages in 1536 and 1539 respectively.[22] The declared charge against a third incumbent, Robert Vaws of Over Wallop (Hants) who lost his benefice in 1538, was failure to proceed to orders,

---

[18] e.g. Dns. Edmund Denny, rector of Beeston, and Dns. Richard Fowler, rector of Melton and Saxlingham; NNRO AI (1532-3, 1538).

[19] See NNRO ACT 5, fo. 243. In this case, however, proceedings were transferred to the consistory court at the instance of the defendant himself.

[20] Above, pp. 29, 31.

[21] 2 & 3 Edward VI, c. 21.

[22] NNRO ACT 5, fos. 111-113; *Reg. Gardiner et Poynet*, 70-1, 114; *LP* xiv. pt. i, 120.

but the diocesan authorities no doubt took his marriage into account.[23] During Bishop Rugge's 1537 visitation it was discovered that two Ipswich chaplains had recently got married; by the following year, marriage was reputedly spreading more widely among the Suffolk clergy.[24] The act of six articles (1539, modified in 1540) laid down harsh penalties for priests' marriages, but enforcement of the relevant provisions of the act has left no traces in the records of these two dioceses.[25]

Legitimate marriage immediately proved popular among the clergy; it spread most rapidly in London diocese, and in the county of Essex 28 per cent of beneficed men took advantage of the Edwardian legislation between 1549 and 1554. In the diocese of Norwich the proportion was about a quarter.[26] It is impossible to calculate the proportion in the diocese of Winchester because of the loss of part of the relevant episcopal register and of records of disciplinary proceedings.

The Marian regime tackled the problem of clerical marriage soon after parliament had repealed the Edwardian religious legislation. The wholesale purge of the married clergy early in 1554 was the first example of an operation of this type and scale in the history of the English church. One of the remarkable features of the process was the speed with which it was carried out. The deprivation of married clergy was ordered in the royal injunctions which were issued on 4 March 1554. It is clear even from the incomplete record of proceedings in the Norwich court books that at least a third of those deprived or dismissed from cures had been dealt with by the end of March. Yet a substantial majority of the clergymen whose answers to the question are known would not separate voluntarily from their wives, and about half of the married clergy of Norwich diocese who made wills in the years

[23] *Reg. Gardiner et Poynet*, 71-4, 113; *LP* viii. 20; HRO CB 7, 27 July 1538.
[24] NNRO ACT 5, fo. 212; Charles Wriothesley, *A Chronicle of England during the Reigns of the Tudors*, ed. W. D. Hamilton (Camden Soc. n. s. xi, 1875), 83.
[25] 31 Henry VIII, c. 14; 32 Henry VIII, c. 10.
[26] H. E. P. Grieve, 'The Deprived Married Clergy in Essex 1553-61', *TRHS* 4th ser. xxii (1940), 142; G. R. Baskerville, 'Married Clergy and Pensioned Religious in Norwich Diocese, 1555', *EHR* xlviii (1933), 45.

1553-58 made provision for their partners.[27] The diocesan authorities could not afford to relax their vigilance after the initial wave of deprivations. During the metropolitical visitation of the diocese in 1556, Bishop Hopton and his chancellor deprived two clergy who had continued to consort with women despite previous proceedings against them, and discovered that two women, one of whom was forced to do penance, were still being supported with food and money by their former husbands.[28]

This drastic measure was no doubt intended to restore clerical discipline and morale. But in the eyes of those of the married clergy who were committed neither to the old faith nor to the new (perhaps the majority) it must have seemed above all the last in a long series of humiliations of the clerical order. The very fact that the process had been carried out with an admirable impartiality, thus affecting 'Rich or poor, learned or unlearned, godly or ungodly' meant that some natural pillars of the old order among the learned pluralists, and even a former diocesan official, had their feelings bruised.[29] At least a third of the deprived clergy of Suffolk and Essex are known to have found other benefices.[30] It is nevertheless likely that a large proportion of those who had originally shown their unwillingness to be separated from their wives left the church altogether, thus contributing to the serious shortage of clergy which was to develop during Mary's reign.

The commissioners who carried out the royal visitation of 1559 were instructed to restore those 'unlawfully' deprived under Mary. Forty-two incumbents of Norwich diocese who had been deprived for marriage in 1554 are known to have

---

[27] *Documentary Annals*, ed. Cardwell, i. 123-4; J. F. Williams, 'The Married Clergy of the Marian Period', *Norfolk Archaeology*, xxxii (1961), esp. 87-8, 90-2.

[28] NNRO ACT 8, fos. 174-5, 238^v-9; ORR 1(b), fos. 11^v-3; cf. VIS 1 (1555), fo. 87.

[29] Grieve, 'Deprived Married Clergy', 152; William White (Baskerville, 'Married Clergy', 49) had been commissary in the archdeaconry of Norwich.

[30] For Essex, see Grieve, op. cit. 153-4. The Suffolk proportion is based on the list in Baskerville, 'Married Clergy', 57-64, and R. Freeman Bullen, 'Catalogue of Beneficed Clergy of Suffolk, 1551-1631', *Proceedings of the Suffolk Institute of Archaeology*, xxii (1934-6), 294-320.

sued the men who had displaced them, or simply *omnes contradictores*. Plaintiffs in the better recorded cases exhibited letters certificatory of their institutions and copies of their 'pretended' deprivation processes. Favourable sentences were quickly given in at least thirty-one of these cases, and probably in others.[31] Other men probably recovered their livings after the visitation. By 1561-2 41 per cent of the incumbents in the archdeaconry of Norwich had married and 21 per cent and 32 per cent of those in the archdeaconries of Winchester and Surrey respectively.[32] These men knew that they were *ipso facto* supporters of the Elizabethan settlement, whose future was at this point far from assured. The events of Mary's reign had made it clear that if the new settlement were reversed, they would be deprived of their livings and compelled to undergo penance. Another important consequence of the very rapid spread of marriage among the clergy after Elizabeth's accession was that clerical incontinence, the most prominent disciplinary problem on the eve of the Reformation, now became one of the least important. Henceforth the diocesan authorities were to be free to devote their main attention to the improvement of pastoral care.

NON-RESIDENCE AND PLURALISM

Perhaps the most fundamental task of those responsible for diocesan administration was to ensure that each cure of souls was properly served. At the beginning of Elizabeth's reign there was a shortage of clergy so severe that many parishes had no ministers to take care of them. But this situation was quite exceptional. Usually the main problem was not one of finding enough clergy to serve cures, but of deploying the available clerical manpower to the church's best advantage. Unfortunately this was not easy. Many patrons, above all the

[31] H. Gee, *The Elizabethan Clergy and the Settlement of Religion, 1558-1564* (Oxford, 1898), p. 92; Bayne, 'Visitation of the Province of Canterbury', 645-6; PRO PROB 34/1, fos. 16ᵛ-7, 28, 46, 65, 69, 70, 71, 72, 73, 74, 75, 93ᵛ, 94, 95ᵛ, 96ᵛ-7, 98, 100, 101ᵛ, 102ᵛ, 103, 104ᵛ, 105, 107, 119ᵛ, 128, 134ᵛ, 136ᵛ.
[32] Cambridge, Corpus Christi College MS. 97, fos. 198-210; Goodman, 'Cathedral Church and Archdeaconry of Winchester in 1562'; G. Baskerville and A. W. Goodman, 'Surrey Incumbents in 1562', *Surrey Arch. Collections*, xlv (1937).

king, but also noblemen and bishops, regarded benefices primarily as means of rewarding their servants and dependants. Such men formed a large proportion of the pluralists, that is those who held more than one benefice. Pluralism was the biggest single cause of non-residence in early sixteenth century England, others (often but not always coupled with pluralism) were service of patrons and study at one of the universities.[33] When a benefice was held by an absentee, the cure was usually served by a stipendiary priest much less well qualified than the incumbent. Only rarely did non-residents fail altogether to provide for the service of the cure. The vast majority of parishioners probably did not expect learning in their clergy, and it is unlikely to have mattered much to them that their parish priests were less well-qualified than the non-resident incumbent. Nevertheless, they probably resented paying tithes into the pocket of a man they never saw, and non-residence may have caused some parishes, particularly larger ones, to be undermanned.

The extent of non-residence on the eve of the Reformation has recently been examined by Mr. Heath and Mrs. Bowker. Visitation records so far analysed suggest that the proportion of clergy which was non-resident might vary from one diocese to another between 10 and 25 per cent, but the extent of effective as opposed to nominal non-residence is hard to define precisely because a number of men who were resident in theory appear to have spent much time away from their parishes in practice.[34]

The Lincoln evidence analysed by Mrs. Bowker is far superior to anything which has survived among the Norwich or Winchester records of the period. Measures taken in the diocese of Norwich to keep track of the extent of pluralism and non-residence on the eve of the Reformation have left few traces. Some notes of licences granted are to be found scattered through early sixteenth-century registers. One of them tells us that the bishop or his chancellor 'not licensing, allowed by word of mouth' one man to be absent from his

---

[33] Heath, *English Parish Clergy*, pp. 50–6; Bowker, *Secular Clergy*, p. 97.
[34] Ibid., pp. 90–1; Heath, op. cit., pp. 56–7.

benefice.[35] The absence thus informally sanctioned was one must hope a short one. Only one early sixteenth-century diocesan visitation record survives at Norwich (that of Nykke's 1532 circuit) and this is incomplete. In it the names of seven non-residents were entered; three of them were warned to reside upon their benefices, the fourth to produce his plurality licence; the fifth showed a letter from the duke of Suffolk certifying that he had taken the man into his service, and no action was recorded in the case of two others, one of whom was studying at Cambridge.[36] The impression created by this meagre evidence differs markedly from that gained by reading, for example, the record of Nykke's monastic visitations. Fuller separate records relating to non-residence may have vanished.

More pre-Reformation visitation material has survived at Winchester than at Norwich. Diocesan visitations took place annually, and it was probably felt to be unnecessary to make a note of all non-residents each year, especially if their dispensations had been examined in the recent past. So we should not expect any one visitation to reveal as much non-residence as was recorded during the less frequent visitations of the diocese of Lincoln. One of the fullest early sixteenth-century visitation records to survive at Winchester was drawn up in 1527. In that year, ten non-resident incumbents were noted in Winchester archdeaconry.[37] One of them exhibited a dispensation issued by Wolsey's authority. Two more were simply warned to reside; five to exhibit dispensations or say why sequestration should not be ordered. No action in respect of the last two was recorded. There is no mention here of men who held satisfactory episcopal dispensations; perhaps it was simply not the administrative custom at Winchester to make note of them. The production of dispensations issued by authorities outside the diocese was not a mere formality. In at least one case a doubtful dispensation turned out to be unsatisfactory. The dispensation under

---

[35] NNRO institution book xiv, fos. 60 r, s, t; SUN 1(b), fo. 24v.
[36] NNRO ACT 4B, fos. 19v, 42v, 56v, 94, 102, 106, 115. The figure does not include the non-resident chantrist mentioned on fo. 135.
[37] HRO VB 3, pp. 30, 44, 45, 50, 56, 69, 81, 84, 86, 101.

Wolsey's seal exhibited by a fellow of Winchester College in May 1527 suggested that his fellowship was a *beneficium compatibile*, whereas in fact, as he confessed, it required continual residence. The man was ordered to explain why he should not be declared to have incurred the appropriate canonical penalty for the misrepresentation.[38]

Having gained information about non-residence (presumably by means of visitation or inquisition) bishops and their chancellors sometimes published warnings to a number of incumbents to come into residence by a certain date, but this procedure has left few traces in the records. In 1508 Fox sent a mandate to the archdeacon of Winchester ordering him to issue one such warning; another, dated 1552, survives in the book of forms compiled by the Norwich scribe Humfrey Rant.[39]

The statute 21 Henry VIII, c. 13 (1529) was ostensibly intended to curb pluralism and non-residence, but, while restricting the number of substantial benefices each man might hold, it permitted a large number of clergy to take more than one. In a petition of 1554 in which they sought its repeal, the lower house of convocation alleged that by reason of the statute 'a larger liberty or licence is geven to a great multitude of priests and chaplleyns to be absent from their benefices with cure, than was ever permitted by the canon laws ...' Mr. Heath has noted that the average number of plurality dispensations granted annually by the Faculty Office between 1534 and 1548 was considerably larger than the number granted by the papal curia in sample years during the mid-fifteenth century, and Mrs. Bowker has demonstrated that non-residence in the diocese of Lincoln, which had declined sharply between 1518 and 1530, was increasing once more during the 1530s.[40]

Whatever the effects of the 1529 statute, they were probably overshadowed in the long run by those of a fall in the numbers of the clergy. In the mid-1530s there was a sudden sharp decline in the number of men coming forward

---

[38] HRO CB 4, fo. 63ᵛ.

[39] HRO Reg. Fox, ii, fo. 98; BL Harley MS. 1253, fo. 179.

[40] *Synodalia*, ed. Cardwell, ii. 435; Heath, *English Parish Clergy*, p. 60; M. Bowker, 'The Henrician Reformation and the Parish Clergy', *BIHR* 1 (1977), 44.

for ordination in the diocese of Lincoln, the biggest in England; a similar development is known to have taken place at about the same time in other dioceses.[41] This sudden fall bears stark witness to the deterrent effects of the dissolution and heavier clerical taxation. In Henry's later years and under Edward the clergy were subjected to a series of increasingly abrupt and drastic changes which undermined their status and economic position. Many of the clergy deprived for marriage under Mary probably left the church for good. Towards the end of her reign, an influenza epidemic caused a very heavy mortality. Then the religious settlement was reversed yet again, and a further, smaller, wave of deprivations followed. In this uncertain atmosphere clerical morale slipped to its nadir, and a career in the church ceased to be attractive. During Mary's reign a shortage of clergy began to develop which in the early 1560s was to cause administrative problems beside which those caused by pluralism and non-residence on the eve of the Reformation paled into insignificance.

A detailed study of pluralism in the diocese of Canterbury has shown that there it increased very rapidly between 1559 and 1561, when it was at its most widespread.[42] The personal unions of benefices granted by the bishops of Norwich also reflected the growing shortage of clergy. Between 1542 and 1553 only twenty were granted altogether. Twenty-nine were granted in the two years 1554-5, a measure of the disruption caused by the deprivations of married clergy. In 1556 the number fell, only to rise to twenty-five in the year 1557; thirty, the largest number of all, were conceded in 1560.[43] These figures indicate that the problem of filling benefices began to develop in the diocese of Norwich, too, under Mary, but that it was at its most acute after Elizabeth's accession, when new deprivations, resignations from the ministry and reluctance to enter it because of the prevailing uncertainty probably contributed to the crisis.

A unique document, the official transcript of certificates

---

[41] Bowker, loc. cit., 33-4.
[42] J. I. Daeley, 'Pluralism in the Diocese of Canterbury during the Administration of Matthew Parker', *JEH* xviii (1967), 49.
[43] *Registrum Vagum*, i. 54-61; above, p. 162.

sent by diocesan officials in answer to a questionnaire about the state of the clergy sent out by Archbishop Parker in October 1561, throws a flood of light on the critical position of the church at a time when the Elizabethan settlement had already endured over two years. An analysis of the returns relating to the archdeaconry of Norwich and the two archdeaconries of the diocese of Winchester reveals the scale of the problems confronting Horne and Parkhurst.[44]

The certificates suggest that about 15 per cent of benefices with cure were vacant in the archdeaconries of Norwich and Winchester.[45] Non-residence affected 35 per cent of the 'full' benefices in Winchester archdeaconry, 22 per cent of those in Surrey archdeaconry, and 21 per cent of those in Norwich archdeaconry. A large proportion of the incumbent clergy held more than one benefice; this proportion was highest in the archdeaconry of Norwich (54 per cent, compared with 21 and 22·5 per cent in the other two archdeaconries). The proportion of pluralists amongst the Norwich beneficed clergy makes the percentage of benefices in that archdeaconry reported to be affected by non-residence surprisingly small. The latter was in fact due to the readiness of those who drew up the returns to consider a man who held two benefices near to each other as resident upon both. In this archdeaconry nearly one-third of the listed clergy were pluralists whose benefices lay next to each other. This state of affairs was due to the very large numbers of 'personal unions' granted by bishops of Norwich in the recent past. The problem posed by a shortage of clergy could only be dealt with, however unsatisfactorily, by allowing churches to be served by the incumbents of neighbouring parishes. In general the bishops of Norwich seem to have used their power to grant personal unions with care and discrimination. Yet although the

[44] *Documentary Annals*, ed. Cardwell, i. 309; Cambridge, Corpus Christi College MS. 97, fos. 198–210; Goodman, 'Cathedral Church and Archdeaconry of Winchester in 1562', Baskerville and Goodman, 'Surrey Incumbents in 1562'.

[45] The percentages of vacant parishes are only rough estimates. The Parker certificates give incomplete information on vacant churches, and my percentages have been arrived at by subtracting the numbers of full benefices named in the certificates from the numbers of parishes in each archdeaconry given in returns sent in by the bishops in 1563 (BL Lansdowne MS. 6/60; Harley MS. 595, fo. 258).

adoption of some such solution was almost inevitable, it was practically certain to reduce the standard of cure experienced by the inhabitants of the parishes concerned. The situation could indeed be worse from their point of view when a 'local pluralist' who held two neighbouring parish churches tried to serve both than it was when a frank absentee paid a full-time curate.

Local pluralism existed on a very much larger scale in the diocese of Norwich than it did in that of Winchester. But it does not follow that the standard of cure was very much higher in the latter diocese. Norwich diocese, and Norwich archdeaconry in particular, contained many small parishes and relatively few subordinate chapelries, while in Winchester diocese the reverse was true. The typical equivalent in the latter diocese of the small, poor parish held by a 'local pluralist' was probably the neglected dependent chapelry. In 1563 sixty-two out of eighty chapels of ease in Winchester diocese were vacant.[46] Here too, of course, there were some poor parishes. Bishops were allowed by ecclesiastical law to unite poor livings permanently, subject to the consent of interested parties, and their power to do so in certan cases had received statutory confirmation in 1545. Some unions were sanctioned in our period in both dioceses. But the necessity of gaining the agreement of all those involved could make such unions difficult to carry out, as Horne found at the beginning of his episcopate when he hoped to unite some of the poor parishes of Winchester city in order to combat what he viewed as popery and superstition.[47]

In the first few years of Elizabeth's reign, the acute shortage of clergy put bishops who wished to tackle the associated evils of pluralism and non-residence in a weak position. Within a few years, however, as it became increasingly likely that the settlement would endure, the number of men coming forward for ordination in the less conservative southern and eastern areas of the country grew rapidly, though areas like Lancashire continued to suffer from an acute shortage of

[46] BL Harley MS. 595, fo. 258.
[47] 37 Henry VIII, c. 21; HRO CB 4, fo. 165; CB 16, fo. 1; *Registrum Vagum*, i. 53; PRO SP 12/21/7.

ministers for many years to come.[48] From 1561 onwards, Parkhurst and his chancellors sharply reduced the numbers of new licences to hold benefices in personal union granted to incumbents in the diocese of Norwich each year.[49] Even this step demanded some firmness on the part of diocesan authorities, as was demonstrated by an incident of 1571 in which Parkhurst was involved. A man who had leased his first benefice on terms which smacked strongly of simony was presented to him for institution to a second benefice. He was notorious for his unseemly behaviour and suspect religious opinions, and after personal examination had revealed his complete ignorance of the scriptures, Parkhurst refused to admit him. The presentee appealed against Parkhurst's decision, and he seems in the end to have been unable to prevent the man's gaining the living.[50] In the light of this incident it is hardly surprising that the bishop should have treated already ensconced pluralists with circumspection. In his visitation of 1569 three pluralists incumbent in the arch-deaconry of Norwich were reported to be without dispen-sations. One of them (whom previous commissary's inqui-sitions had already shown to be inefficient) was merely warned to get one, and no recorded action was taken in respect of the other two.[51]

Matthew Parker was deeply shocked by the state of affairs discovered in his native diocese by the commissioners who carried out the metropolitical visitation in 1567.[52] In October of that year they ordered sixty-one allegedly long-term non-residents to reside on their benefices within six months on pain of deprivation, and fifty-two of these men were later formally deprived.[53] So far as can be seen these men had escaped the net of diocesan discipline, and even Parker's commissioners had only limited success in dealing with them. It is clear that some of those concerned appealed against the

[48] Haigh, *Reformation and Resistance*, p. 239.
[49] *Registrum Vagum*, i. 62-4.
[50] *Letter Book of Parkhurst*, 97-100.
[51] NNRO VIS 1 (1569), fos. 9, 51, 64ᵛ; NAGB 2A (1560), Helmingham; (1564), Ringland.
[52] Above, p. 36.
[53] *Registrum Matthei Parker*, ii. 748-61.

sentence; at least one gained restitution. Over the next few years a number of those sentenced apparently died in possession of their benefices or resigned them freely. Many others, if indeed they lost their livings, had no successors in them whose institution was recorded in Parkhurst's register. Only nine can be said beyond a shadow of doubt to have been effectively deprived. The real number was probably a good deal larger than this, but surviving evidence does not allow one to say how large.[54]

SIMONY

Patrons bore a large share of the responsibility for pluralism and non-residence. Their presentations enabled clergy to accumulate benefices. All too often their actions suggested that they saw ecclesiastical livings simply as a convenient source of income for men who were doing other sorts of work for them. The act of 1529 sanctioned the continuance of pluralism, especially through the exemptions in favour of the chaplains of important people which it contained.[55] In 1562 the marquess of Winchester, a conservative opportunist in matters of religion, and the most powerful magnate in Hampshire, had in his service three non-resident incumbents of Winchester diocese who between them held at least four benefices with cure.[56] He was only one of many such patrons.

During the Reformation, crown grants and leases transferred large amounts of church patronage from ecclesiastical into lay hands. Whether laymen who now gained an increasingly tight grip over the church were more or less discriminating patrons than the monasteries had been has yet to be shown.[57] But with their families and other dependants to provide for, they were probably less disinterested. Letters exchanged in 1573 between Bishop Parkhurst and one of his allies amongst the gentry show that even a strongly Protestant patron, a known favourer of the puritan clergy, was capable of viewing a clerical career as a suitable means of providing

[54] NNRO institution book xix, fos. 143–210; additional details from SUN 3, fos. 137ᵛ-8 (list of those sentenced with some notes of subsequent events).

[55] Above, p. 186.

[56] Goodman, 'Cathedral Church and Archdeaconry of Winchester in 1562', 68, 70, 73, 85.

[57] Cf. above, p. 162.

for a broken-down old husbandman incapable of further work.[58]

The use of ecclesiastical patronage as a means of providing for friends, servants and dependants was a form of exploitation of the patron's position, which, though normal and accepted, often had unfortunate results. A more brutal form of exploitation was simony, the grant of a benefice in return for payment either open or disguised. We do not yet know whether increasing lay control over the church led to an increase in simony. But both Protestants and Catholics stressed the seriousness of the problem. The existing church law provided that guilty clergy were to be suspended from office and lose benefices so obtained. The royal injunctions of 1547 and 1559 reinforced this provision: all who bought benefices, or came by them by fraud or deceit, were to be deprived, and made incapable of further spiritual preferment. Patrons were to lose their right of presentation for that turn.[59] The Marian convocations showed concern with the problem, and one of Pole's legatine constitutions of 1555 condemned a wide range of simoniacal practices and laid down an oath to be sworn by all candidates for institution certifying that they had not obtained the benefice by simony.[60]

Of all the bishops who ruled the two dioceses in our period, only Bishop Hopton of Norwich seems to have made anything like a determined effort to tackle the problem. Two incumbents of Winchester diocese were cited to answer articles connected with simony in the time of Bishop Fox, and the names of a further two who were said to have gained their benefices by this means were noted in 1551, probably as a result of the visitation, but nothing is known to have come of these proceedings. In the one known pre-Marian prosecution for simony in the diocese of Norwich, privately

[58] *Letter Book of Parkhurst*, 191-3.
[59] *Visitation Articles and Injunctions*, ii. 128, iii. 18.
[60] *Documentary Annals*, ed. Cardwell, i. 189-90; *Synodalia*, ed. Cardwell, ii. 435, 439, 455, 461, 479, 480, 509.

undertaken, a peaceful settlement was (somewhat incongruously) attempted.[61]

In Norwich diocese at least twenty clergymen are known to have been prosecuted for simony in Mary's reign, fourteen of them in 1555. These prosecutions were concerned with agreements of many types, some of which had been concluded many years before. In many cases there were other charges besides simony. The results of most of these cases are not known. Three men, however, were certainly deprived (though in two of these cases the sentence was technically given on account of contumacious non-appearance) and others probably were. Two resigned, probably under pressure, and only one of those proceeded against is known to have purged himself of the charges against him.[62]

It is clear from personal answers and depositions that a lease of the benefice to the patron or his nominee lay behind about half the cases of suspected simony dealt with at Norwich.[63] Payments by the incumbent, whether in the shape of a lump sum or an annual charge or pension, were less often suggested. Many of the defendants were at some pains to stress that they had not striven to obtain their benefices, but that they owed them to the efforts of friends or employers, or to the initiative of the patron concerned. We learn for instance that a Mrs. Townshend, desirous that her chaplain become vicar of Westhall (Suffolk) had broached the matter over supper with the patron, Mr. Bohun, who had

[61] HRO CB 3, fo. 2ᵛ; CB 4, fo. 5; CB 9, 16 Oct. 1551, Alton, Mottisfont; NNRO DEP 5A, fo. 291; DEP 5B, fos. 56-9; ACT 7B, fo. 6 (the evidence of simony in this case is admittedly somewhat slender).

[62] (All refs. to NNRO.) See proceedings against *Brake*, ACT 8, fos. 239, 244; *Browne*, DEP 6A, fo. 193; institution book xviii, fo. 194; *Brownsmith*, ORR 1(b), fos. 25ᵛ-6; *Cootes*, DEP 6A, fo. 50ᵛ; *Crosbye*, ACT 8, fos. 305ᵛ, 310ᵛ; *Gippes*, ibid., fo. 169ᵛ; institution book xviii, fo. 121ᵛ; *Haugh*, ACT 8, fos. 208ᵛ, 236ᵛ; *Jaksonne*, ibid., fo. 202ᵛ; *Lache*, DEP 6B, 14 July 1556; *Lincoln*, DEP 4B, fo. 76; ACT 8, fo. 288; *Punder*, ibid., fos. 246ᵛ, 293; *Slater*, VIS 1 (1555), fo. 106; *Stancliff*, ACT 8, fo. 266ᵛ, *Startwhaite, Stevins*, ibid., fo. 294; *Stormes*, ibid., fo. 250ᵛ; institution book xviii, fo. 183ᵛ; *Taylor*, DEP 6A, fos. 222ᵛ-4; *Turner*, ACT 8, fo. 284; institution book xviii, fo. 140ᵛ; *Welles*, DEP 6B (June or July 1556?); *Wright*, ACT 8, fos. 239ᵛ-40. See also PRO PROB 34/1, fo. 95.

[63] In the royal injunctions of March 1554, the bishops were enjoined to do all they could to prevent the decay of benefices through unreasonable leases; *Documentary Annals*, ed. Cardwell, i. 122-3.

known the chaplain when they had both been in the duke of Suffolk's service. She had given Bohun an old coin and an apple to obtain the presentation (a playful gesture which suggests that their relationship may not have been a matter of business alone) and had agreed that he should have ten pounds. One of these cases suggests that the dissolution of the chantries had strengthened the hands of unscrupulous patrons in dealing with men seeking benefices. Mr. James Calthorpe had approached William Brownsmith after the dissolution of the latter's chantry, and had suggested how pleasant it would be if Brownsmith had a little something to live on besides his pension. He had a benefice, he said, which was 'not a living without his help'. Brownsmith should have 5 marks a year and food and drink if he agreed to lease the benefice to Calthorpe.[64]

The early Elizabethan bishops' articles and injunctions included provisions designed to tackle simony, but there is little evidence of punitive action taken in either of the two dioceses with which we are concerned. According to Matthew Parker, writing in 1568, Norfolk was then so far infected with simony that some patrons were 'fleecing' as many as eight benefices at a time. In the same letter, Parker complained that Lord Keeper Bacon himself had been guilty of near simony in connection with a prebend in Norwich cathedral, and in 1571 Parkhurst reported that one of Bacon's relatives supposedly intended to bestow a benefice upon the highest bidder. Parkhurst claimed to have done more to check simony than his predecessors had done; presentees took an oath that they had not been guilty of it, and in a memorandum drawn up not long before the end of his episcopate, he urged his chancellor to take heed of it in certain specific cases, but not more than four clergymen are known for certain to have been prosecuted on this score during his first twelve years at Norwich; of these only one was certainly deprived, and he was suspected of other offences besides simony. Only one

---

[64] See the references in fn. 62, p. 193. above, under *Lincoln, Brownsmith*.

prosecution is known to have been initiated at Winchester during Horne's first decade as bishop,[65]

NEGLECT OF THE CURE

Non-residence was only one of the causes of neglect of the cure, and not always the most important. Mrs. Bowker has shown that unsupervised curates in the diocese of Lincoln in the first twenty years of the sixteenth century were only marginally more likely than their supervised brethren to get into trouble for misconduct or neglect of their duties.[66] Incompetence, old age, and lack of adequate vocation also contributed to neglect. When there were too few clergy to go round, poor parishes and dependent chapelries often had to be served, as we have seen, by men who were already beneficed in the neighbourhood who might well prove unequal to the burdens of a second cure.

Whether or not failure to discharge the cure came to the notice of the authorities depended in the first instance on the parishioners. They were naturally interested first and foremost in the performance of the basic pastoral duties, much less in the intellectual calibre of their clergy. Throughout the period, the commonest complaint on this score made against the clergy by parochial representatives was that particular services had not been said at the proper time, in due fashion or not at all. Failure to perform rites connected with the great crises of life understandably caused considerable bitterness; a number of clergymen were presented in the first half of the period for not ministering the eucharist to pregnant women nearing their time, or for delaying the administration of extreme unction. Betrayal of confessions, omission from the mass of prayers for the dead and failure to visit the sick were also

---

[65] *Visitation Articles and Injunctions*, iii. 102; *Correspondence of Parker*, 311–12; *Letter Book of Parkhurst*, 97, 138–9, 257; NNRO VIS 1 (1569), fos. 66ᵛ, 79ᵛ, 82ᵛ, 84; proceedings against *Cootes*, NNRO ACT 11, 11 Nov. 1567, 23 Mar. 1568; DEP 9, fo. 246; *Plumpton*, NNRO DEP 13A, fo. 122; DEP 11B, 20 June 1570; HRO CB 12, fo. 98.

[66] Bowker, *Secular Clergy*, pp. 107–9.

mentioned.[67] The reasons for neglect are not always apparent from the record. Disagreement over dues or personal hostility sometimes lay in the background. Some men were clearly unfitted by temperament for pastoral work. Inadequate training was presumably the reason why one priest of Norwich diocese was warned in 1520 not to celebrate mass till he had achieved better knowledge of the *verba effectualia* of the sacraments, of the ten commandments, and other things required in confession. Another man was ordered during the visitation of 1532 to go away and say masses for the dead, leaving his cure to be discharged by a competent chaplain.[68] But some of the complaints that the cure had been inadequately served came even in the first half of the period from the dependent chapelries of Winchester diocese and from the small and poor parishes in Norwich diocese which were being served by 'local pluralists'.[69] The plight of these poorer units of pastoral care grew worse towards the end of the period, as has already been pointed out. Of twenty-one men known to have been presented for serious neglect of cures in Norwich archdeaconry in the 1560s, nearly two-thirds were 'local pluralists'.[70] Many incumbents were sued at Winchester by the inhabitants of dependent chapelries in the same decade. A number of them, in their answers to the charges, attributed their failure to discharge their obligations to their inadequate incomes and inability to find chaplains.[71]

One gets the impression (though this may simply be due to the survival of different types of record in the two dioceses) that parishioners' complaints about the clergy were more numerous and better recorded in Winchester than in Norwich

---

[67] HRO CB 2, fo. 25; CB 3, fos. 5ᵛ, 10, 49, 66ᵛ, 156ᵛ, 169; CB 4, fos. 41, 44ᵛ, 53, 56, 197; CB 7, 14 Oct. 1536, *Elys*; 22 June 1538, *Went*; 5 Dec. 1538, *Overton*, 7 May 1541, *OP (Smyth) c. Gardner*; NNRO ACT 3B, fo. 105; ACT 4A, fo. 157ᵛ; ACT 4B, fos. 97-8, 102ᵛ; ACT 5, fo. 19ᵛ; ACT 7B, fo. 290ᵛ; Bury and West Suffolk Record Office, 1st act book of archdeaconry of Sudbury, fos. 7, 30, 44, 51.

[68] NNRO DEP 3, fos. 226ᵛ-8; ACT 3B, fo. 16; ACT 4B, fo. 24.

[69] HRO CB 7, 21 Mar. 1539, *OP (Baker and Newlyn) c. Bentley*; 5 Dec. 1538, *Elys*; CB 6, pp. 512-13; *Reg. Gardiner et Poynet*, 89-91; NNRO ACT 4B, fos. 97, 124.

[70] Figure based on NNRO NAAB 1, 2; NAGB 2A; VIS 1 (1569).

[71] HRO CB 12, fos. 82, 91ᵛ, 101, 126ᵛ; CB 19, pp. 99-108, 111-22, 145-8, 164, 167, 173, 175-6.

diocese, at least in the first half of the period. This may have been due to the frequent visitations carried out in the former diocese by the bishop's chancellor, a more important and possibly less partial figure than the commissary whose rounds were the main vehicle for the enforcement of discipline in Norwich diocese.[72] In the six (later seven) years which elapsed between visitations in Norwich diocese it was more difficult for parishioners to bring their complaints to the attention of the bishop or his chancellor. They might be reluctant to face the technicalities of an instance suit in the consistory court. In 1520, the parishioners of Hardingham (Norfolk) exhibited in the consistory court a bill of articles in English against their parish priest, but they failed to propound them in legal form, and the chancellor dismissed him with a mere injunction.[73]

Both before and after the Reformation parishioners' complaints against their clergy seem all too often to have achieved no worthwhile result. We have already seen how reluctant diocesan authorities were to use the weapon of deprivation before the religious changes. One or two particularly striking cases show how difficult it was to secure effective disciplinary measures against inadequate clergy in Norwich diocese under the weak Bishop Rugge. A priest sued by his parishioners in Rugge's court of audience in 1543 was alleged to have neglected services, betrayed confessions, and postponed the extreme unction of a dying girl until after dinner, by which time he was drunk. His case was merely submitted to arbitration.[74] This was to shy away in the most pusillanimous manner from tackling a serious disciplinary problem. This same year Christopher Calthorpe, patron of the Norfolk benefice of Langham Parva, alleged in course of suit in the court of Arches against the rector for neglect of services on Sundays and feast days that the bishop's commissary (to whom the complaint had originally been taken) had refused to compel witnesses to testify against the rector.[75]

---

[72] Above, pp. 29, 33.
[73] NNRO ACT 3B, fo. 105.
[74] Audience *acta* in NCC will register Thyrkyll; sessions of 22 June and 14 Dec. 1543.
[75] BL Add. MS. 38651, fo. 67.

In both dioceses the first Elizabethan bishops were much readier to use the weapon of deprivation than their pre-Marian predecessors had been. Episcopal registers show that at least thirty-seven men in each diocese had benefices with cure taken from them in the first twelve years of Elizabeth's reign.[76] These figures do not include those Marian 'intruders' who lost their livings to the married men whom they had replaced. They never appeared in episcopal registers as deprived. Because the number of benefices in the diocese of Winchester was less than a third of the number in that of Norwich, it is clear that the rate of deprivation was about three times as high in the former diocese as it was in the latter.

Unfortunately the records do not make clear in the majority of cases why deprivations took place. Non-residence and neglect of the cure were the commonest ascertainable reasons; open disaffection towards the new settlement was much less important except in Winchester diocese before Horne's arrival.[77] Probably antipathy towards the new order underlay a number of the cases of non-residence which were dealt with by means of deprivation, especially during the early years. In the diocese of Winchester most of the deprivations took place in the years up to 1563; the process reached its climax during the first two years of Horne's episcopate. In a letter which he wrote to Cecil during his primary visitation, Horne indicated that he meant to proceed against 'wilful' absentees, whom he

---

[76] Gee, *Elizabethan Clergy*, pp. 281-2, 285-6, 290-1, 292. The real numbers of those deprived were higher than these, but how much higher it is difficult to say. A number of sentences of deprivation were recorded in court books and in Matthew Parker's register, but it is not clear exactly how many of these became effective in the end. For some such sentences against men not included in Gee's lists, see HRO CB 12, fos. 94, 97ᵛ; NNRO ACT 9, 25 Mar. 1563, *T. Thakham*; ACT 10, 27 Apr. 1564, *C. Melton*; 28 June 1564, *W. Farlande*. Further deprivations are mentioned by Goodman, 'Winchester Archdeacory', 73, 79, and by Baskerville and Goodman, 'Surrey Incumbents', 106.

[77] Non-residence or neglect were the stated reasons for at least nine of the sentences of deprivation given in the Winchester consistory court in 1561 (HRO CB 12, fos. 84-5, 90-1, 94, 102ᵛ-3, 120ᵛ) and for the sentences of deprivation given against Norwich incumbents as a result of the metropolitical visitation of 1567 (*Registrum Matthei Parker*, ii. 755-7, 760-1); men like John Seaton and Thomas Harding (Gee, *Elizabethan Clergy*, p. 285) lost their livings for refusal to accept the new settlement.

probably suspected of disaffection towards the settlement.[78] In the diocese of Norwich, however, the heaviest concentration of deprivations occurred at the end of the sixties, largely as a result of the metropolitical visitation of 1567 and the jolt it gave Parkhurst.[79]

The early Elizabethan bishops may have been readier than most previous prelates to deprive men of livings, but one gets the impression that the majority of complaints of negligence made by parishioners were still not tackled satisfactorily. The problems faced by Horne, Parkhurst, and their colleagues in the field of pastoral care were far greater than anything encountered by their predecessors within living memory. There was all too often little that could be done about the neglect that sprang from the shortage of clergy or the poverty of livings or chapelries. The supply of clergy was later to improve steadily as it gradually became increasingly clear that the Elizabethan settlement would last. But the augmentation of livings and stipends, never easy, had almost certainly been made much more difficult by the massive shift of advowsons into lay hands.[80] Even the vigorous Bishop Horne seems to have been at a loss to know how to raise the standard of cure in dependent chapelries, if the numerous Winchester consistory court proceedings concerned with the problem are anything to go by. Most of them petered out inconclusively. In only one case do we find clear evidence that steps to augment the incumbent's portion so that he could afford to pay a chaplain were envisaged.[81] Few if any of the complaints made against 'local pluralists' by their parishioners in Norwich diocese resulted in effective action.

PREACHING AND TEACHING

Medieval legislation had provided for the quarterly instruction of the people in the rudiments of their faith. Bishop Fox followed closely the relevant provincial canons in a mandate which he issued to the archdeacon of Winchester in July

---

[78] PRO SP 12/17/23.
[79] Above, pp. 36, 190.
[80] Heath, *English Parish Clergy*, pp. 165-6, 179-80; Hill, *Economic Problems*, pp. 69-70.
[81] HRO CB 12, fo. 82.

1508. This reminded him of his duty to make sure amongst other things that clergy had a sound understanding of the services they recited and that they expounded the articles of faith, ten commandments, gospel precepts, works of mercy, seven deadly sins, seven principal virtues, and seven sacraments to the people in English four times a year. But there is no other evidence in the records of either diocese to show that this aspect of the clergy's work was effectively supervised in the early sixteenth century.[82]

The Reformation brought a new stress on the preaching and teaching functions of the clergy and on the responsibility of ordinaries to see these discharged. Amongst the provisions of successive royal injunctions were the teaching of the Lord's Prayer, articles of faith, and ten commandments to the young (1536); quarterly sermons and the quarterly reading of the royal injunctions (1538) and the reading of homilies every Sunday (1547).[83] The first convincing evidence of attempted enforcement of these duties in the diocese of Norwich is to be found in the earliest surviving court book of the official of the archdeacon of Sudbury, to whom a few incumbents were presented in 1544-5 for failing to provide sermons for a year, or, in one case, two years.[84] In the very much fuller records of the archdeaconry of Norwich, evidence of the impact upon the clergy of the changes of Cromwell's vicegerency and Edward's reign is extremely meagre. A very few parishes complained of their priests' inability to preach or failure to teach the catechism and expound the scriptures; the men concerned seem to have got off lightly.[85] Very little evidence survives of the efforts made by the diocesan authorities at Winchester to see that the clergy fulfilled the duties laid down in the royal injunctions before the arrival of John Ponet in 1551,[86] which (though he was no John Hooper)

---

[82] Lyndwood, *Provinciale*, pp. 49-51, 54-5; HRO Reg. Fox, ii, 97ᵛ-8. Cf. Bowker, *Secular Clergy*, pp. 113-14 (a few reports of neglect from Lincoln diocese).

[83] *Visitation Articles and Injunctions*, ii. 6-7, 37, 40-1, 128-9.

[84] Bury St. Edmund's and West Suffolk Record Office, first act book of archdeaconry of Sudbury, fos. 15, 30, 51, 60.

[85] NNRO AI (1538), Shereford; (1548), Ormesby; (1549), Repps; (1550), Repps, Scoulton.

[86] Though see HRO CB 7, 21 Mar. 1539, *OP (Baker and Newlyn) c. Bentley*.

brought a draught of change into the diocese. After his primary visitation twenty-one clergy or farmers of benefices were noted for failing to provide quarterly sermons, five for failing to teach their parishioners' children the catechism.[87] Most of these men were dismissed with a monition. One curate, summoned before the commissary general because he had served two cures without a licence, was warned to learn the second chapter of the gospel according to Matthew before the next visitation — the sort of task whose assignment was to be favoured by the Elizabethan bishops.[88] Further cases were entered in the act book before the end of Edward's reign. An effort to ensure that sermons were provided, of a type not seen in Norwich archdeaconry before the 1560s, seems to have been undertaken. But it had started late in the day, and does not seem to have been nearly as thorough as the campaign in the neighbouring diocese of Salisbury.[89]

The demands made of the clergy by the royal injunctions of 1559 were more substantial and more precise than those made in previous injunctions. It was hoped that incumbents who were qualified to do so would provide a sermon every month, or at the very least every quarter. The clergy were enjoined to instruct and examine the youth of their parishes in the Lord's Prayer, creed, ten commandments, and catechism and were themselves to be examined in their studies by their ordinaries during visitations. The injunctions which John Parkhurst administered in his primary visitation of Norwich diocese in 1561 were largely based upon those of 1559, but were in some respects stricter or more specific. The clergy were to peruse two chapters of the New Testament each week, and teach the catechism every Sunday. To encourage the clergy to fulfil their teaching functions, Parkhurst added provisions of his own. Young people were not to be married till they could say the articles of faith, the Lord's Prayer and the ten commandments. No one ignorant of the necessary points of religion was to be admitted to communion. The earliest surviving Winchester articles of Elizabeth's reign

[87] HRO CB 9, 16 Oct., 7 Dec. 1551.
[88] Ibid. (16 Oct. 1551?), curate of Hawkley.
[89] Ibid. 18, 19, Nov. 2, 9 Dec. 1552; 14, 20 Jan. 1553; *VCH Wilts.* iii. 30.

show that by 1570 Horne expected those of his clergy who were under the degree of master of arts to be reading a chapter of the Bible in Latin and English every day. He also asked whether monthly sermons were preached against superstition, works of men's device, and papal authority.[90]

The certificates returned in 1561-2 show that some of the elements of the programme sketched out in the early articles and injunctions were quite unrealistic in the conditions which obtained at the beginning of Elizabeth's reign.[91] The certificates provided an assessment of the learning of incumbents by placing them in one of five or six categories. Unfortunately, the ways in which the categories were used varied so markedly from one diocese to another (and sometimes within the same diocese) that this section of the returns must be considered unreliable even for comparative purposes. The degrees men held, even if they tell us little about their pastoral effectiveness, at least provide us with rather more solid information than these subjective assessments. The percentages of men with degrees in the three archdeaconries of Winchester, Surrey and Norwich were 24, 14, and 18 respectively; nearly two-thirds of them were bachelors or masters of arts. Only a fifth of the men with degrees were theologians (though it is worth noting that two-thirds of these theologians were married men, a sure indication by now of their commitment to the new order). The number of graduates among the clergy of southern England was perhaps smaller than it had been on the eve of the Reformation. In Essex the proportion of presentees to livings with degrees had fallen during the years of turmoil and uncertainty from a high point reached in the 1520s to a dismally low level in Mary's reign.[92] The proportion of learned clergy was to increase slowly in the first half of her successor's reign, and as the universities produced more young men of sound faith and learning the Elizabethan bishops were able to impose stricter standards for entry to the ministry. By August 1560

[90] *Visitation Articles and Injunctions*, iii. 9-10, 13-14, 22, 59-60, 98-100; *Articles to be ministred by Robert Bishop of Winchester*, sig. A2-4.

[91] For full references, see above, pp. 156, 183.

[92] Heath, *English Parish Clergy*, p. 81; J. E. Oxley, *The Reformation in Essex to the Death of Mary* (Manchester, 1965), pp. 265-6.

Archbishop Parker already felt able to forbid the ordination of unlearned men hitherto of menial occupation, and by 1564 Parkhurst was reported to be enforcing this mandate in his ordinations at Norwich. In 1571 convocation passed a canon insisting that ordinands be men trained in good letters and versed in the scriptures, and parliament a statute which provided that ordinands must be able to render an account of their faith in Latin, or have special gift or ability to be a preacher.[93]

The proportion of clergy described as preachers in the certificates returned to Archbishop Parker ranged from 8 per cent in the archdeaconry of Norwich (the proportion was very similar in the diocese of Norwich as a whole) to 16 per cent in the archdeaconry of Winchester. But some even of these men were absent from their dioceses, and others preached only in their own parishes. Among the remainder were priests ill affected to the new order, such as John Stokes, prebendary of Norwich, an opponent of the eucharistic doctrine favoured by most of the English bishops, who had to be warned not to preach in the very year that the certificates were returned.[94]

The certificates from Norwich and Winchester suggest that the prospects for effective pastoral reformation were, in the short run at any rate, extremely dim. The clergy qualified to expound Protestant doctrine were too few to meet even the minimum requirements laid down in the royal injunctions of 1547 and 1559. We can calculate, for example, that each of the men listed as preachers in the certificate for the archdeaconry of Norwich would have had to preach nearly ninety sermons a year in order to provide each parish in the archdeaconry with a quarterly sermon. Yet few would have been able to meet this target even amongst the preachers, some of whom were in any case unreliable.

The vigour with which the goal of regular sermons was pursued varied from diocese to diocese, and from one part

[93] *Correspondence of Parker*, 120-1; *Calendar of State Papers, Domestic, 1601-3, Addenda, 1547-65* (1870), 552; *Synodalia*, ed. Cardwell, i. 113; 13 Elizabeth I, c. 12.
[94] Cambridge, Corpus Christi College MS. 97, fo. 198; MS 102, p. 247; NNRO ACT 9, 17 Sept. 1561.

of a diocese to another. Surviving records show that rather more than fifty clergy were presented in the archdeaconry of Norwich in the 1560s for their failure to provide sermons, and a similar number in the archdeaconry of Winchester.[95] Since it seems probable that a far higher proportion of the Winchester records of the early years of Elizabeth's reign has been lost, including all those relating to archidiaconal visitations, it is fairly safe to assume that many more men were presented on this account in Winchester archdeaconry than were presented in Norwich archdeaconry. Nearly 40 per cent of the men presented in the archdeaconry of Norwich were beneficed in the one deanery of Ingworth. Few presentments were made in the remote deanery of Lynn. Enforcement was uneven; the records of Ingworth deanery, where a special effort may have been made on account of its proximity both to Norwich and to the episcopal residence at Ludham, provide the most reliable indications of what was a typical state of affairs. Winchester presentments were more evenly spread over the archdeaconry as a whole, and the action taken upon them seems to have been at once more thorough and more constructive. If the number of sermons provided (either by the incumbent or by visiting preachers) had fallen short of the required four, the incumbent would be warned to compensate for the shortfall in the coming year. Some second offenders were warned to pay substantial sums to charitable uses. The difficulties faced by individual incumbents were however taken into account. Those who held especially poor benefices might be allowed to read homilies even in lieu of the quarterly sermons, or alternatively their parishioners might be given permission to attend other churches in order to hear sermons. A more positive step was to order the clergy of a given deanery to confer together in order to meet the expenses of a deanery preacher, paying according to a rate probably based on the values of livings.[96]

Of the obligations imposed by royal and episcopal

[95] Figure based on NNRO NAAB 1, 2, NAGB 2A, and VIS 1 (1569); HRO CB 17, 25, 27, 29, 31.

[96] HRO CB 17, pp. 48, 58; CB 25, fos. 27, 76, 78, 80; CB 27, pp. 8ᵛ, 85ᵛ; CB 29, fos. 1, 26ᵛ, 29ᵛ.

injunctions, the provision of regular sermons was the one to which the authorities in these two dioceses paid most attention. Even more important was the religious instruction of the young. Many more presentments concerning it seem to have been made in Winchester archdeaconry than in Norwich archdeaconry, but in neither were reports as numerous as those about preaching. This almost certainly reflects the difficulties of supervision and enforcement rather than a satisfactory level of achievement.[97]

The goal of a preaching and teaching ministry could be brought nearer not only by attracting better qualified candidates for ordination but also by the 'in service training' of existing incumbents. Horne in 1570 expected his archdeacons to take stock of the scriptural learning of the clergy of each deanery in every synod, when they were to set new tasks to those below the rank of master of arts. In 1572, the bishop's commissary, visiting the archdeaconry of Winchester during a vacancy, ordered the clergy of each deanery to learn the epistle of Paul to Timothy, and to render an account of it if required. An order for an exercise of the clergy in Winchester archdeaconry, apparently issued by Horne in August 1573, was entered in one of his visitation books. The beneficed clergy were warned to buy Calvin's *Institutes*, and a work by Musculus (his *Common places of Christian Religion*?) and to learn what they had to say about justification by faith. The curates were to buy the New Testament and learn three chapters of St. Matthew's gospel and three chapters of St. Paul's epistle to the Romans in six weeks. Meetings of the clergy were to take place in each deanery every six weeks in future, and in addition the beneficed clergy were to exhibit every quarter original notes of all the sermons preached in their parishes. Early in 1574 the names of at least five clergy who had failed to attend exercises were entered in the consistory act book, and one of them was warned to be more diligent in future and to learn the third chapter of the Epistle

[97] HRO CB 25, fos. 63, 71ᵛ; CB 27, p. 73ᵛ; CB 29, fo. 6; CB 31, fos. 36, 64ᵛ, 75ᵛ; CB 35, fos. 97, 107, 115ᵛ, 121, 154, 156ᵛ, 163ᵛ, 193ᵛ, 220, 225ᵛ, 238, 258; NNRO VIS 1 (1569), fos. 2, 8ᵛ, 13.

to the Romans by the following session.[98] No evidence
survives to show that Parkhurst ever laid down such detailed
instructions for the conduct of an exercise in his diocese,
though an exercise had already been established in Norwich
by 1564; others were set up later at Holt and Fakenham in
north Norfolk, and at Bury in Suffolk. None of these exercises is mentioned in the surviving church court records of
Parkhurst's time. When he sanctioned the establishment of
the Bury exercise in 1573, however, Parkhurst empowered
the moderators to summon 'the hole clergie there aboutes' to
take part, giving his commissary notice of the names of the
disobedient.[99]

In each diocese, the cathedral chapter should ideally have
been in the vanguard of reform, a group of preaching and
teaching clergy whose godly life provided a model for other
ministers. In both dioceses the chapters fell short of this
ideal, but the situation was better at Winchester in the early
years of Elizabeth's reign than it was at Norwich, partly
because more members of the Marian chapter were deprived
at Winchester than at Norwich, and partly because Horne exercised closer supervision over his chapter than did Parkhurst.
Of the Marian chapter of Winchester, six or seven members
were deprived, most of them in 1559. Their replacements
included two future Elizabethan bishops and a distinguished
Marian exile and moderate puritan, Michael Reniger. But
even so, the chapter left much to be desired. Only four of the
eleven prebendaries named in the certificate returned to
Archbishop Parker were listed as preachers.[100] Horne's
expectations of his cathedral clergy were set out in the injunctions he delivered to them in May 1562. A twice weekly
divinity lecture was to be established. The prebendaries
were to see that a sermon was preached in the cathedral every
Sunday, and each prebendary was himself to preach at least
once a year. A library was to be established in the cathedral,

[98] *Articles to be ministred by Robert Bishop of Winchester*, sig. A4^v; HRO VB
11, at the end of each deanery record; VB 12 (13 Aug. 1573?); CB 39, fos. 148,
152, 157^v.
[99] *Letter Book of Parkhurst*, 46-7, 164-5; *Calendar of State Papers, Domestic
1601-3, Addenda 1547-65*, 552; Inner Temple Library Petyt MS. 538/47, fo. 28.
[100] Goodman, 'Archdeaconry of Winchester', 65-6.

and the funds to be set aside for it were specified. The minor canons and choristers were given a programme of biblical reading on which they were to be examined regularly.[101] Just over a year later he carried out a thorough visitation of the cathedral whose record has no parallel at Norwich. He personally examined the choristers and minor canons on their progress in scriptural studies and punished those of the latter whose performance he found unsatisfactory. He charged the chapter with celebrating holy communion less often than they should have done (which they had to admit). Four of the prebendaries then resident admitted that they had not preached in person according to Horne's injunctions; the bishop then laid down in detail who was to preach the sermon each Sunday for the next quarter, and ordered that each preacher certify his fulfilment of the order to him within three days of the due date.[102] Improvement was slow. During his visitation of 1571, Horne charged the minor canons with neglect of their scriptural studies, the prebendaries with continued slackness in preaching and frequent refusal to attend chapter meetings. Two of them did not reside in the close as long as they were supposed to. The dean was charged with failing to attend sermons when at home, with preaching in the cathedral only once a year, and with favouring superstitious religion more than the true religion now received. In the administration of the cathedral and close and their physical maintenance Horne found much else to complain of. In his new injunctions he laid particular stress on the duty of the chapter and other members of the cathedral staff to attend sermons and participate in communion.[103]

Only one member of the Norwich chapter lost his benefice after Elizabeth's accession, but despite their outward acceptance of the Elizabethan settlement, nearly all the Norwich prebendaries of 1559-61 may be described as conservatives or at best as neuters in religion. Only one of the prebendaries named in the return sent to Archbishop Parker was a staunch

Protestant, and he was a non-resident.[104] Only gradually did
the complexion of the chapter change during the following
decade, as old prebendaries died off. One of the new appointees, George Gardiner, an ambitious man ostentatiously
zealous for reformation, reported the slackness of some of his
chapter colleagues to the metropolitical visitors appointed in
1567,[105] and subsequently instigated a royal visitation of the
cathedral by commissioners who reported in January 1569.
Three prebendaries were neither priests nor preachers, there
was no divinity lecture in the cathedral, no library for
students, no statutes. Goods were wasted, and the administration of the chapter lands was in chaos. Injunctions later
given the chapter by Parkhurst in about 1571 covered some
of the defects here reported. He laid down stricter rules for
the administration of chapter property and ordered amongst
other things that the divinity lecture was to be 'read and continued' and that the petty canons should be examined from
time to time by its reader in order to find out how they had
benefited from what he had had to say.[106] But Parkhurst's
injunctions were very much less comprehensive than those
issued by Horne some nine years before. Nothing was said in
them of regular preaching by the prebendaries; there was no
provision for regular examination of the minor canons or
choristers on their progress in scriptural studies. Parkhurst
had completely failed to give his cathedral chapter the firm
lead which Horne had from the beginning set out to provide.
George Gardiner, self-appointed champion of efficiency and
reform within the chapter, pressed his own claim to the
dean's place when it fell vacant in 1573 by alluding to
Parkhurst's 'softe natur' and, despite the bishop's opposition,
Gardiner gained the position he coveted.[107]

Comparisons between cathedral chapters are difficult to
make because numbers of prebends, average prebendal incomes, and the scope allowed to episcopal initiative by the

---

[104] Gee, *Elizabethan Clergy*, p. 281; Cambridge, Corpus Christi College MS.
97, fo. 198. The strong Protestant was Percival Wyborn.
[105] J. Strype, *The Life and Acts of Matthew Parker* (Oxford, 1821), iii. 159–
61.
[106] *Visitation Articles and Injunctions*, iii. 217-18, 316-17.
[107] BL Lansdowne MS. 18/15; *Letter Book of Parkhurst*, pp. 37-42.

statutes varied so much from one cathedral to another. But conservatism, non-residence, and neglect of duties, particularly that of preaching, reduced the effectiveness as potential vehicles of reformation of nearly all cathedral chapters during the early years of Elizabeth. The greatest foundations in England, including York and Lincoln, suffered to a degree from the same malaise as the poorest.[108] Yet amongst the cathedrals of south-eastern England Norwich does seem to have been exceptionally badly run. There may have been even worse abuses in such remote cathedrals as Hereford and Carlisle, but at least the bishops concerned, powerless though they might be to effect reforms, gave early warning of the state of affairs they had encountered.[109] Horne (an erstwhile dean himself) tackled the problems of his cathedral with a vigour which equalled that of the most effective Elizabethan bishops. At the same time he avoided the charges of partisanship and irregularity which went far to nullify the efforts at capitular reform of the impetuous Bishop Curteys of Chichester.[110]

CONCLUSION

The task of supervising the clergy properly was a formidable one to which only the most energetic and zealous of diocesan administrators were equal at the best of times. Routine inquiries laid stress in practice on only a few aspects of the cure of souls. Regular and careful assessment of the efficiency with which all the clergyman's obligations had been discharged was beyond the resources of the church courts. The prevention of unlicensed absenteeism, the punishment of immorality, and the correction of gross negligence were the aims to which church-court judges tended to limit themselves. The Elizabethan church added to these disciplinary objectives the new and positive aim of the provision of regular sermons. In this great enterprise it was hindered not only by the shortcomings of diocesan machinery (grave though these often

---

[108] R. B. Walker, 'Lincoln Cathedral in the Reign of Queen Elizabeth I', *JEH* xi (1960); C. Cross, '"Dens of Loitering Lubbers"; Protestant Protest against Cathedral Foundations, 1540-1640', *SCH* ix (1972), esp. 234-7.

[109] *Letters of the Bishops to the Privy Council*, 20-1; Strype, *Grindal*, p. 125.

[110] Manning, *Religion and Society*, pp. 72-6.

were) but also, in the early years of the reign, by a serious shortage, not only of educated clergy, but of clergy of any sort. It is hardly surprising that the achievement fell far short of the aim.

There can be no doubt that the effective personal participation of the bishop was of very great importance in maintaining proper clerical discipline. Mrs. Bowker has already suggested that a resident bishop brought to bear in his dealings with the more powerful of negligent patrons and well-connected non-resident clergy an authority which his subordinates could not hope to wield. The increase in the variety and number of reported cases of priestly negligence and indecorum in the time of Bishop Atwater of Lincoln (a resident bishop who often visited in person) is strikingly apparent from the figures which Mrs. Bowker has published.[111] Robert Sherburne of Chichester, another early Henrician resident bishop, dealt with clerical failings (particularly non-residence) with unusual thoroughness and severity. Yet he also understood the problems which the clergy faced, and took an exceptional interest in the augmentation of poor vicarages.[112] From his letters and the records of his administration it is clear that Richard Fox, though reluctant to take really severe measures, shared Sherburne's fatherly concern.[113] Of course not all dioceses were fortunate enough to be supervised by bishops like these in the first part of Henry's reign: a number were neglected by non-residents.

The Reformation made episcopal leadership in the field of pastoral care even more important than before. Residence now became the rule, but not all bishops were equally well fitted to deal with the much greater problems which now confronted them. No other bishop matched the example set by John Hooper at Gloucester. Amongst the outstanding features of his ministry were a visitation accompanied by inquiries of unprecedented thoroughness concerning clerical learning, exceptionally close supervision of his consistory court, and a series of impromptu journeys by means of which

---

[111] Bowker, *Secular Clergy*, pp. 19-21, 114, 116.
[112] Lander, 'Church Courts and the Reformation', pp. 223-5.
[113] Above, pp. 21, 31, 175.

Hooper gained first-hand acquaintance with the problems of his diocese.[114] Though he was by no means Hooper's equal, the extent of his personal participation in visitations (especially of his cathedral), his interest in correctional proceedings, his readiness to wield the weapon of deprivation against non-residents, and his furtherance of clerical scriptural studies through synods and exercises clearly enable us to set Horne in the group of most effective early Elizabethan bishops which also included Grindal, Jewel, and Cox. Ponet, too, though he was not at Winchester very long, made an effort to secure the preaching of sermons which was not matched at Norwich in the time of the conservative and absentee Thirlby. John Parkhurst, however, though a man of integrity and goodwill who was concerned that cures should be well served, proved unequal to the task before him.

Parkhurst's problems were exacerbated by the diocesan routines and structure which he inherited. The medium-sized diocese of Winchester, visited annually, was far easier to control than the large diocese of Norwich, visited every six or seven years. Where it is possible to compare the operation of the archidiaconal jurisdiction with that of the diocesan, one gets the impression that the latter was the more efficient. Clergy suspected of sexual lapses were more effectively dealt with in the consistory courts than in the court of the archdeaconry of Norwich.[115] Parishioners' complaints about the negligence of their clergy were more likely to be followed up if brought to the attention of bishop or chancellor during a visitation than if they were made in the archdeaconry court.[116] It follows that greater over-all efficiency was achieved in the diocese where central control was tighter. Although the records dealing with pluralism and non-residence are insufficiently complete for either diocese to enable one to produce a convincing comparison between them, it does seem that they were more closely monitored in the diocese of Winchester than in that of Norwich. In Elizabeth's reign more vigorous efforts seem to have been made in the former than

---

[114] Price, 'Gloucester Diocese under Hooper', 77–8, 99–104.
[115] Above, p. 179.
[116] Above, pp. 196–7.

in the latter diocese to enforce the provision of quarterly sermons by the clergy.[117]

The ruler of a large diocese had to be able to delegate a large part of his pastoral responsibilities to trustworthy subordinates. Parkhurst was perhaps exceptionally unlucky in his choices[118] and in his inability to replace archdeacons who were not of his choosing, but in other dioceses too it proved difficult to find lesser officials who could be counted upon to enforce official policies efficiently. Bishops such as Bentham of Lichfield and Cooper of Lincoln took a close interest in their clergy's discharge of their pastoral duties, but both had perforce to leave much of the work of supervision to local officers. Bentham saw this clearly, stressed the archdeacons' responsibilities and attempted to reinvigorate the office of rural dean.[119] On the other hand Richard Cox of Ely was able to achieve through synods and visitations an exceptionally close supervision of his parochial clergy. The smallness of his diocese facilitated his drive to secure regular teaching of the catechism as well as his campaign against non-residence, more ruthless and effective even than Horne's.[120]

Some of the most intractable pastoral problems were due to defects in the parochial structure. In this respect our two dioceses occupied a middling position. In parts of the diocese of Norwich there were exceptionally large numbers of small, poor parishes: in that of Winchester there were many large parishes in which dependent chapelries were pastoral units of great importance. In both dioceses a number of parishes were inadequately served for some time after Elizabeth's accession. In some dioceses, such as those of Bath and Wells and Ely, the numbers of unserved parishes and chapelries were reduced more swiftly than they were in our two dioceses, in large part because the distribution of pastoral units was more satisfactory.[121] The university of Cambridge lay in the latter

---

[117] Above, pp. 183-6, 203-5.

[118] Above, pp. 24-5, 53.

[119] M. R. O'Day, 'Thomas Bentham: A Case Study in the Problems of the Early Elizabethan Episcopate', *JEH* xxiii (1972), esp. 148-52.

[120] Heal, 'Bishops of Ely', 113-15, 116, 133-4.

[121] H. N. Birt, *The Elizabethan Religious Settlement* (1907), pp. 376, 388, 391.

diocese, and from very early in the reign Bishop Cox was able at the examination of ordinands to insist on much higher standards than most other bishops.[122] But in poorer and remoter areas of the country, the situation was much worse than it was in either of the dioceses here studied. Lancashire, for example, a county of very large parishes and numerous dependent chapelries, had been ill served even before the Reformation; a number of the parochial benefices had fallen into the hands of non-resident pluralists, while many of the chapelries afforded too poor a living to attract any save the less well-qualified members of the clerical proletariat. Here the shortage of reliable clergy early in Elizabeth's reign was so severe that episcopal efforts to reform the ministry could only begin a generation later than in the south.[123] There was a limit to what bishops and diocesan officials could do, and a fundamental reform of parochial structure lay outside their power. After the Reformation the tightening grip of lay patrons made it increasingly difficult even to tinker with the existing structure.

[122] Heal, 'Bishops of Ely', 108, 124-5.
[123] Haigh, *Reformation and Resistance*, pp. 26-45, 239-40.

8

THE COURTS AND THE MAINTENANCE
OF RELIGIOUS UNIFORMITY

Before the Reformation and for a long time after it the church courts played an important part in the correction of those who failed to participate in the prescribed observances of the national church, or challenged its doctrines. The Reformation, however, changed not only the national faith but also the official attitude towards those who dissented from established doctrines or failed to participate in prescribed observances and the role of the church courts in their control and punishment.

Before the Reformation, those found guilty of teaching contrary to the articles of faith or the doctrines of the Roman church, especially those concerning the sacraments and such practices as the adoration of images and the performance of pilgrimages, were held to be heretics. They were ordered to abjure their errors, and if they failed to do so, or later relapsed into them, they were sentenced to death. Those who failed to take part in obligatory rites and observances also incurred the suspicion of heresy, and might well be called upon to perform fairly severe penances even if they cleared themselves completely.

After the Reformation the penalties of heresy were suffered only by a very few extremists who rejected certain basic doctrines held by both Catholics and Protestants. The act of supremacy of 1559 laid down that nothing was henceforth to be determined to be heresy unless so judged by authority of the scriptures and by the earliest general councils, or by

parliament with the assent of the clergy in convocation.[1] The
main challenges to the settlement established came not from
extremist heresy but from the adherents of the old faith and
from those within the church who wished to carry the process
of reformation further, and these challenges took shape
gradually. The punishments incurred by opponents of the
church settlement whose objections to it were not in the new
sense 'heretical' varied in severity according to the vigour
with which their opposition was expressed. They ranged from
spiritual penalties and small fines (often not levied in practice)
for failure to attend church to large fines or imprisonment
for open criticism of the established order of service or maintenance of an alternative form. Only those who brought the
authority of the crown in question by refusal to accept the
royal supremacy were liable to suffer death, and they not as
heretics but as traitors, whose punishment did not belong to
the church courts.

The Protestant Reformation reduced and simplified the
observances whose performance was obligatory for every
orthodox christian. Before it, participation in the eucharist,
preceded by confession, was supposed to take place three
times a year, once at the very least. Every faithful Christian
partook of the sacraments of baptism, confirmation, and
extreme unction, and sought the blessing of the church upon
his marriage. He attended mass with due regularity. Within
the church the parishioner was supposed to bear himself
decorously, show due reverence towards the sacrament of the
altar and the holy name, participate in such ceremonies as the
kiss of peace during the eucharist, and receive the sacramental
holy bread. The duty of avoiding all corporal labour save
what was absolutely necessary upon Sundays and a number
of feast days was strictly enjoined. Fasting was obligatory
during Lent, the Ember days, and on the eves of the major
feasts. A cycle of other rituals of greater or less importance
marked the passage of the Christian year. As we have already
seen, the parishioner had also to pay a wide range of tithes and
offerings, and sometimes the act of offering assumed the character of a ritual, as when candles were offered on Candlemas

[1] 1 Elizabeth I. c. 1.

Day. Fulfilment of the basic duties remained after the Reformation the most readily observable evidence of orthodoxy, but they were now fewer and simpler. Participation in the eucharist was still supposed to take place three times a year, but auricular confession ceased to be obligatory, only the eucharist and baptism retained the status of sacraments, and the numbers of holy days and ceremonies were greatly reduced.

During the Reformation the church courts continued to play a part in the enforcement of religious uniformity, but their activity in this field was placed under important limitations. The duty of ecclesiastical judges to deal with religious dissidence had been laid down in the first place by the common law of the church and reiterated in provincial canons.[2] In the reigns of Richard II and his two successors, when heresy had for the first time manifested itself as an important problem with political implications, the powers of ordinaries to deal with it, and the duty of secular authorities to co-operate in its suppression had been set out in a series of parliamentary statutes.[3] The most important of these, the notorious statute *De Haeretico Comburendo* (2 Henry IV, c. 15) covered all teachers of heresy and writers and keepers of heretical books. It empowered bishops to arrest suspected heretics on the basis of fame alone and to detain them in prison until they purged themselves or abjured heretical doctrine. Heretics refusing to abjure, or relapsing after abjuration, were to be handed over to the secular court for execution in accordance with the canon law. Other convicted persons not canonically liable to capital punishment might be kept in the bishop's prison as long as might seem expedient. Sheriffs and chief municipal officers were to aid the spiritual judges against heretics at all stages. The statute 2 Henry V, c. 7 drew a wide range of secular judges still further into the work of suppressing heresy by empowering them to initiate inquiries as to heretics and their supporters.

No further changes were made in the statute law relating

---

[2] Especially those issued under Thomas Arundel in order to counter the Wycliffite threat: see Lyndwood, *Provinciale*, pp. 288-305.

[3] The first of these, passed in 1382, was 5 Richard II, st. 2, c. 5.

to the punishment of heresy till 1534, when the statute 25 Henry VIII, c. 14 repealed the act *De Haeretico Comburendo*. The nub of this new act lay in its provisions that ecclesiastical courts were in future to act only upon a presentment made by two witnesses, and that suspects were to answer in open court. No longer was it possible to arrest simply upon suspicion. An even more substantial reduction in the powers of ecclesiastical courts soon followed. The act of six articles, which inflicted a range of new penalties for the offences which it covered more severe than those hitherto incurred under canon law, was to be enforced by commissions appointed in each county which were to keep sessions at least four times a year, inquire by the oaths of twelve men, and receive accusations made by two men. The common-law procedure followed in cases of felony was adopted. The ecclesiastical judges of the diocese were to be among the commissioners appointed; but the independent role of ecclesiastical jurisdiction (placed on a level, in this respect, with the jurisdiction of the justices of the peace) was now restricted to preliminary inquiry.[4]

The statute 34-5 Henry VIII, c. 1 *for the Advancement of the true Religion* provided for the punishment of a wide range of miscellaneous offenders, including those who printed, sold or kept certain heretical books or opposed doctrines set forth by the king, plebeian readers of the Bible, and those who expounded it without authorization. Offenders might be convicted before two councillors, before commissioners appointed by the king or before the ordinary and two justices of the peace. Within a year the law was to be modified in a way which further whittled down ordinaries' power to deal with heresy. The statute 35 Henry VIII, c. 5, seeking to remedy the evils of secret accusation, laid down that no man was to be arraigned for heresy save on presentment by twelve men before commissioners, justices of the peace, or justices of oyer and terminer.

In 1547, the very first statute of Edward VI's reign empowered justices of the peace to proceed against those who spoke contemptuously of the sacrament of the altar upon the

---

[4] 31 Henry VIII, c. 14.

oaths and depositions of at least two persons and to punish them by fine and imprisonment upon the verdict of a quarter session jury. They were to require the ordinary to appear at the proceedings in person or by deputy to give expert advice. In the same parliament all other legislation against heresy was swept away, and for over a year this remained the only act on the statute book by means of which erroneous opinions might be suppressed.

The Edwardian acts of uniformity[5] provided that clergy refusing to use the Books of Common Prayer and those who spoke in derogation of the Books or prevented ministers from using them should be punished either by certain secular justices or by ecclesiastical judges. The second act laid down for the first time in statutory form the basic duty of attendance at services and sermons, which was to be enforced by ordinaries by means of ecclesiastical censures. Participation in other rites than those prescribed was however to be punished by lay justices. No legislation in force during Edward's reign provided for the capital punishment of heretics. This did not however prevent the burning of two extremist religious dissidents one of whom denied the divinity, the other the humanity of Christ. They were punished by commissioners appointed by the crown by virtue of a royal power to punish heretics older than the anti-Lollard legislation.[6]

Mary's first parliament entrusted the punishment of those who interrupted the celebration of mass or behaved irreverently towards the sacrament of the altar to the justices of the peace. Her third, however, restored the anti-Lollard laws, which now facilitated the most intense religious persecution ever witnessed in England. In this, the ecclesiastical courts worked more closely with lay officials than ever before, and many of those who died were condemned not by ecclesiastical judges acting on their own but by joint commissions established by the Marian government, which in this respect was following Henrician and Edwardian precedents. These commissions included laymen connected with the government,

---

[5] 2 & 3 Edward VI, c. 1; 5 & 6 Edward VI, c. 1.
[6] Maitland, *Roman Canon Law in the Church of England*, pp. 158–79; Jordan, *Threshold of Power*, pp. 327–30.

bishops, and common and ecclesiastical lawyers. The powers with which those named were entrusted varied in detail from one commission to another, but they were usually enabled to inquire of heresies and a wide range of associated offences, to fine, imprison, and to bind to appear by recognizance.[7]

The development of royal commissions to enforce religious uniformity reached its furthest point under Elizabeth I. The act of supremacy (1 Elizabeth I, c. 1) placed on a statutory basis the Queen's power to delegate the exercise of her ecclesiastical jurisdiction. Her first commission (closely modelled on one of Mary's) was issued the same year to a mixed body of churchmen and laymen. Separate commissions were later to be issued covering the northern province and individual dioceses.[8] These played an important part in dealing with conservative opposition to the religious settlement; later they were used as a weapon with which to counter the puritan threat as well.

This statute also repealed, this time for good, the medieval heresy legislation revived by Mary. By the Elizabethan act of uniformity (1 Elizabeth, c. 2), as by its predecessor of 1552, absence from church on Sundays and holy days was to be punished by means of ecclesiastical censures; a new provision was that churchwardens were to levy 1s. to the use of the poor from each individual for each absence. The bishops were urged to be diligent in executing the act and authorized to punish all offences specified in it, which included participation in alternative forms of worship. The passage of the thirty-nine articles by convocation in 1563 may be said to have completed the Elizabethan settlement. An act of 1571 laid down that clergy who had undergone a Catholic ordination, and all ministers subsequently to be admitted to benefices with cure, should subscribe those of the articles which concerned doctrine and read them publicly, on pain of deprivation. Clergy maintaining views contrary to those set forth in the articles were also made liable to deprivation.[9]

---

[7] 1 Mary I, st. 2, c. 3; 1 & 2 Philip and Mary, c. 6; Usher, *Rise and Fall of the High Commission*, pp. 20-5; Foxe, *Acts and Monuments*, viii. 301-3.
[8] Usher, op. cit., pp. 27-31, 287-8.
[9] 13 Elizabeth I, c. 12.

Most of the crown's major attempts to impose uniformity of doctrine and practice within the church after the break with Rome were supported by statute. But royal proclamations, too, had an important part to play in the maintenance of due uniformity. The most significant proclamations from our point of view were those which gave fresh impetus to the church courts' work. Perhaps the most important of these was the proclamation of 1530 which spoke of the danger from Lutheran heresy and reiterated the provisions of the medieval anti-Lollard legislation. Its issue made clear the determination of Thomas More, the recently appointed chancellor, to repress heresy.[10] Another proclamation, incorporating Mary I's injunctions of March 1554, spoke of the diverse as yet uncorrected enormities committed in the realm under Edward VI and commanded the bishops to execute the queen's injunctions without fear of the laws, or of being noted as presumptuous.[11] Even after the revival of the statute of 1401, the Marian government felt that the courts needed further encouragement, as is shown by a proclamation of June 1555 which complained that the statute had been disregarded. This proclamation was particularly concerned with the threat posed by heretical literature, and empowered both ordinaries and lay officials to search the houses of those suspected of keeping unorthodox books.[12] Elizabeth, too, felt the need on occasion to urge the ecclesiastical judges to greater activity in the enforcement of her church settlement. In October 1573, for instance, the government issued a proclamation, directed primarily against the puritans, which deplored attacks made on the Prayer Book, and the employment of alternative rites. The queen, so the proclamation alleged, plainly understood 'the negligence of the bishops and other magistrates' to be responsible for these disorders, and after ordering the more rigorous enforcement of the act of uniformity, it concluded with a 'most special

[10] *Tudor Royal Proclamations*, ed. P. L. Hughes and J. F. Larkin (1964-9), i. 181-6; for its correct date see Elton, *Policy and Police*, p. 218; R. W. Heinze, *The Proclamations of the Tudor Kings* (Cambridge, 1976), pp. 132-3. See ibid., pp. 255-6 for some examples of enforcement of Henrician proclamations concerning religion by ecclesiastical judges.

[11] *Tudor Royal Proclamations*, ii. 35-8.

[12] Ibid. 57-60.

and earnest charge' to all ecclesiastical judges to proceed severely against offenders.[13]

Many of the duties laid upon clergy and people by the development of the crown's religious policy were set out in the royal injunctions of 1536, 1538, 1547, 1554, and 1559 for whose enforcement ecclesiastical judges were primarily responsible. Their execution was not however always entrusted to ordinaries alone: an injunction of 1538, for instance, ordered that those who hindered the reading or preaching of the Word of God were to be reported to certain specified lay authorities, perhaps because the vicegerent doubted whether the predominantly conservative body of ecclesiastical judges had the power or the will to take appropriate measures. In March 1554 Mary I ordered her bishops *inter alia* to work hard to suppress heresies and unlawful publications which engendered hatred and discord amongst the people, to see that ceremonies were observed, and to enforce church attendance. The most comprehensive Protestant injunctions were those of 1559, which forbade amongst other things the maintenance of heresy or false doctrine, rash and contentious discussion of the scriptures, the use of abusive terms such as 'papist' or 'schismatic', and the interruption of services or sermons.[14]

It is clear that ecclesiastical judges continued during the years of the Reformation to bear much of the responsibility for the maintenance of religious uniformity. But the scope of their jurisdiction was reduced. After 1534, except during the brief interlude of the Marian reaction, the hitherto dreaded power of ecclesiastical judges to condemn heretics to death was restricted. Successive governments entrusted lay agents with much of the burden of enforcing the religious policies of the crown, either by including them in mixed commissions for the exercise of its ecclesiastical jurisdiction or by creating concurrent lay jurisdiction over offences hitherto or ecclesiastical cognisance. It was also in this area of their *ex officio* activity that the weakening of the moral authority of ecclesiastical judges mattered most. It was difficult for zealous

[13] Ibid. 379-81.
[14] *Visitation Articles and Injunctions*, ii. 1-11, 34-43, 103-30, 322-9; iii. 1-29, esp. 20-4.

Protestants to trust or respect judges who, though sufficiently
pliant to serve regimes which enforced sharply opposing
religious policies, seemed happiest when they were the agents
of reaction. Until well after Elizabeth's accession the majority
of chancellors and commissaries were men of this stamp.[15]

THE MAINTENANCE OF THE OLD FAITH

The church courts' role in the preservation of religious uniformity was so profoundly modified by the Reformation that
it is as well to consider separately the part they played in
maintaining uniformity under the old faith and the ways in
which they were used in support of the new. The years when
the courts were helping to uphold the old faith may be
divided into three main phases. The first ended in 1534 when
the passage of the act for the punishment of heresy curtailed
the courts' powers. The climate of the years of Cromwell's
supremacy was unfavourable to the exercise even of such
powers as they retained. Even when in 1539 an act was
passed which was much more seriously intended as a weapon
against heretics than the act of 1534, it all but ended for the
time being the autonomy of the church courts in this field.
Under Queen Mary, on the other hand, whose reign may be
considered the third phase, the courts received from the lay
power support for their work in the suppression of heresy
even more wholehearted than that given them in the days of
the Lancastrian kings.[16]

Before the Reformation as after it those who appeared
before the church courts as active dissenters from established
orthodoxy were normally few compared with those whose
careless neglect of their duties had got them into trouble.
Thus during proceedings which followed the episcopal visitation of the archdeaconry of Winchester in 1527 at least
nineteen people were charged with failing to come to church,
four with neglect of Sabbath observance, one with non-
reception of the sacrament of the altar and one with non-
participation in a Rogationtide procession.[17] Over half of

---

[15] On conservatism of chancellors, see above, pp. 24–5.

[16] On the relevant legislation, see above, pp. 216–8.

[17] HRO CB 4, fos. 76v–8, 79v, 83, 90v, 94–6v, 100v, 102v–3v, 113, 131v,
133v–4, 141.

those presented received penances, but no charges of heresy resulted. Most of the pre-Reformation correctional records of the diocese of Norwich have perished. But the fact that a man of the diocese incurred a suspicion of heresy in 1511 simply through failing to confess or receive the sacrament at Easter in 1509, and the stiff penace assigned in 1522 to one woman, despite her claim that her son had been ill, for frequent absences from church and non-participation in the eucharist at Easter, suggest that routine discipline was by no means lax.[18]

Some more serious offenders against religious orthodoxy were however dealt with on the eve of the Reformation at both Norwich and Winchester. The body of evidence which survives at Winchester is much the more complete. Here the most important *acta* in heresy cases seem to have been recorded neatly in the episcopal register, a practice not apparently followed at Norwich. The recorded cases were heard in the consistory courts, on visitation or in episcopal residences. The chancellor took the leading part in most proceedings.

In most cases the preliminary investigation or report which furnished the material upon which the articles objected to the suspect were to be based has left no trace. Information came to the authorities by presentment during visitations, by means of private report or accusation, by common fame, and through inquiry in the course of investigation. Some of the heretics dealt with during Bishop Nykke's last visitation of 1532 had presumably been presented in the normal way. One female heretic of Wymondham (Norfolk) proceeded against in the consistory court in 1519 was accused by a man who had been closely acquainted with her for over twenty years. Two important groups of heretics in Winchester diocese may have come to Bishop Fox's notice because he was given information about key members of them by other bishops. Some expressions of unorthodox opinion were too public to be ignored. A Norfolk priest proceeded against in 1521 had been rash enough to voice his opinion that personal tithes were not due by divine law in the presence of a number of his colleagues, who had probably assembled for a visitation.

[18] NNRO ACT 1, fos. 151^V, 168^V; ACT 4A, fo. 28^V.

Thomas Bilney, returning to Norwich in 1531, courted martyrdom through his preaching. Additional information often came to light in the course of proceedings, since suspects were normally asked to reveal the names of all other heretics of whom they knew, especially of those from whom they had received their opinions. Under interrogation, one man proceeded against by Bishop Nykke in 1532 described how three other men had uttered unorthodox views.[19]

Most of the suspects who were convicted in the two dioceses before 1534 confessed their delicts, though not always at once. One man who came before Nykke during his 1532 visitation would at first make no direct answer, whereupon he was sent back to the episcopal prison (in which heretics were normally kept during preliminary investigations). He had changed his mind by the following day. Since a suspect could be condemned on the basis of his own confession, readiness to admit charges made the formal production of witnesses superfluous. The name of a witness, at first included in the last article against another heretic dealt with by Nykke in 1532, was later struck out, probably because as it turned out the defendant's confession made it unnecessary to call him. Whether or not witnesses were produced in the majority of cases, their depositions were seldom included in the record.[20]

Not all defendants were convicted. At least one Winchester suspect purged himself and was warned to avoid in future two things which had occasioned suspicion: the possession of certain books in English and contact with another suspect.[21]

The parts of the heresy process best illustrated by the surviving evidence are the abjuration and penance. Most of the heretics whose cases are recorded in the act books were ready to abjure their opinions after making their confessions. After his abjuration in court the heretic was absolved and enjoined a solemn public penance, often to be performed on two days. If a double penance was enjoined, part of it was often to be

---

[19] NNRO ACT 3A, fos. 67ᵛ-9ᵛ; ACT 4B, fos. 34, 35ᵛ-7; DEP 3, fos. 89, 171ᵛ-2ᵛ; Thomson, *Later Lollards*, pp. 88-9; Foxe, *Acts and Monuments*, iv. 642.
[20] But for exceptions see NNRO ACT 3A, fo. 69ᵛ, ACT 4B, fo. 35ᵛ.
[21] HRO CB 4, fos. 174, 177, 178.

performed in a local market-place, the other part in the heretic's own church. The penance was to be explained to the onlookers by the penitent, or a priest, or both. Winchester penitents sometimes received fustigation at the four corners of the market-place. They usually bore faggots, and sometimes heretical tracts and scriptural translations which at the end of the ceremony they threw onto a fire. Abjured heretics were often restricted to their house or parish for the future, ordered to present themselves regularly to the diocesan authorities, and forbidden to leave the diocese without permission. In addition they sometimes had to carry a faggot badge embroidered on their clothes. One Southwark woman (the first suspect known to have been dealt with by Bishop Fox) had to have the letter 'H' branded on her hand.[22]

In the first quarter of the century, some half-dozen people were burnt in the diocese of Norwich, and at least four others abjured heretical opinions or performed penance, while in the diocese of Winchester one man was burnt and abjuration was imposed on eleven other people.[23] The majority of those involved were proceeded against in the years 1510–14, years which saw a drive against heretics in a number of dioceses. The opinions most characteristic of later medieval Lollardy, hostility towards the sacrament of the altar, or at least the church's doctrines concerning it, dislike of images, and reluctance to attribute special powers to priests, in particular that of absolution, were well represented amongst the suspects.

The influence of the teaching of continental reformers is extremely difficult to distinguish from that of the native heretical tradition in the surviving records of the 1520s. In 1526 a Suffolk gentleman named Anthony Yaxley renounced certain heretical opinions, the most important of which seems to have been that every layman was a priest and had sufficient authority to preach, hear confessions and

[22] HRO Reg. Fox, ii, fo. 87; iii, fos. 71, 73; iv, fo. 19; v, fo. 166; NNRO ACT 3A, fo. 67ᵛ; ACT 4B, fos. 36–7.
[23] Blomefield, *Norfolk*, iii. 182, 193; Foxe, *Acts and Monuments*, iv. 773; Thomson, *Later Lollards*, p. 136; NNRO ACT 3A, fo. 67ᵛ; ACT 3B, fo. 226; ACT 4A, fo. 2; HRO Reg. Fox, ii, fos. 87–8; iii, fos. 70, 72–6ᵛ; iv, fo. 19; v, fos. 108ᵛ–9.

absolve.[24] Yaxley was superior in social status to the usual
Lollard, and his work as a common lawyer may have brought
him into contact with a wider world in which new doctrines
were circulating. His most important opinions have the
appearance of being a distorted version of the Lutheran
doctrine of the priesthood of all believers. But we cannot be
sure. As early as 1514, a Hampshire heretic had had to renounce very similar opinions: that a priest had no power but
to preach, teach and give good advice, as all other men had,
for all men should know God's scriptures.[25] Had a really
thorough investigation been carried out in either Winchester
or Norwich diocese during the twenties, it would probably
have revealed, as did proceedings supervised by the vicar
general of the bishop of London in 1527-8, that the great
majority of heretics had as yet been barely influenced by new
ideas.[26] Nevertheless, the focus of the bishops' attention
shifted towards new sources of heretical doctrine in the
twenties. Nykke claimed in a letter written in 1530 that the
two major sources of heretical ideas were books which had
infected people living near the sea, and Gonville Hall in
Cambridge.[27] The Winchester authorities paid most attention to foreigners and the inhabitants of ports in the last
years before the Reformation.

Nykke's preoccupation with the danger from Cambridge
may have dated from 1521, when Robert Butteler, vicar of
Mattishall Burgh (Norfolk), already under investigation because of his expression of unorthodox views on personal
tithes, confessed that he had had books by Luther which he
had already surrendered in Cambridge.[28] The most important
Cambridge man to influence the diocese during the twenties
was Thomas Bilney. His purpose as a preacher was to remind
his audience that Christ had come to earth to save sinners,
though his fierce attacks on abuses connected with saints'

[24] E. T. Musket, 'The Recantation of Anthony Yaxley', *East Anglian Notes
and Queries*, n. s., iii (1887), 380-1.
[25] HRO Reg. Fox, iii, fo. 73v.
[26] J. E. Oxley, *The Reformation in Essex to the Death of Mary* (Manchester,
1965), pp. 7-14.
[27] BL Cotton MS. Cleo. E v, fo. 360.
[28] NNRO ACT 3B, fos. 214v, 219; ACT 4A, fo. 2; DEP 3, fos. 89, 171v-2v.

cults may have made a more powerful impression on some of his hearers. At least two preaching tours took him into Norwich diocese. In about 1526 Wolsey made him swear not to preach Luther's opinions, and in November 1527 he was tried before Bishop Tunstall of London, convicted of heresy and forced to abjure. In 1531 he returned to Norwich and there, in August, he was burnt as a relapsed heretic.[29] Shortly beforehand Nykke had been hoping to secure an abjuration from Nicholas Shaxton, another Cambridge man.[30] Yet the ten suspects whom Nykke unearthed in his last visitation (in 1532) were nearly all humble men. The only specified offences (the expression of hostility towards images, and fast breaking) could have been committed by Lollards a century earlier, though one of the two chief offenders claimed that he owed his views to Bilney.[31]

In the diocese of Winchester the more important suspects who attracted the attention of the diocesan authorities between 1525 and 1534 were either foreigners or inhabitants of ports. Two foreigners who appeared before the courts in 1527-8 had both read the scriptures in their own tongues. A German or Dutch servant living in Southwark had ridiculed the sacrament of confirmation, and a German living in Winchester had denied the prescription by divine law of confession and fasting, the value of prayer to saints, and the existence of purgatory. He had said that priests should get married and work for their livings.[32] Two cases originated in Southampton. One of the men involved, John Caplyn, possibly a leading citizen of the town in later years, was charged in 1529 with bringing back from Antwerp an English translation of, or book about, the gospels and two of Tyndale's works.[33] The other, an illiterate man who had come from Rye in Sussex, had denied that the sacramental wine was the blood of Christ.[34]

[29] Foxe, *Acts and Monuments*, iv. 621-2, 624-32, 635-6, 641-3; Dickens, *English Reformation*, pp. 79-81.
[30] Foxe, *Acts and Monuments*, iv. 679-80.
[31] NNRO ACT 4B, fos. 34, 35ᵛ, 36-7, 93ᵛ.
[32] HRO Reg. Fox, v, fos. 122, 165-6; CB 4, fo. 169.
[33] Ibid., fo. 187; *VCH Hants* iii. 483, 503, 508, 527.
[34] *Reg. Gardiner et Poynet*, 30-3.

Between 1526 and 1534, despite growing episcopal concern with the threat posed by foreign heresy and the sharp hostility towards unorthodoxy shown by Thomas More after be became chancellor in 1529, persecution in the two dioceses appears to have been far milder than it had been in the first five years of Henry's reign. The one burning of this period in either diocese (Thomas Bilney's) was attended by difficulties of which a full account fortunately survives.[35] Bilney, a once convicted heretic, had returned to the diocese of Norwich to preach doctrines he had already abjured. His action was one which the diocesan authorities could not possibly ignore, and it sealed his fate in the eyes of the church. Nevertheless, Mayor Rede of Norwich was apparently accused of obstructing due process by insisting that the chancellor must accept Bilney's vague and ambiguous replies to questions put to him in the form in which they were first made and by trying to take Bilney into his charge when the latter appealed to the king. This appeal was quite irregular, but Rede had supposedly found a pretext for his action in the king's 'new title', that is the supreme headship of the church, given qualified recognition by convocation in February 1531. Finally, when Bilney had been condemned and handed over to the secular arm, the sheriff of Norwich failed to tell Chancellor Pelles when the execution would take place, probably in order to frustrate his attempt to secure a public recantation. At the stake, when Bilney had spoken to the people, Pelles urged him to read the recantation. Bilney probably read at least part of it, possibly the whole, but in a very low voice, before making a more audible declaration of his own devising. The actions of the secular arm had diminished the intended salutary effect of the execution. Rede's behaviour should probably be attributed to anticlericalism rather than to any sympathy with heresy as such. He had had a brush with a previous chancellor of Norwich,[36] and his service in parliament would have made him aware of the anticlerical feeling in the Commons, encouraged for his own ends by the king. It is in fact hardly surprising that ordinaries under pressure from king and

---

[35] Foxe, *Acts and Monuments*, iv, appendices i–vi (unpaginated).
[36] PRO Star Chamber, 2/34/124.

parliament should have hesitated to arouse popular antagonism by large-scale proceedings against heretics. Even before the first statutory limitations on the powers of the church courts in this field had been enacted, the last serious attempt to stem the spread of heresy before the break with Rome had gone off at half cock.

Between 1534 and Henry's death there were no abjurations or burnings in either diocese of which record remains in the act books or registers, though Foxe tells us that three Suffolk men were burnt in 1537-8 and two more in 1545. These last two executions were, however, apparently the work of a joint commission of laymen and clergy set up in accordance with the provisions of the act of six articles. Three heretics were executed just outside Southwark in the spring of 1540, but there is nothing to show that any of them had previously been connected with Winchester diocese.[37]

In this period a number of people, mostly laymen, who had expressed unorthodox opinions or neglected observances were presented to the church courts in the two dioceses. Failure to offer the customary candle on Purification Day, to receive holy bread or ashes, to kneel before the cross or to confess, fast breaking, and repeated absences from church were the commoner offences. One man had denied transubstantiation, another the existence of the devil, a third had read Tyndale's banned translation of the New Testament.[38] Offences which, a few years earlier, would have been followed by the most searching investigation now led to the imposition of a simple penance or purgation with three or four compurgators. No effective action at all seems to have been taken in many cases. The man who came nearest to performing a heretic's penance was one of the two clergymen who was proceeded against in Norwich diocese in the thirties for opposing the adoration of images. He was ordered to confess his errors before his parishioners and to make obeisance to

---

[37] Foxe, *Acts and Monuments*, v. 253-4, 530-3; *Reg. Gardiner et Poynet*, x-xi.

[38] HRO CB 7, 1 Apr. 1536; 23 Feb., 9 Mar. 1537; 9 Mar., 7 Nov., 7 Dec 1538; 7 June 1539; 27 Oct., 19, 26 Nov. 1540; 25 June, 2 July 1541; 18 Feb., 3 Mar. 1542; Bury and West Suffolk Record Office, first act book of the archdeaconry of Sudbury, fos. 4v, 12v, 15, 33v, 34, 35v, 39v, 43, 49v, 59.

the cross whose adoration he had tried to prevent.[39] In 1546 the radical clergyman Thomas Hancock, then curate of Amport (Hants) was charged by the chancellor's deputy with an implicit denial of transubstantiation. But he suffered nothing worse than suspension from his cure.[40] During this time of growing religious uncertainty the church courts in the two dioceses ceased to play an effective part in eradicating heresy, and even their enforcement of routine observances was carried out more half-heartedly than hitherto.

During this period several of those who expressed unorthodox opinions were proceeded against by lay courts, especially if their utterances seemed likely to arouse public controversy. Thus, for instance, the Norwich mayor's court books tell us far more about the currents of unorthodox opinion in the city in the years 1534-47 than do the consistory court act books which cover the same period.[41] The justices of assize and justices of the peace are also known to have proceeded against heretics in these years. In 1535 the parson of Over Wallop (Hants) was indicted for (amongst other things) refusing to allow his parishioners to maintain lights before images in the parish church and disparaging the saints. The diocesan authorities finally deprived him of his benefice in 1538, but for his failure to proceed to priest's orders rather than for his unorthodox views.[42]

Many local disputes over religion were reported to members of the privy council, especially to Thomas Cromwell, either by protagonists in them or by the local authorities who had to deal with them. In 1539, for instance, a citizen of Norwich challenged what the bishop had taught concerning free will in a Lenten sermon in the cathedral. A local magnate wrote to Cromwell a report highly favourable to Rugge's challenger. A subsequent obsequious letter from Rugge to Cromwell shows that the latter had given the bishop cause to fear the loss of his favour. In the summer of that year, when a priest who had apparently expressed heretical views was sent to Rugge

[39] NNRO ACT 5, fos. 105, 122^v, 134, 206^v.

[40] *Narratives of the Reformation*, 71.

[41] NNRO Norwich mayor's court book 1534-40, fos. 15-17, 21-6^v, 108; 1540-9, fos. 320, 323.

[42] *LP* viii. 20; *Reg. Gardiner et Poynet*, 71-4.

by the Suffolk justices, he appealed to Cromwell, and the bishop took care to report the case to the vicegerent.[43]

The act of six articles seemed at first to presage more effective measures against heretics. Yet there is in the records of the courts of Norwich and Winchester no evidence that they co-operated with commissioners appointed to execute the act, as for example by passing on relevant presentments to them or by binding accusers to appear before them, as did a commissary of the bishop of London on at least one occasion.[44] Not until Mary's reign were the courts of either of these dioceses again to play a prominent part in the suppression of religious dissent.

Even in Mary's reign, however, the pattern of events differed markedly from diocese to diocese. The diocese of Norwich underwent the sharpest persecution it had ever known, while that of Winchester seems to have escaped almost completely. The Norwich evidence relates in the main to individuals who abjured their opinions or were burnt for obdurate persistence in error. The bulk of the less spectacular, more time-consuming, but equally important work of enforcing the proper observance of Catholic rites was probably left to the archdeaconry courts in this diocese, and their Marian records have perished. Those who abjured their beliefs or suffered for them were but the tip of an iceberg composed for the most part of petty offenders, as the records of other better documented dioceses make clear. A London correction act book whose contents have recently been analysed is of outstanding interest because it covers the months from November 1554 to March 1555, just after the re-enactment of the anti-Lollard legislation, when the Marian reaction began in earnest.[45] Particularly significant are the entries which reveal the subterfuges resorted to by people who, though at bottom opposed to the prevailing order, attempted to keep overt gestures of opposition to the discreet minimum necessary to assuage their consciences. A group of people in

---

[43] *LP* xiv. pt. 1, 526, 531, 865; pt. 2, 75.

[44] Hale, *Precedents*, pp. 131-2.

[45] M. Jagger, 'Bonner's Episcopal Visitation of London, 1554', *BIHR* xlv (1972).

the parish of St. Stephen Walbrook 'do use eyther to hange downe theyre heddes at sacrynge tyme of the masse or elles to sytte in suche a place of the churche that theye cannot see the sacrynge.' By means of similar artifices, many religious conservatives were to reconcile themselves to continued church attendance after Elizabeth's accession. Very large numbers of people were presented for failing to attend services, for non-observance of rites or opposition to them. Of the ninety charged with hostility to the sacrament of the altar, two-thirds denied the accusation; only six certainly admitted it.[46] We may be fairly sure that those suspects whose names appear in the Norwich consistory court act books belonged to the small minority whose conduct had aroused really serious misgivings.

A handful of people charged with neglect of ceremonies or non-participation in the Easter eucharist appeared in the Norwich consistory court in the spring of 1554, shortly after the issue of Mary's royal injunctions.[47] This was a false start. Those involved were dismissed with monitions or assigned penances. The Norwich persecution began in earnest in the spring of 1555. Thereafter it followed a spasmodic course. Instead of a steady, even succession of trials there were four major bursts of activity — in the spring and summer of 1555, the spring of 1556, the winter of 1556-7, and the spring of 1558. These claimed between them the great majority of victims. The outbreak of the first bout of persecution immediately preceded Bishop Hopton's primary visitation; the second developed during the metropolitical visitation of 1556.[48] The last two cannot be related to diocesan or provincial routine. Possibly their timing was dictated by local pressures or considerations of administrative convenience which cannot now be discerned. Many of those who were tried in 1558 were dealt with by a court sitting at Bury in Suffolk.[49] The presiding judge, the chancellor, Miles Spenser, was also archdeacon of Sudbury; he may have decided to use his dual position to deal directly with what appears to have

[46] Ibid. 307-9.
[47] NNRO ACT 8, fos. 90, 116, 123.
[48] Above, p. 36.
[49] BL Harley MS. 421, fos. 140-1.

been the area of the diocese worst infected with heresy. During the course of Mary's reign over thirty people were condemned to death in the diocese.[50]

The co-operation of the lay authorities played a crucial part in the Marian persecution. According to one historian's analysis of it, nearly 60 per cent of the arrests described in Foxe's account were due to the initiatives of justices of the peace and constables.[51] The formal records of trials in the Norwich act books tell us nothing of how suspects were arrested, but we learn from the chance survival of one memorandum (probably one of many) that a local gentleman had reported a number of people for failing to receive the sacrament of the altar at Easter.[52] The act books also show that gentlemen and municipal dignitaries were present at some sentences and formal abjurations at Norwich.[53] Laymen co-operated even more closely with ecclesiastical judges as members of the local commissions set up by the crown to deal with heretics and other offenders.[54] Such a commission was almost certainly issued for the diocese of Norwich, probably in 1556, though no copy of it is known to exist. Foxe published a remarkable petition which was allegedly drawn up by certain inhabitants of Norfolk and Suffolk early in 1556 in response to the commencement of the commissioners' activities, as well as a list of people who had fled from Ipswich for religious reasons which was probably exhibited to the commissioners at Beccles in May that year. The commission was still active in the diocese in April 1557, when three commissioners (the bishop, his chancellor, and a local gentleman) took a bond for further appearance.[55]

The diocesan records tell us little about the process of

---

[50] The major sources for the history of the Marian persecution in Norwich diocese are NNRO ACT 8, fos. 204, 237ᵛ, 240ᵛ, 246, 250, 252, 263-4ᵛ, 267, 273ᵛ, 291, 292-4, 305, 321ᵛ, ORR 1(b), fos. 8-9, 13ᵛ, 21ᵛ, 29; BL Harley MS. 421, fos. 140-217; PRO C 85/141/4-6, 10, 12, 19, 20, 23, 25, 27, 28, 30, 33, 36, 37, 39.

[51] Hughes, *Reformation in England*, ii. 274.

[52] NNRO ACT 8, fo. 238ᵛ.

[53] Ibid., fos. 263, 267, 291, 293.

[54] Above, pp. 218-9.

[55] Foxe, *Acts and Monuments*, viii. 121-30, 598-600; PRO E 379/94, Norfolk and Suffolk. It is possible that the commissioners active in East Anglia had been named in a commission covering more than one diocese.

investigation and interrogation that commenced once a suspect had been arrested. Only personal answers are to be
found in the court books and the transcripts made for John
Foxe, mostly from other court records which have now
perished. The depositions of witnesses, if they were taken,
have not survived. The personal answers preserved in the
records are for the most part ones which reveal clearly
whether the defendant's position was heretical or not. In one
case the record shows that such answers were not elicited at
once, but only as the result of two interrogations. Another
suspect probably escaped formal recantation altogether by a
change of heart after the preliminary questioning which
enabled her to produce the 'right' answers when formally
interrogated about her beliefs.[56] We learn hardly anything
from the act books of the efforts that went into securing an
abjuration once it had become clear that a suspect held
heretical beliefs. But Foxe's eye-witness accounts of proceedings reveal how ready Bishop Hopton was to wrestle with
suspects in long and tedious arguments in order to save them
from the consequences of error.[57]

The formal penance to be performed after abjuration was
usually less elaborate than had been enjoined before the
Reformation. Some were ordered to bear faggots, but others
were simply told to make public confessions of error, usually
in their parish churches. No one underwent fustigation. After
abjuration in court in April 1556, John Husbonde of Mulbarton (Norfolk) was ordered to pay the bishop £4 towards
the erection of a new grammar school within the precincts of
Norwich cathedral and meet the expenses of a preacher
whom the bishop should appoint to preach against his heresies
in Mulbarton church.[58]

The aim of interrogation was to discover whether the
suspect assented to certain basic Roman Catholic tenets.
There was apparently no attempt to uncover the whole structure of a given individual's thought. All were asked whether
they believed the official doctrine concerning the eucharist.

[56] BL Harley MS, 421, fos. 141, 193, 195.
[57] Foxe, *Acts and Monuments*, vii. 328, 381-2; viii. 157-8, 161-3, 585-9.
[58] NNRO ACT 8, fos. 240ᵛ, 246ᵛ (a more elaborate penance), 267ᵛ; ORR
1(b), fo. 13ᵛ; BL Harley MS. 421, fo. 173.

The majority were also asked about their beliefs with regard to ceremonies and auricular confession. Other important matters of controversy such as invocation of the saints and prayers for the dead were rarely touched upon, so far as one can see from the surviving records. Only one suspect is known to have been questioned about the crucial but complicated problem of the extent of man's free will.[59]

The surviving evidence does not usually enable us to decide whether suspects derived their beliefs from a 'Lollard' tradition or from the more recent teaching of clergy conversant with the doctrines of the Protestant Reformation, or from both. A few suspects showed clearly that they held 'Protestant' views concerning the eucharist by asserting that Christ's presence in the sacrament was spiritual, or that it depended upon the faith of the recipient.[60] Many more said merely that the elements remained bread and wine or that the eucharist was commemorative. We may suspect that many of those who answered in this fashion had been influenced by 'Lollard' ideas. Yet the opinions which underlay many of these statements may have been debased or simplified versions of doctrines sanctioned by authority in Edward's reign. Those who called the sacrament an 'idol' may have been attacking the doctrine of transubstantiation rather than all forms of eucharistic rite. The suspects were probably not, for the most part, very well educated, and most of them may have shrunk from attempting to give a fuller statement of their beliefs lest they get entangled in a theological argument in which they might be worsted. The impression left by the records of proceedings in court is that after its first few months the persecution was a crude, haphazard drive to enforce basic Catholic observances, in particular participation in the eucharist, by punishing those bold enough to abstain from them, unaccompanied by any careful and systematic investigation of the roots of heresy.

The Marian authorities believed that heresy would wither away without sustenance from false teachers, and the per-

[59] BL Harley MS. 421, fo. 161. Yet see *Acts and Monuments*, viii. 146, for Foxe's statement that an article concerning free will was 'commonly' objected to those condemned in Norwich diocese.

[60] NNRO ACT 8, fo. 264; ORR 1(b), fo. 20^V; BL Harley MS. 421, fos. 155-6.

secution began with an attempt to neutralise or liquidate the major known purveyors of Protestant doctrine. Rowland Taylor, rector of Hadleigh (Suffolk) was probably the Protestant minister who had had most influence in the diocese of Norwich. He was one of the first victims of the Marian persecution, though because his parish was an archiepiscopal peculiar he was not condemned by a diocesan court.[61] A preaching deacon of Nayland (Suffolk) and two other well-known clergymen were amongst those dealt with at Norwich in 1555. Official records claim that all three abjured. One of the clergymen, Thomas Rose, confessed according to the act book that after the words of consecration had been spoken by the priest Christ was really present in the sacrament of the altar. Rose was later to tell John Foxe that he had placed a completely different interpretation on this formula from that intended by his judges, and the case serves to illustrate how men with sufficient theological knowledge and pliable consciences could escape payment of the supreme penalty.[62]

Apart from the handful of known teachers of heresy, those who suffered most heavily in the course of the persecution were from the start those most vulnerable by virtue of their humble origins or place of residence. A majority of those whose occupations are known were husbandmen or workers in the clothing trades. No gentlemen and only one merchant appeared before the courts of Norwich diocese. It is significant that the latter, who came from West Norfolk, was arrested in Norwich, not near his home, and that his view of the eucharist was apparently more sophisticated than that of most of the humble heretics questioned in court: he held that the presence of Christ in the sacrament depended upon the faith of the recipient.[63] It was educated men of his class, able to some extent to study and understand the new doctrines, who were already among the more important supporters of Protestantism. They posed a more insidious threat to the established church than did the humble suspects who bore the brunt of the persecution.

[61] Foxe, *Acts and Monuments*, vi. 690–700.
[62] NNRO ACT 8, fos. 263, 267, 293ᵛ-4; *Acts of the Privy Council*, iv (1892), 383; Foxe, *Acts and Monuments*, viii. 581-90.
[63] Foxe, *Acts and Monuments*, viii. 380-1; BL Harley MS. 421, fos. 155-6.

The persecution was also geographically limited. The major towns of the diocese, with the exception of Ipswich, were hardly affected. Here there was a large Protestant community many of whose members fled the town at least temporarily in order to avoid persecution. Yet Foxe tells us that during the visitation of 1556 Bishop Hopton left Ipswich without completing his enquiries, much preferring to deal with heretics from rural mid-Suffolk. The diocesan authorities seem to have been remarkably reluctant to grasp the nettle of urban dissent. Foxe's accounts show that some of the few urban victims drew attention to themselves by public gestures of defiance which could not be ignored. The incidence of persecution was probably determined to some extent by the attitudes of local figures of weight. Suffolk may have provided a somewhat more fertile soil for heresy than did Norfolk, but this alone can hardly explain why Suffolk should have furnished over two thirds of the victims of the Marian persecution in the diocese. It is significant that according to Foxe's account there were a large number of persecuting justices of the peace in Suffolk. One of the very few parishes in Norfolk known to have experienced persecution was Aylsham. Foxe laid the responsibility squarely on the shoulders of the strongly conservative vicar, John Bury, who was at this time the commissary of the bishop in the archdeaconry of Norwich.[64]

The diocese of Winchester was left almost untouched by the Marian persecution. Hampshire and Surrey were almost certainly more conservative in religion than East Anglia, yet, as we have already seen, they had by no means escaped the contagion of heresy.[65] Both the Marian bishops of Winchester, Gardiner and White, took part in the trial of heretics arrested elsewhere in the country, and there is nothing to show that either of them disapproved of the policy of persecution in principle, though Gardiner may have become convinced of its futility before his death.[66] It may well have been official

[64] Foxe, *Acts and Monuments*, vii. 371; viii. 145-7, 158, 223-5, 381, 424-5, 427-8, 463-6, 493, 598-600; NNRO ORR 1(b), fo. 13ᵛ.
[65] Above, pp. 223-5, 227.
[66] Foxe, *Acts and Monuments*, vi. 704.

policy to concentrate attention upon those dioceses known to be most severely infected by heresy. Such a strategy would help to explain why a comparatively conservative diocese such as Winchester should have escaped persecution despite the fact that both Lollardy and Protestantism had won some converts within it. Certainly no commission is known to have been appointed by the crown to deal with heresy within the diocese.

Most of the meagre surviving evidence of the judicial enforcement of the Marian settlement in the diocese of Winchester is to be found in a record of the chancellor's visitation of the archdeaconry of Winchester in the autumn of 1555 and an office act book of the consistory court covering the summer and autumn of 1556. None of the misdemeanours which were reported (fast-breaking, failure or refusal to follow processions, to offer candles on Purification Day, or to receive holy bread) seems to have led to serious proceedings. The breach of observance most commonly reported was the comparatively trivial one of working on Sundays or feast days.[67]

The only outstanding figure recently active in the diocese who suffered death in the persecution was John Philpot, the Edwardian archdeacon of Winchester and member of a Hampshire family. A leading 'false teacher', he was arrested on account of his bold opposition to the doctrine of transubstantiation in the first convocation of Mary's reign. He was tried by royal commissioners sitting in London, not by a diocesan court.[68] Another inhabitant of the diocese, an obscure gentleman named Thomas Benbrigge, suffered for his beliefs after his condemnation in the consistory court in June 1558. The act book contains no more than a bare record of the final stage of interrogation and the condemnatory sentence, but the signification of his condemnation sent to Chancery attributed the sentence especially to his defence of beliefs contrary to the real presence in the eucharist. According

---

[67] HRO CB 10, 1 Aug. 1556, *Marche, Wavell, Machell*; 8 Aug., *Hakeley*; Faringdon (three cases); Easton (four cases); 22 Aug., *Wafylde*; Twyford, Chalton, Idsworth (ten cases in all); 29 Aug., *Carpenter*; VB 8, 16 Sept. 1555, *Foxe*.
[68] Foxe, *Acts and Monuments*, vii. 606-9, 683-5.

to Foxe, Benbrigge gave unsatisfactory answers to other articles put to him, including ones concerning five more of the sacraments, purgatory and the authority of the church. Benbrigge apparently showed himself read to recant when already at the stake, but the sheriff of Hampshire earned himself a sharp rebuke from the privy council for deferring his execution, and before his death Benbrigge withdrew his recantation.[69]

Surviving records are too patchy to enable one to make a confident judgement in broad terms about the effectiveness of the church courts as instruments for the maintenance of Roman Catholic uniformity. But it is quite clear that the degree of effectiveness varied from time to time and from one diocese to another. The intensity and direction of the courts' activities in this sphere were determined in part by the priorities of individual bishops, in part by general political conditions and the degree of support to be expected from the lay power. Major drives against heresy were infrequent. One, which affected these dioceses and many others,[70] was undertaken during the early years of Henry VIII's reign by a number of bishops in whose eyes orthodoxy and the church's liberties were closely linked. During the 1520s it appears that the authorities in both dioceses came to regard heretical ideas from abroad as the major threat to orthodoxy, though the experience of the neighbouring diocese of London suggests that native heresy was as vigorous as ever. The York evidence of the years 1528-35, carefully analysed by Professor Dickens, suggests that there too judges were concentrating their attention on heretics with foreign origins or connections.[71] After 1529, unfavourable political conditions prevented the fully effective repression of heresy hoped for by certain bishops and Sir Thomas More, though persecution was sufficiently vigorous between 1529 and 1532, particularly in the diocese of London, to sharpen lay hostility towards

[69] HRO CB 12, fo. 2ᵛ; PRO C 85/158/6; *Acts of the Privy Council*, vi (1893), 361, 371-2; Foxe, *Acts and Monuments*, viii. 490-2.
    [70] Thomson, *Later Lollards*, pp. 88-9, 135-7, 238.
    [71] A. G. Dickens, *Lollards and Protestants in the Diocese of York, 1509-58* (Oxford, 1959), pp. 17-29.

the bishops and produce the demands for restriction of episcopal powers contained in the *Commons' Supplication*.[72]

The act of 1534, which met some of the Commons' demands, left the bishops with what were on paper still considerable powers to proceed against heresy, now undoubtedly growing in strength. But the prevailing uncertainty and the attitude of Thomas Cromwell combined to make ordinaries reluctant to take firm action. Even Essex, a hotbed of heresy where Lollardy and Lutheranism mingled, remained almost free of persecution in these years.[73] After the passage of the act of six articles, commissions appointed by the crown, rather than the church courts themselves, took the major part in persecution. This was certainly the case in the diocese of London. Colchester archidiaconal visitation records of the 1540s tell us remarkably little about religious dissent; they betray few signs of even preliminary inquiry, though a report that fewer than half the houseling people of St. Giles's parish in Colchester attended church on Sundays and holy days reveals something of the scale of the problem with which the authorities were confronted. Only at York has recent research so far unearthed evidence of fairly vigorous activity on the part of an episcopal court of audience during the period when the act of six articles was in force, and even here a 'relatively notable incidence of prosecutions during the years 1539-43 was succeeded by three years of quiescence.'[74]

The Marian government restored the powers of ecclesiastical courts, but undertook the over-all direction of the campaign against heresy, and by means of special commissions and repeated directives to local authorities sought to bring the co-operation of the secular and spiritual arms to a new pitch of efficiency. Persecution was fiercest in those dioceses such as London, Canterbury, Rochester, and Norwich where commissions appointed by the crown are known to have been at work. In Essex, Suffolk, and especially Kent, as as reading of Foxe makes clear, groups of Catholic gentlemen

[72] Foxe, *Acts and Monuments*, v. 26-44; *Documents Illustrative of English Church History*, ed. Gee and Hardy, pp. 147-8, 151-2.

[73] Oxley, *Reformation in Essex*, pp. 90-1, 139-44.

[74] Ibid., pp. 145-9; Foxe, *Acts and Monuments*, v. 440-53; Dickens, *Lollards and Protestants*, pp. 36-52; Hughes, *Reformation in England*, ii. 11-12.

took a willing and active part. Certain areas seem to have
escaped close attention, either because the government and
the hierarchy did not think that they had been sufficiently
contaminated to warrant it, or because local support for persecution was lacking. They included not only the conservative
diocese of Winchester but such counties as Buckinghamshire,
a veritable stronghold of Lollardy, and, in the future, of
radical nonconformity. Within the diocese of Norwich the
towns, almost certainly the strongest centres of religious
dissent, yielded comparatively few victims to persecution. In
the neighbouring diocese of London the inhabitants of
Colchester, a major hotbed of heresy, neglected the observances of the church and clergymen were openly mocked in its
streets as late as December 1556.[75] The brunt of the persecution fell on smaller towns and the countryside in the
diocese of Norwich; after its early stages, here as elsewhere,
the heretics who suffered were in the main the poorest and
those who made the most obvious gestures of defiance.

Court records of proceedings against heretics vary greatly
in their completeness and usefulness to the historian.[76] The
neat transcripts in Bishop Fox's registers, for instance, tell us
very much more about suspects and their opinions and contacts than do the short and often enigmatic entries in the
court books of the later thirties and forties. Even the records
of the Marian persecution (at least so far as they concern the
diocese of Norwich) tell us relatively little about suspects and
their beliefs. The sheer scale of the task before the authorities
precluded the comparatively leisurely, careful and solemn investigations of the early years of Henry's reign. The aim
seems to have been at this stage not so much to uncover the
structure of heretical groups and ideas as to secure abjurations
of certain key errors. Only the fullest entries in the court
books of our period (a small proportion of the total) provide
clear indications as to whether the accused derived their ideas
from a 'Lollard' tradition or from Protestant sources. Church

[75] Foxe, *Acts and Monuments*, viii. 383. Colchester, however, witnessed more
persecution than any of the towns in Norwich diocese; see ibid. 303-10, 384-93,
420-3, 467-8.
[76] Above, pp. 223, 229-32, 233-5.

court books will have to be studied in conjunction with a very wide range of other sources before the story of Lollardy and Protestantism in the period of the Reformation can be told.

THE ENFORCEMENT OF PROTESTANT UNIFORMITY

In the latter part of Edward's reign, and more particularly after Elizabeth's accession, it became clear that those who wished to enforce Protestant uniformity were faced with disaffection or opposition on two fronts. On the one hand, a large number of religious conservatives manifested their dissatisfaction by absenting themselves from church or failing to participate in Holy Communion as well as by performing old rituals or maintaining the tenets of the old faith. On the other hand were those Protestants who, though doctrinally at one with the leading members of the hierarchy, felt that the removal of Catholic ceremonies and vestments had not gone far enough. Whatever the extent of lay sympathy with this point of view, its clerical proponents were more likely to attract the attention of the courts in the first place, for it was they who conducted services. In the period covered by this study, ordinaries rarely encountered separatism or radical heresy. In dealing with the clergy, ecclesiastical judges had at their disposal the useful sanctions of deprivation and suspension from celebration, but against most of the laity they could only use increasingly ineffective spiritual sanctions and (from 1559) the 1s. fine for absence from church. During Elizabeth's reign, therefore, lay authorities and commissions established by the crown took an ever increasing share of the responsibility for the maintenance of lay uniformity, though ordinaries continued to provide the government with useful information about the religious attitudes of the laity long after their own coercive discipline had lots its bite.

The Edwardian Reformation developed rapidly and unpredictably. Offical policy was not always unambiguous and consistent. Some dioceses remained till the end of the reign under the control of conservative bishops, while others fell under the sway of radicals. Under these conditions, uniformity was exceptionally difficult to enforce.

Interesting descriptions of the early stages of the Edwardian changes in Gardiner's diocese are to be found in the depositions of those of his servants who testified on his behalf at his trial in 1551.[77] The wary reader is however haunted by an uneasy feeling that the picture painted in such glowing colours by these friends and dependants of 'wily Winchester' is rather too good to be true. The whole hierarchy of conservative officials, headed by that 'expert chancellor' Dr. Stuarde, were it appears bursting with zeal to execute the government's latest directives. Apparitors set out hot-foot from the consistory court to carry mandates to the rural deans, spurred on by the promise of extra payments for their diligence; the commissary in the Isle of Wight saw 'in his own person' to the introduction of innovations into the churches of his jurisdiction. John White, warden of Winchester College and future Marian bishop, was one of those who described the alacrity with which the 1548 order against Candlemas ceremonies was accepted; at Southampton, so he had heard, one priest stopped in the very act of hallowing the candles. Gardiner and Stuarde had done their best to secure the obedience of doubters and waverers; at the episcopal seat of Farnham the bishop himself had, early in 1548, appeased with a timely sermon people angered by the removal of images. But however speedy their compliance with the formal requirements of the Edwardian Reformation, there can be little doubt that these officials were able to impart precious little of its spirit to the people of the diocese. Gardiner had strenuously (though privately) opposed the very first changes of the Edwardian Reformation, and disturbances over religion in which his servants had supposedly had a part led to his recall to London in 1548.

There are disappointingly few signs in the court books of the ways in which religious conservatism manifested itself during the confused years of the Edwardian Reformation. In the archdeaconry of Norwich there was however a significant increase in 1548-9 in the number of people presented for absence from church; many of them, it was alleged, would not hear the scriptures read or the Word of God preached,

---

[77] Foxe, *Acts and Monuments*, vi. 202-4, 206, 208-14, 216-20, 223, 227, 248-50, 251-2.

and one woman was presented for leaving her parish church
during the reading of the homily.[78] In 1549, there were
forty-one presentments for failure to communicate at the
proper time, compared with only three the previous year.
Some and perhaps the majority of these originated in petty
financial wrangles over the cost of the elements, which had
been increased by the concession of the cup to the laity and
the provision of the 1549 Prayer Book that at least one
parishioner should always communicate with the priest when
he celebrated the communion. The Prayer Book suggested
that the cost of the elements be met by the householders of
the parish in turn. But one man refused to communicate at
the time appointed for him and his household, another said
it had not yet come to his household's turn, a third thought
his wife could receive on his behalf, and a fourth said angrily
that it was better not to communicate than to suffer want.[79]
There were many fewer presentments on this score in subsequent years, presumably because the initially irksome
routine had become established. The Norwich and Winchester
court books also show that a few lay people were presented
for telling their beads, one priest for baptizing on a weekday,
another for elevating the chalice during the communion
service.[80] These few trivial entries suggest that the authorities
did not really get to grips with obdurate conservatism in
either of the two dioceses in the reign of Edward. This impression is supported in the case of the archdeaconry of
Norwich by the fact that the notoriously conservative commissary John Bury held office for over half the period covered
by the exceptionally good run of surviving Edwardian act
books.[81] One rector beneficed in the archdeaconry of
Norfolk was presented to the justices for saying services
according to the use of Sarum after the introduction of the

[78] NNRO AI (1548?), Norwich St. Margaret Westwick; (1548), Cley, Wells,
Aylsham; (1549), Burgh, Thetford St. Peter, Sharington, Snoring; (1551),
Hempstead.
[79] First and Second Prayer Books of Edward VI, p. 230; NNRO AI (1549),
Thornage, Briningham, Scoulton, Merton, Caston.
[80] HRO CB 9 (16 Oct. 1551?), Eliot; 7 Dec. 1551, Francis.
[81] On Bury, see Foxe, Acts and Monuments, viii. 465-6; NNRO NCC will
register Ingold, fos. 132-5; Norwich archdeaconry will register Aleyn, fos. 273ᵛ-4.

first Edwardian Prayer Book, and it is hard to believe that his was an isolated case.[82]

During Edward's reign, judges in Norwich diocese took steps to restrain the zeal of three Protestant clergymen serving urban cures, one in Yarmouth and two in Norwich. The first refused to obey an order to face the East during the communion service (in spring 1551, before the second Edwardian Prayer Book had ordered that the minister stand at the north side of the holy table). He told the commissary, John Bury, that he was 'popishe and a maynteyner of papistrye'. The second clergyman told his parishioners that he would not abstain from meat on the eve of St. John the Baptist's day, while the third wore his cope inside out, presumably as a protest against its use. The only clergyman of the diocese of Winchester presented in Edward's reign for deviating from the prescribed order of service may have done so under pressure from certain members of his congregation. It was apparently in order to satisfy them that he had placed bread in the hands of communicants instead of in their mouths as the Prayer Book directed and had on one occasion allowed members of his flock to communicate standing up.[83]

The Elizabethan settlement was enforced in the first place by the commissioners who carried out the royal visitation in the autumn of 1559. In the diocese of Norwich there was astonishingly little overt resistance. Veiled hostility towards the settlement amongst the parish clergy was no doubt widespread; although the diocese contained some 1,200 parishes, only about 500 clergy are known to have accepted the royal supremacy by subscription at this stage.[84] No prominent conservatives appear to have lost their livings during the visitation as a result of open opposition to the new order. A number (foremost amongst whom was John Harpsfield, dean

[82] NNRO Norfolk sessions rolls, 1549.
[83] NNRO AI (1551), Yarmouth/*J. Hikkes; First and Second Prayer Books of Edward VI*, p. 377; NNRO ACT 7A, fos. 132, 156, 161ᵛ, 168ᵛ, 182, 195, 208; ACT 7B, fo. 102ᵛ; HRO CB 9, 5 Feb. 1552, *E. Kene*. For Stephen Gardiner's own concern that popular radicalism in his diocese should not be allowed to outstrip official change, see *Letters of Stephen Gardiner*, ed. J. A. Muller (Cambridge, 1933), pp. 272-6.
[84] Hughes, *Reformation in England*, iii. 40-1; Gee, *Elizabethan Clergy*, pp. 96-7.

of Norwich) did so because they had usurped the places of
married priests. Four known conservatives of the diocese, all
of whom signed their acceptance of the royal supremacy,
were questioned about the religion now established. They all
confessed it to be true and according to the use of the
primitive and apostolic church and were ordered to preach
corroboratory sermons.[85]

Despite the paucity of evidence from the diocese of
Winchester, it seems almost certain that resistance to the
settlement was more vigorous there. Six or seven members
of the cathedral chapter were deprived early in the reign. The
number of parochial incumbents who lost their benefices
before the middle of 1561 was almost twice as high in the
diocese of Winchester as in that of Norwich.[86] There were
thus from the start clear differences between the patterns of
conservative resistance observable in the two dioceses. It is
these differences, as well as the contrasting temperaments of
Horne and Parkhurst, which help to explain why the former's
clashes with conservatism were sharper and more numerous
than the latter's.

The first Elizabethan bishops were able to get to grips with
conservative apathy and resistance more effectively than had
been possible in the brief space of time allowed their
Edwardian predecessors. As a result, the early Elizabethan act
books contain much more evidence of attempted enforcement
of prescribed observances and of measures taken to deal with
those who made positive gestures of dissent.

Reports both of failure to attend church and of non-
participation in communion were more numerous in the
1560s than under Edward, though the numbers made naturally
varied from year to year and from one archdeaconry to
another. In both dioceses there was something like a drive to
secure better church attendance towards the end of the 1560s.
In 1569 some 180 people were presented on this score in the
archdeaconry of Norwich, the following year 116 in that of

[85] PRO PROB 34/1, fos. 76, 98ᵛ; Gee, op. cit., pp. 109, 112, 114, 115.

[86] Gee, op. cit., pp. 281, 285. The fullest published account of religious con-
servatism in Hampshire is in J. E. Paul, 'Hampshire Recusants in the time of
Elizabeth I, with special reference to Winchester', *Proceedings of the Hants Field
Club*, xxi (1958-60).

Winchester.[87] The act of uniformity empowered church-wardens to levy a fine of 1*s.* for each day's absence. Towards the end of his episcopate, Parkhurst complained that the fines were not levied in the archdeaconry of Norfolk, then under the supervision of a notoriously ineffectual commis-sary; but no churchwardens were proceeded against for neg-ligence in the consistory court, as they were at Winchester.[88] Early in his episcopate Horne seems to have enjoined the sending in of lists of non-communicants. In June 1563 in-cumbents and churchwardens who had failed to do so were excommunicated in the consistory court, and in 1568 one incumbent was called upon to justify his bill of non-communicants on oath.[89] Both bishops made some effort to enforce participation in communion three times a year; in practice, however, an annual communion seems still to have been regarded as sufficient in many parishes. The claim made in a Norwich archdeaconry act book in 1569 that one man had given a bad example by failing to communicate more than once a year was quite exceptional for this diocese.[90]

The act books show that the reasons for non-reception ranged from crude scepticism to conservatism or even recu-sancy. One woman of the diocese of Norwich who asked why she should 'goe guppinge uppe to the prest for a peece of Bread a Suppe of Wyne', when she could have more than that at her mistress's, probably stood at the former end of the scale. A man of Headbourne Worthy (Hants) who tried to dissuade a relative of his from participation with the words 'Take heed good Cozen for godes sake, for as it is nowe it is of none effecte and cleane againste godes institution', clearly stood near the latter.[91]

In the early years of Elizabeth's reign it was still possible to hope that some persistent non-participants might be won over by argument. In 1569 Richard Knight of Godshill (Isle

[87] Paul, 'Hampshire Recusants', p. 67; NNRO NAAB 1, 2; NAGB 2A.
[88] *Letter Book of Parkhurst*, 259; HRO CB 29, fos. 98, 119; CB 35, fos. 90ᵛ, 106ᵛ, 110, 123, 225ᵛ, 231ᵛ, 257ᵛ, 260, 267.
[89] HRO CB 17, p. 9; HRO CB 29, fo. 36ᵛ.
[90] NNRO NAAB 1 (1567), Griston; NAAB 2 (1569), Barney; HRO CB 35, fos. 237ᵛ, 240ᵛ, 246, 251ᵛ, 304, 305ᵛ.
[91] NNRO NAAB 2 (1570), Cley; HRO CB 24, fos. 41–2.

of Wight) confessed that he had failed to take part in the communion in his parish church since 1562, but said that he was ready to do so if he could first be told in what he would be participating. Horne told him that 'the bread we break is participation in the body and the chalice we drink is participation in the blood of the Lord, and our fathers ate the same food.' The record may not have done justice to the subtleties of Horne's argument: on the face of it he ran the risk of blurring the difference between Protestant and Catholic eucharistic doctrines in order to win the outward conformity of a recalcitrant conservative. That it was too easy for humble people to read the old meaning into the eucharistic rite is shown by the case of a Norwich woman who, ten years or more after Elizabeth's restoration of Protestantism, could still declare that she could not accept in her conscience that the bread remained bread after consecration.[92]

Parishioners were not supposed to receive communion till they had mastered at least the rudiments of the new faith. The court books show that the catechism was being taught in some parishes, but it is impossible to tell from them how widespread or effective such teaching was. Occasionally parishioners were presented in both dioceses for failing to bring or send their children to learn it, but it was a quite exceptional drive in North Walsham (Norfolk) which produced as many as fifteen such presentments during the episcopal visitation of 1569. It was very rare indeed for an incumbent to be cited to explain why he had admitted a parishioner to communion despite his ignorance, as was the vicar of Holkham (Norfolk). Little could be done to remedy the ignorance of a large proportion of the adult population. The Winchester practice of ordering offenders to learn the catechism in lieu of penance was a small step in this direction.[93]

A wide variety of ceremonies, customs and private devotional practices survived the Elizabethan settlement despite official hostility. Presentments were made about them in

[92] HRO CB 31, fo. 98; NNRO NAAB 1 (1569), Norwich St. Peter Hungate.
[93] *Visitation Articles and Injunctions*, iii. 3; NNRO VIS 1 (1569), fos. 24^V-5, 26^V; NAAB 2 (1569), Holkham; HRO CB 29, fo. 118^V; CB 31, fos. 59, 84, 100^V, 114; CB 35, fos. 90^V, 112^V, 182^V, 224^V.

both dioceses in the early years of the reign, though the reports recorded in the Winchester court books were more numerous and often more detailed. The celebration of funerals in the old manner troubled both Parkhurst and Horne. The latter thought it important enough to warrant the issue of a special prohibition given in his presence by the chancellor in October 1561 to all the churchwardens and parishioners then in court, though it is clear that this was not immediately effective.[94] Clergy were also proceeded against for accompanying the Rogationtide processions with the old trappings.[95] Larger numbers of people were presented for ringing bells on the night of All Saints and for lighting bonfires at Midsummer or on the feast of St. James in what was in the short run an almost certainly abortive attempt to eradicate these popular customs. Individual laymen were punished for amongst other things saying the Lord's Prayer in Latin, using Latin breviaries, praising the use of holy water, and invoking the aid of the Virgin Mary.[96]

In the darkest hour of the Roman Catholic faith in England it was difficult indeed to shun compromise altogether. But some people, while maintaining a toehold within the institutional structure of the national church, showed their continuing loyalty to the old religion by celebrating certain of its rites and by maintaining its doctrines. Of course the clergy alone could conduct services, and it was probably they too who gave the clearest expositions of Catholic doctrine. It was for example the parson of Faccombe (Hants) who in Lent 1563 maintained the doctrine of transubstantiation in a sermon which he gave in his parish church.[97] But it is clear that some of the laity were also capable of defending old doctrines. Thus Thomas Travers, a yeoman of Alresford (Hants) first gave notice of the resistance to the new order

[94] HRO CB 12, fos. 95ᵛ, 99ᵛ, CB 27, p. 31; CB 29, fo. 86ᵛ, CB 31, fo. 36ᵛ; NNRO ACT 9, 12 May 1562, *Davys*. For celebration of a christening with popish trappings, see HRO CB 17, p. 6.

[95] HRO CB 16, fo. 72ᵛ; CB 29, fo. 118ᵛ; CB 35, fo. 79.

[96] HRO CB 12, fo. 104ᵛ; CB 16, fo. 72; CB 27, pp. 11ᵛ, 15, 22ᵛ, 23, 27ᵛ, 30; CB 29, fos. 33ᵛ, 36ᵛ, 47, 49, 54, 116, 122, 124ᵛ, 126; CB 31, fo. 8ᵛ; CB 35, fos. 248ᵛ-50; NNRO NAGB 2A (1563), Sall; (1564), Wighton; (1568), Caister; NNAB 2 (1569), Blofield, Blickling, Aylsham; VIS 1 (1569), fo. 89.

[97] HRO CB 16, fo. 74.

which he was to maintain throughout Horne's episcopate when in 1562 he denounced publicly what the curate had taught. A gentleman of the county who appeared with Travers on a list of recusants prepared by Horne in 1577 had been responsible for the conversion of another layman to the old faith in the 1560s. Other laymen of Hampshire had in their possession copies of works by the Catholic controversialists Harding and Dorman, both men connected with the diocese.[98]

In Winchester diocese clergy were often presented, particularly at the beginning of the 1570s, for failing to read the principal articles of religion set forth in 1559, and those of them who were suspected of doctrinal unsoundness were frequently ordered to preach or provide sermons against those tenets towards which they were believed to have leant.[99] In the last resort diocesan judges could deprive popishly inclined incumbents of their benefices, and thereby of their livelihood and, probably, a large part of their influence. Yet many if not most of those who got into trouble in the courts for the expression of popish views retained their benefices. Men of Roman Catholic sympathies may of course have been amongst those deprived in the sixties for non-residence or for other reasons not specified in the record. By making such men renounce their opinions in more or less explicit fashion, bishops like Horne prevented their becoming convincing agents of counter-Reformation within the church. But episcopal inability to discard men of this type altogether meant that there were within the ranks of the clergy conservatives hostile towards the policies of the Elizabethan bishops, stumbling-blocks in the way of 'godly reformation'.

There is little evidence of action taken against the popishly inclined clergy by judges in Norwich diocese during Parkhurst's episcopate. The career of Peter Kylburne, rector of Hepworth (Suffolk) illustrates the bishop's slackness in dealing with them. After the episcopal visitation of 1569, he was summoned

---

[98] Ibid., fos. 41, 63; CB 17, p. 51; CB 25, fo. 61; CB 29, fo. 119v; CB 35, fos. 79v, 114v; *Diocesan Returns of Recusants for England and Wales*, ed. P. Ryan (Catholic Record Soc. xxii, 1921), 40-1. All the major Catholic controversialists of the early years of Elizabeth's reign had been educated at Winchester College; Bayne, 'Visitation of the Province of Canterbury', 649n.

[99] HRO CB 16, fos. 4v, 8v; CB 17, p. 8; CB 29, fo. 114; CB 35, fos. 143-7.

to undergo interrogation because of his long-standing neglect of his cure and his failure to take the oath to observe the royal supremacy after Elizabeth's accession. Yet he not only managed to hang on to his living, but continued to absent himself from it, living in the cathedral close at Norwich, where he kept beads, images, and a mass book in his lodgings and acted as a link between various Norfolk papists. Not till 1573 were his activities discovered, and then only in the course of investigations into the whereabouts of a recusant gentleman which had been ordered by the high commissioners in London.[100]

The conservative laity were even harder than the clergy to tackle effectively. Their excessive workload and the lack of respect for spiritual sanctions made it difficult for the lesser ecclesiastical courts to deal with them. Proceedings were nevertheless initiated in the Winchester courts against a number of substantial recusants and crypto-papists in the 1560s. Sometimes judges could not even make the people in question appear in court, despite the use of excommunication. Warnings and orders to do penance were followed by backsliding in a number of cases. Some men of substance, such as Thomas Travers of Alresford and the Tichbornes of Hartley Mauditt and West Tisted, were presented repeatedly in visitations before their inclusion in the diocesan return of recusants drawn up in 1577. But at least the Winchester courts attempted to grasp the nettle of recusancy; so far as one can see, those in the diocese of Norwich did not.[101]

The Elizabethan bishop could not make much headway towards the elimination of recusancy if he relied upon the diocesan courts alone. In order to achieve the best results, he had to be ready to draw on other sources of information, and to co-operate as closely as possible with the privy council and the justices of the peace. At the beginning of 1562, and again in 1564, Horne in his correspondence with Cecil and the council laid great stress on the strength of conservatism

---

[100] *Letter Book of Parkhurst*, 139, 175-9; NNRO VIS 1 (1569), fo. 68; cf. ibid., fos. 12ᵛ, 67ᵛ; PRO E 135/25/36.

[101] HRO CB 29. fos. 34ᵛ-5, 63ᵛ, 87ᵛ, 88ᵛ, 93ᵛ, 117, 123; CB 31, fos. 22ᵛ, 29ᵛ, 39ᵛ, 84ᵛ, 107ᵛ; CB 35, fo. 114ᵛ.

in Winchester town, and in November of the latter year, the mayor and other citizens were summoned before the council and imprisoned for a short spell because of their failure to assist in the arrest of an obdurate excommunicate.[102] Horne also began to use his position as a justice of the peace almost as soon as he arrived at Winchester. Writing to Cecil in August 1561, he described how, acting together with leading gentle men of his division, he had called together the constables of the hundreds in their charge and had appointed days on which they were to supply lists of offenders in each parish. By this means, he claimed, more had been discovered than would have been possible in an ecclesiastical visitation, and Horne suggested that such certificates be called for by the council.[103] When Horne and Parkhurst sent reports to the privy council in 1564 describing the religious sympathies and competence of the justices of their respective dioceses, Horne's was much the fuller.[104] Parkhurst's failure to keep himself adequately informed was to get him into trouble before long. In the autumn of 1569 certain privy councillors wrote Parkhurst a stinging letter of complaint of the 'evill governance' of his diocese, due to his slackness in executing the laws. Of three gentlemen of East Anglia whom they had recently examined, so they told Parkhurst, two had not been to church for four or five years, the third had not participated in the communion for ten years. The 'reformation' of the hapless bishop himself was threatened if he failed to take effective action. After this, Parkhurst made some effort to tighten discipline. He insisted that the commissaries reform or punish without respect of persons those who would not hear service or attend communion. But even in the letters urging conformity which he wrote in 1572-3 to prominent conservatives of the diocese Parkhurst betrayed his distaste for harsh measures.[105]

Few religious radicals came to the notice of the church

[102] PRO SP 12/21/7; *Letters of the Bishops to the Privy Council*, 54, 56; *Acts of the Privy Council*, vii (1893), 156, 162, 164, 166.
[103] PRO SP 12/19/36.
[104] *Letters of the Bishops to the Privy Council*, 47-8, 53-7, 58-9.
[105] PRO E 135/25/31, fo. 13; *Letter Book of Parkhurst*, 93-4, 118-19, 121-2, 188.

courts in the early years of Elizabeth's reign. Those who did
belonged to one of two main types. Either they were un-
tutored humble heretics who sometimes belonged to some
underground sect, or clergy who held positions within the
established church, most of them either former Marian exiles,
or younger, newly ordained men who wished to see the
Elizabethan settlement pushed further in a Protestant
direction. Men of the first type seem to have remained very
largely beyond the ken of the Elizabethan church courts,
probably because those in authority were concerned with
more immediate and obvious challenges. Men of the second
type, whom we may call puritans, were very thin on the
ground before the 1570s. There were almost certainly more
of them in the diocese of Norwich than in that of Winchester,
but Parkhurst was of all bishops the one most likely to turn a
blind eye to their activities. Rather did he see them as valuable
allies in the struggle against popery and superstition.

The Elizabethan settlement did not eradicate the popular
scepticism, anti-clericalism and erratic individual speculation
which had characterized pre-Reformation Lollardy. Gestures
of irreverence such as the washing of hands in the font were
occasionally reported; more frequently, anti-clerical feelings,
which were perhaps expressed most vehemently by a parishioner of Burgh in Flegg (Norfolk), who had declared that
he hoped to see the day when he should be one of those who
would bite the parson to pieces, along with a hundred more
villains like him. One man's scriptural reading led him to the
conclusion that a child need not have a godfather.[106] The
heresy of Thomas Lovell of Hevingham (Norfolk), for which
he was presented in the commissary's inquisition in 1563,
was much more fundamental. He did not believe in God the
Son. Those who had persecuted Jesus had done 'better
than we do'. Later in the century, two Norfolk heretics
were to be burnt for denying the divinity of Christ, but
there is nothing to show that there was any connection
between them and Lovell. The latter appears to have escaped

---

[106] NNRO Norfolk archdeaconry act book (1560), Trimingham; NAGB 2A
(1563), Burgh in Flegg/*T. Smyth*; NAAB 2 (1569), Beetley; NAAB 1 (1571),
Weston in Sparham deanery.

punishment.[107] The only heretics known to have been active
in Winchester diocese in the early years of Elizabeth's reign
were a group of sectaries in Surrey who were investigated by
William More of Loseley in 1560-1 at the behest of the privy
council.[108] In the autumn of 1570 a note was made in a
Winchester consistory court act book that Mr. More was
going to investigate words spoken against the doctrine of the
creation by a man of Witley (which lay near the haunts of the
other Surrey heretics), but unfortunately the outcome of the
case does not appear to have been recorded.[109] It may well
have been heretics of one of these groups against whom
Parkhurst preached in his native Guildford before his elevation
to the see of Norwich, but in August 1561 Cecil complained
to Matthew Parker that he had been informed that Parkhurst
'winked' at schismatics and anabaptists.[110] There was great
variety in ministration and 'the ministers follow the folly of
the people, calling it charity to feed their fond humour.'
Such ministers formed a bridge between popular radicalism
and incipient puritanism. There is no sign that Parkhurst
uncovered any 'anabaptist' groups, but not long after this
two Suffolk ministers were cited before the consistory court
charged with the sort of behaviour which Cecil may have had
in mind. One of them had baptized in a manner contrary to
the order of the Prayer Book; the other had allegedly originated popular errors concerning baptism. The first was
suspended; the second, who was only a deacon, was deprived
of his benefice.[111]

One of Cecil's complaints against Parkhurst was that sur-
plices were not tolerated in his diocese, and in 1567 Parkhurst
was one of the few bishops commended to Heinrich Bullinger
of Zürich for their 'kind forbearance' towards nonconformists.[112] It may have been largely for this reason that

[107] NNRO NAGB 2A, *VCH Norfolk*, ii. 275-6.
[108] *VCH Surrey*, i. 382.
[109] HRO CB 35, fo. 244v.
[110] *The Zurich Letters* ed. H. Robinson (Parker Society, vii, 1842), 30; *Correspondence of Parker*, 148-9.
[111] NNRO ACT 9, 27 Nov. 1561, *R. Nunne*; 5, 25 May 1563, *R. Buttell*; DEP 4B, fo. 307; Gee, *Elizabethan Clergy*, p. 282.
[112] *Zurich Letters (2nd ser.)* ed. H. Robinson (Parker Soc. viii, 1845), 151.

Parker determined upon his metropolitical visitation of Norwich diocese in 1567, charging the commissioners who were to carry it out to bring the clergy to a uniform order in ministration and preaching.[113] From this time onwards, more proceedings against clergy who had failed to conform in dress, preaching or ministration were recorded in the Norwich act books.[114] But this trickle of prosecutions gave no hint of the crisis which the diocese was shortly to witness. In the autumn of 1573, after the government had issued a proclamation insisting upon religious uniformity, commissions of enforcement were issued to bishops and gentry. Next year, Matthew Parker, urged by the queen to put down the exercises of the clergy, singled out Parkhurst and Norwich diocese for especially heavy pressure. These events revealed that there was by now a substantial puritan party among the clergy of the diocese which enjoyed strong gentry support. Yet previous correctional *acta* tell us hardly anything of the growth of this group. In the winter of 1573-4, Parkhurst sent up to the archbishop lists (almost certainly incomplete) of those ministers of the diocese who failed to wear the surplice. The list covering the archdeaconry of Norwich is the fullest, and of the sixteen men who appear on it, only one is known for certain to have been in trouble during our period for hostility towards the hated vestment.[115]

Although Horne shared Parkhurst's desire for further change in the church, and claimed in one letter to Zürich that he had done his best to get rid of vestments, he insisted that the Queen's authority be upheld in matters indifferent.[116] Yet some enigmatic remarks written by the archbishop after the metropolitical visitation of Winchester diocese in 1575 suggest that he was not altogether satisfied with the support he

[113] *Visitation Articles and Injunctions*, iii. 197.
[114] NNRO NAGB 2A (1568) Norwich (St. Peter Permountergate, St. Julian, St. John Ber Street, St. Peter Mancroft), Stanfield; VIS 1 (1569), fo. 82; NAAB 2 (1569, 1571), Walsingham Magna/*T. Punt.*
[115] *Tudor Royal Proclamations*, ii. 35–8; above, p. 220; BL Harley MS. 380, fo. 69; *Letter Book of Parkhurst*, 45-6, 219-21, 229-30.
[116] Collinson, *Elizabethan Puritan Movement*, pp. 66, 73; *Zurich Letters*, i. 177.

received from Horne, at least within the latter's own diocese.
The visitation, he claimed, had

> wrought such a contentation for obedience, that I do not yet repent me
> of it, though the bishop be told that his clergy was sifted, and the
> thorn was put in his foot; but he will so pluck it out that it should be so
> in other men's feet that they should stamp again, as I am credibly
> informed. The Isle of Wight and other places of that diocese be now
> gone again from their obedience. If this be a good policy, well, then let
> it be so.[117]

A number of cases of nonconformity, for the most part in
failing to wear the surplice or square cap, had been dealt with
between 1566 and 1570.[118] None of the offenders is known
to have received more than a monition. The fact that nearly
half the reports of clerical disobedience in the court books
originated in the Isle of Wight bears out Parker's impression
of the distribution of nonconformity. Most of the evidence
of early puritanism in Southwark, almost certainly a centre
of vigorous nonconformity, has perished with long-lost
Surrey visitation and archidiaconal act books. Yet the clearest
surviving evidence of lay puritanism in the diocese at this
time comes from St. Saviour's in that town, where in 1566-7
one parishioner refused to participate in the communion
because the minister wore the square cap.[119] In 1570, John
Edwyn, the puritan minister of nearby Wandsworth, was
warned to perform all services according to the ecclesiastical
laws of the kingdom. It was in this parish, not long afterwards, that the radical puritan John Field and his associates
established their presbyterian 'Order'.[120]

CONCLUSION

One of the most valuable results of recent local studies of the
progress of the Reformation has been the production of new
evidence of the strength of popular conservatism. A tendency
to equate resistance to Protestantism with recusancy has led
some historians to overestimate the ease with which the

---

[117] Strype, *Parker*, ii. 422-4; *Correspondence of Parker*, 478.
[118] HRO VB 10, fo. 43; CB 27, pp. 39ᵛ, 40; CB 29, fo. 40ᵛ; CB 35, fos. 27, 76ᵛ, 78, 193ᵛ-4.
[119] HRO VB 10, fo. 26.
[120] HRO CB 35, fo. 27; Collinson, *Elizabethan Puritan Movement*, pp. 138-9.

religious transformation of England was accomplished. Resistance took many shapes, most of them a good deal less obvious than overt recusancy. The great majority of conservatives were for many years after Elizabeth's accession 'church papists' who sought to retain something of the old religion within the framework of the national church.[121] Even more numerous were the 'neuters', apathetic, bewildered, tired of change. In their efforts to enforce the new settlement, the early Elizabethan bishops could count on the wholehearted support of no more than a minority. In pockets of East Anglia, over large areas of Hampshire and Sussex, as in most of Lancashire, the inherited mould of popular observance was only slowly changed.

The ecclesiastical courts provided useful, perhaps indispensable channels for the communication of official requirements to the people. But however efficient in this respect diocesan officials were (and on this score there is no reason to doubt the testimony which Gardiner's Winchester officers gave at his trial) most of them were fundamentally incapable of communicating to the people the *spirit* of the new faith. The hearts of a predominantly conservative body of diocesan officials were not in the task of reformation. A convinced conservative such as commissary Bury of Norwich archdeaconry, a future persecutor of heretics who was under Edward accused to his face of maintaining papistry by a Protestant minister against whom he had proceeded for outstripping by a narrow margin the development of official policy, must have viewed with profound distaste many of the changes he was supposed to enforce.[122]

Reformation was not simply a matter of passing on with all speed the latest official directive. It entailed sustained pressure and supervision. The courts' workload and units of administration were too large to permit the adequate discharge of all aspects of their work, and this was clearly seen by those who wished to enhance the role of the rural dean.[123] The

[121] See esp. Manning, *Religion and Society*, pp. 35-47, 151-65, 241-62; Haigh *Reformation and Resistance*, pp. 209-94; J. T. Cliffe, *The Yorkshire Gentry from the Reformation to the Civil War* (1969), pp. 168-9.
[122] Above, pp. 243, 245.
[123] Strype, *Annals*, ii, pt. 2, 695-701.

number of their other tasks, the speed of their transit, prevented chancellors and commissaries from gaining anything
but a comparatively superficial view of the life of each parish.
It was entirely characteristic of the system that trivial offences
should be presented while more serious ones probably went
unreported, and that the only trace in the records of the
momentous concession of the cup to the laity should have
been caused by paltry disputes over the cost of the elements.[124] Visitation articles ranged over nearly every aspect
of popular religious life. In practice, visitors concentrated on
the fundamental duties of attendance and participation.
There was no effective inquiry in either diocese, so far as one
can tell, into such matters as popular progress in mastery of
the rudiments of the new faith. The same pattern is strikingly
apparent from the statistics (based on the visitation records
of four counties) which Dr. Marchant has drawn up.[125] Even
in the tasks on which they concentrated the courts were not
entirely effective. In Norfolk (as in Lancashire) many churchwardens ignored with impunity the requirement that they
fine absentees from church.[126] All too often, neglect of
prescribed religious duties did not fall within the category of
offences in whose prosecution the local community was most
interested. Over half of those presented in the court of the
commissary in the archdeaconry of Norwich towards the end
of the 1560s for failure to attend church or participate in
Holy Communion were dismissed without further proceedings.[127]

Amongst the clergy relatively few lost their livings on
account of overt opposition to the new settlement. But many
more remained hostile towards it, and of these a number
manifested their opinions by word or gesture. The strength
and importance of this 'fifth column' has recently been
underlined in studies of the enforcement of the settlement in
Lancashire and Sussex.[128] The appalling shortage of ministers

---

[124] Above, p. 244.
[125] Marchant, *Church under the Law*, p. 219.
[126] Haigh, *Reformation and Resistance*, p. 270.
[127] See appendix 3.
[128] Haigh, *Reformation and Resistance*, pp. 216–19, 257–8; Manning, *Religion and Society*, pp. 43–5.

of any sort ruled out any early attempt to purge the parish clergy systematically, but at least it was possible to weaken or destroy the moral authority of many of these men by making them do penance or by securing from them explicit repudiations of 'popish' views. Horne's proceedings against clergy of this sort were altogether more vigorous than Parkhurst's. In part this was due to the differences between the structures of the two dioceses: commissaries could not, as we have seen, dangle over the heads of recalcitrant clergy the threat of deprivation; their right to order sequestrations was dubious, and they must often have been tempted to overlook all but the most flagrant examples of defiance. At a slightly later date the puritan ministers of London diocese were, between episcopal visitations, to benefit from the 'salutary neglect' experienced by the crypto-papist clergy of Norwich diocese. The annual visitations carried out in Hampshire and Surrey enabled bishop and chancellor to exercise much closer control over the parish clergy, and to grapple more closely with a wide range of pastoral problems.[129]

The first Elizabethan bishops saw the main challenges which faced them in popular conservatism and ignorance, in clerical inadequacy, and in various shades of papistry. Bickerings with godly ministers, their natural allies, over things indifferent, entailed a tragic waste of time and energy when problems so much vaster in the bishops' eyes withstood solution. Neither Parkhurst nor Horne welcomed the task of imposing uniformity upon the errant brethren; their act books tell us of trivial delicts of obscure clerics presented haphazardly and usually dismissed with no more than a warning.[130] We can learn little from them of the true extent or nature of puritanism in either diocese.

Despite its uneven and often superficial character, the pressure exerted through the church courts over many years did much to help transform England into a Protestant country. But far more vital in their influence were such things as the presence of groups of godly merchants and

[129] J. P. Anglin, 'The Essex Puritan Movement and the "Bawdy" Courts, 1577–94', in *Tudor Men and Institutions*, ed. A. J. Slavin (Baton Rouge, 1972) pp. 193–4; above, pp. 29, 160, 176.
[130] Above, pp. 254–6.

gentry and links with strongly puritan colleges in the universities. Despite Horne's zeal and Parkhurst's inefficiency,
economic and social facts beyond the control of any bishop
made Protestantism more vigorous in the diocese of Norwich
than in that of Winchester. In the former were to be found
(despite its many dark corners) some of the main bastions of
the new faith; the latter remained one of the most conservative dioceses in southern England.

CONCLUSION

Today many of the forms of action once brought in the church courts have vanished from the judicial scene as completely as the assumptions on which they were based, while others have been altered beyond recognition. There is as yet an established church in England, but few now believe that salvation is to be attained only through it or churches in communion with it. The greater part of the population can still claim by virtue of baptism to belong to it, yet only a small fraction of this nominal membership attends church at all regularly. Many of the things which the church still regards as sinful are no longer crimes: no court in England today has the power to punish fornication or adultery. No longer is every Englishman bound to give the church economic support; tithes are things of the past.

Defamation of character, marital status, and the validity of testaments are still matters for judicial decision, but ecclesiastical judges have long since ceased to be concerned with them, and cases concerning the first two are handled in a manner which would be practically incomprehensible to Lyndwood or Swinburne. In the sixteenth century he who was found guilty of defamation automatically incurred excommunication, the church's ultimate penalty; for the health of his own soul as well as to restore the good name of the man he had defamed he was compelled to perform penance.[1] Those who entered a valid marriage, however informally, could not free themselves from it till death parted them.

The modern courts are not concerned with the health of the souls of those who come before them. Those who sue for

---

[1] Above, pp. 81–3.

defamation still seek restoration of their good name, but the extent of such restoration is now measured by the size of the damages awarded, not the solemnity of a penance enjoined. The law of the land no longer accepts that marriage is indissoluble. Until a few years ago it was still possible to recover damages for breach of promise of marriage: now that action too has been abolished.[2] Today marriages which break down can be dissolved with very little difficulty if both parties so desire; the divorce courts are no longer concerned with the original validity of unions. The bewildered sixteenth-century lawyer would find himself on more familiar ground when he turned to consider the testamentary jurisdiction of the modern courts, though even here he would find the law greatly changed. He would note, for instance, that the construction and interpretation of wills is now governed by rules far more rigid and formal than those which guided him, and a recent recommendation that greater weight should be given to extrinsic evidence of the testator's intentions would no doubt appeal to him.[3]

Although the procedures of the sixteenth-century ecclesiastical courts and the assumptions on which they were based were remote from twentieth-century conditions, the criteria by which one may judge their efficiency are basically the same as those which we would apply to present day institutions. How close did they come to achieving the purposes for which they were designed? How well did they adapt to the changing needs and expectations of the society in which they functioned? It was always difficult to satisfy both these criteria, and in the period of the Reformation the contradictions between them suddenly grew very much greater, placing the inherited structure of ecclesiastical jurisdiction under intolerable strains. The repudiation of papal supremacy, the attacks on clerical privileges and sacerdotal powers, the hardening reality of religious division, all these struck at the very roots of the moral authority of the church courts in England. The most obvious result of these blows was a

---

[2] By the Law Reform (Miscellaneous Provisions) Act (1970, c. 33).

[3] Made in Parliamentary Papers 1972-3 (Cmnd 5301) xiv, 637 *Law Reform Committee: Nineteenth Report: Interpretation of Wills.*

dramatic decline in the effectiveness of spiritual censures. Some aspects of the courts' work fared better than others. Buoyed up by popular demand, the courts would continue for a long time to come to offer indispensable 'social' services. It was as buttresses of the established church that they suffered their worst shocks. It is of course impossible to separate the two spheres of activity completely; the parish church was a vital centre of social as well as religious life.

In their settlement of matrimonial and testamentary suits and their correction of those who threatened parochial harmony, the courts continued to perform work which was guided by old ideals yet useful to contemporary society. Judges' reluctance to give adjudicatory sentences in cases concerned with matrimonial contracts helped to discourage people from entering into ill-attested agreements before solemnization. It is clear, despite suggestions often made to the contrary, that they rarely dissolved solemnized marriages. The ecclesiastical laws, as enforced in the sixteenth-century church courts, tended to promote the security and stability of the matrimonial partnership.[4] In testamentary suits, whether validity or difficulties of execution were at issue, judges were guided by a real concern that the wishes of the dead should be enforced, tempered by a readiness to allow interested parties to come to mutually satisfactory agreement.[5] Of all the elements of the courts' *ex officio* work, the correction of fornicators, adulterers, quarrellers and common defamers probably received the largest measure of popular support, and the solemn penances which judges imposed gave satisfaction to the congregation and cleansed the festering sores of local enmity.[6]

But the Reformation made the courts' work in support of church and clergy very much more difficult. The decline in popular respect for priests, the sharp rise in agricultural prices and the legislation of the 1540s led to an enormous increase in tithe litigation. The confiscation of parochial endowments and the clumsy official attempts to divert popular piety from

[4] Above, pp. 64–75.
[5] Above, p. 112.
[6] Above, pp. 46–8, 86–7.

its traditional channels made the maintenance of the parish church and its furniture and ornaments a bigger problem than it had been hitherto. The transformation of a Catholic priesthood into a Protestant ministry was a colossal task made all the more formidable by the temporary reversal of official policy under Mary and the severe shortage of clergy at the beginning of Elizabeth's reign. Finally, the events of our period made the outward show of religious unity very much harder to sustain. Before the Reformation, the church courts were dealing with relatively small heretical groups. Fifty years later popular heresy had by no means disappeared; at the opposite end of the spectrum, Catholic recusancy had already taken shape; in between, a national church which sheltered both radical puritans and church papists was bursting at the seams.

In all these spheres of their activity the courts were dealing with vastly greater problems with sanctions of much diminished strength. Perhaps no agency was as well fitted as the visitation courts to enforce the purchase of new equipment and supervise the clergy's performance of new duties. Yet these tasks were added to an already excessively large administrative and correctional burden; they entailed new directive pressures upon the local community from outside, at a time when old habits of obedience had been undermined. What was worse, the personnel of the courts remained in great part apathetic, if not downright hostile, towards the programme of reform.

Historians have often regretted the increased scale, complexity and impersonality of later medieval diocesan administration while conceding their inevitability. The Reformation tended to make court personnel harder to control. The proportion of the episcopal bench which possessed experience of diocesan administration fell sharply after about 1550. Some bishops showed themselves naturally apt to rule, but all were to a greater or lesser extent dependent upon the very much greater experience of scribes and lawyers who had continued the courts' work through successive religious changes and long vacancies or periods of episcopal absence. It was of course in the interests of registrars and proctors to foster litigation and to spin it out by procedural ingenuity, and bishops without a grounding in canon or civil law were less able to overrule what court personnel might choose to present as local custom. As Thomas Yale observed, 'handling of causes is made an art of gain, and prolonging of suits a point of cunning; style and customs formed for commodity [are] observed as laws ...'[7] More litigation meant more lawyers; at Norwich the number of full-time proctors working in the consistory court more than doubled during the century. More lawyers in turn tended to create more litigation; as Chancellor Nevinson pointed out in 1569, '... if wee had more ravens wee must haue more carion ...'[8] Yet the burgeoning weeds of litigation did not altogether hide from view the ancient aim of reconciliation. A very small proportion of cases went as far as sentence throughout the period, and arbitration and compromise continued to play a major part in the termination of disputes.

The fact that administrative and judicial structures and customs varied greatly from diocese to diocese has been stressed repeatedly in the course of this study. The relative smallness of Winchester diocese and the exceptional frequency of Winchester diocesan visitations made possible much closer episcopal oversight and control than the bishops of Norwich could hope to achieve over their great diocese. The authority of the bishops of Winchester within their diocese must also have been strengthened by the fact that they were the greatest episcopal landowners in England. On the eve of the Reformation public opinion in the diocese of Winchester appears to have tolerated procedures which had dropped out of use in the diocese of Norwich. At Winchester corporal punishment of sexual offenders was still a fairly common sight. Judges dealt *ex officio* with many of those who withheld their tithes, and continued as late as the 1540s to handle such cases in a more brisk and summary manner than their Norwich counterparts.[9] But it is possible to lay too much stress on differences of administrative and judicial practice. They were overshadowed by interdependent developments which in our

---

[7] Strype, *Grindal*, p. 308; above, pp. 43, 51-2.
[8] Marchant, *Church under the Law*, p. 16; PRO E 135/25/31, fo. 7.
[9] Above, pp. 46, 138.

period affected all dioceses, such as the decline in the effectiveness of spiritual sanctions and the upsurge in litigation. During the Reformation Winchester judges ceased, as their colleagues elsewhere had done earlier, to use corporal punishment; the proportional increase in the amount of litigation they had to settle was even greater than at Norwich, and they faced with a similar, though admittedly rather more slowly growing, contempt for excommunication. On the other hand, the fact that the bishops of Winchester were able to supervise their diocese more closely than most of their colleagues weighed very little in the balance against the strength of conservatism within its boundaries; the popular Reformation made greater progress in East Anglia than in Hampshire.

The ecclesiastical courts emerged from the Reformation gravely weakened. Their jurisdiction was hedged about, too, with new statutory limitations. Amongst the most far-reaching of these were contained in the tithe statutes of the 1540s. The stipulation that the more important tithes be paid henceforth as had hitherto been customary was to provide litigants before the courts with a most important new ground for seeking prohibitions.[10] For some time, the courts continued to do their work with comparatively little interference, but by the end of the century the number of prohibitions had greatly increased, and more than 75 per cent of them were issued in tithe cases.[11] Difficulties which arose from executors' sales of land and gifts or promises made *inter vivos*[12] were to allow scope for the issue of prohibitions in testamentary causes too. The tendency of many scribes and lawyers to exploit procedure for their own benefit and the decline in popular respect for the courts can only have increased people's readiness to seek alternative means of redress. The judges of the temporal courts gradually developed the scope of writs of prohibition in response to a swelling demand. But there is little sign that they were inspired by a conscious desire to curtail ecclesiastical jurisdiction before the closing years of Elizabeth's reign. It was then that, for the first time, bishops and ecclesiastical judges complained loudly about the

[10] Above, pp. 120-2, 142-3.
[11] Levack, *Civil Lawyers in England*, p. 76.
[12] Above, pp. 90, 102-3, 110-1.

encroachments of the common law. In 1598 the bishops and certain other ecclesiastical judges drew up a list of points regarding the issue of prohibitions which they desired the Lords and other judges of the realm to consider. A further series of complaints was to be submitted to the privy council by Richard Bancroft in 1605.[13] The bishops' attempted defence of their jurisdiction only angered the common law judges; they responded by extending their claims. Their power to interpret statutes laid nearly all the church courts' work open to their scrutiny, since few aspects of it had not been touched by act of parliament during the Reformation.

A second major threat to the courts came from militant Protestantism. The notorious conservatism of the majority of scribes and lawyers made them natural objects of suspicion and distaste in the eyes of the godly.[14] The queen's insistence on uniformity brought the courts into direct conflict with the puritans, who directed their most vituperative attacks against chancellors and commissaries. The courts, they could claim, had been taken over unreformed from the popish church. They were burdened with a whole range of tasks which could be more appropriately discharged by lay courts. Their structure and procedures were inimical to the exercise of the intimate fraternal discipline which was one of the hall-marks of a true reformed church. Excommunication, the church's weightiest censure, was made the penalty for the most trivial offences.[15]

The challenges to the courts from the puritans and the common lawyers were utterly different in character. The puritans' attack was explicit and ideologically inspired. The common lawyers' piecemeal encroachment upon the ecclesiastical courts was actuated (in so far as the process was deliberate) by pedantic opportunism and professional rivalry. Yet when the puritans turned to the common lawyers for help in questioning the procedures of the high commission,

[13] Strype, *Whitgift*, ii. 397-400; Coke, *Second Part of the Institutes*, pp. 601-18.
[14] Above, pp. 24-7.
[15] See esp. *Zurich Letters (2nd ser.)*, 128-30, 358-60; *An Admonition to the Parliament* in *Puritan Manifestoes* ed. W. H. Frere and C. E. Douglas (1954), 15-18, 30-4.

the two came together, and it was against what threatened to be a most dangerous alliance that in 1591 Richard Cosin aimed his *Apologie*. The efforts of the apologists for ecclesiastical jurisdiction had however an effect which was the reverse of what they had hoped for. By forcing the temporal judges to think more clearly about the wider implications of their actions, they unwittingly opened the way to a more formidable attack upon a wider front.

It was natural that the bishops should have looked to the crown to help them in fending off attacks upon their jurisdiction. The break with Rome, it was pointed out in the episcopal protests of 1598 and 1605, had made the church courts courts of the crown in the fullest sense. But the Tudors had done hardly anything to invigorate or overhaul the ecclesiastical courts. No doubt they were conscious of the potential unpopularity of measures to strengthen ecclesiastical jurisdiction in a country impatient of clerical guidance and control. In order to enforce their religious policies they had developed that curious hybrid the commission for ecclesiastical causes. Powers to fine and imprison which it was perhaps politically impossible to grant to the ecclesiastical courts were granted to bodies which included both laymen and clerics, temporal and ecclesiastical lawyers. Within a few years of the establishment of the first commissions, bishops were pressing for the establishment of further diocesan commissions in order to combat popery. As Horne pointed out in an early letter to Cecil, the men of Hampshire feared 'punishment by the purse more than of Goddes curse'.[16] Both Parkhurst and Horne sought grants of local commissions early in the second decade of the queen's reign, and the latter had gained one by 1572.[17]

Hopes of a new era of harmonious co-operation between churchmen and laity were however doomed to disappointment. Increasingly preoccupied with the puritan challenge to their authority, the second generation of Elizabethan bishops found the prospect of alliance with the militant Protestant

[16] PRO SP 12/19/36.
[17] BL Lansdowne MS. 12, fos. 63, 74; *Letter Book of Parkhurst*, 134–5; Paul, 'Hampshire Recusants', 67–8.

gentry less alluring than their predecessors had done. After 1581, when new and severer penalties were imposed on recusants, their control and punishment were increasingly entrusted to lay agencies. Soon after this, Whitgift began to use the high commission in London as one of his main weapons in the struggle to secure puritan conformity, while the diocesan commissions became increasingly concerned with routine ecclesiastical court business. At both national and diocesan level laymen played a diminishing part in the commissions' work. As the most recent historian of the commissions has written, the 'disaffection of the gentry and the reconstitution of diocesan ecclesiastical commissions as just another species of church court dominated by clerics and civilians suggests that these extraordinary grants of royal power failed to achieve their original purpose.'[18] Whitgift's immediate aims were largely achieved, but at the price of giving the high commission much unfavourable and ultimately damaging publicity; and the government proved unable or unwilling to check the steadily increasing flow of prohibitions which in the 1590s began to hamper the work of all ecclesiastical courts, including the high commission.

James I, and to an even greater extent his son, sought to check the erosion of ecclesiastical jurisdiction and supported the church courts more wholeheartedly than Elizabeth had ever done. But their support came too late to restore the moral authority lost during the Reformation and the Elizabethan years of neglect, or to reverse the inroads made by prohibitions in the quarter century after 1590. The important part played by the courts in the enforcement of Laudian policies could only increase their unpopularity; it led, briefly, to their abolition after the downfall of the monarchy. The long-term effect of the events of the interregnum was however to delay the ultimate drastic pruning of ecclesiastical jurisdiction. What appeared to be radical excesses discredited the cause of judicial reform. The church courts, restored after Charles II's return, were to survive in their old shape (despite the further

[18] R. B. Manning, 'The Crisis of Episcopal Authority during the Reign of Elizabeth I', *Journal of British Studies*, xi (1971), 25.

diminution of their correctional powers as a result of the Toleration Act of 1689) for nearly 200 years.

In urging further drastic reforms, the nineteenth-century critics of the ecclesiastical courts used three arguments of particular weight: that the courts' structure was full of anomalies; that the existing boundary between secular and ecclesiastical jurisdiction was extremely inconvenient; and that much of the business dealt with by the church courts was not properly the concern of ecclesiastics.[19] None of these points was new. As early as the 1530s would be reformers of the church had called for rationalisation of its judicial structure. The inconveniences caused by the division of jurisdiction over disposal of property at death had been apparent since at least the sixteenth century. In certain papers drawn up shortly after the break with Rome, it had been claimed that much, if not most, of the business before the church courts was temporal in nature and could more conveniently be dealt with by other tribunals.[20] The fusion of judicial and pastoral responsibilities, it was argued, hampered the true work of the church, while in some types of case, such as those brought for the recovery of tithes, ecclesiastical judges could not be impartial. Similar arguments had been used by puritan critics in Elizabeth's reign. But these old criticisms of the courts drew new force from the changed circumstances of the early nineteenth century. Long-overdue judicial and administrative reforms were now at last removing some of the hoariest anomalies of the common law and local government. Above all, the church faced new and more vigorous assaults on her privileged position. Those outside the Anglican fold pressed for full civil rights with increased insistence, while the radicals attacked the hierarchy for misuse of the church's still substantial endowments. Whig reforms such as tithe commutation, the inauguration of civil marriage and the establishment of national registration of births, marriages and deaths were supported both by those who sought institutional reform and rationalization and by those who

---

[19] This paragraph is heavily indebted to A. H. Manchester, 'The Reform of the Ecclesiastical Courts', *American Journal of Legal History*, x (1966).
[20] BL Cotton MS. Cleo. F. ii, fos. 250-4ᵛ; *LP*, ix. 1071.

wished to see the church shorn of privilege and power. The
commutation act of 1836 brought to an end the church's
jurisdiction over tithe.[21] In 1855 suits for defamation were
taken away.[22] In 1857, the very mainstay of the courts, their
probate powers, were given to a new tribunal, and they lost
all jurisdiction in matrimonial causes.[23] The great shearing
which some common lawyers had hopefully anticipated over
three centuries before had at last come to pass.

* * * * *

Two main questions face the historian of the church courts in
the period of the Reformation. First, did they merit the
exceptionally bitter criticism to which they were subjected at
this time? Secondly, how were they affected by the break
with Rome and the changes which followed in its wake?
Plenty of evidence can be adduced in support of the view
that the courts were partial, oppressive, corrupt, and parasitic.
Some of the most colourful can be found in their own
records. In about 1565 the chancellor of Winchester diocese
allegedly made a remark which could have been culled from a
satire written by an enemy of the courts. He was reported to
have said of certain parishioners engaged in complex litigation
with their vicar that they 'shuld be eased of ther monye well
enoughe, and be never the nere of ther purpose nether ...'[24]
The words do not ring entirely false; he may have spoken
them. No doubt ecclesiastical judges were not always impartial, and there was probably much petty corruption and
inefficiency amongst the personnel of the courts. No doubt
the same could be said of most courts at this time. But it has
been argued in this study that ecclesiastical court procedure
was a good deal more speedy, flexible, inexpensive and readily
understandable than has commonly been allowed, and that
insufficient weight has been given to the peaceful settlement
of causes by compromise and arbitration. It has also been

[21] 6 & 7 William IV, c. 71.
[22] 18 & 19 Victoria, c. 41.
[23] 20-1 Victoria, cc. 77, 85.
[24] HRO CB 19, p. 309.

suggested that the correctional work of the courts, particularly in matters of social discipline, received a great deal more popular support than their critics have been prepared to admit.

The effects of the Reformation upon the ecclesiastical courts were undoubtedly adverse. Their jurisdictional losses were, on the face of it, small. The full implications of the tithe legislation of the 1540s were not at once apparent, and less was taken from them than was taken by the decisions of the temporal courts under Henry VII or during the later years of Elizabeth. But their moral authority suffered a series of blows from which it never really recovered. Loss of respect for their spiritual sanctions left the courts' coercive procedures in Whitgift's words 'a carcasse without a soul'. Religious unity was an essential pre-requisite of general acceptance of the exercise of judicial powers over all members of the commonwealth by officers of the established church. Yet abrupt changes in royal policy went far towards cracking the facade of doctrinal harmony.

Henry VIII's assumption of ecclesiastical jurisdiction gave the crown a unique opportunity to curtail or reform ecclesiastical jurisdiction. By failing to do either, mid-Tudor governments, especially those of Henry VIII and Elizabeth I, took what must at the time have seemed the easiest course, but laid up trouble for the future. Hardly anything was done to tackle the admitted weaknesses of ecclesiastical law, to tighten up its procedures where necessary, to overhaul the church's judicial structure, to replace ineffective spiritual sanctions or to guard against haphazard and arbitrary interference by temporal judges. Elizabeth's government implicitly recognized, when it granted ecclesiastical commissions, the need to involve laymen of substance more closely in the work of the courts, but the odium which the bishops incurred through trying to enforce her timid and devious religious policies went far towards cancelling out the commissions' good effects. The moment of opportunity passed, and the piecemeal erosion of ecclesiastical jurisdiction continued unchecked.

APPENDIX 1

LITIGATION IN THE CONSISTORY COURTS

x = gaps in the *acta* of the years indicated. The unidentified causes of these years have not been counted.

'Matrimonial' here refers to all litigation concerned with marriage, not only to causes brought to enforce matrimonial contracts. '

(a) Causes brought in the Norwich consistory court at the instance of parties and *ex officio promoto*.

Year	Matri-monial	Defa-mation	Tithes	Testa-mentary	Other	Unidenti-fied	Total
1519	7	33	12	20	3	22	97
1520	16	10	11	5	3	51	96
1521ˣ	11	21	12	5	1		
1522ˣ	7	8	10	5	3		
1523	15	13	8	3	5	31	75
1524	12	19	10	14	1	43	99
1534	13	6	3	12	2	13	49
1535	18	1	4	14	3	20	60
1536	13	7	18	11	—	13	62
1537	13	7	10	12	2	23	67
1538	14	7	12	9	2	26	70
1545	5	4	12	26	—	59	106
1546	5	4	4	27	1	68	109
1547	1	—	6	16	1	47	71
1548	5	2	11	18	—	70	106
1549	3	1	8	7	2	41	62
1550	23	3	44	13	2	83	168
1551	34	9	54	38	6	98	239
1552	23	7	30	40	1	102	203
1553	9	4	26	30	1	82	152
1554	12	4	26	17	—	100	159

Year	Matri- monial	Defa- mation	Tithes	Testa- mentary	Other	Unidenti- fied	Total
1555ˣ	15	4	34	34	10		
1561	21	8	37	103	7	180	356
1562	26	18	49	50	8	178	329
1563	25	19	45	39	9	185	322
1567	6	13	34	47	4	118	222
1568	15	16	59	53	2	174	319
1569	13	14	55	54	8	144	288

(b) Causes brought in the Winchester consistory court at the insistance of parties and *ex officio promoto* which were recorded in the instance act books of the court.[1]

Year	Matri- monial	Defa- mation	Tithes	Testa- mentary	Other	Unidenti- fied	Total
1527	3	5	2	2	6	18	36
1529	7	3	3	3	2	20	38
1541	13	7	12	2	—	24	58
1543	14	20	6	2	—	27	69
1545	8	17	19	7	—	7	58
1547	2	11	11	—	1	2	27
1560ˣ	14	17	18	10	2		
1563	13	24	27	27	7	16	114
1566	15	30	50	43	14	17	169

[1] A considerable number of office cases promoted by individuals, many of them concerned with testaments and legacies, were entered in the office act books. It was however thought best to base this table in the instance act books alone, first because large gaps in both series prevent their effective collation, and secondly because it was judged impossible to draw a line between those *ex officio promoto* cases which were essentially concerned with private interests and those which were really correctional in character. Procedure *ex officio promoto* was more often used at Winchester than it was at Norwich, and all sorts of cases were instituted in this way, including even the charge of heresy brought against Thomas Benbrigge in 1558 (HRO CB 12, fo. 2ᵛ).

APPENDIX 2

OUTCOMES OF THE SUITS OF THE FOUR MAJOR TYPES BROUGHT IN THE CONSISTORY COURTS

Key

a. Outcome unknown (the numbers in brackets refer to suits removed by inhibition to a higher court and not subsequently remitted). Many of the suits under this head may have ended satisfactorily.

b. Hope of agreement. Here are grouped all cases which ended with the nomination of arbiters, or with a note such as *sub spe concordie*.

c. Peaceful conclusion, indicated by an entry such as *Pax in causa*. This column includes formal renunciations of matrimonial proceedings.

d. Terminal or definitive sentences, decrees, court orders and monitions.
A = Actor (plaintiff); R = Reus (defendant); ←1→ = a sentence or order given in part for each party. A question mark indicates that the record of sentence does not make clear for whom it was given.

e. Appeals from sentences.

f. Inhibitions from higher courts. Figures in brackets indicate remissions.

Note: Not all matrimonial litigation was concerned with contracts. The numbers of matrimonial causes given in this table are smaller than those in appendix 1.

Norwich

Date / Type	Yearly average to nearest whole number	Total (a–d)	a	b	c	d A	d R	e	f
1519–1524									
Mat. Contracts	10	63	25 (3)	2	2	8	26	6	
Defamation	17	104	54	3	20	17	10	12	4 (1)
Tithes	10	63	41 (1)	6	6	6	4	5	2
Testaments	9	52	34 (1)	8	3	1	6	1	1
1534–1538									
Mat. Contracts	12	58	22 (1)	2	4	5	24 / 1?	1	
Defamation	6	28	17	3	4	4			
Tithes	9	47	32	9	2	3	1	2	
Testaments	12	58	34	10	9	4	1	2	
1545–1549									
Mat. Contracts	3	16	13				3		
Defamation	2	11	2	3	1	5		3	
Tithes	8	41	16	10	10	4	1	3	
Testaments	19	94	59 (3)	17	13	3	2	1	
1550–1555									
Mat. Contracts	15	91	30			18	37 / 6?		
Defamation	5	31	10	3	7	8	3	1	
Tithes	36	214	99	26	46	37	2 / ←3→ / 1?	17	2
Testaments	29	172	86	12	44	9	18 / 3?	2	2 (1)
1561–1563									
Mat. Contracts	19	56	17 (2)	2	5	10	22	6	
Defamation	15	45	18	5	12	8	2	3	
Tithes	44	131	48 (2)	19	43	14	7	6	
Testaments	64	192	78 (1)	17	36	24	33 / ←1→ / 3?	25	6 (2)
1567–1569									
Mat. Contracts	7	21	10	1	1	4	5	5	
Defamation	14	43	19	7	14	3		3	2
Tithes	49	148	71	14	44	18	1	6	1
Testaments	51	154	69	23	41	14	7	11	4 (1)

Winchester[1]

Date / Type	Yearly average to nearest whole number	Total (a–d)	a	b	c	d A	R	e	f
1527 and 1529									
Mat. Contracts	5	9	2			4	3	1	
Defamation	4	8	3		1	4		1	
Tithes	3	5	1		2	2			
Testaments	3	5	4		1				
1541, 1543, 1545, 1547									
Mat. Contracts	9	36	7		8	5	16		
Defamation	14	55	17	4	14	20		1	
Tithes	12	48	15 (2)	8	13	11	1	1	
Testamentary	3	11	3	1	5	2			
1560, 1563, 1566									
Mat. Contracts	11	33	20		2	2	9	2	
Defamation	24	71	50	1	9	6	5	4	
Tithes	32	95	63	3	8	16	5	5	
Testaments	20	80	50	5	8	11	6	1	

[1] This section of the table does not include inhibitions.

APPENDIX 3

CORRECTIONAL ACTIVITY OF THE COMMISSARY IN THE ARCHDEACONRY OF NORWICH

Key

T : Total number of offences.
a : Ultimate outcome of proceedings unknown.
b : Monitions, dismissals and decisions to take no further action.
c : Successful purgations.
d : Orders to do penance.
e : Pecuniary penalties, commuted penances etc.

1532–1533

	T	a	b	c	d	e
Sexual misbehaviour causing pregnancy	14	6			5	3
Other sexual misbehaviour	49	29		4	12	4
Encouraging or conniving at sexual misbehaviour	1		1			
Delaying solemnization of marriage	2	1	1			
Leaving, maltreating spouse	2	2				
Defaming neighbours, sowing discord	9	5	1	1	2	
Testamentary	6	3	3			
Detention of church goods						
Detention of public dues	2	1	1			
Non-reception of communion						
Non-observance of Sabbath, saints' days	19	13	2	1	3	
Absence from church	3	2			1	
Working etc. during service						
Disturbance in church	4	2	1		1	
Defiling churchyard	1		1			
Defects in chancel, rectory	3	3				
In church: furnishings						
In church: fabric						
In churchyard	3	2	1			
Neglect of duties by clergy	2	2				
Reviling questmen						
Total so far listed:	120	71	12	6	24	7
Cases of other types:	2					
Grand total:	122					

1538-39						1549-1550					
T	a	b	c	d	e	T	a	b	c	d	e
24	15	1		7	1	42	26	2	1	9	4
61	38	13	4	6		46	30	7	1	1	7
1	1					5	3	2			
2	2					1	1				
1		1				2	2				
14	10	4				14	9	5			
32	18	14				10	2	8			
						1	1				
2	1	1				6	2	4			
						17	11	4		1	1
9	6	2			1	1	1				
1	1					19	14	5			
2	2										
6	5		1			4	1	2		1	
5	3	2				3	3				
6	5	1				6	6				
2	2					40	17	23			
						2		2			
3	3					4		4			
						5	4				1[x]
1		1									
172	112	40	5	13	2	228	133	68	2	12	13
						2					
172						230					

[x] Sequestration of the fruits of Wiveton because the cure had been left unserved.

1551–1552

	T	a	b	c	d	e
Sexual misbehaviour causing pregnancy	25	15	3	2	3	2
Other sexual misbehaviour	52	23	18	7	3	1
Encouraging or conniving at sexual misbehaviour	9	4	5			
Delaying solemnization of marriage	2	1	1			
Leaving, maltreating spouse	4	2	1			1
Defaming neighbours, sowing discord	12	4	8			
Testamentary	10	2	8			
Detention of church goods	3	1	2			
Detention of public dues						
Non-reception of communion	2	2				
Non-observance of Sabbath, saints' days	6	1	4			1
Absence from church						
Working etc. during service	1	1				
Disturbance in church	8	4	4			
Defiling churchyard	1	1				
Defects in chancel, rectory	7	5				2
In church: furnishings	13		12		1	
In church: fabric						
In churchyard	2	1	1			
Neglect of duties by clergy						
Reviling questmen						
Total so far listed:	157	66	68	9	7	7
Cases of other types:	4					
Grand Total:	161					

1560-1561 (see note below)						1569-1570					
T	a	b	c	d	e	T	a	b	c	d	e
18	8	2		7	1	38	19	3	4	12	
24	8	11	2	3		60	35	18	2	5	
						7	3	2	2		
1		1				2	1		1		
1		1				3	1	2			
21	3	11	4	3		46	14	22	4	6	
9	2	6		1		5	2	3			
1		1				9	5	4			
1		1				10	3	7			
21	3	9	1	7	1	7	2	3			2
15	3	11	1			47	11	27		2	7
1		1				33	6	18	1	3	5
9	2	3	1	3		16	1	11		4	
5	2	2		1		2	1				1
9	2	7				23	7	16			
66	12	54				30	4	26			
11	3	8				9		9			
10	2	8				20	1	19			
6	3	3				21	17	4			
2	1			1		1		1			
231	54	140	9	26	2	389	133	195	14	32	15
4						22					
235						411					

Note: These statistics are based on the records of inquisitions held in the deaneries of Ingworth, Holt, Walsingham, Brisley, and Toftrees, i.e. five of the thirteen deaneries of the archdeaconry of Norwich, save in the case of 1560-1. Ingworth and Holt records do not survive for this year. Most of the records for individual years appear to have been begun in the spring and to have recorded correctional action taken during the following year. Those for 1532-3 and 1551-2 seem however to have been begun in the autumn and to have recorded correctional action taken during the following six months. This table is not therefore a reliable guide to the *volume* of correctional business at different times, but it gives some indication of its changing character and of the efficiency of the court in dealing with it.

BIBLIOGRAPHY

1. MANUSCRIPT SOURCES

Bury St. Edmund's and West Suffolk Record Office
Act books of the archdeaconry of Sudbury.
Cambridge, Corpus Christi College
    MS. 97   Parker Certificates.
    MS. 114   Letters sent to Archbishop Parker.
Durham University Department of Palaeography and Diplomatic
    DR III   Act books of the Durham consistory court.
London
British Library
    Additional MS. 12, 483 Record of visitation of the archdeaconry of Winchester carried out by the archdeacon's official in 1543.
    Additional MS. 38,651 Cases before the court of Canterbury in 1543-4.
    Additional MS. 48,022 Transcripts of entries from a register of Thomas Cromwell's vicegerential court.
    Cotton MSS.
    Harley MS. 421   Transcripts of Marian proceedings against heretics.
    Harley MS. 1253   Humfrey Rant's book of forms.
    Lansdowne MSS.
Greater London Record Office
    DL/C   Act books of the London consistory court.
    DW/PA/2 Court books of the archdeaconry of Surrey.
    DW/PA/5 Original wills of the archdeaconry of Surrey.
    DW/PA/7 Registered wills of the archdeaconry of Surrey.
    Microfilm X 11 Act book of an episcopal court sitting in Southwark, 1511-15.
Lambeth Palace Library
    Archiepiscopal registers of Thomas Cranmer and Reginald Pole.
Public Record Office
    C 85   Significations of excommunication.
    DEL 4/1   First act book of the court of delegates.
    E 135   Exchequer ecclesiastical miscellanea.

PROB 11   Registered wills proved in the prerogative court of Canterbury.

PROB 34/1 Act book of royal visitation of the eastern dioceses, 1559.

Star Chamber 2 Proceedings (t. Henry VIII).

SP 12   State Papers, Domestic (t. Elizabeth I).

SP 15   Additional State Papers (Edward VI–James I)

Norwich, Norfolk and Norwich Record Office

Diocesan Records

ACT   Act books of the consistory court (*Item, not box numbers have been cited*). This series covers in full or in part the years 1508-12, 1518-25, 1534-8, 1544-55, 1560-4 and 1567-72 in thirteen volumes. ACT 4B is not a consistory court act book but the record of an episcopal visitation of 1532.

CON 1   Consistory court papers, including register of sentences on oaths of compurgators.

DEP   Consistory court deposition books (*Item, not box numbers have been cited*). This series covers the years 1499-1512, 1518-71 in nineteen volumes, some of which are almost certainly incomplete. DEP 11B contains acts of 1569-70.

HAR   Collections of Anthony Harison.

ORR 1(b)   Contains record of visitation of the diocese in 1556 carried out by Bishop Hopton on behalf of Reginald Pole.

REG   Bishop's registers or institution books (referred to as institution books).

SUN   Sundry documents including registers of accounts, dispensations etc.

VIS   Visitation records.

Will registers of the consistory court.

Dean and Chapter Records

Dean and chapter patent book 1.

Norwich archdeaconry records

The act books of visitations or inquisitions really form a single series, but they are to be found in a number of boxes with different and misleading labels, and it is often difficult to ascertain the original arrangement of the series. The number of inquisitions covered in one set of acts differs from one book to another. The years I have given in footnotes are those in which individual act books were apparently begun. *Many books could only be tentatively dated.*

AI   Archdeaconry inquisitions, 1532-3, 1538-9, 1548-52.

NAGB   Norwich archdeaconry general books.

NAAB   Norwich archdeaconry act books.

           These two series between them contain material from nearly all years of the 1560s.

Norwich archdeaconry will registers.
Norfolk archdeaconry records
Act book, 1560-2.
Norfolk archdeaconry will registers.
Norwich city records
Mayor's court books.
Oxford, Bodleian Library
Rawlinson MS. D.1088   Book of forms and precedents from
Norwich diocese.
Winchester, Hampshire Record Office
B/1/A   Visitation Books (referred to as VB).
CB   Consistory court books. The first 35 volumes in the
series cover the period up to 1570. The books are of
three main types:
(i) Instance act books (1513-16, 1526-31, 1541-9,
1558 onwards).
(ii) Deposition books (1531-47, 1561 onwards).
(iii) Office act books (1520-9, 1534-42, 1548-53,
1556-7, 1558-64, 1566 conwards).
Bishops' registers.
Winchester archdeaconry will registers and original wills.
Winchester cathedral
Dean and chapter ledger books.

PRINTED SOURCES

Primary Sources

Act Book of the Archdeacon of Taunton, ed. C. Jenkins (Somerset
Record Society, xliii, 1928).
Acts of the Privy Council of England, ed. J. R. Dasent (1890-1907).
An Admonition to the Parliament in *Puritan Manifestoes*, ed. W. H.
Frere and C. E. Douglas (1954).
The Archdeacon's Court, Liber Actorum, 1584, ed. E. R. C. Brinkworth
(Oxfordshire Record Society, xxiii-iv, 1942-6).
Archdeacon Harpsfield's Visitation, 1557, ed. L. E. Whatmore (Catholic
Record Society, xlv-xlvi, 1950-1).
*Articles to be ministred by the right Reuerend ... Robert ... Bishop of
Winchester ... in his Visitation, to be kept and holden ... Anno 1570*
(1570).
BASKERVILLE, G. R., 'Married Clergy and Pensioned Religious in
Norwich Diocese, 1555', *EHR*, xlviii (1933).
— and GOODMAN, A. W., 'Surrey Incumbents in 1562', *Surrey Ar-
chaeological Collections*, xlv (1937).
*A Collection of Original Letters from the Bishops to the Privy Council,
1564*, ed. M. Bateson (Camden Society, n. s. liii, 1895).
Correspondence of Matthew Parker, ed. J. Bruce and T. T. Perowne
(Parker Society, xlii, 1853).

Councils and Synods, with other documents relating to the English Church, ii, *A.D. 1205-1313*, ed. F. M. Powicke and C. R. Cheney (Oxford, 1964).

The Courts of the Archdeaconry of Buckingham, 1483-1523, ed. E. M. Elvey (Buckinghamshire Record Society, xix, 1975).

The Demands of the Rebels led by Ket, in *English Economic History, Select Documents*, ed. A. E. Bland, P. A. Brown, and R. H. Tawney (1914).

Depositions and other Ecclesiastical Proceedings from the Courts of Durham, extending from 1311 to the Reign of Elizabeth, ed. J. Raine (Surtees Society, xxi, 1845).

Documentary Annals of the Reformed Church of England, 1546-1716, ed. E. Cardwell (Oxford, 1844).

Documents Illustrative of English Church History, ed. H. Gee and W. J. Hardy (1896).

Ecclesiastical Terriers of Warwickshire Parishes, ed. D. M. Barratt (Dugdate Society Publications, xxii, xxvii, 1955 and 1971).

An Episcopal Court Book for the Diocese of Lincoln, ed. M. Bowker (Lincoln Record Society, lxi, 1967).

Faculty Office Registers, 1534-49, ed. D. S. Chambers (Oxford, 1966).

The First and Second Prayer Books of Edward VI (Everyman Edition, 1949).

GOODMAN, A. W., 'The Cathedral Church and the Archdeaconry of Winchester in 1562', *Papers and Proceedings of the Hampshire Field Club and Archaeological Society*, xiv (1940).

HALE, W. H., *A Series of Precedents and Proceedings in Criminal Causes, 1475-1640* (1847).

Hampshire Churchwardens' Accounts, ed. J. F. Williams (1913).

Lambeth Churchwardens' Accounts, i. ed. C. Drew (Surrey Record Society, xviii, 1941).

The Letter Book of John Parkhurst, Bishop of Norwich, ed. R. A. Houlbrooke (Norfolk Record Society, xliii, 1974-5).

Letters and Papers, Foreign and Domestic, of the Reign of Henry VIII, 1509-47, ed. J. Brewer, J. Gairdner and R. Brodie (1862-1932).

Letters of Richard Fox, 1486-1527, ed. P. S. and H. M. Allen (Oxford, 1929).

Letters of Stephen Gardiner, ed. J. A. Muller (Cambridge, 1933).

London Consistory Court Wills, 1492-1547, ed. I. Darlington (London Record Society, xii, 1967).

MORE, A. P., 'Proceedings of Ecclesiastical Courts in the Archdeaconry of Leicester, 1516-35', *Associated Architectural Societies' Reports and Papers*, xxviii (1905-6).

MYRC, J., *Instructions for Parish Priests*, ed. E. Peacock (Early English Text Society, xxxi, 1868, revised 1902).

Narratives of the Days of the Reformation, ed. J. G. Nichols (Camden Society, o. s. lxxvii, 1859).

Norwich Consistory Court Depositins, 1499-1512 and 1518-1530, calendared by E. D. Stone, arranged by B. Cozens-Hardy (Norfolk Record Society, x, 1938).

The Paston Letters, 1422-1509, ed. J. Gairdner (Edinburgh, 1910).

PURVIS, J. S., *Tudor Parish Documents of the Diocese of York* (Cambridge, 1948).

The Reformation of the Ecclesiastical Laws, ed. E. Cardwell (Oxford, 1850).

Registra Stephani Gardiner et Johannis Poynet, ed. H. Chitty and H. E. Malden (Canterbury and York Society, xxxvii, 1930).

Registrum Johannis Whyte, Episcopi Wintoniensis, ed. W. H. Frere (Canterbury and York Society, xvi, 1914).

Registrum Matthei Parker, transcribed by E. M. Thompson, edited by W. H. Frere (Canterbury and York Society, xxxv, xxxvi, and xxxix, 1928-33).

Registrum Thome Wolsey, ed. H. Chitty (Canterbury and York Society, xxxii, 1926).

The Registrum Vagum of Anthony Harison, ed. T. F. Barton (Norfolk Record Society, xxxii, xxxiii, 1963-4).

ST. GERMAN, C., *Doctor and Student*, ed. T. F. T. Plucknett and J. L. Barton (Selden Society, xci, 1974).

Select Sixteenth Century Causes in Tithe from the York Diocesan Registry, ed. J. S. Purvis (Yorkshire Archaeological Society Record Series, cxiv, 1949).

Synodalia: A Collection of Articles of Religion, Canons and Proceedings of Convocations, ed. E. Cardwell (Oxford, 1842).

Tudor Royal Proclamations, ed. P. L. Hughes and J. F. Larkin (1964-9).

Valor Ecclesiasticus temp. Henrici VIII, Auctoritate Regia institutus, ed. J. Caley and J. Hunter (Record Commission, 1810-34).

Visitation Articles and Injunctions of the Period of the Reformation, ed. W. H. Frere and W. P. M. Kennedy (Alcuin Club Publications, xiv-xvi, 1910).

Visitations in the Diocese of Lincoln, 1517-31 ed. A. H. Thompson (Lincoln Record Society, xxxiii, xxxv, xxxvii, 1940-7).

Visitations of the Diocese of Norwich, ed. A. Jessopp (Camden Society, n. s. xliii, 1888).

Wills and Inventories from the Registers of the Commissary of Bury St. Edmund's and the Archdeacon of Sudbury, ed. S. Tymms (Camden Society, old series, xlix, 1850).

The Zurich Letters, comprising the Correspondence of several English Bishops and others during the early part of the Reign of Queen Elizabeth, ed. H. Robinson (Parker Society, vii, 1842).

The Zurich Letters (2nd ser.) ... (Parker Society, viii, 1845).

Books on law and court procedure published before 1800

BURN, R., *Ecclesiastical Law* (1763).

CLARKE, F., *Praxis in Curiis Ecclesiasticis* (Dublin, 1666).

COKE, E., *The Second Part of the Institutes* (1669).

CONSET, H., *The Practice of the Spiritual or Ecclesiastical Courts*, (2nd edn. 1700).
COSIN, R., *An Apologie: of, and for Sundrie Proceedings by Jurisdiction Ecclesiasticall* (1591).
DEGGE, Sir S., *The Parson's Counsellor, with the Law of Tithes or Tithing* (1676).
GIBSON, E., *Codex Juris Ecclesiastici Anglicani* (Oxford, 1761).
GODOLPHIN, J., *Repertorium Canonicum or An Abridgement of the Ecclesiastical Laws* (1680).
LYNDWOOD, W., *Provinciale seu Constitutiones Angliae* (Oxford, 1679).
RASTELL, W., *A Collection of Entrees, of Declarations, Barres, Replications* (1596 edn.).
SWINBURNE, H., *A Brief Treatise of Testaments and Last Wills* (1590-1).
—— *A Treatise of Spousals or Matrimonial Contracts* (1686).
Tithes and Oblations according to the Lawes established in the Church of England (1595).

Indexes

BULLEN, R. FREEMAN, 'Catalogue of Beneficed Clergy of Suffolk, 1551-1631', *Proceedings of the Suffolk Institute of Archaeology*, xxii (1934-6).
Index of Wills Proved in the Consistory Court of Norwich, 1370-1550 and 1550-1603, ed. M. A. Farrow (Norfolk Record Society, xvi, xxi, 1943-5, 1950).
List of Early Chancery Proceedings, X (Public Record Office Lists and Indexes, 55, 1936).
Survey of Ecclesiastical Archives, ed. L. M. Midgley (Pilgrim Trust, 1951).

Biographical Registers

Dictionary of National Biography, ed. L. Stephen and S. Lee (1885-1900).
EMDEN, A. B., *Biographical Register of the University of Oxford to A.D. 1500* (Oxford, 1957-9).
—— *Biographical Register of the University of Oxford, A.D. 1501-40* (Oxford, 1974).
FOSTER, J., *Alumni Oxonienses, 1500-1714* (Oxford, 1891-2).
LE NEVE, J., *Fasti Ecclesiae Anglicanae 1300-1541*, iv. comp. B. Jones (1963).
—— *Fasti Ecclesiae Anglicanae 1541-1857*, iii. comp. J. Horn (1974).
VENN, J. and J. A., *Alumni Cantabrigienses*, Part I (Cambridge, 1922-7).

Secondary Works

ADAMS, N., 'The Writ of Prohibition to Court Christian', *Minnesota Law Review*, xx (1935-6).

288 BIBLIOGRAPHY

ADAMS, N., 'The Judicial Conflict over Tithes', *EHR* lii (1937).

ADDY, J., *The Archdeacon and Ecclesiastical Discipline in Yorkshire, 1598-1714* (St. Anthony's Hall Publication, xxiv, York, 1963).

ANGLIN, J. P., 'The Essex Puritan Movement and the "Bawdy" Courts, 1577-94', in *Tudor Men and Institutions*, ed. A. J. Slavin (Baton Rouge, 1972).

ATKINSON, T., *Elizabethan Winchester* (1963).

BAYNE, C. G., 'The Visitation of the Province of Canterbury, 1559', *EHR* xxviii (1913).

BINDOFF, S. T., *Ket's Rebellion, 1549* (Historical Association Pamphlet, G 12, 1949).

BIRT, H. N., *The Elizabethan Religious Settlement* (1907).

BLOMEFIELD, F. and PARKIN, C., *An Essay towards a Topographical History of the County of Norfolk* (2nd edn. 1805-10).

BOWKER, M., *The Secular Clergy in the Diocese of Lincoln, 1495-1520* (Cambridge, 1968).

—— 'The Commons' Supplication against the Ordinaries in the light of some Archidiaconal *Acta*', *TRHS* 5th ser. xxi (1971).

—— 'The Supremacy and the Episcopate: The Struggle for Control, 1534-1540', *HJ*, xviii (1975).

—— 'The Henrician Reformation and the Parish Clergy', *BIHR* l (1977).

BRINKWORTH, E. R. C., 'The Study and Use of Archdeacons' Court Records, illustrated from the Oxford Records (1566-1759)', *TRHS* 4th ser. xxv (1943).

BURNET, G., *History of the Reformation of the Church of England*, ed. N. Pocock (Oxford, 1865).

The Canon Law of the Church of England ... the Report of the Archbishops' Commission on Canon Law, together with Proposals for a Revised Body of Canons (1947).

CHURCHILL, I. J., *Canterbury Administration* (1933).

COLLINSON, P., *The Elizabethan Puritan Movement* (1967).

—— 'Episcopacy and Reform in England in the later Sixteenth Century', *SCH* iii (1966).

Continuity and Change: Personnel and Administration of the Church in England 1500-1642, ed. M. R. O'Day and F. Heal (Leicester, 1976).

COX, J. C., *Churchwardens' Accounts* (1913).

COX, J. C., and HARVEY, A., *English Church Furniture*

CUTTS, E. L., *Parish Priests and their People in the Middle Ages in England* (1898).

DAELEY, J. I., 'Pluralism in the Diocese of Canterbury during the Administration of Matthew Parker', *JEH* xviii (1967).

DERRETT, J. D. M., *Henry Swinburne (?1551-1624) Civil Lawyer of York* (Borthwick Paper, xliv, York, 1973).

DEVEREUX, E. J., 'The Publication of the English *Paraphrases* of Erasmus', *Bulletin of the John Rylands Library*, li (1968-9).

DIBDIN, L., and HEALEY, C. E. H. CHADWYCK, *English Church Law and Divorce* (1912).

DICKENS, A. G., *Lollards and Protestants in the Diocese of York, 1509-1558* (Oxford, 1959).
— *The English Reformation* (1964).
DONAHUE, C., Jr., 'Roman Canon Law in the Medieval English Church: Stubbs vs. Maitland re-examined after 75 years in the light of some records from the Church Courts', *Michigan Law Review*, lxxii (1974).
DUNCAN, G. I. O., *The High Court of Delegates* (Cambridge, 1971).
DUNNING, R. W., 'The Wells Consistory Court in the Fifteenth Century', *Proceedings of the Somerset Archaeological and Natural History Society*, cvi (1962).
— 'Rural Deans in England in the Fifteenth Century', *BIHR* xl (1967).
EASTERBY, W., *The History of the Law of Tithes in England* (Cambridge, 1888).
ELTON, G. R., *The Tudor Constitution* (Cambridge, 1960).
— *Policy and Police* (Cambridge, 1972).
— *Reform and Renewal: Thomas Cromwell and the Common Weal* (Cambridge, 1973).
— 'The Evolution of a Reformation Statute', *EHR* lxiv (1949).
EMMISON, F. G., *Elizabethan Life: Morals and the Church Courts* (Chelmsford, 1973).
FLAHIFF, G. B., 'The Writ of Prohibition to the Court Christian in the Thirteenth Century', *Medieval Studies*, vi-vii (1944-5).
FOXE, J., *Acts and Monuments*, ed. J. Pratt, with introduction by J. Stoughton (1877).
GEE, H., *The Elizabethan Clergy and the Settlement of Religion, 1558-1564* (Oxford, 1898).
GRIEVE, H. E. P., 'The Deprived Married Clergy in Essex, 1553-61', *TRHS* 4th ser. xxii (1940).
HAIGH, C., *Reformation and Resistance in Tudor Lancashire* (Cambridge, 1975).
HAUGAARD, W. P., *Elizabeth and the English Reformation* (Cambridge, 1968).
HAW, R., *The State of Matrimony* (1952).
HEATH, P., *The English Parish Clergy on the Eve of the Reformation* (1969).
— 'The Medieval Archdeaconry and the Tudor Bishopric of Chester', *JEH* xx (1969).
HELMHOLZ, R. H., *Marriage Litigation in Medieval England* (Cambridge, 1974).
— 'Canonical Defamation in Medieval England', *American Journal of Legal History*, xv (1971).
HILL, J. E. C., *Economic Problems of the Church* (Oxford, 1956).
— *Society and Puritanism in Pre-Revolutionary England* (1964).
HOCKADAY, F. S., 'The Consistory Court of the Diocese of Gloucester', *Transactions of the Bristol and Gloucestershire Archaeological Society*, xlvi (1924).
HOLDSWORTH, W. S., *A History of English Law* (1922-72).

HUDSON, W. S., *John Ponet (1516?-1556) Advocate of Limited Monarchy* (Chicago, 1942).
HUGHES, P., *The Reformation in England* (5th edn. 1963).
HURSTFIELD, J., *The Queen's Wards: Wardship and Marriage under Elizabeth I* (1958).
IVES, E. W., 'The Common Lawyers in Pre-Reformation England', *TRHS*, 5th ser. xviii (1968).
JAGGER, M., 'Bonner's Episcopal Visitation of London, 1554', *BIHR* xlv (1972).
JONES, W. J., *The Elizabethan Court of Chancery* (Oxford, 1967).
JORDAN, W. K., *Edward VI: The Threshold of Power* (1970).
KELLY, H. A., *The Matrimonial Trials of Henry VIII* (Stanford, 1976).
KELLY, M. J., 'The Submission of the Clergy', *TRHS*, 5th ser. xv (1965).
KITCHING, C. J., 'The Probate Jurisdiction of Thomas Cromwell as Vicegerent', *BIHR*, xlvi (1973).
LEHMBERG, S. E., *The Reformation Parliament, 1529-1536* (Cambridge, 1970).
— 'Supremacy and Vicegerency: A Re-examination', *EHR*, lxxxi (1966).
LEVACK, B. P., *The Civil Lawyers in England, 1603-1641* (Oxford, 1973).
LITTLE, A. G., 'Personal Tithes', *EHR* lx (1945).
LOBEL, M. D., *The Borough of Bury St. Edmund's* (Oxford, 1935).
LOGAN, F. D., *Excommunication and the Secular Arm in Medieval England* (Toronto, 1968).
— 'The Henrician Canons', *BIHR* xlvii (1974).
MAITLAND, F. W., *Roman Canon Law in the Church of England* (1898).
MANCHESTER, A. H., 'The Reform of the Ecclesiastical Courts', *American Journal of Legal history*, x (1966).
MANNING, R. B., *Religion and Society in Elizabethan Sussex* (Leicester, 1969).
— 'The Crisis of Episcopal Authority during the Reign of Elizabeth I', *Journal of British Studies*, xi (1971).
MARCHANT, R. A., *The Church under the Law: Justice, Administration and Discipline in the Diocese of York, 1560-1640* (Cambridge, 1969).
MILSOM, S. T. C., *Historical Foundations of the Common Law* (1969).
MORRIS, C., 'The Commissary of the Bishop in the Diocese of Lincoln', *JEH* x (1959).
— 'A Consistory Court in the Middle Ages', *JEH* xiv (1963).
MULLER, J. A., *Stephen Gardiner and the Tudor Reaction* (1926).
MUSKET, E. T., 'The Recantation of Anthony Yaxley', *East Anglian Notes and Queries*, n. s. iii (1887).
O'DAY, M. R., 'Thomas Bentham: A Case Study in the Problems of the Early Elizabethan Episcopate', *JEH* xxiii (1972).

OWEN, D. M., *The Records of the Established Church in England* (British Records Association: Archives and the User, i, 1970).

OWEN, D. M., 'Synods in the Diocese of Ely in the latter Middle Ages and the Sixteenth Century', *SCH* iii (1966).

— 'Ecclesiastical Jurisdiction in England 1300-1550: The Records and their Interpretation', *SCH* xi (1975).

OWEN, H. G., 'The Episcopal Visitation: Its Limits and Limitations in Elizabethan London', *JEH* xi (1960).

OXLEY, J. E., *The Reformation in Essex to the Death of Mary* (Manchester, 1965).

Parliamentary Papers 1845 (249), xxxvi, *Returns relating to the Titles and Jurisdiction of all Courts empowered to grant Probates of Wills ... (reprinted from former Returns).*

Parliamentary Papers 1831-2 (199), xxiv, *The Special and General Reports of the Commissioners appointed to inquire into the Practice and Jurisdiction of Ecclesiastical Courts.*

Parliamentary Papers 1883 (c. 3760), xxiv, *Report of the Commissioners appointed to inquire into the Constitution and Working of the Ecclesiastical Courts.*

PAUL, J. E., 'Hampshire Recusants in the time of Elizabeth I, with special reference to Winchester', *Proceedings of the Hampshire Field Club*, xxi (1958-60).

PETERS, R., *Oculus Episcopi: Administration in the Archdeaconry of St. Albans, 1580-1625* (Manchester, 1963).

PLUCKNETT, T. F. T., *A Concise History of the Common Law* (5th edn. 1956).

POLLARD, A. F., *Wolsey* (1929).

PRICE, F. D., 'Gloucester Diocese under Bishop Hooper', *Transactions of the Bristol and Gloucestershire Archaeological Society*, lx (1939).

— 'The Abuses of Excommunication and the Decline of Ecclesiastical Discipline under Queen Elizabeth', *EHR* lvii (1942).

— 'An Elizabethan Church Official — Thomas Powell, Chancellor of Gloucester Diocese', *Church Quarterly Review*, cxxviii (1939).

— 'Elizabethan Apparitors in the Diocese of Gloucester', *Church Quarterly Review*, cxxxiv (1942).

— 'Bishop Bullingham and Chancellor Blackleech: A Diocese divided', *Transactions of the Bristol and Gloucestershire Archaeological Society*, xci (1972).

PURVIS, J. S., *An Introduction to Ecclesiastical Records* (1953).

REDSTONE, V. B., 'South Elmham Deanery', *Proceedings of the Suffolk Institute of Archaeology*, xiv (1912).

RIDLEY, J., *Thomas Cranmer* (Oxford, 1962).

RITCHIE, C. I. A., *The Ecclesiastical Courts of York* (Arbroath, 1956).

SCARISBRICK, J. J., *Henry VIII* (1968).

— 'The Pardon of the Clergy, 1531', *CHJ*, xii (1956).

— 'Clerical Taxation in England, 1485-1547', *JEH*, xi (1960).

SHEEHAN, M. M., *The Will in Medieval England* (Toronto, 1963).
—— 'The Formation and Stability of Marriage in Fourteenth-Century England: Evidence of an Ely Register', *Medieval Studies*, xxxiii (1971).
SHIRLEY, T. F., *Thomas Thirlby, Tudor Bishop* (1964).
SMITH, A. H., *County and Court: Government and Politics in Norfolk, 1558-1603* (Oxford, 1974).
SMITH, A. L., *Church and State in the Middle Ages* (Oxford, 1913).
SMITH, L. B., *Tudor Prelates and Politics, 1536-1558* (Princeton, (1953).
SPUFFORD, M., *Contrasting Communities: English Villagers in the Sixteenth and Seventeenth Centuries* (Cambridge, 1974).
SQUIBB, G. D., *Doctors' Commons. A History of the College of Advocates and Doctors of Law* (Oxford, 1977).
STOREY, R. L., *Diocesan Administration in the Fifteenth Century* (St. Anthony's Hall Publication, xvi, 2nd. edn., York, 1972).
STRYPE, J., *Ecclesiastical Memorials relating chiefly to Religion and the Reformation of it under King Henry VIII, King Edward VI and Queen Mary* (Oxford, 1822).
—— *Annals of the Reformation and Establishment of Religion ... during Queen Elizabeth's Happy Reign* (Oxford, 1824).
—— *The Life and Acts of Matthew Parker* (Oxford, 1821).
—— *The Life and Acts of Edmund Grindal* (Oxford, 1821).
—— *The Life and Acts of John Whitgift* (Oxford, 1822).
THOMAS, K. V., *Religion and the Decline of Magic* (1971).
THOMPSON, A. Hamilton, 'Diocesan Organisation in the Middle Ages: Archdeacons and Rural Deans', *Proceedings of the British Academy*, xxix (1943).
—— *The English Clergy and their Organisation in the Later Middle Ages* (Oxford, 1947).
THOMSON, J. A. F., *The Later Lollards, 1414-1520* (Oxford, 1965).
—— 'Tithe Disputes in Later Medieval London', *EHR*, lxxviii (1963).
TIERNEY, B., *Medieval Poor Law: A Sketch of Canonical Theory and its Application in England* (Berkeley and Los Angeles, 1959).
USHER, R. G., *The Rise and Fall of the High Commission*, introd. P. Tyler (Oxford, 1968).
WARE, S. L., *The Elizabethan Parish in its Ecclesiastical and Financial Aspects* (Baltimore, 1908).
WILLIAMS, J. F., 'The Married Clergy of the Marian Period', *Norfolk Archaeology*, xxxii (1961).
WOODCOCK, B. L., *Medieval Ecclesiastical Courts in the Diocese of Canterbury* (Oxford, 1952).
ZELL, M. L., 'The Personnel of the Clergy in Kent, in the Reformation Period', *EHR*, lxxxix (1974).

Unpublished theses

ANGLIN, J. P., 'The Court of the Archdeacon of Essex, 1571-1609: An Institutional and Social Study' (California Univ. Ph. D., 1965).

BARRATT, D. M., 'The Condition of the English Parish Clergy from
the Reformation to 1660' (Oxford Univ. D. Phil., 1949).
HEAL, F. M., 'The Bishops of Ely and their Diocese, 1515-c. 1600'
(Cambridge Univ. Ph. D., 1972).
HOULBROOKE, R. A., 'Church Courts and People in the Diocese of
Norwich, 1519-1570' (Oxford Univ. D. Phil., 1970).
KELLY, M. J., 'Canterbury Jurisdiction and Influence during the
Episcopate of William Warham, 1503-32' (Cambridge Univ. Ph. D.,
1963).
MILDON, W. H., 'Puritanism in Hampshire and the Isle of Wight from
the Reign of Elizabeth to the Restoration' (London Univ. Ph. D.,
1934).
O'DAY, M. R., 'Clerical Patronage and Recruitment in England during
the Elizabethan and Early Stuart Periods, with special reference to
the Diocese of Coventry and Lichfield' (London Univ. Ph. D., 1972).

INDEX

Fox, Richard, (*cont.*)
175, 186, 192, 199, 210, 223, 225,
241
Foxe, John, 229, 233, 234, 235n, 236,
237, 239, 240
free will, 230, 235
Frere, W. H., 6
Frodsham, 87
Fuller, John, 42, 71, 79, 147, 166
funerals, 249

Gambylfelde, Elizabeth, 106
Gambylfelde, Joan, 106
Gambylfelde, John, father and son,
106
Gambylfelde, Richard, 106
Garboldisham, 135
Gardiner, George, 208
Gardiner, Stephen, 22, 25, 26, 27, 153,
237, 243, 245n, 257
Gascoigne, Edward, 53n
gifts *inter vivos*, 102, 113, 266
gilds, parochial, 154
Gloucester, 2, 26, 49, 53, 210
Godshill, 94, 247
Gonville Hall, 226
Grigges, Helen, 69
Grindal, Edmund, 23, 43, 115, 211
Guildford, 254
Gunvile, Richard, 98

Hadleigh, 236
Hale, W. H., 2
Halesworth, 123
Hampshire, 5, 105, 127, 128, 130, 132,
139, 152, 154, 166, 191, 226, 237,
238, 239, 250, 257, 259, 266, 268
Hancock, Thomas, 230
Harding, Thomas, 198n, 250
Hardingham, 197
Harpsfield, John, 245
Hartley Mauditt, 251
Haverhill, 125
Heacham, 123n
Headbourne Worthy, 159, 247
Heath, P., 175, 176-7, 178, 184, 186
Helmholz, R. H., 44, 85, 87
Henry VII, 9, 11, 272
Henry VIII, 8, 9, 11, 12, 13, 14, 17,
37, 72, 74, 125, 147, 187, 210,
228, 239, 241, 272
Hepworth, 250
Hereford, 209

heresy, suppression of, 11, 22, 48,
214-242, 253-4, 264
Hevingham, 253
Hill, J. E. C., 149, 162
Hobart, Sir James, 90
Hockaday, F. S., 2
Holkham, 248
Holt, 206, 281n
holy bread, 215, 229, 238
Holy Communion, 207, 216, 244-5,
247, 248, 258
admission to, 201, 248
bread and wine used in celebration
of, 150, 244, 258
failure to receive, 47, 242, 244, 246,
247, 252, 256, 258, 278-81
holy water, 249
holy water stoups, 167, 168
homilies, 163, 164, 165, 169, 171,
200, 204, 244
Hooper, John, 75, 200, 210, 211
Hopton, John, 22, 36, 166, 182, 192,
232, 234, 237
Horne, Robert, 22-3, 24, 26, 31, 33,
111, 169, 188, 189, 195, 198, 199,
202, 203, 205, 206, 207, 208, 209,
246, 247, 248, 249, 250, 252, 255,
256, 259, 260, 268
Horningtoft, 137
houses of clergy, repair of, 158-9,
278-81
Howard, Catherine, 72
Hunne, Richard, 9, 10, 11
Husbonde, John, 234

images, 163, 165, 168, 169, 171, 214,
225, 227, 229, 230, 243, 251
impediments
affinity, 71, 74, 75, 84, 85
coercion (force and fear), 62, 64, 73
consanguinity, 74, 75, 84, 85
nonage, 62, 73-4
pre-contract, 71-3, 75, 84, 85
imprisonment
of clergy, 176
of heretics, 216, 218, 219, 224
incontinence, punishment of, 39, 47,
55, 56, 60, 64, 65, 75-9, 86-7,
261, 263, 278-81, *and see* clergy,
incontinence amongst
Ingworth, 204, 281n
injunctions, episcopal, 30, 194, 206-7,
208

Thirlby (*cont.*):
 165, 214
thirty-nine articles, 219
Thompson, A. Hamilton, 2, 40
Thurgarton, 136
Tibenham, 134
Tichborne family, 251
tithes
 agreements concerning, 127, 128,
  133, 134–7
 cases concerning, 15, 17, 39, 48, 64,
  65, 83, 117–50, 263, 265, 270,
  271, 273–7
 commutation of, demanded, 147
 customary ways of paying, 119, 121,
  122, 126–35, 138, 140, 142, 147,
  148, 149, 266
 disputed rights to receive, 134–5, 141
 exemptions from, 120, 121, 127–8,
  129, 132, 135–6, 141, 142, 143,
  148
 mixed, 118, 121, 130–2, 149
 of cheese, 118, 131, 136, 140, 148
 of corn, 118, 121, 126–8, 136, 140,
  142, 148
 of fish, 132, 146
 of gardens, 133
 of hay, 128–9, 148
 of milk, 118, 131, 140, 148
 of mills, 120, 128, 141
 of minerals, 120, 133
 of pannage, 129–30
 of pasture, 120, 129–30, 141, 142,
  147, 148
 of wild animals, 120, 132
 of wood, 120, 132, 141, 142, 143
 of wool, 118, 131–2, 134–5
 of the young of animals, 118, 130–1,
  134, 148
 personal, 118, 121, 122–3, 124, 125,
  148, 223
 plaintiffs suing for, 134, 143–6
 predial, 118, 121, 122, 128
 scriptural foundation and early
  development, 117–8
Toftrees, 281n
tokens of marriage, 60–1
Townshend, Mrs., 193
transubstantiation, denial of, 225, 229,
 232, 234–5, 236, 238
Travers, Thomas, 249–50, 251
Trent, Council of, 57
Tunstall, Cuthbert, 26, 227

Tyndale, William, 227, 229

unions of benefices
 permanent, 162, 189
 personal, 162, 187, 188–9, 190
unmarried mothers, payments to, 77–8
usury, 40

Valor Ecclesiasticus, 122, 123, 144
Vaws, Robert, 180
vestments, 163, 167, 242, 245, 254–6
violence to clergy, 48
visitations, 40, 80, 137, 173, 178, 184,
 190, 252
 archidiaconal, 33, 137, 167, 168,
  204, 240
 episcopal, 6, 21, 27, 29–30, 31, 37,
  138, 152, 157, 159, 160, 161, 163,
  166, 170, 175, 178, 181, 185, 186,
  192, 196, 197, 198, 201, 205, 207,
  210, 211, 212, 222, 223, 224, 227,
  232, 238, 248, 250, 251, 258, 259,
  265
 legatine, 8
 metropolitical, 13, 27, 36, 165, 166,
  167, 170, 182, 190, 198n, 199,
  208, 232, 255
 royal, 13, 14, 27, 36, 164, 167, 176,
  182–3, 208, 245

Walsingham, 281n
Wandsworth, 256
wardship, 62
Warham, William, 9, 10, 91n
West, Nicholas, 22
Westhall, 193
West Tisted, 251
White, John, 22, 237, 243
White, William, 182n
Whitgift, John, 50, 116, 269, 272
Whitsede, William, 138
Whytforde, Richard, 66
widows, remarriage of, 106–7
Wiggenhall St. Mary, 135
Wight, Isle of, 132, 176, 243, 256
wills
 cases concerning, 39, 48, 64, 65, 83,
  89–116, 261, 262, 263, 273–7,
  278–8
 clerical advice on making, 101–2
 falsification of, 100
 forgery of, 109, 114
 probate of, *see* probate

wills (*cont.*):
validity of, 98–100, 116
Winchester
archdeaconry of, 27, 29, 31–4, 92,
143, 144, 152, 156, 157, 159, 161,
163, 166, 174n, 175, 178, 183, 185,
188, 202, 203, 204, 205, 222, 238
cathedral, 206–7, 211
city of, 124, 133, 189, 227, 252
College, 186, 243, 250n
dean and chapter of, 206–7, 246
diocese of (general description), 4–6
marquess of (William Paulet), 191
mayor of, 252
witchcraft, 40
Witley, 254
witnesses, 40–1, 51, 57, 58, 60, 65, 84,
91, 92, 93, 97, 98, 100, 109, 110,
112, 123, 131, 134, 140, 141, 161,

witnesses (*cont.*):
197, 217, 224, 234
Wiveton, 279n
Wolsey, Thomas, 10, 11, 91, 185, 186,
227
Woodcock, B. L., 2, 3, 51n
Woodhouse, Sir Roger, 79
Wyborn, Percival, 208
Wymondham, 223

Yale, Thomas, 265
Yarmouth (Great Yarmouth), 5, 132,
245
Yaxley, Anthony, 225, 226
York, 3, 19, 26, 27, 31, 37, 42, 65, 86,
87, 115, 144, 149, 176, 177, 178,
209, 239, 240

Zürich, 254, 244